William Stroud

The physical cause of the Death of Christ :

and its relation to the principles and practice of Christianity

William Stroud

The physical cause of the Death of Christ :
and its relation to the principles and practice of Christianity

ISBN/EAN: 9783743356795

Manufactured in Europe, USA, Canada, Australia, Japa

Cover: Foto ©ninafisch / pixelio.de

Manufactured and distributed by brebook publishing software (www.brebook.com)

William Stroud

The physical cause of the Death of Christ :

THE PHYSICAL CAUSE

OF THE

DEATH OF CHRIST,

AND

ITS RELATION TO THE PRINCIPLES AND PRACTICE OF CHRISTIANITY.

BY

WILLIAM STROUD, M. D.

WITH A LETTER ON THE SUBJECT
BY SIR JAMES Y. SIMPSON, BART. M. D.

NEW YORK:
D. APPLETON AND COMPANY,
549 & 551 BROADWAY.
1871.

SKETCH OF THE AUTHOR'S LIFE.

BY JAMES MORISON, D. D.

Dr. William Stroud, the author of the following work on *the Physical Cause of the Death of Christ*, was a highly accomplished and remarkable man. He was a licentiate of the Royal College of Physicians, London, "and continued," says Dr. Hodgkin, "to grace that section of the Doctors of Medicine in the Metropolis until his death."[*] He was born at Bath on the third of July, 1789. Before he was five years of age, his grandfather presented to him a folio copy of Fox's Book of Martyrs, as a reward for his diligence in perusing it. On leaving school, where he had highly distinguished himself, he commenced preparation for the medical profession. He resided, first of all, for several years, with Mr. R. Stocker, Apothecary of Guy's Hospital, London. He then studied at the University of Edinburgh, where he took, with much *éclat*, his degree of M. D. in 1819. His Latin thesis on *gout* was a volume of eighty printed pages, and elicited the highest commendation from the late Dr. Gregory, Professor of the Practice of Medicine. After taking his degree, he continued for two or three years in the northern metropolis, as clinical clerk to the late Prof. Duncan, who bore the highest testimony to the singular

---

[*] Biographical Sketch of Dr. William Stroud, 1858.

ability with which he discharged his duties. "I rather learned from him, than taught him," says Dr. Duncan, "and, in the clinical wards, his treatment saved the lives of patients who would have slipped through my own hands." During this prolonged sojourn in Edinburgh he became one of the Presidents of the Royal Medical Society, and took an active and prominent part in its discussions. He had great facility in speaking extemporaneously; and Dr. Hodgkin says of him, that "his speeches, for their arrangement and accuracy of diction, as well as for their amount of learning, and soundness of reasoning, might have been taken down *verbatim* and printed as essays." On leaving Edinburgh, he went to Paris, where he took advantage, for about the space of two years, of the Classroom prelections, and Hospital practice, of the most illustrious of the French Teachers and Practitioners. He then travelled, making in particular an extensive tour in Italy, and spending in its famous cities weeks or months, as the case might be, in studying art, or making himself acquainted with the most important of its medical schools, and the most eminent of its literati.

At length he returned to London, and became Physician to the Northern Dispensary, where Dr. Roget, Dr. Tweedie, and Dr. Theophilus Thomson, were successively his colleagues. He frequented his Alma Mater, Guy's Hospital, and often took part in the meetings of various Medical Societies.

He never, however, did very much in the way of private practice, though, when his aid was called in, he scarcely ever failed to shed light on the most obscure disorders, and to throw out the most valuable suggestions for treatment.

From an early period in his intellectual development he took a special interest in biblical pursuits; and on them he expended a large proportion of the zeal and energy of his maturer years. He entered into extensive investigations, more particularly, in reference to *the Gospels*, and, as the result of the labor of thirty years, he published *a Harmony of the Four Gospels in Greek*,* accompanied with a long and interesting Introduction, and Critical Notes, embodying the results of learned, minute, extensive, and most painstaking and laborious investigations.

His most important work, however, is his *Treatise on the Physical Cause of Christ's Death*. It is, in its own place, a master-piece, and must continue to be a standard work in theology for many years to come. It could have been composed only by a man characterized by a combination of singular endowments. It required, on the one hand, a profound acquaintance with medical subjects and medical literature. It required, on the other, an equally profound acquaintance with the Bible, and with theology in general. It required, too, in addition, a profound veneration for Christ, and a devoted attachment to Christianity. All these qualities—so rarely combined—met and were eminent in Dr. Stroud. He was as good as he was great. He took an interest in every Christian and philanthropic movement. He was a member of the Committee of the British and Foreign Bible Society. He toiled daily in giving gratuitous medical attendance on the poor. It is pleasing to add that, in the midst of his profound religious reverence and piety, he was ever humanely genial, and brimming over with innocent gayety and "pun." He was never married, but was truly "a family man," says Dr. Hodgkin, amid the children of relatives, who had been bereaved of their own parents. "In a gentlemanly courtesy," says Dr. Theophilus Thomson, "he could not be surpassed, but he would never allow temptations to compliance to thwart his unswerving aim at theoretical perfection." "He was never driven by prejudice, nor beguiled by any fascination, from

* London : Samuel Bagster & Sons, Paternoster Row.

the plain course of duty; and I shall always remember him as moving calmly onward toward the haven of truth and peace." He died suddenly, in his own house, on the twenty-ninth day of June, 1858, and his remains were interred in the cemetery at Highgate, on the sixth of July.

SIR JAMES Y. SIMPSON, Bart., M.D.,

ON DR. STROUD'S VIEW

OF THE PHYSICAL CAUSE OF THE DEATH OF CHRIST.

Reprinted, by permission, from Dr. Hanna's "Last Days of our Lord's Passion."

MY DEAR DR. HANNA:—Ever since reading, some ten or twelve years ago, Dr. Stroud's remarkable treatise *On the Physical Cause of the Death of Christ*, I have been strongly impressed with the belief that the views which he adopted* and maintained on this subject are fundamentally correct. Nor has this opinion been in any way altered by a perusal of some later observations published on the same question, both here and on the Continent.

That the immediate cause of the death of our blessed Saviour was—speaking medically—laceration or rupture of the heart, is a doctrine in regard to which there can be no absolute certainty; but, assuredly, in favor of it there is a very high amount of circumstantial probability.

Let me try to state the arguments for this view in the form of a few brief propositions:

I. His death was not the mere result of crucifixion; for,
1. The period was too short; a person in the prime of life,

---

* Dr. Stroud himself points out that Russell, Edwards, Rambach, and other writers, had more or less correctly anticipated him in the belief that Christ had died from rupture or breaking of the heart.

as Christ was, not dying from this mode of mortal punishment in six hours, as He did, but usually surviving till the second or third day, or even longer. 2. The attendant phenomena, at the time of actual death, were different from those of crucifixion. The crucified died, as is well known, under a lingering process of gradual exhaustion, weakness, and faintness. On the contrary, Christ cried with a loud voice, and spoke once and again—all apparently within a few minutes of His dissolution.

II. No known injury, lesion, or disease of the brain, lungs, or other vital organs could, I believe, account for such a sudden termination of His sufferings in death, except (1) arrestment of the action of the heart by fatal fainting or syncope; or (2) rupture of the walls of the heart, or larger blood-vessels issuing from it.

III. The attendant symptoms—particularly the loud cry and subsequent exclamations—show that death was not the effect of mortal fainting, or mere fatal arrestment of the action of the heart by syncope.

IV. On the other hand, these symptoms were such as have been seen in cases of rupture of the walls of the heart. Thus, in the latest book published in the English language on Diseases of the Heart, the eminent author, Dr. Walshe, Professor of Medicine in University College, London, when treating of the symptoms indicating death by rupture of the heart, observes, "The hand is suddenly carried to the front of the chest, a piercing shriek uttered," etc., etc. The rapidity of the resulting death is regulated by the size and shape of the ruptured opening. But, usually, death very speedily ensues, in consequence of the blood escaping from the interior of the heart into the cavity of the large surrounding heart-sac or pericardium; which sac has, in cases of rupture of the heart, been found, on dissection, to contain sometimes two, three, four, or more pounds, of blood accumulated within it, and separated into red clot and limpid serum, or "blood and water"—as is seen in blood when collected out of the body in a cup or basin in the operation of common bloodletting.

V. No medical jurist would, in a court of law, venture to assert, from the mere symptoms preceding death, that a person had certainly died of rupture of the heart. To obtain positive *proof* that rupture of the heart was the cause of death, a *post-mortem* examination of the chest would be necessary. In ancient times, such dissections were not practised. But the details left regarding Christ's death are most strikingly peculiar in this respect, that they offer us the result of a very rude dissection, as it were, by the gash* made in His side after death by the thrust of the Roman soldier's spear. The effect of that wounding or piercing of the side was an escape of "blood and water," visible to the Apostle John, standing some distance off; and I do not believe that any thing could possibly account for this appearance, as described by that Apostle, except a collection of blood effused into the distended sac of the pericardium in consequence of rupture of the heart, and afterward separated, as is usual with *extravasated* blood into those two parts, viz. (1), crassamentum, or red clot, and (2) watery serum. The subsequent puncture from below of the distended pericardial sac would most certainly, under such circumstances, lead to the immediate ejection and escape of its sanguineous contents in the form of red clots of blood and a stream of watery serum, exactly corresponding to that description given in the sacred narrative, "and forthwith came there out blood *and* water"—an appearance which no other natural event or mode of death can explain or account for.

VI. Mental emotions and passions are well known by all to affect the actions of the heart in the way of palpita-

---

* Its size may be inferred from the Apostle Thomas being asked to thrust not his "finger," but his "hand" into it.—John xx.

tion, fainting, etc. That these emotions and passions, when in overwhelming excess, occasionally, though rarely, produce laceration or rupture of the walls of the heart, is stated by most medical authorities, who have written on the affections of this organ; and our poets even allude to this effect as an established fact—

. . . . . . "The grief that does not speak
Whispers the o'erfraught heart, and bids it break."

But if ever a human heart was riven and ruptured by the mere amount of mental agony that was endured, it would surely—we might even argue *a priori*—be that of our Redeemer, when, during these dark and dreadful hours on the cross, He, "being made a curse for us," "bore our griefs, and carried our sorrows," and suffered for sin, the malediction of God and man, "full of anguish," and now "exceeding sorrowful even unto death."

There are theological as well as medical arguments in favor of the opinion that Christ in reality died from a ruptured or broken heart. You know them infinitely better than I do. But let me merely observe that—

VII. If the various wondrous prophecies and minute predictions in Psalms xxii. and lxix., regarding the circumstances connected with Christ's death, be justly held as literally true, such as, "They pierced my hands and my feet," "They part my garments among them, and cast lots upon my vesture," etc., why should we regard as merely metaphorical, and not as literally true also, the declarations in the same Psalms, "Reproach hath broken my heart," "My heart is like wax, it is melted in the midst of my bowels?" And—

VIII. Death by mere crucifixion was not a form of death in which there was much, if indeed any, shedding of blood. Punctured wounds do not generally bleed; and the nails, besides being driven through parts that were not provided with large blood-vessels, necessarily remain plugging up the openings made by their passage. The whole language and types of Scriptures, however, involve the idea that the atonement for our sins was obtained by the *blood* of Christ shed for us during His death on the cross. "Without shedding of blood there is no remission." This shedding, however, was assuredly done in the fullest possible sense, under the view that the immediate cause of His dissolution was rupture of the heart, and the consequent fatal escape of His heart and life-blood from the central cistern of the circulation.

It has always appeared—to my medical mind at least—that this view of the mode by which death was produced in the human body of Christ intensifies all our thoughts and ideas regarding the immensity of the astounding sacrifice which He made for our sinful race upon the cross. Nothing can possibly be more striking and startling than the appalling and terrible passiveness with which God as man submitted, for our sakes, His incarnate body to all the horrors and tortures of the crucifixion. But our wonderment at the stupendous sacrifice only increases when we reflect that, while thus enduring for our sins the most cruel and agonizing form of corporeal death, He was ultimately "slain," not by the effects of the anguish of His corporeal frame, but by the effects of the mightier anguish of His mind; the fleshy walls of His heart—like the veil, as it were, in the temple of His human body—becoming rent and riven, as for us "He poured out His soul unto death;" —"the travail of His soul" in that awful hour thus standing out as unspeakably bitterer and more dreadful than even the travail of His body.

Believe me, my dear Dr. Hanna,

Ever sincerely yours,

J. Y. SIMPSON, M.D.

EDINBURGH, *May* 1 1862.

AUTHOR'S PREFACE.

Whatever faults may justly be attributed to the following treatise, crudeness and precipitation will scarcely be among their number; for, since its original conception first occurred to the author, more than a quarter of a century has elapsed, during the greater part of which period it has often been the subject of his thoughts, and not unfrequently of his conversation and correspondence.

Its chief object is to demonstrate an important physical fact connected with the death of Christ, and to point out its relation to the principles and practice of Christianity; but, although the subjects discussed and the conclusions deduced from them are, it is hoped, of no inconsiderable value in a devotional point of view, the treatise itself is rather argumentative than sentimental, and more concerned with the foundation of evangelical religion than with its superstructure. The fact is not indeed now announced for the first time, having been more or less correctly anticipated by several pious and excellent writers during the last century; but, as, in matters of such solemn import, conjecture and probability are not a sufficient ground for conviction, the author has labored to supply a demonstration of the fact, which he trusts will be found both new and satisfactory. He has, accordingly, been careful not to assume any thing which is not generally acknowledged; and has supported every point of the argument with proofs and evidences so combined, as apparently to leave no other alternative than that which is here maintained. Should the attempt have been successful, it will furnish a fresh proof of the value of inductive reasoning; which, like a sounding-line let down into the ocean of time, has thus, from the depth of eighteen hundred years, brought up to the surface a pearl of great price.

In executing this design, the author has derived much advantage from his medical studies, whereby he has been enabled to bring forward many anatomical and physiological details which, although absolutely necessary for the demonstration, would scarcely have been within the reach of the merely theological inquirer, however in other respects able and well-informed. Some of the facts concerned in this investigation are either of such rare occurrence, or have been so seldom verified and recorded, that a few of them only could be adduced; but, as these are fully authenticated, and free from ambiguity, they are sufficient for the end in view; and, on account of the peculiar nature of the subject, it would be alike fruitless and unreasonable to demand a much greater number. He has also introduced many quotations from authors of eminence, in order that, on all points requiring positive and special information, the reader may be furnished with valuable documents; and may, perhaps, in some instances be better satisfied of the truth and pertinency of statements, by perceiving that the original writers had no concern with the argument here pursued, and could not even have conjectured the purpose to which their remarks have been applied. He takes this opportunity of recording his acknowledgments to several friends who have supplied him with useful materials; but whose names, being for the most part inserted in the treatise itself, need not now be repeated. Should the work ever reach a second edition, he shall feel much obliged by any communications tending to its further improvement, with which he may in the mean time be favored.

He has likewise had occasion to refer very copiously to the Scriptures, both of the Old and the New Testament. In doing this, he has, at the risk of incurring some censure for tediousness and repetition, often quoted the passages at large; fearing that, unless he adopted this plan, the effect which he was anxious to produce would in many cases have been much impaired, if not wholly defeated. Few readers can, in fact, be trusted to examine and collate a mere list of biblical references, and to make that careful and intelligent use of them which is requisite for the purpose of demonstration. It will, however, be generally admitted that, in enouncing the truths of Scripture, no course can be so proper as to cite the words of Scripture; which, in respect to beauty, energy, and perspicuity, as well as to authority, far excel all human compositions whatsoever. In quoting from the Old Testament, he has seldom departed from the text of the English Vulgate; partly, because his acquaintance with the

Hebrew language is too limited to qualify him for the task of translating from it; and partly, because it is allowed on all hands that, in this portion of the Bible, the authorized version stands in little need of improvement. But, in the New Testament, which, as being the code of Christianity, is the most important part of the sacred volume, and of which the original language is more easily and more commonly acquired, he has often ventured to deviate from that version, and attempted to express with greater clearness and force the sense of the apostolical writings. For practical purposes the authorized version is sufficiently correct, and frequently indeed as perfect as could be desired; but the passages are neither few nor unimportant, more especially in the epistles, wherein, as competent judges will admit, it is susceptible of improvement, both in point of accuracy and of style. Such, however, is the force of long custom and early association, that a modified version, even when confessedly preferable, appears to most persons, and particularly to those who are not much accustomed to critical researches, strange and repulsive. It ought at the same time to be understood that, although some of the Biblical translations here introduced may serve to elucidate and confirm the peculiar views proposed in this work, none of them is essential to their demonstration; which would have been equally certain, had the common version been exclusively employed. An early section of this treatise, describing the sufferings and death of Christ, besides being a necessary foundation for the reasonings and deductions which follow, furnishes a fair specimen of such translation, as likewise of another work, in which the author has also been for many years more or less engaged; namely, a Harmony of the four Gospels. This he hopes before long to publish, in the first instance in Greek; and afterward, if he has reason to hope that such a performance will be acceptable to the public, in English.

Of the subsequent portions of the treatise the professed object is to propose a peculiar, and as it were physical demonstration of the great truths of the Gospel, derived from internal evidence. Such, however, is the variety of human characters and dispositions, that to some persons its arguments may possibly appear defective, and to others superfluous, or even presumptuous. Both parties may, however, be reminded that the subject is encompassed with difficulties and obscurities which, as they tend to impair its legitimate influence, it is desirable to diminish or remove. Some of these, lying entirely beyond the range of the human faculties, at least in the present stage of existence, the author has intentionally left untouched; but others, depending chiefly on confusion of ideas, or the want of sufficient information, he has endeavored to dispel. Yet, although he trusts his arguments may have some weight, even with persons of a careless or skeptical temper, he does not profess to have written a work specifically adapted to their case. He assumes, for instance, at the outset the truth and divine origin of the canonical Scriptures; but still, in the course of the subsequent disquisition, subjects these Scriptures to so close and searching an investigation, as serves fully to justify the confidence provisionally placed in them; since, had they been spurious or erroneous, such a trial would infallibly have led to their refutation. This process is, indeed, the converse of that which is often employed in mathematical works, under the appellation of the *reductio ad absurdum;* and, supposing the reasoning to be correct, the conclusions deduced from this source are universally allowed to be valid. On the other hand, the humble and practical Christian, whose religious convictions are chiefly founded on the direct statements of the Scriptures, and on his personal experience of their happy effects when cordially embraced, will not regret to find that, by pursuing a particular course of research, the truth and wisdom of divine revelation may be illustrated to a greater extent than he might perhaps have originally expected; and that, when carefully and rationally investigated, its salutary doctrines approve themselves no less to the understanding than to the heart. To all classes of readers, the author, therefore, respectfully commends his treatise; and, without troubling them with any further preliminary remarks, fervently hopes that, in a matter of the highest interest and importance, it may, under the divine blessing, in some degree contribute both to their satisfaction and their advantage.

TABLE OF CONTENTS.

SKETCH OF THE AUTHOR'S LIFE,	3
SIR JAMES SIMPSON ON THE DEATH OF CHRIST,	7
PREFACE,	13
INTRODUCTION,	21

PART I.

INVESTIGATION OF THE IMMEDIATE CAUSE OF THE DEATH OF CHRIST.

CHAPTER I.

Evangelical Narrative of the Death of Christ, . . 27

CHAPTER II.

Summary of the Principal Circumstances which attended the Death of Christ, ... 46

CHAPTER III.

Rejection of Erroneous Explanations of the Death of Christ, . 51

CHAPTER IV.

Demonstration of the Immediate Cause of the Death of Christ, . 83

PART II.

ELUCIDATION OF SCRIPTURAL TRUTH, BY THE FOREGOING EXPLANATION OF THE DEATH OF CHRIST.

CHAPTER I.

On the Doctrine of Atonement, in Relation to the Death of Christ, 157

CHAPTER II.

On the Types and Prophecies of the Old Testament, in Relation to the Death of Christ, ... 215

CHAPTER III.

On the Narratives and Symbols of the New Testament, in Relation to the Death of Christ, ... 252

CHAPTER IV.

On the Doctrines and Precepts of Christianity, in Relation to the Death of Christ, ... 279

CHAPTER V.

On the Peculiar Evidence of the Truth of Christianity, furnished by the Foregoing Explanation of the Death of Christ, . 306

CONCLUSION, ... 318

NOTES AND ILLUSTRATIONS:
    I.—On the Erroneous Readings of the Vatican Manuscript, 330
    II.—On Crucifixion, ... 334
    III.—On Agony and Bloody Sweat, . . . 342
    IV.—On Rupture of the Heart from Mental Emotion, . 349
    V.—On the Blood and Water which flowed from the Side of Christ, ... 355
    VI.—On the Darkness of the Sun and Moon during the Sufferings of Christ, ... 370
    VII.—On Peter's Denials of Christ, . . . 386
    VIII.—On the Scriptural Use of the Terms Covenant and Testament, ... 397

LIST OF AUTHORS AND WORKS, . . . 415

INTRODUCTION.

Of the facts on which Christianity is based, and of the doctrines and precepts wherein it mainly consists, the death of Christ on the cross is the common centre, to which all the other parts of the system bear so special and intimate a relation, that without it they would be unconnected and inefficient. In proportion as this momentous event is duly appreciated, the Christian religion may be expected to prosper; but, could the fact as related in Scripture be disproved, the religion would fall to the ground. Hence, the apostle Paul termed the preaching of the gospel—"the preaching of the cross;" and, in the discharge of his ministry both among Jews and Gentiles, resolved to build on no other foundation than—"Christ crucified."* Such being indisputably the case, it must be regarded as a remarkable circumstance, that of this cardinal fact the precise nature and immediate cause have never yet been fully explored. That the subject is involved in considerable obscurity is not unfrequently admitted; and yet, with the exception of a few neglected hints and conjectures, little progress has been made during more than eighteen hundred years toward its complete elucidation. The solutions proposed by commentators,

* 1 Corinth. chap. 1, v. 17, 18; chap. 2, v. 1, 2; Galat. chap. 3, v. 1; chap. 5, v. 11; chap. 6, v. 12-14, etc.

both ancient and modern, are for the most part borrowed from each other without sufficient proof or acknowledgment; and, as will hereafter be shown, are either inadequate, or erroneous. This deficiency of research on a point so interesting and important may be attributed, partly to the difficulty of obtaining an accurate view of all the conditions concerned, and partly to all ill-founded apprehension that such inquiries are either presumptuous and impracticable, or, at best, rather curious than useful. Whether the present attempt will be more successful than those by which it has been preceded, the event must determine; but that it is neither improper, superfluous, nor unimportant, may easily be proved. It is not improper, because there are numerous intimations in Scripture which so strongly invite attention to the subject, that it is impossible to ascribe to them any other use or design; a circumstance in strict accordance with the general character of the sacred volume, which demands from its readers reflection as well as docility, and is alike opposed to credulity and to skepticism. It is not superfluous, because hitherto the subject has been either imperfectly examined, or wholly misunderstood; and, with few exceptions, has received so little illustration from expositors, that their remarks concerning it are more calculated to excite doubt than to afford satisfaction. It is not unimportant, because it tends to present the Saviour's death in the most impressive and affecting point of view, and to furnish new and powerful evidence of the truth and value of revelation.

There is little reason to regard such an inquiry as presumptuous, since it is suggested by the Scripture itself; which, moreover, assigns no other limits to the acquisition of knowledge than the capacity of the mind, and the means of information placed within its reach. The Father of lights, from whom descends every good and perfect gift, has no jealousy of his rational creatures knowing too much; but they are unhappily prone to limit themselves, by neglecting the advantages which he grants them for this end. It is true that in religion, pure and elevated affections are the principal object of pursuit; but, as a means both of exciting and of exercising these affections, sacred knowledge is essential; and, although a small amount of such knowledge may be sufficient for salvation, pious persons are not encouraged to rest satisfied with low attainments in this respect, but exhorted to grow in wisdom and understanding, as well as in all other spiritual endowments. Mankind, indeed, whether pious or profane, are throughout Scripture reproached for their indifference and inattention to the operations of God; while, on the other hand, he is represented as approving the conduct of those who take pleasure in examining his works and ways. Much may be learned from the intelligent contemplation of nature and providence, but it is in the Christian dispensation that the divine character is most conspicuously displayed; and the more attentively its discoveries are studied, the greater inducement will there be to yield the heart to their salutary influence.

Such is precisely the object of the ensuing explanation of the immediate cause and mode of the death of Christ; an explanation which is recommended to the reader's favorable regard by the following considerations: In the first place, it is not only in perfect harmony with all the facts and doctrines of the Gospel, but also serves to elucidate and confirm them. Secondly, it demands no assent except on the ground of demonstration, and involves no reflection on the piety of those by whom it may be doubted, or declined. Thirdly, if admitted, it claims no higher merit for the author than that of having jointly cultivated to some extent physiological and biblical studies—a combination of which, although indispensable for such purposes, is not perhaps often realized; and lastly, after having been for several years submitted to private examination, it has received the assent of many competent judges in each of those branches of knowledge, without encountering any material objection. In pursuing this inquiry, a regular and inductive method will be observed. Since there cannot be conclusive reasoning on any subject without a connected view of all the facts relating to it which may be supplied by direct observation, a continuous narrative of the sufferings and death of Christ, collected from the separate accounts of the four evangelists, will first be proposed. In order to concentrate attention on the most essential points of this narrative, a short summary of its principal circumstances will next be presented, and employed as a chart to direct the course of the subsequent investigation, and as a criterion to determine the value of the several opinions adduced. These opinions will then be reviewed; and, after acknowledging such portions of truth as they may be found to contain, will be severally shown to be either insufficient or untenable. The explanation which remains after every other alternative has been excluded will finally be demonstrated; and the rest of the treatise will be occupied in pointing out some of the useful purposes to which it may be applied.

That the subject is deserving of profound attention will not be disputed. All the works of the Deity are entitled to the most respectful regard; but some of them are so obscure and mysterious as to be in a great measure beyond the reach of investigation. Others, like the phenomena of Nature, appear magnificent even to the naked eye, but still more so when minutely and scientifically examined. Just so it is with the death of Christ on the cross. To render it available for practical purposes, the most ordinary contemplation is sufficient; but, under close and critical inspection, it becomes far more intelligible and affecting. With the inspired narratives and doctrines concerning this solemn event the students of Scripture may well be content; but, by penetrating a little beneath the surface, he finds himself in contact with awful realities, more impressive than the most authentic reports, and which may be as distinctly recognized at all times as at the moment of their original occurrence. The entire system of evangelical religion hence acquires new evidence and attraction, tending to produce a deeper conviction of its truth, and a more cordial compliance with its invitations. Should the following attempt to develop this evidence contribute in any degree to promote such effects, the wishes of the author will be amply fulfilled.

PART I.

INVESTIGATION OF THE IMMEDIATE CAUSE OF THE DEATH OF CHRIST.

CHAPTER I.

EVANGELICAL NARRATIVE OF THE DEATH OF CHRIST.

Having been divinely anointed as the prophet, priest, and king of his people, Christ successively assumed, during his life on earth, each of those sacred characters; his prophetical office having commenced at his baptism, his priesthood at the last supper, and his kingdom at his resurrection. When his public ministry in Jerusalem was concluded, he entered on his priestly functions by celebrating the passover with his apostles; whom, under the influence of the most generous affection, he continued till the last moment to instruct and console. After predicting the events which were immediately to befall him, and commending himself, his disciples, and his cause in solemn prayer to the Father, he closed the hallowed engagement, and spontaneously proceeded to the scene where his sufferings were to begin. The apostle John, by whom alone this prayer is recorded, thus connects it with the sequel:

. . . .

When Jesus had spoken these words he went forth

with his disciples, and having sung a hymn they repaired, as usual, to the Mount of Olives. He then said to them, "All of you will this night be offended by me, for it is written,—*I will smite the shepherd; and the sheep of the flock will be scattered;*—but after I am risen [from the dead], I will go before you to Galilee."—Peter answered him,—" Though all [others] should be offended by thee, I will never be offended."—Jesus said to him,—" I tell thee truly that to-day, [even] this very night, before the cock crows the second time, thou wilt disown me thrice:"—but he spoke the more positively,—" Though I should die with thee, I will never disown thee:"—So likewise said all the disciples. Then came Jesus with them to a place beyond the brook Kidron, called Gethsemane, where was a garden, into which he and his disciples entered. And Judas also, who betrayed him, knew the spot, for Jesus and his disciples often assembled there. On arriving at this place he said to them,—" Sit here whilst I go and pray yonder, [and] pray that ye may not fall into temptation."—Then taking apart with him Peter, and the two sons of Zebediah, James and John, he was seized with consternation and distress : * and said to them,—" My soul is exceedingly sorrowful, even unto death : remain here, and watch with me."—And he hastily withdrew from them about a stone's cast,† and kneeling down, threw himself on his face, and prayed that, if it were possible, the hour might pass from him, saying—" Abba! [that is] Father! if it be possible, let this cup pass from me; nevertheless not my will, but thine be done."—Returning to

---

The portions of the four Gospels here harmonized are,—Matt., chap. 26, v. 30–75 ; chap. 27;—Mark, chap. 14, v. 26–72 ; chap. 15 ;—Luke, chap. 22, v. 39–71 ; chap. 23 ;—and John, chaps. 18 and 19.

* ἤρξατο ἐκθαμβεῖσθαι καὶ ἀδημονεῖν. Mark, chap. 14, v. 33.

† Καὶ αὐτὸς ἀπεσπάσθη ἀπ' αὐτῶν ὡσεὶ λίθου βολήν. Luke, chap. 22, v. 41.

DEATH OF CHRIST.

the disciples he found them asleep, and said to Peter,—"Simon! sleepest thou? Are ye thus unable to watch with me a single hour? Watch and pray that ye may not fall into temptation. The spirit indeed is willing, but the flesh is weak."—Again withdrawing, he prayed a second time, saying the same words;—"My Father! if this cup cannot pass from me unless I drink it, thy will be done."—On returning, he found them asleep again, for their eyes were heavy, and they knew not what to answer him. Again withdrawing from them, he prayed a third time, saying the same words; and there appeared to him an angel from heaven, strengthening him. Then, falling into an agony, he prayed most earnestly, and his sweat became, as it were, clots of blood dropping to the ground. Rising from prayer, he returned a third time to the disciples, and found them asleep through sorrow, and said to them,—"Do ye sleep and rest till the last moment? Rise, and pray that ye may not fall into temptation. There is no longer time. The hour is come.[*] Behold! the Son of man is betrayed into the hands of sinners. Rise, let us go. Behold! he that betrayeth me is at hand."

While he was yet speaking, behold! Judas, one of the twelve, having taken the Roman guard,[†] besides officers from the chief priests and Pharisees, came thither with lanterns, and torches, and weapons. And he had appointed them a signal, saying,—["The man] whom I shall kiss is he, seize him, and lead him away securely."—So he instantly went up to Jesus, and said—"Hail, Rabbi!"—and earnestly kissed him: but Jesus said to him,—"Companion! for what purpose art thou come? Judas! dost thou betray the Son of man by a kiss?"—Then Jesus, knowing all that was about to befall him,

---

[*] Ἀπέχει, ἦλθεν ἡ ὥρα. Mark, chap. 14, v. 41.
[†] λαβὼν τὴν σπεῖραν. John, chap. 18, v. 3.

went forth and said to them,—"Whom seek ye?"—They answered him,—"Jesus of Nazareth;"—Jesus said to them,—"I am he."—And Judas also who betrayed him was standing with them. As soon then as he had said to them,—"I am he,"—they drew backward, and fell to the ground. Then he asked them again,—"Whom seek ye?"—They said,—"Jesus of Nazareth."—Jesus answered,—"I have told you that I am he: if therefore ye seek me, allow these men to depart;" thus fulfilling the declaration which he had made,—"Of those whom thou gavest me I have not lost one."—Then they advanced, laid hands on Jesus, and seized him. On this, those who were with him, perceiving what was about to happen, said to him,—"Lord, shall we smite with the sword?" and Simon Peter having a sword drew it, and smote the high priest's slave, and cut off his right ear: the slave's name was Malchus. Then said Jesus to Peter,—"Put the sword into the scabbard, for all who take the sword will perish by the sword. The cup which the Father hath given me, shall I not drink it? Thinkest thou that I cannot even now request my Father, and he would send to my aid more than twelve legions of angels?—[but] how then would the Scriptures be fulfilled, [which declare] that thus it must be?"—And he said,—"Suffer [me] thus far:"—and, touching the ear of Malchus, he healed him. Then said Jesus to the chief priests, commanders of the temple [guard], and elders, who had come forth against him,—"Are ye come forth as against a robber, with swords and staves, to seize me? I sat daily among you, teaching in the temple, and ye did not seize me; but this is your hour, and the power of darkness, in fulfilment of the writings of the prophets."—Then all the disciples forsook him, and fled.

So the guard, and [their] commander, and the officers

of the Jews,* seized Jesus, and bound him. And there followed him a certain youth having no other clothing than a linen sheet, and the young men seized him; on which leaving the sheet he fled from them naked. They led Jesus, in the first instance, to Annas, for he was father-in-law of Caiaphas, who was high priest that year. Caiaphas was he who had counselled the Jews that it was expedient one man should die for the nation. Annas sent Jesus bound to Caiaphas, the high priest, at whose palace all the chief priests, scribes, and elders were assembled. Now Simon Peter had followed Jesus at a distance; another disciple also [followed him]: that disciple was known to the high priest, and entered with Jesus into the palace, but Peter stood without at the gate; so the other disciple who was known to the high priest went out, and spoke to the maid-servant who attended the gate, and obtained admission for Peter. Then said the maid-servant to Peter,—"Art not thou also [one] of this man's disciples?"—He said,—"I am not:"—and he went in, and joined the officers, to see the end. The slaves and officers were standing round a fire of embers which they had kindled in the midst of the hall, for it was cold, and were warming themselves, and Peter stood with them, and warmed himself. While he was there, one of the maid-servants of the high priest came, and seeing Peter sitting at the fire, after looking steadfastly at him, said,—"This man also was with him,—Thou also wast with Jesus of Nazareth:"—but he disowned him before them all, saying,—"Woman, I know him not, neither do I understand what thou meanest."—A little after another person saw him, and said,—"Thou also art [one] of them:"—but Peter said,—"Man, I am not:"—and he went out into the porch, and the cock crew. While he was there,

* Ἡ οὖν σπεῖρα, καὶ ὁ χιλίαρχος, καὶ οἱ ὑπηρέται τῶν Ἰουδαίων, etc. John, chap. 18, v. 12.

another [maid-servant] saw him, and said to those who were present,—" This man also was with Jesus of Nazareth."—Again he denied [it] with an oath, [saying],—" I know not the man."—Now the high priest questioned Jesus concerning his disciples, and his doctrine. Jesus answered him,—" I spoke openly to the world, I always taught in synagogues, and in the temple, where all the Jews assemble,* and I have not taught any thing in secret. Why askest thou me? Ask those who heard [me] what I spoke to them. Behold! they know what I have spoken."—On his saying this, one of the officers who stood near struck him with his staff, saying,—" Answerest thou the high priest thus?"—Jesus replied to him,—" If I have spoken evil, bear witness of the evil; but if well, why strikest thou me?"—Then the chief priests, and the elders, and the whole Sanhedrim sought for evidence against Jesus, that they might sentence him to death, but were unable to obtain it; for although many witnessed falsely against him, their charges did not agree. At length two false witnesses came forward, and declared,—" This man said,—I am able to destroy the temple of God, and in three days to build it again.—We heard him say,—I will destroy this temple made with hands, and in three days I will build another not made with hands:"—yet even thus their evidence did not agree. Then the high priest, standing up in the midst, questioned Jesus, saying,—" Dost not thou make any answer? What is it that these men witness against thee?"—but he continued silent, and returned no answer; on which the high priest said to him,—" I adjure thee by the living God to tell us whether thou art the Christ, the Son of God."—Jesus said to him,—[" It is as] thou hast said; [and] I further tell you, Hereafter ye shall see the Son of man sitting at the

* ὅπου πάντες οἱ Ἰουδαῖοι συνέρχονται. John, chap. 18, v. 20.

right hand of the Almighty,* and coming on the clouds of heaven."—Then the high priest rent his clothes, saying,—" He hath spoken blasphemy: what further need have we of witnesses? Behold! ye have now heard his blasphemy. What think ye?—They all answered,—"He is deserving of death."—[Meanwhile] Simon Peter was standing and warming himself. So they said to him,—" Art not thou also [one] of his disciples?"—He denied [it], and said,—" I am not."—One of the high priest's slaves, a relative [of him] whose ear Peter cut off, said,—" Did not I see thee in the garden with him?"—Again Peter denied [it].—A little after another man confidently affirmed, saying,—" Certainly this man also was with him, for he is a Galilean."—So the bystanders came up, and said again to Peter,—" Certainly thou also art [one] of them, for thy [manner of] speaking is similar, [and] discovereth thee:"—but he began to utter oaths and curses [saying],—" Man, I know not what thou meanest: I know not this man of whom ye speak:"—and instantly, while he was yet speaking, the cock crew the second time. And the Lord turned and looked on Peter; and Peter remembered what the Lord had said to him,—" Before the cock crows the second time thou wilt disown me thrice;"†—and he went out, and wept bitterly. The men who guarded Jesus mocked him, and beat him: some began to spit on him, and to blindfold him, and to buffet him, and the officers struck him [with their staves], saying,—" Divine to us, Christ: Who is it that smote thee?"— and many other blasphemies uttered they against him.

* καθήμενον ἐκ δεξιῶν τῆς δυνάμεως. Matt. chap. 26, v. 64.

† Before the second cock-crowing Peter denied Christ seven times. Four times he declared that he was not one of his disciples, and three times that he did not know him. It was the latter mode of denial which Christ had specially predicted. Luke, chap. 22, v. 34.

As soon as it was morning, all the chief priests, with the elders of the people, and the scribes, held a consultation against Jesus, to put him to death; and having brought him again into their Sanhedrim, they said,—" Tell us whether thou art the Christ."—He said to them,—" If I tell you ye will not believe, and if I question [you] ye will neither answer me, nor release [me]. Henceforth the Son of man will sit at the right hand of the Almighty."— On this they all said,—"Art thou then the Son of God?" —He replied to them,—" Ye say what I am."—They said, —" What further need have we of evidence, since we ourselves have heard [enough] from his own mouth?"—And the whole assembly of them rose up, and having bound Jesus, led [him] away, and delivered him to Pontius Pilate, the governor. When Judas who had betrayed him found that he was condemned, he regretted [what he had done,]* and brought back the thirty pieces of silver to the chief priests and elders, saying,—" I have sinned by betraying innocent blood."—They replied,—" What [is that] to us? See thou [to that]:"—on which he threw down the silver pieces in the temple, and went away, and hanged himself. The chief priests took the money, and said,—" It is not lawful to put it into the treasury, because it is the price of blood:"—and after consulting, they purchased with it the potter's field, as a burial-ground for strangers; on which account that field is to this day called a field of blood. Then was fulfilled what was spoken by the prophet Jeremiah:—*And I took the thirty pieces of silver, the price of him who was appraised, whom some of the sons of Israel appraised,†* and *I gave them for the potter's field, as the Lord commanded me.*—So they led Jesus from [the palace] of Caiaphas to that of the Roman gov-

* μεταμεληθείς. Matt. chap. 27, v. 3.

† τὴν τιμὴν τοῦ τετιμημένου, ὃν ἐτιμήσαντο ἀπὸ υἱῶν Ἰσραὴλ. Matt. chap. 27, v. 9;—Zech. chap. 11, v. 12, 13.

ernor,* and it was early. They did not themselves enter the governor's palace, lest they should be defiled, and prevented from keeping the passover.† Pilate therefore went forth to them, and said,—" What accusation do ye bring against this man?"—They answered him,—" If he were not a malefactor we should not have delivered him to thee."—Pilate said to them,—" Take him yourselves, and judge him according to your law."—The Jews said to him,—" We have no authority to put any one to death;" —thereby fulfilling what Jesus had said, when intimating what kind of death he was to die. Then they began to accuse him, saying,—" We found this man perverting the nation, and forbidding to pay tribute to Cæsar, declaring himself to be Christ [the] king."—And Jesus stood before the governor: so the governor asked him,—" Art thou the king of the Jews?"—He answered him,—[" It is as] thou sayest:"—and on being accused by the chief priests and elders, he made no reply. Then Pilate asked him again,— "Dost not thou make any reply? See how many charges they bring against thee:"—but Jesus still made no reply, whereat the governor wondered exceedingly. Then Pilate returned into the palace, and having called Jesus, said to him,—" Art thou the king of the Jews?"—Jesus answered,—" Sayest thou this of thyself, or have others told it thee concerning me?"—Pilate replied,—" Am I a Jew? Thine own nation, and the chief priests have delivered thee to me. What hast thou done?"—Jesus answered,—" My kingdom is not of this world. If my kingdom were of this world, my followers would have striven that I should not have been delivered to the Jews; but now [it is evident that] my kingdom is not of this world?"‡

---

* ἀπὸ τοῦ Καϊάφα εἰς τὸ πραιτώριον. John, chap. 18, v. 28.

† ἀλλ' ἵνα φάγωσι τὸ πάσχα. John, chap. 18, v. 28;—not the paschal supper, which had been celebrated the evening before, but the paschal festival regarded as a whole.

‡ νῦν δὲ ἡ βασιλεία ἡ ἐμὴ οὐκ ἔστιν ἐντεῦθεν. John, chap. 18, v. 36.

—Pilate said to him,—" Art thou a king then?"—Jesus answered,—[" As] thou sayest, I am a king. For this purpose was I born, and for this purpose came I into the world, that I should bear witness to the truth. Whosoever is of the truth obeyeth my voice."—Pilate said to him,—" What is truth?"—Having thus spoken, he again went forth to the Jews, and said to the chief priests, and to the multitude,—" I find no fault in this man:" but they became more urgent, saying,—" He stirreth up the people, and hath spread his doctrine throughout all Judea to this place, beginning from Galilee."—On hearing of Galilee, Pilate asked, " Is the man a Galilean?"*—and having learned that he belonged to Herod's jurisdiction, he sent him to Herod, who also was at Jerusalem during that season. When Herod saw Jesus he was very glad, for he had long wished to see him on account of the numerous reports which he had heard of him, and he hoped to see some miracle performed by him: he therefore asked him many questions, but Jesus gave him no answer. Meanwhile the chief priests and the scribes stood by, vehemently accusing him; but Herod, with his guards, made light of him, and mocked [him], and after dressing him in a splendid robe, sent him back to Pilate. The same day Pilate and Herod were reconciled to each other, for they had previously been at enmity. Then Pilate, having called together the chief priests, with the rulers, and the people, said to them,—" Ye have brought me this man as a perverter of the people, and behold! after examining [him] before you, I have not found him guilty of any of the crimes whereof ye accuse him; neither has Herod, for I sent you to him, and behold! nothing deserving of death has been done by the man.† I will therefore chastise him,

---

* ἐπηρώτησεν,—Εἰ ὁ ἄνθρωπος Γαλιλαῖός ἐστι; Luke, chap. 23, v. 6.

† οὐδὲν ἄξιον θανάτου ἐστὶ πεπραγμένον αὐτῷ. Luke, chap. 23, v. 15—" has done by him."

and release [him]."—Now at each return of the festival the governor had been accustomed to release to the multitude any prisoner whom they chose. And they had at the time a prisoner of note, named Barabbas, a robber, who, on account of a sedition attended with murder which had taken place in the city, was in prison with his accomplices. The multitude then began with loud cries to request [Pilate to do for them] what he had always done: so, as they were assembled, he said to them;—"Ye have a custom that at the passover I should release a [prisoner] to you. Which, therefore, do ye wish me to release to you, Barabbas, or Jesus who is called Christ? Do ye choose that I should release to you the king of the Jews?"—for he knew that through envy the chief priests had delivered him [into his hands]. While he was sitting on the judgment-seat, his wife sent to him, saying,—"Have nothing to do with that righteous man, for I have suffered much in a dream to-day because of him:" but the chief priests and elders persuaded the multitude to demand Barabbas, and destroy Jesus. Then the governor said again to them,—"Which of the two do ye wish me to release to you?"—They all cried aloud in a body,—"Away with this man, and release to us Barabbas."—Desirous to release Jesus, Pilate once more addressed [them],—"What then shall I do to Jesus, who is called Christ, whom ye term king of the Jews?"— They cried out in reply,—"Crucify [him], crucify him."— He spoke to them the third time,—"Why? what evil hath he done? I have not found him guilty of any crime deserving of death, I will therefore chastise him, and release [him]:"—but they were urgent with loud cries, demanding that he should be crucified. Then Pilate took Jesus, and caused him to be scourged:* and the soldiers, after stripping him, threw around him a purple military robe, and having platted a crown of thorns, they put [it] on his

---

* ἐμαστίγωσε. John, chap. 19, v. 1.

head, and a cane* in his right hand, and kneeling before him they mocked him, saying—" Hail, king of the Jews!" and after spitting on him, they took the cane and struck him on the head. Pilate then went out again, and said to the Jews,—" Behold! I bring him forth to you, to let you know that I find no fault in him."—So Jesus came forth, wearing the crown of thorns and the purple robe. And Pilate said to them,—" Behold the man!"—but when the chief priests and the officers saw him, they cried out,—" Crucify [him], crucify him."—Pilate said to them,—" Take him yourselves and crucify [him], for I find no fault in him."—The Jews answered him,—" We have a law, and according to our law he ought to die, because he hath claimed to be the Son of God."†—On hearing this, Pilate became more alarmed, and returning into the palace, said to Jesus,—" Whence art thou?"—but Jesus gave him no answer. Pilate said to him,—" Dost thou refuse to speak to me? Knowest thou not that I have authority to crucify thee, and authority to release thee?"—Jesus replied,—" Thou wouldest not have had any authority at all against me, had it not been given thee from above; therefore he that delivered me to thee hath the greater sin."—Thereupon Pilate endeavored to release him, but the Jews cried out,—" If thou release this man, thou art no friend of Cæsar. Whosoever claimeth to be a king denieth the claims of Cæsar."‡—On hearing these words Pilate brought Jesus forth, and sat down on the judgment-seat in a place called the Pavement,—in Hebrew, Gabbatha. It was the preparation-day of the passover,

---

* κάλαμον. Matt. chap. 27, v. 29. For the convenience of the narrative, the accounts given by Matthew and Mark of the second mockery of Christ by the Roman soldiers are transferred to this place.

† ὅτι ἑαυτὸν υἱὸν θεοῦ ἐποίησεν. John, chap. 19, v. 7.

‡ Πᾶς ὁ βασιλέα ἑαυτὸν ποιῶν ἀντιλέγει τῷ Καίσαρι. John, chap. 19, v. 12.

and about the sixth hour.* And he said to the Jews,—
"Behold your king:"—but they cried out,—"Away with
him, away with him, crucify him."—Pilate said to them,—
"Shall I crucify your king?"—The chief priests replied,—
"We have no king but Cæsar."—When Pilate perceived
that his efforts were of no avail, but that, on the contrary,
a tumult was arising, he took water, and washed his hands
before the multitude, saying,—"I am innocent of the blood
of this righteous man: See ye to it."—All the people replied,—"His blood be on us, and on our children."—And
their clamors, and those of the chief priests prevailed; for
Pilate, desirous to satisfy the multitude, gave sentence
that their demand should be executed. So he released to
them Barabbas, imprisoned on account of sedition and
murder, whom they had desired, and delivered Jesus to
them to be crucified.

Then the soldiers of the governor took Jesus into the
palace, and gathered around him the whole guard; and
when they had [again] mocked him, they stripped him of
the purple robe, put on him his own clothes, and led him
away to crucify [him]. As they went forth, they met
coming from the country a Cyrenian named Simon, the
father of Alexander and Rufus: him they compelled [to
assist, and] laid on him the cross to carry behind Jesus.
And there followed him a great multitude of the people,
as likewise many women, who smote their breasts and
lamented him; but Jesus turned toward them and said,—
"Daughters of Jerusalem, weep not for me, but weep for
yourselves and for your children: for behold! days are
coming wherein they will say, Happy [are] barren women,
wombs which never bare, and breasts which never suckled.
Then will they begin to say to the mountains, Fall on us,

---

* So termed by John, chap. 19, v. 14; probably in reference to some
ecclesiastical computation of the day, equivalent to the third civil hour so
distinctly mentioned by Mark, chap. 15, v. 25.

and to the hills, Cover us; for if they do these things to the green tree, what will be done to the dry [tree]?"— And two malefactors were also led forth to suffer death with him. So bearing his cross, Jesus went forth to the place named after a skull,* and in Hebrew called Golgotha. On arriving at this place, they offered him a draught of wine and myrrh,† [as it were] vinegar mingled with gall; but after tasting he refused to drink [it]. Then they crucified him there, as likewise the malefactors, one on the right hand, the other on the left, and Jesus in the midst; in fulfilment of the Scripture which saith,—*He was ranked among transgressors;*—but Jesus said,—"Father! forgive them, for they know not what they are doing."—Pilate also caused a title denoting the charge against Jesus to be written, and fixed to the cross over his head,—THIS IS JESUS OF NAZARETH, THE KING OF THE JEWS.—Many of the Jews therefore read this title; for the quarter of the city where Jesus was crucified was near,‡ and it was written in Hebrew, Greek, [and] Latin. Then said the Jewish chief priests to Pilate,—"Write not, The king of the Jews; but that he said, I am king of the Jews." Pilate answered,— "What I have written I have written."—When the soldiers had crucified Jesus they took his outer garments, and divided them into four parts, for each soldier a part, as likewise his vest. Now the vest was without seam, woven from the top throughout: so they said one to another,— "Let us not rend it, but cast lots for it, [to settle] whose it shall be;"—in fulfilment of the Scripture which saith,—

---

* ἐξῆλθεν εἰς τὸν λεγόμενον Κρανίου τόπον. John, chap. 19, v. 17. Golgotha is never in Scripture termed a mount.

† ἐσμυρνισμένον οἶνον: Mark, chap. 15, v. 23; here supposed to be equivalent to the vinegar mingled with gall, mentioned by Matt. chap. 27, v. 34.

‡ ὅτι ἐγγὺς ἦν ὁ τόπος τῆς πόλεως ὅπου ἐσταυρώθη ὁ 'Ιησοῦς. John, chap. 19, v. 20; so termed in a general sense, although without the walls of Jerusalem. Heb. chap. 13, v. 11, 12.

They parted my garments among them, and for my vesture they cast lots.—Thus accordingly the soldiers did; for after parting his outer garments, they cast lots for them, [to settle] what each man should take. It was the third hour when they crucified him, and they sat down and guarded him there, while the people stood looking on. And those who passed by reviled him, shaking their heads, and saying,—"Aha! thou that destroyest the temple, and rebuildest [it] in three days, save thyself. If thou art the Son of God, come down from the cross."—In like manner the chief priests also, jesting among themselves, with the scribes and elders said,—"He saved others, [but] cannot save himself. If he is the Christ, the chosen of God, the king of Israel, let him now come down from the cross, that we may see and believe. He trusted in God; let [God] now deliver him if he will have him, for he said, I am the Son of God."—The soldiers likewise mocked him, coming up and offering him vinegar, and saying,—"If thou art the king of the Jews, save thyself."—One even of the crucified malefactors reviled him, saying,—"If thou art the Christ, save thyself and us:"—but the other replied, and rebuked him, saying,—"Dost not thou fear God, since thou art suffering the same punishment?* We indeed [suffer] justly, for we receive the due recompense of our actions, but this man never did any thing amiss."—And he said to Jesus,—"Lord! remember me when thou comest in thy kingdom."—Jesus said to him,—"I tell thee truly, this day thou shalt be with me in Paradise."—Now there stood near the cross of Jesus his mother, and Mary the [wife] of Cleopas, her sister, and Mary of Magdala. Then Jesus seeing his mother, and the disciple also whom he loved standing near, said to his mother,—"Woman! behold thy son:"—then he said to the disciple,—"Behold thy mother:"—and from that hour the disciple received

---

* ὅτι ἐν τῷ αὐτῷ κρίματι εἶ.   Luke, chap. 23, v. 40.

her to his home. When the sixth hour was come a darkness overspread the whole land till the ninth hour, and the sun was obscured. At the ninth hour Jesus cried with a loud voice,—"Eloi! Eloi! lamma sabachthani?"—which when translated is,—"My God! my God! why hast thou forsaken me?"—On hearing [this], some of the bystanders said,—"Behold! he calleth on Elijah."—Then Jesus, knowing that all things were now accomplished, that the Scripture might be fulfilled, said—"I thirst."—And there stood near a vessel full of vinegar: so one of them immediately ran, and took a sponge, and having filled [it] with vinegar, and fastened [it] to a rod of hyssop,* gave him drink; but the rest said,—"Hold! let us see whether Elijah will come and deliver him."—When Jesus had received the vinegar he again cried with a loud voice, saying,—"[All] is accomplished: Father! into thy hands I commit my spirit."—Having thus spoken, he bowed his head and resigned his spirit. And behold! the veil of the temple split asunder in the midst from the top to the bottom, and the earth quaked, and the rocks were rent, and the tombs were opened, and many bodies of holy persons deceased arose, who coming out of the tombs after his resurrection, entered the holy city and appeared to many. When the centurion who stood opposite, and those who were with him guarding Jesus, observed the earthquake and the [other] events, [and] that he expired with such a cry, they feared greatly, [and] gave Glory to God, saying,— "Certainly this man was a son of God."†—And the whole multitude who had come together to this spectacle, on observing these events, returned smiting their breasts. And

---

* καὶ περιθεὶς καλάμῳ. Matt. chap. 27, v. 48;—Mark, chap. 15, v. 36; καὶ ὑσσώπῳ περιθέντες. John, chap. 19, v. 29; supposed to be the stem of a large species of hyssop, probably growing on the spot.

† θεοῦ υἱός. Matt. chap. 27, v. 54:—υἱὸς θεοῦ, Mark, chap. 15, v. 39:—δίκαιος, Luke, chap. 23, v. 47.

all the friends and acquaintance of Jesus stood afar off beholding these things, with many women, among whom was Mary of Magdala, and Mary the mother of James the less, and of Joses, and Salome the mother of the sons of Zebadiah; who had also followed him and ministered to him when he was in Galilee, as likewise many other women who had come up with him to Jerusalem.

Now in order that the bodies might not remain on the cross during the sabbath-day, as it was then the preparation-day, for that sabbath-day was a high day, the Jews requested Pilate that their legs might be broken, and that they might be taken away. So the soldiers came and broke the legs of the first and of the other who was crucified with Jesus; but, on coming to him, as they perceived that he was already dead, they did not break his legs: one of the soldiers, however, pierced his side with a spear, and immediately there came forth blood and water. He that bears [this] testimony saw [the fact *], and his testimony is true, and he is sure that he relates what is true, that ye also may believe: for these things happened in fulfilment of the scripture,—*not one of his bones shall be broken;*—and again, another scripture saith,—*They shall look on him whom they pierced.*—After this, when it was now late, there came a rich man of Arimathea, a city of the Jews, named Joseph, a good and upright man, and a member of the Sanhedrim, but who had not consented to their plot nor to its execution,† being himself one who expected the kingdom of God, and a disciple of Jesus, although secretly through fear of the Jews: this man went boldly to Pilate, and requested that he might take the body of Jesus. Pilate wondered if Jesus were already dead, so calling the centurion, he asked him if he

---

* Καὶ ὁ ἑωρακὼς μεμαρτύρηκε. John, chap. 19, v. 35.
† Οὗτος οὐκ ἦν συγκατατεθειμένος τῇ βουλῇ καὶ τῇ πράξει αὐτῶν. Luke, chap. 23, v. 51.

had been any time dead, and having been assured [of this] by the centurion, he granted the body to Joseph. Then Joseph came, and took the body [from the cross]: Nicodemus, who at first went to Jesus by night, also came bringing a mixture of myrrh and aloes-wood, about a hundred pounds [in weight]: so they took the body of Jesus, and having purchased new linen, bound the body in bandages with the spices according to the Jewish manner of embalming. Now in the place where Jesus had been crucified was a garden, and in the garden a new tomb which [Joseph] had caused to be hewn for himself out of the rock, [but] wherein no one had ever been laid. There then, on account of the Jews' preparation-day, as the sabbath was approaching and the tomb near, they laid Jesus, and after rolling a large stone against the entrance of the tomb they departed. Meanwhile Mary of Magdala, and Mary [the mother] of Joses were sitting opposite, and with the other women observed the tomb, and how the body was laid; after which, returning [into the city], they provided spices and ointments, but rested on the sabbath-day according to the commandment. On the following day, that is [the day] after the preparation-day,* the chief priests and Pharisees went in a body to Pilate and said,—"Sir, we remember that when this impostor was alive he said, Within three days I shall rise [from the dead]. Command therefore that the tomb be secured till the third day, lest his disciples should go and steal him [away], and tell the people, He is risen from the dead; for this last imposture would be worse than the first."—Pilate said to them,—"Take a guard, go [and]

---

* Namely, the sabbath; described in this circumlocutory manner by Matthew, chap. 27, v. 62, apparently to avoid the indecorum of directly charging the chief priests, etc., with sabbath-breaking.

make [every thing] secure in your own way."*—So they went, and after sealing the stone, secured the tomb by the guard.

. . . .

* Ἔχετε κουστωδίαν, ὑπάγετε, ἀσφαλίσασθε ὡς οἴδατε. Matt. chap. 27, v. 65.

CHAPTER II.

SUMMARY OF THE PRINCIPAL CIRCUMSTANCES WHICH ATTENDED THE DEATH OF CHRIST.

Although important explanations of the death of Christ are furnished by other portions of Scripture, the principal information respecting the mode in which it happened must obviously be derived from the narratives of the four evangelists, which, in a combined and harmonized form, have now been presented. The whole transaction was extraordinary and peculiar. On this occasion, as on some others which required a decisive evidence of the truth of revelation, the hand of God was displayed in first appointing, and afterward accomplishing a conjuncture of circumstances so complex and seemingly incompatible, that had it not been actually realized, few persons would have believed its possibility, and none would have ventured to predict its occurrence. Many centuries before the event, the voice of prophecy had proclaimed that the Saviour of mankind would suffer a death at once violent and voluntary, as a criminal, and as a victim, universally approved by God and man, yet loaded with the malediction of both. His death was to be directed by Jewish priests without power, and executed by Gentile rulers without authority, and he was to be condemned on a charge in which, notwithstanding their religious hostility, both parties could unite in attesting and rejecting his claims as the Messiah. He was to suffer the death of the cross, which commonly happened by slow exhaustion, and in Judea was usually hastened by breaking the legs, yet none of his bones was to be broken. His heart was at the same time to be pierced, and he was to die suddenly as a sin-offering by the effusion of his life's blood, the appointed means of atonement, although the former was not essential to the punishment of crucifixion, and the latter was the very reverse of its usual effect. The actual accomplishment of all these intricate and apparently discordant conditions is formally asserted in various parts of the New Testament, not as a casual coincidence, but as indispensably necessary to the fulfilment of prophecy, the veracity of which would have been forfeited had any one of them failed to take place.

To prevent misapprehension, it is proper to state that in the following investigation the union of the divine and human natures in the person of Christ is fully acknowledged, but that, in conformity with the dictates both of reason and revelation, the two natures are regarded as totally distinct, the latter only having been susceptible of suffering and death. Hence, in all that concerns the sufferings and death of the Saviour, attention will be exclusively directed to a pure and perfect human nature, subject to those influences and agencies which the circumstances involved, and which the Scriptures represent. With such a nature specially prepared by the Holy Spirit, and fitted to make an atoning sacrifice for the sins of the world, in the full possession of all his faculties, and in the very prime and vigor of life, a little under thirty-five years of age, the Redeemer entered on his sufferings, which were completed within the space of eighteen hours, and actually occupied eight. The discourses and devotional exercises in which he engaged with his apostles after the paschal supper, probably celebrated in a house on Mount Zion, must have been continued till an advanced hour of the night, since they were of considerable length, and it was already late when they began.* Hence, it could not have been much before midnight when he arrived in the garden of Gethsemane, at the foot of the Mount of Olives. There, during an hour from which he earnestly prayed to be delivered, he was seized with mental anguish of so peculiar and intense a character as to force from him a bloody sweat; and which, had he not been strengthened by supernatural aid, might very possibly have occasioned his death on the spot. During the ten following hours, the greater part of which was passed before the tribunals of the Sanhedrim and of Pontius Pilate, he evinced the utmost firmness and self-possession; and, with the exception of the indignities offered him by the Jewish domestics and the Roman soldiers, his bodily sufferings were chiefly confined to the scourging which generally preceded crucifixion, and in his case was designed to supersede it. Some commentators have imagined that this scourging was unusually severe, but to such a supposition the scriptural narrative gives no countenance, and the respect manifested by Pilate toward a prisoner whom he repeatedly declared to be innocent, and anxiously labored to release, renders it inadmissible. The crucifixion of Christ occupied the exact interval of six hours, between the times of the morning and evening sacrifice in the temple, on the first day of the paschal festival, having commenced at the third hour of the day, and terminated at the ninth.† From some expressions which fell from him, it is evident that during the latter part of this awful period the peculiar sufferings of Gethsemane were re-

---

* On mentioning the retirement of Judas Iscariot, which took place after the paschal supper, and before the commencement of Christ's discourses with the other apostles, John states that—"it was night."—Chap. 13, v. 29, 30.

† Coinciding with nine o'clock in the forenoon, and three in the afternoon, according to modern European computation.

newed, while at the same time his energy of mind and body was displayed by characteristic actions and discourses, and by several loud and pious exclamations uttered immediately before his death, which took place very suddenly, and much earlier than might naturally have been expected. Its speedy and abrupt occurrence accordingly excited the surprise of the centurion who superintended the execution, and of the Roman governor who commanded it. Thus, when Joseph of Arimathea asked permission to remove the body of Jesus for the purpose of interment, Pilate wondered if he were already dead, and it was not until he had ascertained the fact from the centurion, that he granted the request. The two malefactors, crucified at the same time and place, were still living, and, in compliance with the customs of the country, were dispatched and buried before sunset. When, however, the soldiers came for a similar purpose to Jesus, as they found him already dead, they did not break his bones; but, as if to remove all possibility of doubt on the subject, one of them pierced his side with a spear, whereupon, as recorded by the apostle John, an eye-witness of the scene from its commencement to its close,—" immediately there came forth blood and water."—In opposition to various misrepresentations of this momentous fact, originating either from inadvertence or design, the Scriptures plainly state that Christ died the death of the cross, appointed by the Father, accepted by himself, demanded by the Jewish people, and executed by the Gentile government to which they were then subject. In proof of this assertion many passages might be cited, but two will suffice. When addressing the immense multitude of Israelites assembled at Jerusalem from all parts of the world on the ensuing day of Pentecost, Peter distinctly charged the nation with the murder of Jesus:—" Him, having been delivered up by the determinate counsel and foreknowledge of God, ye took, and, by the hands of wicked men, crucified and slew;"—and Paul, writing to the Greek Church at Philippi, says of the Saviour that,—" although in the form of God, and deeming it no robbery to be equal to God, he stripped himself of his glory, assumed the form of a slave, and was made in the likeness of men, and having been found in aspect as a man, humbled himself, and became obedient unto death, even the death of the cross." *—No explanation of the fact can therefore be admitted, in which this condition is not fully acknowledged.

* Acts, chap. 2, v. 22, 23; chap. 3, v. 13–15; chap. 5, v. 29, 30; chap. 7, v. 51, 52;—Philipp. chap. 2, v. 5–8, etc.

CHAPTER III.

REJECTION OF ERRONEOUS EXPLANATIONS OF THE DEATH OF CHRIST.

By a certain class of German theologians who arrogate to themselves the title of Rationalists, the reality of Christ's death on the cross has been questioned, or denied. In the course of this treatise the fact will be incidentally established by new and conclusive evidence, but, for the present, will be simply assumed on the testimony of Scripture, the statements of which concerning this point are so numerous and positive that, could they be disproved, its claims not merely to inspiration, but even to ordinary credibility, would be destroyed, and any further inquiry on the subject would be irrational. The fact being therefore assumed, its explanation will now be attempted, and, in order to exclude mere conjecture, and aim at demonstration, the common rules respecting the assignment of causes will be strictly observed; namely, those causes only will be deemed admissible which actually preceded the effect, were adequate to its production, and perfectly accord with all the circumstances of the case, and the cause in which these conditions are found most completely to concur, will be regarded as the true one. By a majority of those whose knowledge of the subject is chiefly derived from the evangelical narrative, the death of Christ is not unreasonably ascribed to the ordinary sufferings of crucifixion; but as the nature of this punishment is at present very little understood, and no conclusion respecting it can be satisfactory which does not rest on competent information, a short account of it will here be introduced.

The cruel mode of putting condemned persons to death by nailing them to a cross prevailed among various nations of the ancient world, both civilized and barbarous, from the earliest times * till the reign of the Emperor Constantine, by whom, partly from motives of humanity, but chiefly from reverence to Christ, it was finally abrogated throughout the Roman empire.—"His respect for the cross of our Saviour"—says Crevier,—"made him abolish crucifixion, a death which the Greeks and Romans had at all times inflicted upon criminals, particularly slaves. He would not suffer the instrument of our salvation to be dishonored by any use, not only profane, but capable of making men look upon it with horror. He thought it indecent and irreligious that the cross should be used for the punishment of the vilest offenders, while he himself erected it as a trophy, and esteemed it the noblest ornament of his diadem, and military standards. The text of this law, so worthy of the piety of the first Christian emperor, has not been preserved; but the fact is asserted by a pagan writer, and the practice of all the princes and nations who profess Christianity is agreeable to it. The same religious sentiment induced Constantine likewise to forbid breaking the legs of criminals, a punishment often annexed to that of the cross, as appears from the example of the two thieves crucified with Christ."†—Crucifixion, having in consequence scarcely been witnessed in Europe during the last fifteen hundred years, has often been erroneously

---

* The earliest example of crucifixion on record is probably that of Pharaoh's chief baker, said in the authorized English version to have been hanged, but by Josephus to have been crucified.—Gen., chap. 40, v. 16-22;—Whiston's Josephus, vol. i. pp. 65, 66.

† Crevier's History of the Roman Emperors, vol. x. p. 132.

represented by painters, poets, and devotional writers, who have followed the dictates of their imagination, or the guidance of vague tradition, rather than the evidence of facts. In order to obtain correct notions on this subject, it is therefore necessary to consult the records of antiquity, the testimony of which has long since been collected and reported in a very satisfactory manner by two eminent scholars of the seventeenth century, Salmasius and Lipsius. From these and similar authorities it is clearly ascertained that the punishment of crucifixion was peculiarly painful, lingering, and ignominious. The cross consisted of a strong upright post, sharpened at the lower end by which it was fixed in the ground, having a short bar or stake projecting from its middle, and a longer transverse beam firmly joined near its top. As the middle bar, although an important appendage, has been almost universally overlooked by modern authors, it will be proper here to insert the account given of it by some of the early fathers of the Church, and founded on personal observation.—"The structure of the cross,"—says Irenæus,—"has five ends or summits, two in length, two in breadth, and one in the middle, on which the crucified person rests."—Justyn Martyr, in like manner, speaks of—"that end projecting from the middle [of the upright post] like a horn, on which crucified persons are seated;"—and the language of Tertullian, who wrote a little later, exactly corresponds,—"A part, and indeed a principal part of the cross, is any post which is fixed in an upright position; but to us the entire cross is imputed, including its transverse beam, and the projecting bar which serves as a seat."* The criminal condemned to this dreadful mode of death, having first been scourged, was compelled to

---

* Irenæus, Opera, p. 166;—Justinus Martyr, Cum Tryphone Judæo Dialogus, pp. 271, 272;—Tertullianus, Ad Nationes, p. 49;—Adversus Judæos, p. 195.

carry the cross on his shoulders to the place of execution, a circumstance which implies that the scourging was not excessively severe, and that the dimensions of the gibbet did not in general much exceed those of the human body. On arriving at the spot, he was stripped of his clothes; and, after receiving a cup of wine—sometimes medicated, with a view to impart firmness, or alleviate pain—was speedily nailed to the cross, either before or after its erection. In either case he was made to sit astride on the middle bar; and his limbs, having been extended and bound with cords, were finally secured by large iron spikes driven through their extremities, the hands to the transverse beam, and the feet to the upright post. The crucifixion of Christ is thus accurately described by Bishop Pearson:—"The form of the cross on which our Saviour suffered was not a simple but a compounded figure, according to the custom of the Romans, by whose procurator he was condemned to die. In which there was not only a straight and erected piece of wood fixed in the earth, but also a transverse beam fastened unto that toward the top thereof; and, besides these two, cutting each other transversely at right angles, so that the erected part extended itself above the transverse, there was also another piece of wood infixed into, and standing out from, that which was erected and straight up. To that erected piece was his body being lifted up applied, as Moses's serpent to the pole, and to the transverse beam his hands were nailed. Upon the lower part coming out from the erected piece his sacred body rested, and his feet were transfixed and fastened with nails. His head, being pressed with a crown of thorns, was applied to that part of the erect which stood above the transverse beam; and above his head to that was fastened the table on which was written in Hebrew, Greek, and Latin characters, the accusation, according to the Roman custom, and the writing was,—Jesus of Nazareth, the king of the Jews."*—The bodily sufferings attending this punishment were doubtless great, but, either through ignorance or design, have been much exaggerated. The insertion of the cross into its hole or socket, when the criminal was previously attached to it, did not necessarily produce the violent concussion which has been supposed; and, as the body rested on a bar, it did not bear with its whole weight on the perforated extremities. At all events, there have been many examples of persons enduring these sufferings with the utmost fortitude, and almost without a complaint, until relieved from them by death. A fact of importance to be known, but which has not been sufficiently regarded, is that crucifixion was a very lingering punishment, and proved fatal not so much by loss of blood, since the wounds in the hands and feet did not lacerate any large vessel, and were nearly closed by the nails which produced them, as by the slow process of nervous irritation and exhaustion. This would of course be liable to variety, depending on differences of age, sex, constitution, and other circumstances; but for persons to live two or more days on the cross was a common occurrence, and there are even instances of some who, having been taken down in time and carefully treated, recovered and survived. In many cases death was partly induced by hunger and thirst, the vicissitudes of heat and cold, or the attacks of ravenous birds and beasts; and in others was designedly accelerated by burning, stoning, suffocation, breaking the bones, or piercing the vital organs.†

In proof of the lingering nature of crucifixion, and of the courage with which it was often endured, a few instances will be adduced from ancient and modern authors;

* Bishop Pearson, Exposition of the Creed, pp. 203–205.
† Claudius Salmasius, De Cruce, etc., pp. 229–340, etc.;—Justus Lipsius, De Cruce, pp. 98–109, etc.;—Dr. Adam Clarke, The New Testament, with a Commentary, etc.; Comment on Matt. chap. 27, v. 35.

but it is difficult to find many examples of this kind at once sufficiently detailed, and fully deserving of credit. In his elaborate work entitled "The Cross Triumphant," etc., Bosius recites from the Roman Martyrology the crucifixion of the apostle Andrew, who is said to have lived on the cross two days, which he spent in preaching and instructing the people; also that of Victor, bishop of Amiterna, who, although crucified with his head downward, a posture unfavorable to the continuance of life, survived in like manner two days; which, according to Origen and other early fathers, seems to have been the usual period during which crucified persons survived, when their death was not hastened by additional means. He likewise repeats the marvellous story of Timotheus and Maura, a married pair who suffered in the Thebaid about the year 286, under the Diocletian persecution. After enduring many horrible tortures with invincible constancy, these pious persons were, it is said, crucified together; and having hung alive on the cross nine days and nights, mutually exhorting and confirming each other in the faith, expired on the tenth day.* Although this last narrative may justly be suspected of exaggeration, it serves to show that in ancient times, when the punishment of crucifixion was common, it was well known to be a tedious mode of death. The following examples, extracted from the same Martyrology by the Rev. Alban Butler, seem to be more authentic. The same year 286 proved fatal to Marcus and Marcellianus,—" twin brothers of an illustrious family in Rome . . . . who were condemned to be bound to two pillars, with their feet nailed to the same. In this posture they remained a day and a night, and on the following day were stabbed with lances, and buried in the Arenarium, since called their cemetery, two miles out

---

* Jacobus Bosius. Crux Triumphans et Gloriosa, pp. 8, 9, 43, 47, 94, 112-115.

of Rome, between the Appian and Ardeatine roads."— In the year 297, by order of the Emperor Maximian, seven Christians at Samosata were subjected to long and various tortures, and ultimately crucified.—"Hipparchus,"— a venerable old man,—"died on the cross in a short time. James, Romanus, and Lollianus, expired the next day, being stabbed by the soldiers while they hung on their crosses. Philotheus, Habibus, and Paragrus, were taken down from their crosses while they were still living. The emperor, being informed that they were yet alive, commanded huge nails to be driven into their heads,"—by which they were at length dispatched. Under the reign of the same execrable tyrant, Calliopius, a handsome youth, born at Perga in Pamphilia, was put to death in the year 304, at the city of Pompeiopolis in Cilicia. After suffering the most cruel tortures by being scourged, broken on the wheel, and partially burnt, he was crucified with his head downward on the fifth day of the passion-week, and expired on the following or preparation-day, at the same hour.*—The fortitude displayed under crucifixion by Bomilcar is thus described by the pagan historian Justin. After a severe defeat of the Carthaginian army by Agathocles king of Sicily, this African chief had shown a disposition to desert to the enemy;—"for which offence,"— says Justin,—"he was nailed by the Carthaginians to a gibbet in the middle of the forum, that the same place which had been the scene of his honors might now witness his punishment. But Bomilcar bore the cruelty of the citizens with magnanimity, and from the height of the cross, as from a tribunal, declaimed against their crimes, etc. . . . . Having thus spoken with a loud voice amid an immense concourse of the people, he expired."

* Rev. Alban Butler, Lives of the Fathers, etc., vol. vi. pp. 251, 252; vol. xii. pp. 175, 176;—Acta Sanctorum, curâ Bollandi, vol. i. pp. 659-662.

The following testimonies on the same subject are derived from more modern times:—" The capital punishments inflicted in Soudan"—observes Captain Clapperton, writing in 1824,—" are beheading, impaling, and crucifixion; the first being reserved for Mahometans, and the other two practised on Pagans. I was told, as a matter of curiosity, that wretches on the cross generally linger three days before death puts an end to their sufferings." *—When describing the punishments used in Madagascar, Rev. Mr. Ellis remarks,—" In a few cases of great enormity, a sort of crucifixion has been resorted to; and, in addition to this, burning or roasting at a slow fire, kept at some distance from the sufferer, has completed the horrors of this miserable death. . . . In the year 1825 a man was condemned to crucifixion, who had murdered a female for the sake of stealing her child. He carried the child for sale to the public market, where the infant was recognized, and the murderer detected. He bore his punishment in the most hardened manner, avenging himself by all the violence he was capable of exercising upon those who dragged him to the place of execution. Not a single groan escaped him during the period he was nailed to the wood, nor while the cross was fixed upright in the earth. The wooden frame used in the place of a cross resembles a gallows. To this the malefactor is nailed while it remains flat upon the earth, after which it is lifted up with its miserable burden, and fixed in two holes made in the ground for the purpose. Here the sufferer is kept until he dies of cold, hunger, or agony. Some criminals, after being nailed to the frame, have remained for hours for the gaze of the multitude. A fire has oftentimes been placed to windward of them by which they and the cross have been consumed together."—Even the still more horrible punishments of

---

* Justinus, Historiæ Philippicæ, pp. 490, 491;—Denham and Clapperton, Travels in Africa, etc.; Clapperton's Narrative, p. 107.

impalement, and suspension on a hook, whereby the vital organs are severely bruised or lacerated, are longer protracted and better supported than might be imagined. After describing the manner in which the former is executed among the Turks, the Rev. Mr. Maundrell continues as follows:—" The criminal sitting [on the stake] remains not only still alive, but also drinks, smokes, and talks as one perfectly sensible, and thus some have continued for twenty-four hours; but, generally, after the tortured wretch has remained in this deplorable and ignominious posture an hour or two, some one of the standers-by is permitted to give him a gracious stab to the heart, so putting an end to his inexpressible misery." *—Of the same punishment Dr. Russell states,—" It is seldom seen at Aleppo, though a certain Hussein Bashaw is well remembered there, who, some years before, impaled twenty Kurds at one time close to the city. Several of them remained many hours alive on the stake, nor is it known how long they might have survived, liberty having been obtained to put an end to their torture by shooting them." —Referring to numerous executions which took place at Constantinople in 1829, Mr. Slade says—"In many shapes death triumphed during this terrible fortnight. Two wretches, convicted of attempting to fire the new seraglio at Beglerbey on the Bosporus, were impaled; one still breathed on the following day."—The same author thus reports the execution at Salonica in the ensuing year of Chaban, a captain of banditti,—" described by those who saw him as a very fine-looking man, about thirty-five. . . . . . As a preparatory exercise, he was suspended by his arms for twelve hours. . . . The following day a hook was thrust into his side, by which he was suspended to a tree, and there hung enduring the agony of thirst till

* Rev. W. Ellis, History of Madagascar, vol. i. pp. 371, 372;—Rev. H. Maundrell, Journey from Aleppo to Jerusalem, etc., pp. 189-191.

the third evening, when death closed the scene; but before that about an hour the birds, already considering him their own, had alighted on his brow to peck his eyes. During this frightful period he uttered no unmanly complaints, only repeated several times,—'Had I known that I was to suffer this infernal death, I would never have done what I have. From the moment I led the klephte's life I had death before my eyes, and was prepared to meet it, but I expected to die as my predecessors, by decapitation.'"*—A similar account is given by Mr. Morgan of the execution at Algiers, in 1556, of Hassan Corso, who was of moderate stature, and in his thirty-eighth year. Having been cast from a considerable height on the *chingan*, or hook, ... "he remained in that torture three whole days and two nights with the hook through his right-side ribs. . . . At the third day's end he expired." —From the "Chrestomathia Arabica" of Kosegarten, published in 1828, Bishop Wiseman borrows an interesting narrative originally written in Arabic, and remarkably apposite to the present purpose, of the execution of a Mameluke, who was crucified under the walls of Damascus for the murder of his master, and, although quite a youth, was possessed of great strength and prowess. His hands, arms, and feet, having been nailed to the cross, he remained alive from mid-day on Friday to the same hour on Sunday, when he died. He bore his punishment with great firmness, without uttering a groan or changing his countenance, complaining only of thirst during the whole of the first day, after which he was patient and silent till he died.†—Of persons recovering from the effects of cruci-

---

* Dr. Russell, Natural History of Aleppo, vol. i. p. 332;—Slade's Records of Travels in Turkey, Greece, etc., vol. i. p. 417; vol. ii. pp. 417, 418.

† Morgan, Complete History of Algiers, pp. 391, 392;—Bishop Wiseman, On the Connection between Science and Revealed Religion, vol. i. pp. 265-275.

OF THE DEATH OF CHRIST.

fixion when taken in time from the cross, besides a few instances which may be found among the records of insanity, one example is mentioned by Herodotus, and another by Josephus. In describing a singular incident which occurred during the naval warfare between the Greeks and the Persians, the former author states as follows :—" Here, also, it was that the fleet of Xerxes came to anchor [namely, in the gulf of Magnesia]. Fifteen of these, being at a considerable distance from their companions, discovered the vessels of the Greeks, at Artemisium, and, mistaking them for friends, sailed into the midst of them. The leader of these ships was Sandoces, son of Thamasias, the governor of Cyma in Æolia. This man Darius had formerly condemned to the punishment of the cross: he had been one of the royal judges, and convicted of corruption in his office. He was already on the cross when the king, reflecting that his services to the royal family exceeded his offences, ... commanded him to be taken down; thus he escaped the punishment to which Darius had condemned him. His escape now from the Greeks was altogether impossible: they saw him sailing toward them, and, perceiving his error, attacked and took him and his vessels."—In enumerating his various claims to the gratitude of his countrymen, the Jewish historian relates,—" When I was sent by Titus Cæsar with Cerealius and a thousand horsemen to a certain village called Thecoa, in order to know whether it was a place fit for a camp, as I came back I saw many captives crucified, and remembered three of them as my former acquaintance. I was very sorry at this in my mind, and went, with tears in my eyes, to Titus, and told him of them. So he immediately commanded them to be taken down, and to have the greatest care taken of them in order to their recovery; yet two of them died under the physicians' hands, while the third recovered." *

---

* Herodotus, History by Beloe, vol. iii. p. 292; vol. iv. pp. 125, 126; —Josephus, Works by Whiston, vol. iii. pp. 242, 243.

In Palestine, under the Roman government, crucifixion during life was a punishment peculiar to the conquerors. Among the Hebrew people, in whose institutions, owing to their divine origin, justice was tempered with mercy, it was either not practised at all, or only on dead bodies; and in such cases the Mosaic law strictly commanded that the body of a person suspended on a tree should be taken down and buried before sunset.* In the crucifixion of Jesus by their Roman masters the Jewish authorities acquiesced the more willingly, because, like their own national punishment for blasphemy, namely, stoning followed by suspension, it involved the stigma of divine malediction which they were anxious to attach to him. Knowing that the former mode of death was generally protracted, and obliged to comply with the requisitions of their law, more especially as the Sabbath, which began at sunset, was rapidly approaching, they applied to Pilate soon after the ninth hour of the day, and obtained the usual order that the crucified persons should be dispatched and removed. The soldiers appointed to this duty accordingly came, and broke the legs of the two malefactors executed with Jesus. Observing, however, that he was already dead, they did not break his legs; but, to prevent all doubt on the subject, one of them pierced his side with a spear, when the result confirmed their previous decision. The circumstances above stated fully demonstrate that, in whatever degree the ordinary sufferings of crucifixion contributed to his death, they were not its immediate cause. Without the concurrence of other causes they rarely proved fatal in less than two days, whereas Jesus died suddenly after enduring them only six hours. The remarks made on the occasion by the Roman centurion and his soldiers, as well as by Pontius Pilate, all of them competent judges of the fact, and

---

* Levit. chap. 24, v. 10–16;—Deut. chap. 21, v. 22, 23.

interested in ascertaining its reality, plainly show that they regarded **the** death of Christ as having happened much earlier than might have been expected, and coincide with the conclusion deducible from other considerations, **that it was not the** result of crucifixion alone.

Although the matter has never yet been thoroughly investigated, it is interesting to observe that the principal commentators on Scripture, **both** ancient and **modern,** have either openly or tacitly adopted the negative **conclusion** here taken, and that many of them have **even suggested** additional causes by which, **in conjunction with** crucifixion, the Saviour's **death might in their opinion have been induced. These causes have been proposed under various modifications, which are all** reducible to three; namely—supernatural agency,—the wound inflicted by the soldier's spear,—or an unusual degree of weakness, original or acquired. It will be the object of the following remarks to show that neither of these explanations **is** admissible, all of them being at variance with well-known facts, **and that another is therefore absolutely requisite. In the** early times of Christianity, **not long** after its apostolical period, and when **pretensions to** miraculous power **were still made and credited,** it is by no means wonderful that the death **of** Christ should have been ascribed to supernatural influence, which is accordingly **the** solution adopted by **almost** all **the** ancient Christian writers who have considered the subject. The opinion of Tertullian is thus briefly stated: [Christ]— "when crucified spontaneously dismissed his spirit **with a** word, thus preventing the office of the executioner."— That of Origen is more full.—" Since "—says he,—" those crucified persons **who** are not **stabbed** suffer greater torment, and survive in great pain, sometimes the whole of the following night, and even the whole **of the** next day; **and** since **Jesus was not stabbed, and his** enemies hoped that by his hanging long on the cross he would suffer the greater torment, he prayed to the Father and was heard, and as soon as he had called was taken to the Father; or else, as one who had the power of laying down his life, he laid it down when he chose. This prodigy astonished the centurion, who said—' Truly this man was a son of God.'—For it was a miracle that he who would otherwise perhaps have survived two days on the cross, according to the custom of those who are crucified but not stabbed, should have been taken up after three hours, so that his death seems to have happened by the favor of God, and rather through the merit of his own prayer than through the violence of the cross." *—Origen proceeds to observe that the marvellousness of the occurrence was further proved by the surprise of Pilate on hearing that Christ was dead so early, and by his caution in ascertaining the fact from the centurion before he granted the body to Joseph. In commenting on Matt., chap. 27, v. 50, Jerome similarly remarks,—" In the first place, it must be declared that for Jesus to lay down his life when he chose, and to take it again, was an act of divine power. Then the centurion hearing him say to the Father,—' Into thy hands I commit my spirit,'—and perceiving that he immediately dismissed his spirit of his own accord, was struck with the greatness of the miracle, and said,—' Truly this man was a son of God.'"—Cyprian follows in the same track.—" That the Jewish rulers would deliver Christ to Pontius Pilate to be crucified, he had himself predicted, and the testimony of all the prophets had also previously declared that it was necessary for him to suffer, not that he might feel, but conquer death, and after

---

* Tertullianus, Apologeticus, p. 20;—Origines, Opera, vol. ii. p. 237. By misunderstanding the statement concerning—" the sixth hour,"—in John, chap. 19, v. 14, Origen seems to have concluded that the time during which Christ hung alive on the cross was only three hours.

he had suffered to return to heaven, that he might display the power of **the divine** majesty. The course of events corresponded **to** expectation; for when he was crucified **he** dismissed his **spirit** of his own accord, **preventing the office of the** executioner, and also **of his own accord rose from the dead** on the third day."*—Theophylact, **metro**politan **of** Bulgaria, who stands **as it were** midway between the ancients and **the moderns,** exhibits **similar** views in expounding **Luke, chap. 23, v. 46.—" When** [Jesus] had exclaimed **with a loud voice he expired, for** he had **power to lay down** his **life, and to take it again. That exclamation, and other miracles, furnished to the centurion grounds of faith: for [Christ] did not die** like **an ordinary man, but with great** power, **and** called death **a** deposit, like one who was about to take his life again." —So likewise in commenting on Matt. chap. 27, v. 50.— " He lays down his life by his own power. But what was the exclamation?—'Father! into thy hands I commit **my** spirit:'—for he expired **not by** compulsion, but **volunta**rily, this being the signification **of,—'I commit my spirit,' etc.,—and therefore** with **a loud voice he called on death,** which dared **not to come to him** without being **called." †**

Among the **more modern commentators the earlier** generally adopt the **miraculous hypothesis of** their predecessors, but the superior judgment of **a** few is evinced by their expressing themselves **with** becoming reserve on a **subject** which they felt they did not perfectly understand, and some are absolutely silent. Thus Calvin remarks,— " The circumstance that after breaking the legs of the two malefactors **the** soldiers found Christ dead, and therefore did not assail his body, shows an extraordinary operation

---

* Hieronymus, **Opera, vol. iii. pp. 47,** 48 **;**—Cyprianus, Opera :—De idolorum vanitate, p. 228.

† Theophylact, Opera; Comment on Matt., chap. 27, v. 50; Mark, chap. 15, v. 37; Luke, chap. 23, v. 46; and John, chap. 19, v. 30.

of divine providence. Profane persons may indeed say that it is natural for one man to die sooner than another; but whoever carefully examines the whole series of the narrative will be compelled to ascribe the exemption of Christ from the breaking of his legs, by a death beyond all expectation rapid, to the secret counsel of God." *—In commenting on Matt., chap. 27, v. 50.—" Jesus, having again cried with a loud voice, resigned [his] spirit,"—Grotius subjoins,—" in the very act of exclamation, as we have found Tertullian saying,—' He spontaneously dismissed his spirit with a word.'—This exclamation was,—'[All] is accomplished,'—as mentioned by John, and—'Father! into thy hands I commit my spirit.'—This very circumstance,—'that he expired with such a cry,'—was regarded by the centurion as miraculous; for the event itself, immediately responding to the words of Christ, showed that his soul had really been taken by God. His death was in fact accelerated by divine counsel before the failure of his natural strength, otherwise it could not have been expected to occur so soon (Mark, chap. 15, v. 44.); and therefore the malefactors were dispatched by breaking their legs." †—In his discourse on the fourth article of the Apostles' creed, Lightfoot observes,—" Christ could not die, nay I may say he would not die, till all things were fulfilled that were written concerning his death. Therefore, when he had hung above three hours, and knowing it was written,—' They gave me vinegar,' etc.,—he said,—' I thirst.'—He tastes and finds it vinegar, and says,—' It is finished.'—Now, all is accomplished, so he bows his head, and composeth himself to die, and cries,—' Father! into thy hands,' etc.;—and having

---

* Joannes Calvinus, Comment: in quatuor Evangelistas;—John, chap. 19, v. 33.

† Hugo Grotius, Opera, Theologica, etc.; Comment on Matt., chap. 27, v. 50.

so said he let go his soul, and delivered it up into the hands of God. Remember that, John, chap. 10, v. 17, 18, and you see the sense of these expressions;—'I lay down my life that I may take it again. No man taketh it from me, but I lay it down of myself. I have power to lay it down, and I have power to take it again.'—He had life in his own hand, and the Jews could not take it from him, but he let it go himself, and delivered it up.—' When the centurion saw that he thus cried out and gave up the ghost, he said, Surely this man was the Son of God.'— Doubtless this man hath the disposal of his own life. So strong a cry is not the cry of one that is spent and dying through weakness and fainting, but it argues life strong and vigorous to be still in him, and therefore he dies not of weakness, but gives up his life at his own pleasure."— " Jesus"—says the celebrated Bishop Taylor,—" took all his passion with a voluntary susception, God heightening it to great degrees of torment supernaturally, and he laid down his life voluntarily, when his Father's wrath was totally appeased toward mankind."*—Matthew Henry makes the following observations on Matt., chap. 27, v. 50. —" Two things are here noted concerning the manner of Christ's dying; 1st, that he *cried with a loud voice*, as before, v. 46. Now this was a sign that after all his pains and fatigues his life was whole in him, and nature strong. The voice of dying men is one of the first things that fails. With a panting breath and a faltering tongue a few broken words are hardly spoken, and more hardly heard; but Christ just before he expired spoke like a man in his full strength, to show that his life was not forced from him, but was freely delivered by him into his Father's hands, as his own act and deed. He that had strength to cry thus when he died could have got loose from the ar-

* Dr. Lightfoot, Works, vol. i. p. 1354;—Bishop Jeremy Taylor, Works, vol. iii. p. 371.

rest he was under, and have bid defiance to the power of death; but, to show that *by the eternal Spirit he offered himself*, being the priest as well as the sacrifice, he *cried with a loud voice.*"—In his annotations on John, chap. 19, v. 30, the same author remarks,—"'*He gave up the ghost.*' —His life was not forcibly extorted from him, but freely resigned;"—and on v. 33.—"'They supposed him to be dead, and *therefore did not break his legs.*'—Observe here that Jesus died in less time than persons crucified usually did. The structure of his body, perhaps being extraordinarily fine and tender, was the sooner broke by pain; or rather, it was to show that he laid down his life of himself, and could die when he pleased, though his hands were nailed. Though he *yielded* to death, he was not conquered."*—Christ's—"being able to express himself in such a manner,"—says Dr. Gill,—"declared him to be more than a mere man; for after such agonies in the garden, and so much fatigue in being hurried from place to place, and such loss of blood from being buffeted, scourged, crowned with thorns, and nailed to the accursed tree, where being stretched he had hung for some hours, to speak with so loud a voice was more than human, and was a conviction to the centurion that he was a divine person; for—'when he saw that he so cried out and gave up the ghost, he said,—Truly this man was the Son of God;'— (Mark, chap. 15, v. 39), and likewise it shows that he died freely and voluntarily, and not through force and necessity. It was not all that men had done, or could do to him that could have forced his life from him. He died willingly, and when nature was in its full strength, and, which is signified in the next phrase,—'yielded up the ghost,'— or—'dismissed the spirit,'—as the Syriac version truly renders it,—he sent it away. It was not taken from him,

---

* Matthew Henry, Exposition on the New Testament; Comment on Matt., chap. 27, v. 50 · John. chap. 19, v. 30, 33.

he laid down his life of himself as the lord of it, and gave himself freely to be an offering and sacrifice in the room of his people, which is a proof of his great love and amazing grace unto them."—Dr. Doddridge also contends that the phrase—"ἀφῆκε τὸ πνεῦμα,"—in Matt., chap. 27, v. 50, should be rendered,—"he dismissed his spirit;"—and observes,—"Now this expression seems admirably to suit our Lord's words, John, chap. 10, v. 18.—'No man taketh my life from me, but I lay it down of myself,' etc.—showing, as the strong cry which so much impressed the centurion did, that he died by the voluntary act of his own mind, according to the power received from the Father, and in a way peculiar to himself, by which he alone of all men that ever existed could have continued alive, even in the greatest tortures, as long as he pleased, or have retired from the body whenever he thought fit. Which view of the case, by the way, suggests an illustration of the love of Christ manifested in his death beyond what is commonly observed; inasmuch as he did not use this power to quit his body as soon as ever it was fastened to the cross, leaving only an insensible corpse to the cruelty of his murderers, but continued his abode in it with a steady resolution as long as it was proper, and then retired from it with a majesty and dignity never known, or to be known in any other death; dying, if I may so express it, like the prince of life."*

Lastly, Dr. Adam Clarke, taking the same view of the phrase, remarks,—"He himself willingly gave up that life which it was impossible for man to take away. It is not said that he hung on the cross till he died through pain and agony, nor is it said that his bones were broken the sooner to put him out of pain, and to hasten his death, but

---

* Dr. Gill, Exposition of the New Testament; Comment on Matt., chap. 27, v. 50.—Dr. Doddridge, Family Expositor of the New Testament; Comment on Luke, chap. 23, v. 46.

that himself dismissed the soul, that he might thus become not a forced sacrifice, but a free-will offering for sin."*

The quotations above collected plainly show that from an early period of Christianity down to the present day many learned and pious men have agreed in ascribing the death of Christ to supernatural agency. Had not the later writers of this class been guided by an undue deference to the opinions of their predecessors rather than by independent inquiry, it is difficult to understand how so many able divines should have concurred in a view decidedly contradicted by several passages of the New Testament, which positively declare that Christ was slain by his enemies, and died the death of the cross. Thus, when anticipating his crucifixion a few days before its occurrence, the Saviour himself predicted,—"If I be lifted up from the earth, I will draw all men unto me:"—on which the apostle John remarks,—"In thus speaking, he signified the kind of death which he was about to die."—Paul, in like manner, affirms that Christ—"assumed the form of a slave, and was made in the likeness of men, and, having been found in aspect as a man, humbled himself, and became obedient unto death, even the death of the cross."—In his defence before the Sanhedrim, Stephen indignantly asked,—"Which of the prophets did your fathers forbear to persecute? Yea, they slew those who foretold the coming of that righteous person, of whom ye have now been the betrayers and murderers."—Similar statements were on various occasions made by Peter; as, for example, when replying to the Sanhedrim,—"The God of our fathers raised from the dead Jesus, whom ye slew by crucifixion;"—when addressing the vast multitude assembled at Jerusalem on the day of Pentecost,—"Him, having been delivered up by the determinate counsel and foreknowledge of God, ye took, and by the hands of wicked men

---

* Dr. Adam Clarke, Comment on Matt., chap. 27, v. 50.

crucified and slew;"—and in a second address to the same multitude shortly afterward,—" The God of **Abraham, Isaac, and Jacob, the God of** our fathers hath glorified his **Son Jesus, whom ye** delivered up, **and rejected before Pilate, when he had** decided on releasing **him; but ye rejected that** holy and righteous person, and [in his stead] begged for the release of **a murderer, and slew the prince of life, whom God raised from the dead, whereof we are witnesses** .... And **now, brethren, I know that ye did [this] through** ignorance, **as likewise did your rulers;** but those sufferings of **Christ which God foretold by the mouth of all his prophets, he hath thus accomplished."** *—In his " Exposition of the Creed," Bishop Pearson discusses the subject with much ability ; and, although his own explanation is equally objectionable, deserves credit for the soundness of his judgment, in rejecting that which is now under consideration. Christ, he observes,—" died not by, but with a miracle. Should we imagine **Christ to anticipate the time of death, and to subtract** his **soul from future torments necessary to cause an expiration, we might rationally** say the Jews and Gentiles were **guilty of his death, but we could not** properly **say they slew him. Guilty they must be, because they inflicted those torments which in time death must necessarily follow; but** slay him actually they did not, if his death proceeded **from any** other cause, and not from the wounds which they inflicted." †—After a careful **perusal of the passages above cited, it does not require any long or elaborate reasoning to prove that, if the** Saviour humbled himself to death, even the death **of the** cross, if the Father accomplished his designs in **this respect** through the instrumentality of Christ's enemies, and

---

* John, chap. 12, v. 30-34 ; chap. 18, v. 31, 32 ;—Acts, chap. 2, v. 22, 23 ; chap. 3, v. 12-18 ; chap. 5, v. 29, 30 ; chap. 7, v. 51, 52 ; chap. 10, v. 38, 39 ;—Philipp., chap. 2, v. 5-8 ;—Heb., chap. 12, v. 1-3.

† Bishop Pearson, Exposition of the Creed, pp. 212, 213.

if in the midst of their fancied triumph over him they were in reality blindly executing the divine purposes, whatever may be the true explanation of his death, it cannot be attributed to supernatural agency. The opposite opinion has been chiefly deduced from the declaration of Jesus that no man took his life from him, but that he laid it down of himself, and from the expressions of some of the evangelists, that at his death he resigned or dismissed his spirit; but the foregoing passages, in conjunction with several others which might be added, prove the meaning of these expressions to be simply this; that, in fulfilment of the divine plan of human redemption, Christ voluntarily submitted to a violent death which he had it in his power to avoid. That he actually suffered such a death is indeed repeatedly stated, both before and after the event. Thus, in his last journey to Jerusalem,—"he took the twelve aside, and began to apprize them of what was about to befall him, [saying]—Behold! we are going up to Jerusalem, and the Son of Man will be delivered to the chief priests, and scribes, and they will condemn him to death, and deliver him to the Gentiles, who will mock him, and scourge him, and spit on him, and kill him, but on the third day he will rise from the dead."—That it was in the power of Christ to avoid such a death, had he chosen to renounce the object of his mission, is evident, among other reasons, from his miraculous overthrow of the hostile band in the garden of Gethsemane; from his question to Peter,—"Thinkest thou that I cannot even now request my Father, and he would send to my aid more than twelve legions of angels? [but] how then would the Scriptures be fulfilled, [which declare] that thus it must be?"—and from his remark to Pilate,—"Thou wouldst not have had any authority at all against me, had it not been given thee from above."*—In all the scriptural allusions to this sub-

* Matt., chap. 16, v. 21; chap. 17, v. 22, 23; chap. 20, v. 17-19;

ject, the death intimated, although voluntary, is moreover represented not as self-inflicted, but as penal and vicarious. In the very passage which has been thus misinterpreted, the death encountered by the good shepherd for the safety of his flock is ascribed to the wolf from whom the hireling flees. So, when Peter promised to lay down his life for Christ's sake, his meaning is explained to be, that he would follow him both to prison and to death. The true interpretation of this passage is, however, ascertained beyond all doubt by the same apostle who records it; for he declares that, as—" Christ laid down his life for us, we ought also to lay down our lives for the brethren;" —not of course by suicide, but by cheerfully submitting to death from persecution, whenever it may appear necessary for the welfare of the church; an act of self-devotion which the apostle Paul repeatedly professed himself ready to perform, and at last actually accomplished. On such occasions it was usual for Christian martyrs to resign, or commend their spirits to God, in token of their perfect acquiescence in his will, and confidence in his fidelity; and, with the exception of his having been a victim of an infinitely higher order, this was all that was done by Christ himself when he died on the cross. Accordingly, while Matthew and John state that he dismissed or resigned his spirit, Mark and Luke say simply, that he expired.*

From the concurrence of so many pious and learned authors in ascribing the death of Jesus to supernatural

---

chap. 26, v. 51-54;—Mark, chap. 8, v. 31; chap. 9, v. 30, 31; chap. 10, v. 32-34;—Luke, chap. 9, v. 21, 22; chap. 18, v. 31-33;—John, chap. 10, v. 17, 18; chap. 18, v. 1-6; chap. 19, v. 8-11;—1 Thess. chap. 2, v. 14, 15;—Revel. chap. 5, v. 9, 12, etc.

* Luke, chap. 22, v. 33;—John, chap. 10, v. 11-15; chap. 13, v. 36, 37;—Acts, chap. 7, v. 59, 60;—Rom. chap. 5, v. 6-8;—Philipp. chap. 2, v. 17, 18;—Coloss. chap. 1, v. 23, 24;—2 Tim. chap. 1, v. 12; chap. 4, v. 6-8;—1 Peter, chap. 4, v. 12-19;—1 John, chap. 3, v. 16.

agency, one advantage however results, namely, the acknowledgment thereby made that in their opinion this solemn event cannot be satisfactorily explained by any other cause;—neither by the principal, nor the accessory sufferings of crucifixion,—by an extraordinary degree of weakness original or acquired,—nor by the wound inflicted with the soldier's spear;—and this acknowledgment is the more valuable in the case of several of the earlier writers, because they lived in times when all the circumstances attending crucifixion in general, and that of Christ in particular, must have been perfectly known. So much the more remarkable is the fact that certain manuscripts of the Greek New Testament, particularly the Vatican, and the Ephrem, with some others of minor note, contain a various reading which seems to affirm the cause last mentioned, namely, the wound with the soldier's spear; and that a recent and talented author, the late Mr. Granville Penn,* has zealously adopted this reading, which it will be the object of the following observations to show is spurious, and unworthy of regard. It occurs as an additional clause to Matt. chap. 27, v. 48, 49. after the statement that a little before his death Christ uttered the cry,—"Eloi! Eloi! lama sabachthani?"—which some of the by-standers erroneously supposed to be an invocation of the prophet Elijah. In order to do justice to the subject, the original passage, as it stands in the Vatican manuscript, is here subjoined, together with Mr. Penn's translation.—Matt. chap. 27, v. 48. Καὶ εὐθέως δραμὼν εἰς ἐξ αὐτῶν, καὶ λαβὼν σπόγγον, πλήσας τε ὄξους, καὶ περιθεὶς καλάμῳ, ἐπότιζεν αὐτον: 49. οἱ δὲ λοιποὶ ἔλεγον, Ἄφες, ἴδωμεν εἰ ἔρχεται Ἠλίας σώσων αὐτόν: ἄλλος δὲ, λαβὼν λόγχην, ἔνυξεν αὐτοῦ τὴν πλευρὰν, καὶ ἐξῆλθεν ὕδωρ καὶ

---

* Granville Penn, The Book of the New Covenant of our Lord and Saviour Jesus Christ;—Annotations to the Book of the New Covenant, with an Expository Preface, etc.

αἷμα. 50. Ὁ δὲ Ἰησοῦς, πάλιν κράξας φωνῇ μεγάλῃ, ἀφῆκε τὸ πνεῦμα. 48. And straightway one of them ran, and took a sponge, and filled *it* with vinegar, and put *it* on a reed, and gave *it* him to drink: 49. the rest said, Let *him* alone; let us see whether Elijah will come to save him: 50. but another, taking a spear, pierced his side; and there came forth water and blood: and Jesus, crying out with a loud voice, expired."— Mr. Penn supposes this clause to have been expunged from the ancient copies of Matthew's gospel through the influence of Origen. His principal, if not his only reasons for regarding it as an authentic portion of Scripture, are its insertion in the Vatican and Ephrem manuscripts, and its adoption by Chrysostom. The high value which he attaches to it is evinced by the ensuing remarks.—"The restoration of this verse to its due place in the Gospel is the most important circumstance of this Revision;"—and again,—" The recovery of this important record, possibly reserved with a view to rouse and quicken the languor of the Christian Church in this its last age, and its restoration to the evangelical text, is well calculated to fan the embers of Christian devotion, and to cause them to revive with a flame answering to that with which it shone at the first,"*— Notwithstanding so high a eulogium, it will be easy to prove that this clause, excluded by almost all the ancient manuscripts, versions, and fathers, rejected by the principal critics and editors of the Greek New Testament, and stamped with internal marks of inconsistency and falsehood, is an unwarrantable interpolation in Matthew's gospel of words borrowed from that of St. John. In opposition to the weight of adverse evidence on this point, the authorities adduced by Mr. Penn are quite insufficient. That of Chrysostom he himself disregards, in reference to

* Granville Penn, Annotations to the Book of the New Covenant, etc., pp., 176, 184.

a closely-connected passage, and in the present case it is scarcely available; for Chrysostom represents the spear-wound as having been inflicted on the body of Christ when dead, and declares that he laid down his life by his own power. The Ephrem manuscript is probably little more than a duplicate of the Vatican, and for the extraordinary and exclusive deference paid by Mr. Penn to the Roman document no just reason can be assigned. To ascertain the precise age of a manuscript is not a very easy task; but granting that the Vatican is one of the oldest now extant, it by no means follows that all junior manuscripts, some of which must be of nearly equal antiquity, are either derived from it, or of inferior authority. Granting that this clause was known in the fourth century, there is no proof that it existed in the first copies of Matthew's gospel, or that it was expunged by Origen. That distinguished author testifies that in his time, and doubtless long before, the Scriptures of the New Testament presented many various readings, which he judiciously refers to three different sources; namely, the negligence of transcribers, the presumption of heretics, and the officiousness of critics.* To the last of these classes may reasonably be ascribed several of those families, as they have been termed, of manuscripts, which, while agreeing in all essential points, differ considerably with respect to style and diction, in consequence of the simple and Oriental phraseology of the original writings having been, as it seems, variously modified and retouched, to suit the taste of those for whose use they were successively transcribed. That the text of the Vatican manuscript was thus modified, at least in the New Testament, will plainly appear to any competent inquirer who will carefully and candidly examine its peculiar readings. Were such interference with Scripture ever admissible, many of these readings

---

* Lardner (Dr. Nathaniel), Works, vol. ii. pp. 522, 523.

might, in reference to expression, be deemed improvements; but, as might naturally have been expected, when the editor had once engaged in this critical career, he was induced to proceed further than at first perhaps he intended; and not content with correcting the style of the sacred original, presumed in some instances to alter its matter. Thus, for example, he has expunged the clause in Luke, chap. 22, v. 43, 44. which describes the agony and bloody sweat of Christ in the garden of Gethsemane; and has inserted after Matt. chap. 27, v. 49, the clause now under consideration, which attributes the death of Christ on the cross to the wound inflicted by the soldier's spear. In both these alterations, as well as in most other cases, he is implicitly followed by Mr. Penn, who gladly cites the authority of Chrysostom in support of the latter clause, but apparently forgets that the same authority confirms the former one which, in deference to the Vatican manuscript, he himself rejects; and on which this prince of interpreters, as he is styled by Dr. Isaac Barrow and Mr. Penn, makes the following apposite remark:—"Lest heretics should say that [Christ] pretended agony, his sweat was as clots of blood, and an angel appeared strengthening him, and [he showed] many other infallible signs of fear, lest any one should say that [his] words were feigned."*—After stating that this clause was acknowledged as authentic by Justin Martyr and Tatian, in the second century, as well as by other early authors, Dr. Lardner adds that it—"was wanting in some ancient copies, as we learn from Hilary, Jerome, and Photius, which last intimates that the omission of this text was owing to some Syrians. Mill thinks they must have been of the sect of the Jacobites; and Dr. Assemann has particularly observed that this text is quoted by Ephrem the Syrian. Epiphanius likewise says that these two verses

* Joannes Chrysostomus, Opera, vol. vii. p. 791.

were in the ancient copies, before they were corrected and altered by some over-nice Catholics who did not well understand them."*—With the exception of the Alexandrian manuscript, which likewise omits it, this clause is accordingly retained by almost all the ancient editors, critics, and commentators of the New Testament, and is further supported by a well-known passage in the Epistle to the Hebrews, chap. 5, v. 7–10, where, although the sacred writer does not minutely describe the scene in the garden of Gethsemane, he evidently alludes to it in a manner exactly corresponding to the narrative of Luke, with which the statements of Paul generally present a very close and striking coincidence. Speaking of the sufferings of Christ, the apostle remarks that,—"having in the days of his flesh offered prayers and supplications, [accompanied] with tears and loud cries, to him who was able to save him from death, and having been heard on account of his pious fear, although he was a son, he learned obedience from his sufferings; and when [at length] perfected, became the author of eternal salvation to all who obey him." —This allusion, which intimates that previously to his crucifixion Christ piously endured a degree of mental agony which threatened his life, but from which he was for the time delivered by divine succor, in answer to his intense and urgent prayers, furnishes a powerful confirmation, were any wanting, of that important passage in Luke's gospel which the Vatican manuscript has improperly dropped, while with equal impropriety it has admitted into the gospel of Matthew a spurious passage, which disfigures and contradicts the scriptural narrative.† The in-

---

* Lardner, vol. ii. pp. 425, 426.

† In consequence of mistaking the golden censer,—θυμιατήριον,—for the golden altar,—θυσιαστήριον,—the same manuscript has transferred the clause respecting it in Heb. chap. 9, from the fourth to the second verse. This transposition, cited by Mr. Penn as a triumphant proof of

ternal proof of its being spurious is, that the passage is inconsistent with the accounts given both by Matthew and John, as well as with other circumstances belonging to the event. Having stated that about the ninth hour of the day on which he was crucified Jesus uttered the cry, "Eli! Eli! lama sabachthani,—that is,—My God! My God! why hast thou forsaken me?"—Matt. chap. 27, v. 46, the evangelist relates,—v. 47.—" On hearing [this], some of the bystanders said,—This man calleth for Elijah. —48. One of them immediately ran, and took a sponge, and having filled it with vinegar, and fixed it on a reed, gave him drink: 49. but the rest said,—Hold! let us see whether Elijah will come to save him. 50. Having again cried with a loud voice, Jesus expired."—It is between verses 49 and 50, that the Vatican manuscript inserts the clause,—" but another, taking a spear, pierced his side, and there came forth water and blood:"—which clause, short as it is, entirely disagrees both with the immediate context, and with the facts of the case. The bystanders were evidently the Roman soldiers on guard, who knew little of the Hebrew language, but could not have resided long in Palestine without learning something of the great prophet Elijah, and of the expected Messiah of the Jews. Now, after stating that *one* of these men,—εἷς ἐξ αὐτῶν,— on hearing Jesus complain of thirst, (John, chap. 19, v. 28, 29) offered him vinegar, and that *the rest—οἱ λοιποὶ*— desired their comrade not to interfere, but to await the event, what intelligent writer would have introduced *another,—ἄλλος δὲ*,—and that to perform an act in opposition to the wish just before expressed? Besides, the soldiers were not at liberty thus to interfere with the exe-

the superiority of the Vatican manuscript, is in reality another example of its injudicious and unwarrantable interference with the original text. See Rev. chap. 8, v. 1-5.—Granville Penn, Annotations, etc., Preface, pp. 32, 33.

cution at their pleasure, and had any of them presumed to do so, it would have been at the risk of his life. When the Jewish authorities were anxious to have the crucified persons dispatched, and their bodies removed before the sabbath began, that is, before six o'clock the same evening, they were under the necessity of applying to the Roman governor, who gave orders accordingly. That he did not issue any other order is manifest; since after giving this, and when he had reason to believe that it had been carried into effect, Pilate was astonished to hear that Jesus was already dead. By the apostle John, a deeply-interested spectator of the whole scene, the sequel is thus described:—" Now in order that the bodies might not remain on the cross during the sabbath-day, as it was [then] the preparation-day, for that sabbath-day was a high day, the Jews requested Pilate that their legs might be broken, and that they might be taken away. So the soldiers came, and broke the legs of the first and of the other who was crucified with Jesus, but on coming to him, as they perceived that he was already dead, they did not break his legs: one of the soldiers, however, pierced his side with a spear, and immediately there came forth blood and water." —John, chap. 19, v. 28–34. Nothing can be plainer or more complete than this account. The death of Christ happened, not in consequence of his having been stabbed to the heart, but from some other cause, immediately after he had received the vinegar. His side was pierced, not while he was alive, but after he was dead, and as the alternative of breaking his legs, an act which the soldiers were otherwise about to perform; implying that until that moment they were not aware of his death, and even then thought it proper, by wounding him with a spear, to ascertain its reality. It is to be regretted that this very clear and unequivocal statement should have been misrepresented by Mr. Penn, no doubt, unintentionally, and under the influence of an undue partiality for a favorite manuscript. The evangelist's words are as follows,—John, chap. 19, v. 32.—" Ἦλθον οὖν οἱ στρατιῶται, καὶ τοῦ μὲν πρώτου κατέαξαν τὰ σκέλη, καὶ τοῦ ἄλλου τοῦ συσταυρωθέντος αὐτῷ : 33. ἐπὶ δὲ τὸν Ἰησοῦν ἐλθόντες, ὡς εἶδον αὐτὸν ἤδη τεθνηκότα, οὐ κατέαξαν αὐτοῦ τὰ σκέλη : 34. ἀλλ᾽ εἷς τῶν στρατιωτῶν λόγχῃ αὐτοῦ τὴν πλευρὰν ἔνυξε, καὶ εὐθὺς ἐξῆλθεν αἷμα καὶ ὕδωρ.—The following is Mr. Penn's translation :—" 32. Then the soldiers came, and brake the legs of the first, and of the other which was crucified with him; 33. but, coming to Jesus, they brake not his legs, when they saw that he was already dead ; 34. for, one of the soldiers pierced his side with a spear, and immediately came forth blood and water."—Every competent and unprejudiced reader will perceive that the mental substitution in this version of the explanatory particle,—γὰρ, *for*, instead of the distinctive one,—ἀλλὰ, *but*—entirely perverts the meaning of the sentence, which is thereby tacitly acknowledged to be incompatible with the corresponding clause, interpolated in Matthew's gospel by the Vatican manuscript. Far, however, from seeing this, Mr. Penn supposes that in the following verses 35-37, John quotes, and thereby confirms the pretended statement of Matthew, as if it were credible that John, who during the whole scene of the crucifixion stood near the foot of the cross, should have suppressed his own testimony, and given in preference that of Matthew, who, if present at all, must have been stationed at a distance, and consequently far less qualified to bear witness on the subject, Luke, chap. 23, v. 49. It must, on the contrary, be evident that John, who through modesty generally speaks of himself anonymously, and in the third person, is here placing on scriptural record that testimony, which as an eye-witness of these momentous events he had from the first orally delivered, and that previously to citing two remarkable prophecies of the Old Testament respecting them, he accurately describes the occurrences by which they were simultaneously fulfilled,—John, chap. 19, v. 35. "He that bears [this] testimony saw [the fact], and his testimony is true, and he is sure that he relates what is true, that ye also may believe: 36. for these things happened in fulfilment of the Scripture,—*Not one of his bones shall be broken:*—37. and again another Scripture saith,—*They shall look on him whom they pierced.*" *—Other objections might be urged against the allegation that the spear-wound was inflicted on the body of Christ while he was yet alive, such as the immediate effusion of blood and water, and the loud and distinct exclamation,—"[All] is accomplished: Father! into thy hands I commit my spirit,"—neither of which could on this supposition have taken place; but those already adduced will probably be deemed sufficient.

The opinion that the death of Christ was accelerated by supernatural agency originated with some of the early Christian writers; that which ascribes its speedy occurrence to an extraordinary degree of debility, either constitutional or superinduced, is chiefly confined to a small number of modern theologians; and, as will now be shown, is equally untenable with the former, being not only destitute of proof, but positively contradicted by the well-known facts of the case. Both as a priest and as a victim, it was necessary that Christ should possess a human nature absolutely pure and perfect. This perfect nature was accordingly provided by a special interposition of the Holy Spirit, in the manner related by the evangelist Luke; and from such a source it is evident that nothing feeble, vitiated, or defective could have proceeded.†

* Granville Penn, Annotations, etc.; pp. 286, 287.
† Levit. chap. 21, v. 16-24; chap. 22, v. 17-25;—John, chap. 1, v. 29, 36;—Heb. chap. 7, v. 23-28; chap. 9, v. 13, 14; chap. 10, v. 1-11;—1 Peter, chap. 1, v. 18, 19, etc.

As a child, Jesus rapidly grew in wisdom, and in stature, and in favor with God and man; and at the early age of twelve years exhibited a degree of energy and intelligence, which astonished the doctors of the law with whom he conversed in the temple. The subsequent course of his life corresponded to its commencement. Until the age of thirty he chiefly resided in the country, where his occupations, although humble and laborious, were well adapted to promote health and strength. During the three or four years of his personal ministry nothing of a contrary kind occurred. He now took much mental as well as bodily exercise, mingled freely with all classes of society, was often engaged in public speaking, and made frequent journeys on foot; but, under the guardianship of a special providence, appears never to have suffered the slightest accident or indisposition. The notion of his having been weakened and emaciated by continual watchings and fastings is worthy of the monkish writers by whom it was first suggested, but utterly at variance with the evangelical narrative. Whatever might in this respect have been the practice of John the Baptist, who was sent to announce the divine judgments impending over a guilty nation, the Son of Man came, as he himself declares, eating and drinking; his first miracle was performed at a marriage-feast, for the purpose of furnishing a liberal supply of excellent wine; and on all occasions, he readily accepted the hospitalities both of his friends and his enemies. Even his disciples could not fast while he was with them; and the malicious aspersion thrown against him of being a gluttonous man and a wine-bibber, false as it was, served to prove that he did not profess to lead a life of abstinence and mortification. His last sufferings befell him when in the flower of his age, at the period of his greatest vigor and maturity. Those in the garden of Gethsemane, although intense, were of short duration, and he was supernaturally strengthened for the very purpose of enabling him to support them. Those incidental to crucifixion were not more severe in his case than in that of others. His deportment throughout the whole scene, whether in the garden, before the tribunals of the Sanhedrim and of Pilate, or at Golgotha, evinced the utmost piety, fortitude, and self-possession. The circumstance of Simon the Cyrenian having been compelled to assist in bearing his cross, by no means proves that mere weakness disabled Christ from bearing it alone. The contrary appears from his immediately afterward addressing the Jewish women who bewailed his fate, and bidding them weep not for him, but for themselves and their children. On arriving at the fatal spot he refused the cup of medicated wine, usually given as a cordial to crucified persons; and after praying for his executioners, assuring the penitent malefactor of eternal happiness, providing for the future support of his widowed mother, and actively concurring in the fulfilment of prophecy, he suddenly expired amid loud and fervent ejaculations, which alone were sufficient to show that he retained all his faculties of mind and body to the last moment of his life. The opposite opinion is so manifestly unfounded and erroneous, that to illustrate it by quotations from the writings of authors who have taken that view of the subject, would be a mere loss of time and labor. Some of the principal expositions of this class will, however, be stated and refuted in the following chapter.

CHAPTER IV.

DEMONSTRATION OF THE IMMEDIATE CAUSE OF THE DEATH OF CHRIST.

SECTION I.

In the preceding chapter it is presumed to have been demonstrated that neither the ordinary sufferings of crucifixion, nor the wound inflicted by the soldier's spear, nor an unusual degree of weakness, nor the interposition of supernatural influence, was the immediate cause of the Saviour's death. The first of these conditions was inadequate, the second followed instead of preceding the effect, and the third and fourth had no existence. What, then, it will be asked, was the real cause? In conformity with the inductive principles announced at the commencement of this inquiry, it must have been a known power in nature, possessing the requisite efficacy, agreeing with all the circumstances of the case, and by suitable tests proved to have been present without counteraction. It will be the object of the ensuing observations to show that the power in which these characters perfectly and exclusively concurred was AGONY OF MIND, PRODUCING RUPTURE OF THE HEART. To establish this conclusion numerous details will be adduced, but the argument itself is short and simple. In the garden of Gethsemane Christ endured mental agony so intense that, had it not been limited by divine interposition, it would probably have destroyed his life without the aid of any other sufferings; but having been thus mitigated, its effects were confined to violent palpitation of the heart, accompanied with bloody sweat. On the cross this agony was renewed, in conjunction with the ordinary sufferings incidental to that mode of punishment; and having at this time been allowed to proceed to its utmost extremity without restraint, occasioned sudden death by rupture of the heart, intimated by a discharge of blood and water from his side, when it was afterward pierced with a spear.

In reference to their influence on the functions of body and mind, the human passions are naturally divisible into two opposite classes, the exciting and the depressing: the former giving rise to energy and animation, the latter to debility and torpor. Provided they are sufficiently strong or long-continued, passions of either class may induce death, either by simple exhaustion of vital power, or by some special injury to the heart, brain, or lungs. Agony, or the conflict between two exciting passions having opposite objects, is in this respect peculiarly efficacious; and when intense, produces violent palpitation, bloody sweat, oppression of the chest, loud cries, and ultimately rupture of the heart. Such rupture is usually attended with immediate death, and with an effusion into the pericardium (the capsule containing the heart) of the blood previously circulating through that organ; which when thus extravasated, although scarcely in any other case, separates into its constituent parts, so as to present the appearance commonly termed blood and water. In support of these statements several proofs and illustrations will now be proposed, and others will be inserted at the end of the volume. It must not, however, be expected that many distinct examples of this kind can be cited; since, while few it may be hoped have occurred, still fewer have been duly authenticated and recorded. For the satisfaction of persons not familiar with anatomy, it may be proper to premise that the heart is a double muscular bag, of a conical form, lined within and without by a dense membrane, and loosely enclosed in a receptacle of similar material, called the pericardium. It consists of two principle sacs, the right and the left, which lie side by side, and adhere firmly together, so as to form a strong middle wall, but have no internal communication. Each of these is subdivided into two connected pouches, or chambers, termed auricle and ventricle, whereof the auricle is round and thin, the ventricle long and fleshy; the two former constituting the base, and the two latter the body of the organ. Placed in the centre of the vascular system, the heart promotes and regulates the circulation of the blood, received on each side from two or more large veins of a soft and compressible texture, and discharged through a single artery which, being firm and elastic, is kept constantly pervious. Returning from all parts of the body except the lungs, blood of nearly a black color, and become unfit for the purposes of life, is poured by two principal veins, called venæ cavæ, into the right auricle, whence, after a momentary delay, it is transferred to the corresponding ventricle, its reflux being prevented by a membranous valve interposed between them. By the powerful contraction of the ventricle it is transmitted through the pulmonary artery to the lungs, where by minute subdivision, and contact with atmospheric air inhaled through the windpipe, it is purified, and acquires a bright crimson color. Returning from the lungs by the four pulmonary veins, the renovated blood next passes into the left auricle, and from thence in a similar manner and at the same time as on the right side into the left ventricle, by the contraction of which it is distributed with great force through the aorta to the remaining parts of the body, whence it was originally derived.

While undisturbed by accident or disease, the actions

just described are maintained during the whole of life with admirable energy and regularity, but are liable to be deranged or interrupted by various causes, and particularly by the passions of the mind. Thus it is observed by Baron Haller, the father of modern physiology, that excessive grief occasions palpitation, and sometimes sudden death; that the corporeal effects of anger and terror are nearly alike, including increased strength, and violent motions both in the heart and throughout the body, and producing bloody sweats, and other kinds of hemorrhage.*
—"Anger"—says Senac,—"has in certain cases torn the fibres of the heart, and even opened the ventricles. It is not, therefore, extraordinary that it should be followed by palpitation, and, accordingly, various physicians have observed such a result. . . . But fear and terror are not less powerful causes, especially when they seize suddenly. In that case the nerves act with violence on the heart, and derange the order of its movements. The blood is at the same time propelled in these passions by a general shock, or commotion of all the parts of the body: it therefore necessarily accumulates in the two trunks of the venæ cavæ, rushes into the auricles, and overcharges them, as well as the ventricles. Here, then, are two causes, one the consequence of the other, which, as is proved by numerous examples, produce palpitation. Dilatations are, as we have already stated, frequent results of fits of passion. Grief and sadness do not act so suddenly, nor with equal force; but, as we have said, these secret and silent passions induce similar disorder." †—"If any one"—remarks Corvisart,—" can seriously deny, or even doubt the fatal physical influence of the passions on the heart, let it suffice him to know that a fit of anger may produce rup-

* Haller, Element. Physiolog. Corp. Human, vol. v. pp. 50, 583, 586, 587.

† Senac, Traité du Cœur, vol. ii. p. 515.

ture of the heart, and cause sudden death. . . . Complete rupture of the heart has rarely been observed in the sound state of this organ: some examples may, however, be cited of this lesion, in consequence of a violent effort, a fit of anger, an epileptic paroxysm, etc. . . . But of all the causes capable of producing organic diseases in general, and more especially those of the heart, the most powerful beyond dispute are mental affections. . . . No mental affection can, indeed, be experienced without the movement of the heart being either augmented, accelerated, retarded, weakened, or disturbed, without its force in fact being increased, enfeebled, or almost annihilated. Pleasure, pain, fear, anger, in short all the powerful passions, cause the heart to palpitate, to beat more or less frequently, strongly, slowly, or regularly, or to suspend its action momentarily, sometimes even mortally." *

In his admirable dissertations on the nervous system, Sir Charles Bell has not only confirmed these statements, but explained them.—"The language and sentiments of every people,"—he observes,—"have pointed to the heart as the seat of passion, and every individual must have felt its truth. For, though the heart be not in the proper sense the seat of passion, it is influenced by the conditions of the mind, and from thence its influence is extended through the respiratory organs, so as to mount to the throat, lips, and cheeks, and account for every movement in passion which is not explained by the direct influence of the mind upon the features. So we shall find, if we attend to the expression of grief, that the same phenomena are presented, and we may catalogue them as it were anatomically. Imagine the overwhelming influence of grief. The object in the mind has absorbed the powers of the frame; the body is no more regarded, the spirits

* Corvisart, Sur les Maladies du Cœur, etc.; Discours Préliminaire, p. xli. pp. 259, 369, 370.

have left it; it reclines, and the limbs gravitate; the whole frame is nerveless and relaxed, and the person scarcely breathes. . . . Although the heart has not the common sense of touch, yet it has an appropriate sensibility, by which it is held united in the closest connection and sympathy with the other vital organs, so that it participates in all the changes of the general system of the body. But, connected with the heart, and depending on its peculiar and excessive sensibility, there is an extensive apparatus which demands our attention. This is the organ of breathing, a part known obviously as the instrument of speech, but which I shall show to be more. The organ of breathing, in its association with the heart, is the instrument of expression, and is the part of the frame by the action of which the emotions are developed, and made visible to us. Certain strong feelings of the mind produce a disturbed condition of the heart, and through that corporeal influence, directly from the heart, indirectly from the mind, the extensive apparatus constituting the organ of breathing is put in motion, and gives us the outward signs which we call expression. . . . The heart and lungs, though insensible to common impression, yet being acutely alive to their proper stimulus, suffer from the slightest change of posture, or exertion of the frame, and also from the changes or affections of the mind. . . . But it is when the strong are subdued by this mysterious union of soul and body, when passion tears the breast, that the most afflicting picture of human frailty is presented, and the surest proof afforded that it is on the respiratory organs that the influence of passion falls with so powerful an expression of agony."[*] Precisely similar, and somewhat more explanatory, is the testimony of Crichton.—" The internal gratifications and uneasinesses which we call mental, are all"—

---

[*] Sir Charles Bell, On the Nervous System of the Human Body, pp. 170-172;—The Anatomy and Philosophy of Expression, pp. 90-92.

says he,—"felt about the præcordia [the region of the heart], and strictly speaking, therefore, are sensual. It would appear that the sensorial impressions, which all ideas belonging to these causes produce, are communicated by a necessary law of our economy to these parts, affecting particularly the heart, diaphragm, and organs of respiration. It is there that the pleasure or pain is experienced. Nothing can be a more convincing proof of this than the common expressions and actions of mankind when under the influence of one or other of these feelings. *Our heart*, we say, *is relieved from a load,—it is light,—it jumps for joy,—it is oppressed,—it is full,—it is ready to break,—it is touched with sorrow.*"—The involuntary effects of terror on a man are thus described.—" His heart is thrown into greater and more violent action than usual, but the arterial system, so far from corresponding with it in a general sense, is either rendered torpid at its extremities, or else is affected with a spasm; a sudden paleness spreads itself over his countenance, his lips lose the coral tint, and the whole body of the man seems to shrink into a smaller compass, a tremor agitates his whole frame, and he feels as if he had suffered a great diminution of strength. . . . . It happens now and then, when the whole play of the mental faculties is as it were destroyed by the impression of the dreadful object, and no possibility of escape appears, that, volition being then without a stimulus, a person drops down on the earth, as if suddenly bereft of all his animal powers. . . . That the sanguiferous system does sustain great and sudden changes from the influence of the passions, is a fact which common observation is sufficient to prove. In all those which are the offspring of desire it is accelerated, and in all those which spring from aversion it is slower. In sudden joy, in eager hope, in the expectations of love, in the endearments of friendship, the pulse beats quick, the face glows, and the eyes glisten. In grief and sorrow, extreme anger, hatred, jealousy, and envy, the blood stagnates about the heart, a chilling cold spreads itself over the whole surface of the body, the blood forsakes the cheeks, and a tremor ensues. .... The general corporeal effect of all the modifications of grief and sorrow is a torpor in every irritable part, especially in the circulating and absorbent system: hence the paleness of the countenance, the coldness of the extremities, the contraction and shrinking of the skin and general surface of the body, the smallness and slowness of the pulse, the want of appetite, the deficiency of muscular force, and the sense of general languor which overspreads the whole frame. As the action of the extreme branches of the arterial system is greatly diminished, the heart, and aorta and its larger vessels, and the whole system of the pulmonary artery become loaded and distended with blood. The painful sense of fulness which this occasions gives rise to a common expression, which is in some degree descriptive of what really exists. In sorrow the heart is said to be *full*, and in deep sorrow it is often said to be *like to burst*. A sense of oppression and anxiety, a laborious and slow respiration, and the remarkable phenomena of sobbing and sighing, naturally arise from this state of torpor and retarded circulation. . . . The debilitating powers of grief seem to exhaust the irritability of the system, without a previous increase of vascular action. When a person is suddenly informed of some melancholy event that deeply affects his life, fortune, or fame, his whole strength seems at once to leave him, the muscles which support him are all relaxed, and he feels as if his knees gave way under him. In some people the sensorial impression exhausts the irritability so completely as to cause the action of the heart and arteries and organs of respiration to cease, and the person then falls into a swoon, as it is called. . . . When a person is suddenly terrified, the motion of the heart is generally quickened, a kind of spasmodic contraction seizes all the arteries, especially the extreme ones, causing an accumulation of blood in the larger vessels. The sudden and forcible distention of the heart makes it move on its basis, and produces that peculiar sensation, which most people endeavor to express by saying that their heart seems to jump to their throat. . . . In some cases the debility which is produced is so great as to render it impossible for the person to support himself in an erect posture, and he therefore falls down, apparently senseless and speechless, on the ground. In this way the strongest man is often deprived in a few seconds of almost the whole of his natural strength. . . . As soon as burning anger is excited, the impressions are directed to the heart and arteries, and they are stimulated to a preternatural degree of action, the blood is propelled with violence to the surface of the body, and circulates with force and rapidity through the smallest and most extreme arteries, and hence the burning heat which characterizes this sort of passion."*

Of rapid death occasioned by the direct operation either of joy or grief, Robinson, in his work on the spleen, furnishes two examples.—"Mrs. Davise, a lady of consummate virtue, was so sensibly touched with excessive joy on suddenly hearing of the return of her son from the Indies, that the passion was too big for her soul to struggle with, which in a moment disconcerted all the animal springs, and put an everlasting stop to all their motions. . . . Mrs. Chiswell was so extremely affected with sorrow at the departure of her son for Turkey, that she expired that very moment she was about to withdraw her hand from a parting farewell."†—The increased influence of these pas-

---

* Alexander Crichton, On Mental Derangement, vol. ii., pp. 119–121, 127–134, 178, 183, 184, 260, 288, 289.

† Nicholas Robinson, System of the Spleen, etc., pp. 91, 92.

sions, when they abruptly succeed one another, is thus noticed by Dr. Cogan.—"There are many instances on record of sudden death having been occasioned by the hasty communication of very joyful tidings. Like a stroke of electricity indiscreetly directed, the violent percussion has probably produced a paralysis of the heart by the excess of its stimulus. These incidents are most likely to take place in subjects who were at the instant deeply oppressed with the opposite passions of fear and anxiety, by which the natural and salutary action of the heart and arteries was greatly impeded. This of consequence will create a resistance to the impulse, and render it more liable to destroy the tone of that sensible organ. In most of the instances recorded, the persons who have fallen a sacrifice to the excess of joy were in this particular situation, nor was there an opportunity given to soften the agony of fear by a cautious manner of communicating the tidings. . . . Historians present us with many instances of fatal effects from the excess of joy; but it plainly appears from their narratives that the subjects were at the instant preceding under the pressure of extreme anguish of mind. Pliny informs us that Chilo the Lacedemonian died on hearing that his son had gained a prize in the Olympic games. We may consider the excess of joy in this case as an indication of his previous solicitude concerning the issue. (Lib. vii. sect. 7.) But the following instances are more express. Valerius Maximus tells us that Sophocles the tragic writer, in a contest of honor, died in consequence of a decision being pronounced in his favor. (Lib. ix. cap. 12.) Aulus Gellius mentions a remarkable example of what may be termed accumulated joy in [the sudden death of] Diagoras, whose three sons were crowned the same day as victors, the one as a pugilist, the other as a wrestler, and the third in both capacities. (Noct. Attic. lib. iii. cap. 15.) Livy also mentions the instance of an aged matron who, while she was in the depth of distress from the tidings of her son's having been slain in battle, died in his arms in the excess of joy on his safe return. (Lib. xxii. cap. 7.) Not to enumerate more examples, we are told by the Italian historian Guicciardini that Leo X. died of a fever occasioned by the agitation of his spirits on his receiving the joyful news of the capture of Milan, concerning which he had entertained much anxiety. (Lib. xiv.) In all these instances, the previous state of mind, with its pathological effects on the body, made the impulse of joy the stronger, and contributed to render it fatal." *

From the foregoing testimonies of eminent authors, to which many more might be added, it thus appears that one of the principal corporeal effects of the exciting passions is palpitation, or vehement action of the heart; and it will now be shown that, when this action is intense, it produces bloody sweat, dilatation, and ultimately rupture of the heart. By those acquainted with the structure and functions of the animal frame such results might readily be anticipated; but to others, authentic records of their actual occurrence will furnish the best proof of the fact. Perspiration, both sensible and insensible, takes place from the mouths of small regularly-organized tubes, which perforate the skin in all parts of the body, terminating in blind extremities internally, and by innumerable orifices on the outer surface. These tubes are surrounded by a net-work of minute vessels, and penetrated by the ultimate ramifications of arteries which, according to the force of the local circulation, depending chiefly on that of the heart, discharge either the watery parts of the blood in the state of vapor, its grosser ingredients in the form of a glutinous liquid, or in extreme cases the entire blood

* Dr. Cogan, Philosophical Treatise on the Passions, pp. 285, 363, 364.

itself. The influence of the invigorating passions, more especially in exciting an increased flow of blood to the skin, is familiarly illustrated by the process of blushing, either from shame or anger; for during this state the heart beats strongly, the surface of the body becomes hot and red, and if the emotion is very powerful, breaks out into a warm and copious perspiration, the first step toward a bloody sweat. Of the latter affection several instances are related in the German Ephemerides, wherein Kannegiesser remarks,—" Violent mental excitement, whether occasioned by uncontrollable anger, or vehement joy, and in like manner sudden terror, or intense fear, forces out a sweat, accompanied with signs either of anxiety or of hilarity." After ascribing this sweat to the unequal constriction of some vessels and dilatation of others, he further observes,—" If the mind is seized with a sudden fear of death, the sweat, owing to the excessive degree of constriction, often becomes bloody."—The eminent French historian De Thou mentions the case of—" an Italian officer who commanded at Monte-Maro, a fortress of Piedmont, during the warfare in 1552, between Henry II. of France and the Emperor Charles V. This officer, having been treacherously seized by order of the hostile general, and threatened with public execution unless he surrendered the place, was so agitated at the prospect of an ignominious death, that he sweated blood from every part of his body."—The same writer relates a similar occurrence in the person of a young Florentine at Rome, unjustly put to death by order of Pope Sixtus V. in the beginning of his reign, and concludes the narrative as follows.—" When the youth was led forth to execution, he excited the commiseration of many, and through excess of grief, was observed to shed bloody tears, and to discharge blood instead of sweat from his whole body; a circumstance which many regard as a certain proof that Nature con-

demned the severity of a sentence so cruelly hastened, and invoked vengeance against the magistrate himself, as therein guilty of murder."—Among several other examples given in the Ephemerides, of bloody tears and bloody sweat occasioned by extreme fear, more especially the fear of death, may be mentioned that of—" a young boy who, having taken part in a crime for which two of his elder brothers were hanged, was exposed to public view under the gallows on which they were executed, and was thereupon observed to sweat blood from his whole body."
—In his Commentaries on the four Gospels, Maldonato refers to—"a robust and healthy man at Paris who, on hearing sentence of death passed on him, was covered with a bloody sweat."—Zacchias mentions a young man who was similarly affected on being condemned to the flames. Schenck cites from a martyrology the case of—"a nun who fell into the hands of soldiers; and, on seeing herself encompassed with swords and daggers threatening instant death, was so terrified and agitated, that she discharged blood from every part of her body, and died of hæmorrhage in the sight of her assailants;"*—and Tissot reports from a respectable journal that of—"a sailor who was so alarmed by a storm, that through fear he fell down, and his face sweated blood, which during the whole continuance of the storm returned like ordinary sweat, as fast as it was wiped away." †

That several of the instances on record of sudden death from exciting passions were occasioned by rupture

---

* Ephemerid. Acad. Natur. Curios. Ann. 2, p. 34;—Dec. ii. Ann. 10, p. 354;—Dec. iii. Ann. 1, Append. pp. 124, 125;—Ann. 7 and 8, Append. p. 124;—Ibid. edit. 2da. vol. i. p. 84;—vol. viii. p. 184;—Thuanus, Hist. sui Temp. vol. i. p. 373; vol. iv. p. 300;—Joannes Maldonatus, Comment, in quatuor Evangelist. p. 601;—Paulus Zacchias, Quæstiones Medico-legales, lib. iii. p. 154;—Joannes Schenck à Grafenberg, Observ. Medic. etc. lib. iii. p. 458.

† Tissot, Traité des Nerfs, etc., pp. 279, 280.

of the heart, the circumstances which attended them render it impossible to doubt; although, owing to the neglect of examination, the decisive proof afforded by actual inspection is seldom attainable. The following examples may, however, suffice; but, previously to stating them, it seems proper to explain the manner in which, under such agency, rupture of the heart takes place. The immediate cause is a sudden and violent contraction of one of the ventricles, usually the left, on the column of blood thrown into it by a similar contraction of the corresponding auricle. Prevented from returning backward by the intervening valve, and not finding a sufficient outlet forward in the connected artery, the blood reacts against the ventricle itself, which is consequently torn open at the point of greatest distention, or least resistance, by the influence of its own reflected force. A quantity of blood is hereby discharged into the pericardium, and having no means of escape from that capsule, stops the circulation by compressing the heart from without, and induces almost instantaneous death.* In young and vigorous subjects, the blood thus collected in the pericardium soon divides into its constituent parts, namely, a pale watery liquid called serum, and a soft clotted substance of a deep-red color termed crassamentum; but, except under similar circumstances of extravasation, this distinct separation of the blood is seldom witnessed in the dead body. When, however, the action of the ventricle is less violent, instead of bursting under the continued injection from the auricle, it merely dilates; but, as in consequence of this over-distention its power of contraction is speedily destroyed, death takes place with equal certainty, although perhaps with less rapidity, and in this case, as well as in the

---

* Allan Burns, On Diseases of the Heart, pp. 181–186, 223, 224, 251, 255.

former one, the blood remaining within the heart has been found divided into serum and crassamentum.

In exact conformity with the foregoing statement Dr. Hope observes,—"It is generally in the left ventricle that the rupture [of the heart] takes place; a circumstance which at first appears remarkable, since this ventricle is the stronger, but for the same reason it contracts more energetically, and . . . . it is only strong muscles which undergo rupture from the energy of their own contraction. Hence rupture of the auricles is much more rare than that of the ventricles. The exciting causes of rupture are generally considerable efforts, paroxysms of passion, external violence, as falls, etc. . . . Rupture of the heart or great vessels into the pericardium is not always immediately fatal, as a solid coagulum or a fibrinous concretion has in several instances been known to arrest the hæmorrhage for a few hours. Of ten cases mentioned by Bayle, eight died instantaneously, one in about two hours, and another in fourteen."—Among the causes of rupture of the heart Dr. Copland enumerates,—"violent mental emotions, especially anger, fright, terror, unexpected disappointment, distressing intelligence abruptly communicated, anxiety, etc., sudden and violent muscular efforts and laborious or prolonged physical exertions of any kind, particularly in constrained positions . . . . In some cases,"—he observes,—"inexpressible anxiety and pain have been felt in the præcordia and epigastrium, with cold extremities, and cramps, shortly before dissolution. In the majority rupture has produced instant death, but in some this has not been the case . . . . In most of the cases in which the rupture is preceded by violent pain, M. Ollivier thinks that it is produced gradually from the successive laceration of several layers or fasciculi of muscular fibres, and that the pericardium becomes only gradually distended by the effused blood. Where the laceration and aperture are at once large, a copious effusion instantly occurs, fills the pericardium, and abolishes the contractions of the organ."*—The distinguished Italian anatomist Morgagni judiciously remarks, that the cause of death on such occasions is not the mere loss of blood, since under different circumstances a greater quantity may be lost without destroying life, but the sudden compression of the heart, and stoppage of the circulation, in consequence of which, as he says,—" a small hæmorrhage within the pericardium causes death far more rapidly than a much larger one in most other parts of the body." †—This is proved by several examples, in which without any obvious rupture of the heart, blood effused into the pericardium induced sudden death. One is mentioned by Christian Vater, in the German Ephemerides, and another by Van Geuns, in a separate work. Both the subjects were robust soldiers who died of excessive joy, and in whose bodies no morbid condition was afterward found, except a large quantity of clotted blood in the pericardium, by which the action of the heart had been suppressed. The latter author ascribes the effect to sudden distention of the exhalants opening on the inner surface of the membrane. This would correspond to the manner in which bloody sweat is produced; but, as the exhalants of the pericardium are very inferior both in size and activity to those of the skin, it is more probable that in such cases the effusion is due either to rupture of some of the nutrient vessels of the heart itself, termed its coronary vessels, or to hæmorrhage from without, penetrating by a minute or circuitous passage into its capsule. Such at least is the opinion of Morgagni, Zecchinelli, and other anatomists. Of blood thus finding its

---

* Dr. Hope, On the Diseases of the Heart and Great Vessels, pp. 198, 199 ;—Dr. Copland, Dict. of Practical Medicine, Part v. p. 224.

† Morgagni, De Caus. et Sed. Morb. vol. iii. pp. 433-445, 465-467 ;— vol. vii. pp. 654-657.

way into the pericardium by a small aperture, which without great attention might easily escape notice, the former gives several examples; and in the Ephemerides, Dr. Daniel Fischer mentions the case of a soldier who died suddenly after eating a hearty dinner, and in whose body the only morbid appearance discovered on inspection was, —"the pericardium filled and distended with very fluid and florid blood. The membrane having been divided longitudinally, in order to trace more exactly the source of the hæmorrhage, this was found at the base of the heart, where a branch of the coronary artery had ruptured, and from which blood was still actually flowing." *

The lower and more common degrees of injury of the heart from passions of the mind are well adapted to illustrate the higher ones, which are necessarily rare. Thus, Harvey relates the case of a man who, under the long-continued working of indignation which he was compelled to restrain, and of vindictive feelings which he was unable to gratify, fell after some years into a scorbutic or hæmorrhagic state, attended with extreme oppression and pain of the chest, owing to an immense enlargement of the heart and principal arteries, entirely occasioned by mental emotion. Had this emotion been more intense, it is easy to conceive that, instead of a slight oozing of blood from the cutaneous vessels, and a mere enlargement of the central organs of circulation, the result would have been bloody sweat, and rupture of the heart. Dionis gives an interesting account of a French naval officer who labored for several years under disease of the heart, to which he at

---

* Ephemerid. Acad. Natur. Curios. Dec. iii. Ann. 9 and 10.—p. 293; —Ibid. Edit. 2da. vol. v. pp. 141, 142;—Matt. Van Geuns, De Morte Corporea, etc. p. 591;—Zecchinelli, Sulla Angina del Petto, etc. vol. i. pp. 95, 96;—Thurnam, in Lond. Med. Gazette, 1838, pp. 813–817;—Curling, Ibid. pp. 894, 895;—Fitzpatrick, in Lond. Med. Repository, vol. xvii. pp. 295–298.

length fell a victim. On subsequent examination, the right auricle was found as big as the head of a new-born child, and contained nearly a pint and a half of blood, the greater part of which was coagulated. He uniformly ascribed his complaint to the strong efforts which he used twelve or thirteen years before, in suppressing the first motions of a violent fit of anger; for at that time the cardiac symptoms commenced, and continued ever after till the day of his death. In like manner, Tissot quotes from Viridet the case of a merchant, who, in consequence of violent grief was seized with constriction and severe pain of heart, terminating in death. On inspection of the body, —"the heart was found twice as large as it should have been, and the whole of its left cavity filled with blood strongly coagulated."—In another merchant, aged sixty-two years, who suddenly died of grief, Bonet states that the heart and lungs were found greatly distended with blood, which in the right ventricle was almost entirely coagulated. Of the separation of the blood in some of these cases into its constituents, the same author gives two examples.—" A paralytic orphan girl, seventeen years of age, suddenly died of suffocation without any obvious cause. On dissecting the body, I found the heart of twice the usual size, its auricles very large, and, like the veins and arteries, much distended with water, and black clotted blood . . . . In a soldier who suddenly died after long-continued grief, while all the other viscera were healthy, the pericardium was found to contain not only water, but also much coagulated blood." *—The popular use of the terms blood and water, or their equivalents in different languages, to signify the dissevered crassamentum and serum of the blood, is thus explained, and the

* Harvæus, Opera, pp. 127, 128 ;—Dionis, Anatomy of Human Bodies, pp. 270, 445–451 ;—Tissot, Traité des Nerfs, etc. p. 361 ;—Bonetus Sepulchretum, vol. i. pp. 585, 887, 899.

expressions are natural and reasonable; since the crassamentum, or red clotted portion, comprises nearly all the more essential ingredients of the blood, and the serum, or pale-yellow liquid, consists chiefly of water. In commenting on the last case, Morgagni makes the following apposite remark.—" Although you will see it repeated in a note that the heart was loaded both with blood and water, it is by no means necessary that you should believe this water to have been any other than the serum of the blood separated from the coagulated part, as not unfrequently happens to a considerable amount."—An interesting example of the same kind is furnished by Mr. Bedingfield, who observes,—" In persons who die of what is called a broken heart, the auricles will sometimes be found much distended. I remember examining a case of this description in which no trace of disease could be detected except in the right auricle of the heart. This compartment was of three times its natural dimensions. It contained a large quantity of blood which had separated into serum, crassamentum, and coagulable lymph, as perfectly as inflamed blood does when drawn from a vein."—In such circumstances the cause of death is, as Haller and others have explained, a sudden and excessive distention of the cardiac cavity, which thereupon loses its power of contraction, more especially when the contained blood coagulates, and the circulation is in consequence permanently stopped.*

When, however, the distention is followed by violent contraction, the result may be rupture, which, as before stated, generally takes place in the left ventricle; and, unless the vital force happens at the time to be much depressed, the blood thus discharged into the pericardial sac

---

* Morgagni, De Caus. et Sed. Morb. vol. iii. p. 465; Bedingfield, Compendium of Medical Practice, p. 154;—Haller, On the Motion of the Blood, etc., p. 111;—Senac, vol. ii. p. 540.

divides into its constituents more readily than when it remains within its natural receptacles. These constituents are commonly termed blood and water; but in medical writings there is reason to believe the same separation is sometimes intended by the less accurate expression,—"coagulated blood;"—as, perhaps, in the following examples of rupture of the heart, recorded by the late Dr. Abercrombie, of Edinburgh. A man, aged thirty-five years, on stooping forward to lift something, died suddenly. As he had made little previous complaint, except of headache, the case might have been mistaken for apoplexy. On dissection, however, all was sound in the brain, but the pericardium was found distended with coagulated blood. A woman, aged twenty-eight years, died suddenly, after complaining of pain extending from the left side of the chest to the left shoulder. On inspection, the pericardium was found distended with coagulated blood, but there was also some bloody fluid in the left cavity of the chest, and the right lung adhered extensively to the side. In an old man, aged seventy-seven years, who died suddenly, owing to a rupture of the heart from accidental injury, the cavities of the pleura contained about three pounds of fluid, but the lungs were sound. The pericardium appeared greatly distended, and when opened, was found to contain an immense quantity of coagulated blood. The heart was much enlarged, and very flabby. Dr. Thurnam reports a similar—"case of rupture of the heart from external violence, but without any penetrating wound. The pericardium contained several ounces of serum and coagulated blood. There was a considerable rupture of the right auricle, and a smaller one at the apex of the heart."—He also mentions an instance—"of spontaneous rupture of the right auricle and ventricle, attended with great and general softening. The pericardium was filled with liquid blood,"—coagulation having apparently been prevented by the feebleness of the heart's action, which is usually attended with a corresponding condition of the blood.* Dr. Elliotson relates the case of a female who died suddenly with severe pain of the heart. On opening the body, the pericardium was found distended with clear serum, and a very large coagulum of blood, which had escaped through a spontaneous rupture of the aorta near its origin, without any other morbid appearance. This author is nevertheless of opinion that—"ruptures of the heart and aorta rarely occur under the most violent impulse, unless there be disease of substance;"—but the contrary is proved by several eminent pathologists, particularly Portal and Rostan, who have written distinct treatises on the subject, containing the results of numerous observations, which decidedly show that rupture of the left ventricle may take place without any previous alteration of tissue, and while the walls of the heart are perfectly sound.† The following case, furnished by Dr. Fischer, a German physician, confirms this view, and is at the same time a good example of rupture of the heart, occasioned by the slow operation of continued grief.—"A gentleman aged sixty-eight, and apparently possessing every claim to longevity, was, after having spent many years at court, compelled to quit it, and retire to a country residence.... Toward the close of life his attention was occupied by an unpleasant business, which, as interfering with the indulgence of his propensity for solitude, had the effect of aggravating his melancholy.... On the 16th of October, 1817, he was seized, while walking, with a severe pain, which he sup-

---

* Trans. of the Medico-Chirurg. Society of Edinburgh, vol. i. pp. 60–63;—Dr. Thurnam, in the London Med. Gazette for 1838, pp. 813–817.

† Dr. Elliotson, Lumleyan Lectures on Diseases of the Heart, pp. 30–34;—Portal, Sur la Nature de plusieurs Maladies, vol. ii. pp. 7–12, 17;—Rostan, Mémoires sur les Ruptures du Cœur, p. 10.

posed to be cramp at the stomach. [This pain], after returning repeatedly, attended with violent agitation and agony, proved fatal on the evening of the 20th. On examination of the body eighteen hours after death, the only morbid condition of any importance was rupture of the heart. On puncturing the pericardium, which had the appearance of being distended by a substance of a dark-blue color, a quantity of reddish fluid escaped, and afterward florid blood to the amount of two or three pounds. The membrane was then slit up, and the heart seen surrounded by a coagulum more than three pounds in weight. This having been cleared away, a rupture was discovered in the aortic [left] ventricle, which extended upward from the apex, about an inch and a half on the external surface. The internal wound was found but about half an inch in length, and its lips [were] at least as wide again asunder as those of the external breach."* Owing to the smallness of the aperture the fatal result was more protracted, the discharge of blood into the pericardial sac less rapid, and its consequent separation into its constituents less complete than would otherwise in all probability have been the case.

In his treatise on the Influence of the Passions, Mr. Townsend, of New York, remarks,—"Anger, fear, and grief, always occasion distress. The diseases which they produce must necessarily correspond; hence, those which accompany these passions are of the most dangerous and fatal kinds, as rupture of the heart, and of the large blood-vessels, etc. . . . An unfortunate female of this city . . . . literally and truly died of a broken heart, as was found on dissection; and there was every reason to believe that this consummation of her misery was the unavoidable consequence of her exquisite dejection of mind at that particu-

* Dr. Fischer, in the London Medical Repository, etc., vol. xi. pp. 422–427; vol. xii. pp. 161–168.

lar moment."—In this instance,—"the subject was a robust and plethoric female, aged twenty-two years, long addicted to dissolute and intemperate habits. For some time previously to her decease she had complained only of slight, and apparently rheumatic pains; but within a day or two of the fatal event, she had been deserted by a man to whom she was engaged in marriage. In consequence of this, her mind became very deeply affected. After having supped on the preceding night, she retired to rest as usual, and in the morning was found dead in bed. She lay in a bent position on the left side, and was hence supposed at first to be in a profound sleep. Neither the countenance nor the limbs were at all contorted. On dissection, the sac of the pericardium was found filled with about ten ounces of coagulated blood, and two of serum. The heart, on all sides covered by it, was of the ordinary volume, but much loaded with fat. At the summit of the aortic [left] ventricle was discovered the breach, from which the effused blood had issued. It was irregularly lacerated, and measured about half an inch in diameter."*—In this case, the rupture of the heart was combined with some degree of inflammatory affection attributable, it may be presumed, to the same mental cause; but in the ensuing one, communicated by Dr. Williams, of Southampton, and never before published, the rupture, besides being much more extensive, was free from any material complication.—"R. W., a laborer, aged fifty-six years, had generally enjoyed good health, but for ten years had suffered great despondency of mind, owing to the unfaithfulness of his wife. About six months before his death he was troubled with severe cough, which came on in paroxysms, generally at night and early in the

---

* P. S. Townsend, On the Influence of the Passions in the Production and Modification of Disease, pp. 51-56, 65.—London Medical Repository, vol. xi. pp. 427, 428.

morning, and after a fit of this kind was found one morning dead. A *post-mortem* examination took place in the presence of Mr. Boulton, surgeon, of Leamington. On opening the chest, the bag of the pericardium appeared much distended with fluid, and was of a dark-blue color. On cutting into it, a pint at least of transparent serum issued out, leaving the crassamentum firmly attached to the anterior surface of the heart. On further examination to ascertain the source of this hæmorrhage, we found the left ventricle, from the origin of the aorta downward to within an inch of the apex, ruptured. The heart appeared in no way disorganized, there was no softness of its walls, the internal membrane was healthy, and so were the valves of each cavity. Some portions of both lungs were found slightly hepatized,"—that is, consolidated, so as to present an appearance like that of the liver. The following case, related by Mr. Adams, is remarkably similar.— "Thomas Treacher, forty-six years of age, a stout, muscular working-man, who had labored for many years under great mental anxiety, was attacked with severe cardiac symptoms on Sunday evening, November the 5th, 1826, and, after great agony of body and mind, died on November the 9th. On opening the thorax, the pericardium was found distended, and emitted when divided a quantity of serous fluid; but the heart was entirely concealed by an envelope of coagulated blood in three distinct layers, owing to rupture of the left ventricle close to the septum, and nearer the apex than the base of the heart."*

SECTION II.

By the facts and reasonings above adduced it may be regarded as proved that, owing to the natural constitution of the human frame, the exciting passions when violent,

---

* Journal of Morbid Anatomy, Ophthalmic Medicine, etc. Art. v.

and especially when accompanied with agony or conflict, are capable of inducing bloody sweat, and, when still more intense, rupture of the heart; both effects depending on an excessive and irregular action of that organ, occurring in a lower or higher degree. The next step in the process of demonstration is to show, that this natural and adequate agency was really present and operative in the sufferings and death of Christ,—a task which, owing to the fulness and precision of the evangelical narrative, is by no means difficult. The peculiar sufferings of the Saviour commenced in the solitude of Gethsemane, as if it had been the divine purpose to prove, by the absence of every other cause, that at this time they were wholly occasioned by mental distress. His enemies had not yet arrived, and he was still attended by his three principal apostles, Peter, James, and John, when retiring at a late hour of the night to a lonely spot in the garden,—" he was seized with consternation and distress: and said to them,—' My soul is exceedingly sorrowful, even unto death. Remain here, and watch with me.'—And he hastily withdrew from them about a stone's cast, and, kneeling down, threw himself on his face, and prayed that, if it were possible, the hour might pass from him, saying— 'Abba! [that is] Father! if it be possible, let this cup pass from me; nevertheless, not my will but thine be done.' "—The terms used by the evangelists on this occasion are, as competent judges have often noticed, the strongest which the Greek language, one of the most expressive which ever existed, could supply.* Thus the Rev. Archibald M'Lean, in his Commentary on the

---

* Matt. chap. 26, v. 36–42;—Mark, chap. 14, v. 32–36;—Luke, chap. 22, v. 39–42.—Mark's statement, probably derived from Peter, an eye-witness of the scene, is perhaps the most striking,—" Καὶ ἤρξατο ἐκθαμβεῖσθαι καὶ ἀδημονεῖν· καὶ λέγει αὐτοῖς,—Περίλυπός ἐστιν ἡ ψυχή μου ἕως θανάτου· μείνατε ὧδε, καὶ γρηγορεῖτε."—Mark, chap. 14, v. 33, 34.

Epistle to the Hebrews, judiciously remarks,—" We have an account of the exceeding greatness of his soul-sufferings in the garden, as related by the evangelists, and expressed by himself.—' He began to be sorrowful, and very heavy,'—and this he expressed by saying,—' My soul is exceedingly sorrowful, even unto death,'—Matt. chap. 26, v. 37, 38. On which we may observe, 1. That the seat of his sufferings at this time was his *soul*, his body being no otherwise concerned than as it was affected by the distress of his mind, for as yet there was no human hand upon him. 2. The words set forth the greatness of his soul-sufferings. His soul was not only sorrowful, but (περίλυπος) exceeding sorrowful. The word signifies to be *beset with sorrow round about*, and is well expressed in the Psalms,—' The sorrows of death compassed me, and the pains of hell gat hold upon me.'—Psalm 18, v. 5, 6; Psalm 116, v. 3. His soul was now besieged with sorrow and sore amazement on every side, so that there was no evasion for him. Turn which way he will, nothing but the bitter cup presented itself to him, in all its dreadful ingredients. His soul was thus sorrowful, *even unto death*. It was a deadly sorrow, the sorrows of death; and this sorrow seems actually to have killed him before the time in which the tortures of the cross could have effected his death. He is said to be *sore amazed, and very heavy*, Mark, chap. 14, v. 33; which sets forth the greatness of his fear, terror, and consternation. This we may conceive to arise from his clear apprehensions of the evil and demerit of sin, of the infinite opposition of the divine holiness and justice to it, and of the power of God's wrath as the curse threatened against it, which he now saw ready to be inflicted upon him as the devoted victim; for—' the Lord made to meet upon him the iniquities of us all.'—Isaiah, chap. 53, v. 6. In the full view of all this, it is no wonder that his human soul was filled with the most dreadful amazement and fear." *

To the same effect are the observations of the acute and pious Rambach.—" The sorrow of the blessed Jesus is further represented as very bitter and vehement. The evangelists use different phrases to express the anguish of his soul. He began to be overwhelmed with sorrow, to be sore amazed, to be troubled, and seized with fear and dread; as it is said of St. Paul when, frightened by a sudden flash of lightning, he spoke trembling and astonished; and likewise of the women, when surprised by the appearance of an angel at the sepulchre. He began to be sore amazed; which word in the original denotes the most painful anguish of soul, and depression of spirit. . . . The chief seat of his agony was his soul, which was subject to the like passions with ours. See Psalms 18, 40, 69, and 88. And this sorrow was unto death; that is, it was so great that it might have broken his heart, and thus have brought on his death; or because it would not cease till death put an end to it. . . . He prays that, if it were possible, this hour might pass from him. He calls the suffering allotted to him, and of which he had already a foretaste, an hour. It had before been said, His hour was not yet come; but now it was come, as our blessed Lord himself says in his prayer, —'Father, the hour is come.' . . . It more particularly denotes the present hour of his inward agony, his anguish of soul, when the floods of God's wrath were discharged on him, when he stood before the divine tribunal as the greatest criminal, loaded with the oppressive weight of the sins of the whole world. . . . He does not properly petition his Father that all the sufferings he was to undergo may pass from him, as it is commonly expounded; but he means only to obtain, in the present hour of extreme

* Archibald M'Lean, Paraphrase and Commentary on the Epistle to the Hebrews, vol. i. pp. 163, 164.

inward trouble and anguish, an abatement and shortening of the dreadful agony he felt, which might have given offence even to his disciples, who were unacquainted with the mystery of his sufferings. . . . By the cup is to be understood the present excruciating sense of the wrath of God, and the withdrawing of the sensible and comfortable assistance, which at other times his human nature used to enjoy from the divine. Hence, all the evangelists subjoin—'*this* cup.'—All the other cups of his passion he was most willing and ready to drink; but this cup, which he now first began to taste, in which were poured the dregs of the wrath and curse of God, was so extremely bitter that his spotless and feeble humanity shuddered at it. Hence he cries out,—'Let this cup pass from me;'—in which words he only prays for the shortening of the duration of his painful inward agony, that it might soon pass over."

It can scarcely fail to be noticed that under the influence of a sort of pious instinct or sagacity, the result of long-continued and ardent contemplation, these and other authors almost divined the latent cause of the Saviour's death, without possessing a distinct knowledge of those physical facts by which alone it can be fully demonstrated. Thus M'Lean observes that the sorrow of Christ—"seems actually to have killed him before the time in which the tortures of the cross could have effected his death;"—and Rambach affirms,—"it was so great that it might have broken his heart, and thus have brought on his death."—Even Dr. Priestley says the agonies of Christ —"affected him so much, that it would not have been extraordinary if he had actually died in consequence of it; since such consternation and terror as he appears to have been in, is well known to have been of itself the cause of death to many persons."*—A still nearer approximation

* J. Rambach, Considerations on the Sufferings of Christ, translated

to the truth, although intermixed with some errors of detail, was attained by the celebrated President Edwards, who in his Sermon on the excellency of Christ makes the following observation,—" In Christ's great sufferings did his infinite regard to the honor of God's justice distinguishingly appear; for it was from regard to *that* that he thus humbled himself. And yet, in these sufferings, Christ was the mark of the vindictive expressions of that very justice of God. Revenging justice then spent all its force upon him, which made him sweat blood, and cry out upon the cross, and probably rent his vitals, broke his heart, the fountain of blood, or some other blood-vessels, and by the violent fermentation turned his blood to water; for the blood and water that issued out of his side when pierced by the spear seems to have been extravasated blood, and so there might be a kind of literal fulfilment of Psalm 22, v. 14;—'I am poured out like water, and all my bones are out of joint; my heart is like wax, it is melted in the midst of my bowels.'"*—But the most complete statement of this kind has been given by an eminent living divine, Dr. Russell, of Dundee, whose remarks on the subject, had they been accompanied by a competent demonstration of the facts, would have superseded the present work. Speaking of Christ's sufferings at Gethsemane, he says,—" His heart was preternaturally fired within him, so as to force a passage through the body for his rarefied blood; for his sweat was as it were great drops of blood falling down to the ground. The agony of his soul must have been bitter beyond conception, when such was its effect upon his body in the open air, at midnight, and when they who were within found it

from the German; vol. i. pp. 35-37, 48, 49, 55, 56.—Dr. Priestley, Discourse on the Evidence of the Resurrection of Jesus, pp. 12, 13.

* President Edwards, Works, in eight vols. 8vo. Lond. 1817; vol. vi. pp. 413, 414.

necessary to defend themselves against the cold. His firm heart was ready to break, and immediate death was threatened; but knowing that much remained to be accomplished, it was his prayer that the cup might for a time pass from him. His prayer was heard. An angel appeared to strengthen him, and he regained composure to act with propriety before his judges and the people, and to suffer what he endured before he reached the cross. On the cross the scene of Gethsemane was renewed;—the cup was again presented to him, and there he drank it to the very dregs. On Calvary his distress reached its height, and drew from him the bitter exclamation,—'My God! my God! why hast thou forsaken me?'—Matt. chap. 27, v. 46. Mysterious dereliction! only to be accounted for by the nature of his death. . . . He at last expired under the curse, not so much in consequence of the exhaustion of nature by bodily pain and the loss of blood (for in the article of death he cried with a loud voice, and Pilate marvelled when he heard of it), as in consequence of the extreme pressure of mental torture; Matt. chap. 27, v. 50; Mark, chap. 15, v. 44. This was too racking, too exquisite for nature to support,—it literally broke his heart. That sorrow which is the very soul of the curse terminated his life, and thus discovered the nature of his sufferings, together with their great and glorious design."*

The mortal tendency of the mental sufferings of Gethsemane is, however, placed beyond all doubt by the authority of the apostle Paul, who in his epistle to the Hebrews states of Christ, that—"in the days of his flesh he offered prayers and supplications, [accompanied] with tears and loud cries, to him who was able to save him from death, and was heard on account of [his] pious fear:

* Dr. David Russell, Letters, chiefly practical and consolatory, etc.; vol. i. pp. 7-9.

[that thus,] although he was a son, he learned obedience from his sufferings, and when [at length] perfected, became the author of eternal salvation to all who obey him, having been proclaimed by God a high-priest after the order of Melchisedek."—This interpretation of the passage is adopted by the writers above-mentioned, and by many others.—" I apprehend "—says M'Lean,—" that the deprecations and supplications here mentioned, are chiefly those which he offered up in the garden of Gethsemane, and also on the cross."—" It must have been "—observes Rambach,—" a petition in which he was heard, which cannot be said if he prayed for the removal of all his sufferings in general."—" I do not suppose,"—remarks Dr. Doddridge,—" our Lord here prayed to be excused entirely from sufferings and death. It appears to me much safer to expound it as relating to the terror and severity of the combat in which he was now actually engaged. This throws great light on Heb. chap. 5, v. 7;— 'He was heard in that he feared.' "*—" What then "— asks Dr. Moses Stuart,—" was it in respect to which he was εἰσακουσθεὶς, *heard* or *delivered?* The context necessarily limits the *hearing* or *deliverance* to something in his petitions which appertained to *suffering*, which was an object of *dread*. What could it be but the dread of sinking under the agony of being deserted by his Father? Matt. chap. 27, v. 46. Great as his agony was, he never refused to bear it, nor did he shrink from tasting the bitter cup. Luke, chap. 22, v. 42; Matt. chap. 26, v. 39. And does not Luke, chap. 22, v. 43, explain our εἰσακουσθεὶς ἀπὸ εὐλαβείας, [he was heard on account of his pious fear,]—'There appeared unto him an angel from heaven strengthening him, ἐνισχύων αὐτόν.'—This was the only

---

* M'Lean, vol. i. p. 163;—Rambach, vol. i. p. 56;—Dr. Doddridge, Family Expositor of the New Testament, vol. ii. p. 483.—Hebrews, chap. 5, v. 7-10.

kind of deliverance he sought for, or on the whole desired; Luke, chap. 22, v. 42. πλὴν μὴ τὸ θέλημά μου, ἀλλὰ τὸ σὸν γενέσθω· [nevertheless, not my will but thine be done.] The dread in question was, like all his other sufferings, incident to his human nature, and the fact shows that he suffered under it to a high degree; but he did not shrink from it, and so he was *heard* or *delivered* in respect to the object of his petition in regard to it."*

It is indeed sufficiently evident that in this remarkable passage the apostle is speaking of the peculiar mental sufferings of Christ in the garden of Gethsemane, and not of the ordinary sufferings attending his seizure, trial, and crucifixion; which, as is manifest from the sacred narrative, he endured not only without dismay, but with the utmost dignity and firmness. That his mental sufferings proceeded not from men or demons, but from God, was stated by himself, when on his way to the garden he said to his apostles,—"All of you will this night be offended by me, for it is written,—'*I will smite the shepherd, and the sheep of the flock will be scattered;*'"— when he afterward entreated the Father to withdraw from him the fatal cup; and when, as this was impossible, he meekly asked,—"The cup which the Father hath given me, shall I not drink it?"—This language exactly corresponds to his affecting demand on the cross,—"My God! my God! why hast *thou* forsaken me?"—and shows that in their general nature his mental sufferings in both instances were identical. Too violent to last long, they began and ended abruptly, continuing in the first case one hour, in the second three hours, leaving his mind during the interval comparatively calm and self-possessed. The scene at Gethsemane was a wise and necessary prelude to that at Calvary, a foretaste or trial, which prepared him for the

---

* Dr. Moses Stuart, Commentary on the Epistle to the Hebrews, vol. ii. pp. 126, 127, 420–422.—See also Poole's Synopsis.

last awful conflict; and his conduct on the two occasions exhibits a marked and corresponding difference. In the garden these sufferings were absolutely new to him. Never before had his filial communion with God been interrupted. On suddenly losing it, and finding himself exposed without protection to the horrors of his responsibility, and the malignity of the powers of darkness, he was as it were taken by surprise, and nearly destroyed by consternation and distress. So the terms used by the evangelists literally imply. According to the apostle Paul, he had now for the first time to learn this peculiarly difficult lesson of obedience to the divine will, and found it almost insupportable. With tears and cries, he repeatedly prayed for relief to him who alone was able to save him from death, and by supernatural aid was strengthened and delivered. Thus instructed and experienced he endured these sufferings, when renewed on the cross, with less consternation and greater energy than before. Until near the end, when he uttered a few fervent exclamations, he was silent, and opened not his mouth; and, instead of being delivered from death, was left to bear the full weight of the divine malediction in helpless agony, till by the rupture of his heart he completed that atoning sacrifice which he had undertaken to offer, and by which, as the high-priest of his people,—"he became the author of eternal salvation to all who obey him."*

The more minutely the subject is examined, the more perfect will be found the accordance between the sufferings of Christ, and the cause here assigned for them. These sufferings presented two successive stages,—consternation, and agony,—conditions which, although frequently confounded by commentators, are not only differ-

---

* Matt. chap. 26, v. 30, 31, 36-44; chap. 27, v. 45, 46;—Mark, chap. 14, v. 26, 27, 32-39; chap. 15, v. 33, 34;—John, chap. 18, v. 11; —Heb. chap. 5, v. 7-9.

ent, but actually opposite to each other. The natural contrast which subsists between the exciting and the depressing passions, as likewise between their respective effects, has been already mentioned. Excessive fear and grief debilitate and almost paralyze the body, while agony or conflict is attended with extraordinary strength. Under the former the action of the heart is enfeebled; and if, owing to constriction of the cutaneous vessels, perspiration ever occurs, it is cold and scanty. Under the latter the heart acts with great violence, and forces a hot, copious, and in extreme cases a bloody sweat through the pores of the skin. The testimony of Crichton on this subject is so apposite and decisive, that it deserves to be repeated.—"In grief and sorrow,"—he observes,—"in extreme anger, hatred, jealousy, and envy, the blood stagnates about the heart, a chilling cold spreads itself over the whole surface of the body, the blood forsakes the cheeks, and a tremor ensues."—On the contrary, under anger and other invigorating passions,—"the heart and arteries are excited to a preternatural degree of action, the blood is propelled with violence to the surface of the body, and circulates with force and rapidity through the smallest and most extreme arteries, and hence the burning heat which characterizes this sort of passion."—When Belshazzar saw the handwriting on the wall, his—"countenance was changed, and his thoughts troubled him, so that the joints of his loins were loosed, and his knees smote one against another."—When Daniel was accosted in vision by an angel of surpassing majesty,—"his comeliness was turned into corruption, and he retained no strength;"—and when the apostle John saw Christ in his glory,—"he fell at his feet as dead."—On the other hand, when Samson, laboring under the united stings of shame, indignation, and revenge, agonized in the temple of Dagon, he recovered all his original might, threw down the two massy columns which supported the building, and, together with himself, buried thousands of his own and his country's enemies under its ruins.* It has been suggested that the bloody sweat of Christ might be attributed to relaxation of the cutaneous vessels, in conjunction with a dissolved state of the blood; but the explanation is inadmissible, since, as has been shown, his condition at the time was not that of weakness but of **strength**, and the blood which issued with his sweat was not liquid, but clotted. Besides, except under peculiar circumstances, and in connection, there is reason to believe, with violent action of the heart, relaxation of the cutaneous capillaries is not productive of bloody sweat, which on the contrary requires and implies a strong expulsive force.—" In all hæmorrhage "—says Harvey,—" the more vehemently the arteries pulsate, the more speedily will the body be emptied of its blood. Hence also, in all fainting, fear, and similar affections, when the heart beats languidly, weakly, and without impulse, all hæmorrhage is checked and restrained." †—The natural association of bloody sweat with agony and exertion is well exemplified in the case of **Charles IX.** of France, a prince of execrable cruelty, but at the same time of great energy, both of mind and body, who died of a singular complaint in his twenty-fifth year.—" The disease which carried him off"—says Voltaire,—" is very uncommon; his blood flowed from all his pores. This malady, of which there are some examples, is the result either of excessive fear, furious passion, or of a violent and melancholic temperament."—

---

* Crichton, On Mental Derangement, etc., vol. ii. pp. 134, 288, 289; —Judges, chap. 16, v. 23-30;—Daniel, chap. 5, v. 1-6; chap. 10, v. 7-11, 15-17;—Rev. chap. 1, v. 12-17.

† Harvæus, de Motu Cordis et Sanguinis in Animalibus; pp. 118, 119; —Kuinoël, Lib. Historic. Nov. Test. Comment on Luke, chap. 22, v. 43, 44.

The circumstances of the case are graphically described by the old French historian, De Mezeray.—"After the vigor of his youth and the energy of his courage had long struggled against his disease, he was at length reduced by it to his bed, at the castle of Vincennes, about the 8th of May [1574]. During the last two weeks of his life, his constitution made strange efforts. He was affected with spasms and convulsions of extreme violence. He tossed and agitated himself continually, and his blood gushed from all the outlets of his body, even from the pores of his skin, so that on one occasion he was found bathed in a bloody sweat."*

The intense grief and consternation which the Saviour experienced at the commencement of his sufferings in the garden, and under the shock of which he fell prostrate to the earth, might possibly have destroyed him by simple exhaustion, but would never have produced the bloody sweat reported by Luke; who, independently of his guidance by the Holy Spirit, was, as a physician, peculiarly well qualified to notice and record such an occurrence. He therefore ascribes this sweat to a cause by which it is fully and solely explained, namely, the communication of supernatural strength;—"There appeared to him an angel from heaven, strengthening him."—It was then that,—"falling into an agony, [Christ] prayed most earnestly, and his sweat became as it were clots of blood dropping to the ground:"—implying that he was no longer prostrate as at first, but on his knees. Attempts have been made to explain away the strong terms used by the evangelist, but they certainly denote a sweat mixed with blood in a half-coagulated state, so profuse as to fall from the head and neck (the parts chiefly liable to be uncovered, and from which sweat of any kind is most readily fur-

---

* Voltaire, Œuvres complètes; vol. xviii. pp. 531, 532.—De Mezeray, Histoire de France; vol. iii. p. 306.

nished), in thick and **heavy** drops to the ground. Unless Luke meant to convey this meaning, his employment of such expressions is unaccountable.* The fact is well stated by M'Lean.—[Christ] " is said to be *in an agony*. An agony is the conflict of Nature in the extremity of distress. The Lord was now bruising **him, and putting him to grief.** So great was the agony and conflict **of his soul, that it produced the most wonderful effect upon his body;** for we are told that—'his sweat was as it were great **drops of blood falling down to the ground.'**—A common **sweat** in the open air, and **exposed to the cold damp of night,** when **those within-doors required a fire of coals to warm them, must have been the effect of very** great **fear** and agony. What then must **his agony have** been, which induced **a bloody** sweat, and so copious as to fall down in great drops to the ground?"—It was then that, as intimated by the apostle Paul,—" he offered prayers and **supplications** [accompanied] with tears and loud cries, to him who **was able** to save him from death, and was heard on account **of** his pious fear;"—in other words, **these peculiar and overwhelming** sufferings were by divine **interposition** suddenly terminated, **leaving him with restored strength, ready to undergo the trials which next awaited him.†**

Since the scene at Gethsemane was, **as has been shown, a** prelude and foretaste of that **at Calvary, the** same explanation is applicable to **both.** In both, mental sufferings

* Ὤφθη δὲ αὐτῷ ἄγγελος ἀπ' οὐρανοῦ ἐνισχύων αὐτόν· καὶ, γενόμενος ἐν ἀγωνίᾳ, ἐκτενέστερον προσηύχετο· ἐγένετο δὲ ὁ ἱδρὼς αὐτοῦ ὡσεὶ θρόμβοι αἵματος καταβαίνοντες ἐπὶ τὴν γῆν. Luke, chap. 22, v. 43, 44. See, also, Coloss. chap. 4, v. 14; Poole's Synopsis, Schleusner's Lexicon of the New Testament, etc. The force of the term ὡσεὶ, **frequently used by Luke** in a similar sense, evidently is, that Christ's sweat on this occasion consisted **of clotted** blood, not pure, **but** mixed with the usual watery liquid.

† M'Lean, On the Epistle to the Hebrews, vol. i. pp. 163, 164;—John, chap. 16, v. 31, 32;—Heb. chap. 5 v. 7-9.

of a peculiar character and of extreme severity produced on the body of Christ their natural effects,—in the garden a bloody sweat,—on the cross sudden death, followed by an effusion of blood and water from his side, when it was afterward pierced by a spear. In both, the immediate cause of these effects, the link which connected them with their more remote cause, the mental anguish, was violent action of the heart, ultimately proceeding to rupture, the proof being that, of all the causes which can be assigned, this alone fulfils the requisite conditions, having been at once present, adequate, and in strict accordance with the circumstances. The death of Christ cannot be ascribed to the ordinary sufferings of crucifixion, because, far from destroying life in six hours, they often allowed it to be protracted for three or more days; nor to miraculous interposition, because he was slain by his enemies, and died the death of the cross; nor to original feebleness of constitution, because, as the priest and victim of an atoning sacrifice, he was perfect in body and mind; nor to temporary weakness resulting from his recent agony, because his strength was sustained by angelic agency. That his mental sufferings were, on the contrary, adequate to the effect, is evident from their influence at Gethsemane, where, had he not received supernatural aid, they would apparently have proved fatal without the addition of any others; and, if in a lower degree they excited palpitation of the heart so violent as to occasion bloody sweat, it is equally evident that, when aggravated and longer continued, they were capable of producing rupture. That the same sufferings were present in both instances, and arose from a sense of the divine malediction, is proved by his referring them in both to the immediate hand of God, by his allusion in the garden to the cup given him by his heavenly Father, and to the ancient prophecy,—"*I will smite the shepherd, and the sheep of the flock will be scat-*

tered;"—and by his final exclamation on the cross,—" My God! my God! why hast thou forsaken me?"—That rupture of the heart thus induced was in conformity with the circumstances, and actually implied by them, will now be demonstrated.

The ordinary sufferings incidental to crucifixion have been minutely analyzed by Richter, the Bartholines, Grüners, etc., and are often injudiciously exaggerated, in order to account for the speedy occurrence of the Saviour's death. Richter's explanation of them, as quoted in a note of the Pictorial Bible on John, chap. 19, v. 18, is somewhat fanciful and overstrained; yet, after all, the author acknowledges that they were not calculated to accasion rapid death, and concludes as follows:—" The degree of misery is gradual in its increase, and the person crucified is able to live under it commonly until the third, and sometimes till the seventh day. Pilate, therefore, being surprised at the speedy termination of our Saviour's life, inquired in respect to the truth of it of the centurion himself who had the command of the soldiers. (Mark, chap. 15, v. 44.)"—Concurring in this opinion, the editor of the Pictorial Bible observes,—" It may be added, that no act in the punishment of crucifixion was in itself mortal, the sufferer died rather from the continuance and increase of the unutterable anguish and exhaustion of his torturing position;"—and then subjoins the account, already cited from Josephus, of a person known to that historian, who had been crucified apparently for several hours, but having been taken down from the cross, and committed to medical care, survived and recovered. In their laborious attempts to prove that for some time before his death Christ was reduced to a state of extreme debility, the Grüners strongly insist on the accessory or subordinate sufferings of crucifixion, as materially concurring with the principal ones in producing this effect; but, on an impartial examination of the matter, their insufficiency is obvious. The scourging, mockery, and labor of carrying the cross, were not in themselves more distressing to Jesus than to the malefactors who accompanied him;—his fasting and watching had not, at farthest, continued longer than from the preceding evening;—his removal from place to place was not likely to be attended with much fatigue, since all the places lay within a narrow compass;—and heat of climate could not have been very oppressive in Jerusalem at the vernal equinox, to a native of the country; more especially when it is considered that, during the last three hours of his life, from the sixth to the ninth hour, the sun was obscured, and that in the much hotter climate of Central Africa crucified persons usually live three days on the cross.*

But, whatever may have been the severity of the ordinary sufferings of crucifixion, whether principal or accessory, the sacred writers of the New Testament uniformly represent Christ as bearing them with becoming dignity, and without betraying the least weakness either of body or mind; for the circumstance of Simon the Cyrenian having been compelled to assist in carrying his cross, furnishes no sufficient proof that Christ was disabled by mere weakness from carrying it alone. While undergoing the very act of crucifixion, which occurred at nine in the morning, he prayed for his executioners, and during the three following hours evinced the utmost patience and self-possession, assured the penitent malefactor that he should that day be with him in Paradise, and committed his afflicted mother to the care of the beloved disciple, John. At noon, however, a remarkable change took place in this respect, evidently owing to a renewal of the

---

* The Pictorial Bible, by Knight and Co. Note on John, chap. 19, v. 18;—Kuinoël, Lib. Historic. Nov. Test. Comment on Matt. chap. 27, v. 50.

mental sufferings of Gethsemane. On both occasions these sufferings were distinguished from all others, by beginning and ending abruptly, as well as by their peculiar circumstances and effects. On both occasions, the gloom which oppressed the Redeemer's soul was by divine appointment accompanied with external darkness, as its appropriate sign and illustration. When he was in the garden the preceding evening, it appears, from astronomical calculation, that the paschal full moon underwent a natural eclipse; on which account, perhaps, the numerous party which went forth to seize him were provided with lanterns and torches.* Twelve hours later, on the same day, according to the Jewish mode of reckoning, a preternatural darkness overspread the whole land, from the sixth to the ninth hour. Hereby were realized several prophecies of the Old Testament, particularly a most important prediction of Joel, cited by the apostle Peter in his discourse at Jerusalem, on the subsequent day of Pentecost, when describing the principal signs of that eventful time, which intimated the end of the Mosaic, and the commencement of the Christian dispensation.—" It shall come to pass in the last days, saith God, that I will pour out of my Spirit on all flesh, and your sons and your daughters shall prophesy, your young men shall see visions, and your old men shall dream dreams. And also on my servants and on my handmaids will I pour out of my Spirit in those days, and they shall prophesy. And I will show wonders in the heaven above, and signs on the earth beneath, blood, and fire, and vapor of smoke. The sun shall be turned into darkness, and the moon into blood, before the coming of the great and illustrious day of the Lord; and it shall be that whosoever shall call on the name of the Lord shall be saved."—In conformity with this prophecy, on one and the same day, the day of

---

* John, chap. 18, v. 1-3.

Christ's death according to Jewish reckoning, the two luminaries of heaven were successively darkened; first, the moon by an ordinary eclipse, which, on account of the dusky red color with which it is attended, is in figurative language compared to blood; and, afterward, the sun, most probably by a dense shower of volcanic ashes, accompanying the repeated shocks of earthquake by which, owing to divine interposition, Palestine, and perhaps some of the adjacent countries were then convulsed.* Such at least is the scriptural explanation of a similar occurrence exhibited among the apocalyptic visions to the apostle John, when, on the central pit or abyss of the earth being laid open, it is said,—"there came up a smoke out of the pit, like the smoke of a great furnace, and the sun and the air were darkened by the smoke of the pit."—Such also is the description, addressed by God himself to the prophet Ezekiel, of the prodigies which would mark the downfall of Pharaoh Hophrah; and a similar explanation may be given of—"the palpable darkness,"—which constituted one of the plagues of Egypt at an earlier period.—"And when I shall put thee out I will cover the heaven, and make the stars thereof dark. I will cover the sun with a cloud, and the moon shall not give her light. All the bright lights of heaven will I make dark over thee, and set darkness upon thy land, saith the Lord God." †

The darkness which now enveloped the cross of Christ but faintly represented that which overwhelmed his soul,

---

* Joel, chap. 2, v. 28-32;—Amos, chap. 8, v. 9;—Zechar. chap. 14, v. 3-7;—Matt. chap. 27, v. 45, 51;—Luke, chap. 23, v. 44, 45;—Acts, chap. 2, v. 14-21;—Rev. chap. 6, v. 12.—In the last passage the phraseology is more adapted to European usage;—The sun became black as sackcloth of hair, and the moon became *as blood*.

† Exodus, chap. 10, v. 21-23;—Ezek. chap. 32, v. 1-8;—Revel. chap. 9, v. 1, 2.

under a renewed sense of the divine abandonment. During three hours he endured in silent agony the tremendous infliction. At length about the ninth hour, the hour of sacrifice, feeling his end approach, he uttered the loud cry which expressed the most exalted piety, combined with the severest mental anguish; and, having committed his spirit into the hands of his heavenly Father, suddenly bowed his head and expired. At the same time the darkness cleared away, the mystery which had so long veiled the scene terminated, and the evening sun, shining on Golgotha with renovated splendor, revealed to the world the momentous fact of the Saviour's death. The solemn spectacle was not, however, to be long contemplated. That day was the preparation-day, and at six in the evening the Sabbath began; previously to which it was necessary, in compliance with the laws of Moses, that the crucified persons should be dispatched and removed. The Jewish authorities, therefore, made the usual application to Pilate, and obtained the necessary order. It was probably between four and five in the afternoon when the Roman soldiers came, and broke the legs of the two malefactors who were crucified with Jesus. On finding him already dead, they abstained from offering this needless violence to his corpse; but, as if to make sure, one of them with a spear pierced his side, whence, says the beloved disciple, an eye-witness of the transaction,—" immediately there came forth blood and water,"—and with peculiar solemnity remarks that the whole took place under the superintendence of divine providence, in fulfilment of two ancient prophecies concerning Christ, one of which declared that none of his bones should be broken, and the other, that the guilty people of Israel should look on him whom they had pierced. Like the brazen serpent in the wilderness he was now lifted up from the earth, that whosoever looked to him with sincere penitence and cordial faith might not perish, but have eternal life.*

Taken in conjunction with the events, these predictions imply that the Saviour's death happened in an extraordinary manner, and earlier than could naturally have been expected. Its immediate cause was more fully intimated by the flow of blood and water from his wounded side, a remarkable occurrence, with which a true explanation must of course perfectly agree. Owing to the necessary exclusion of all other causes, as formerly shown, two only now remain to be considered; namely, exhaustion and rupture of the heart. That death may result from exhaustion, or simple failure of vital power, occasioned either by loss of blood, over-excitement, violent exertion, or depressing passions, cannot be doubted, since many cases of this kind are on record, but the circumstances which attended the death of Christ are incompatible with such causes, and with such an effect; while on the other hand they are in perfect accordance with rupture of the heart, followed as a necessary consequence by effusion of blood into the pericardium, and sudden suppression of the circulation. That the ordinary sufferings of crucifixion were not sufficient to destroy a young and vigorous person, either by exhaustion or in any other manner, within the short period of six hours, has already been demonstrated; as likewise that, with the exception of his first feelings of consternation at Gethsemane, which seem never to have recurred, the mental sufferings of Christ were not of a debilitating, but of an exciting nature, consisting in a severe agony or struggle between two opposite motives, the desire of deliverance from the intolerable sense of divine malediction, and the desire of fulfilling the will of

---

* Exodus, chap. 12, v. 43-46;—Numb. chap. 21, v. 4-9;—Deut. chap. 21, v. 22, 23;—Zechar. chap. 12, v. 10;—John, chap. 3, v. 14, 15; chap. 12, v. 30-34; chap. 19, v. 31-37;—Revel. chap. 1, v. 7.

DEATH OF CHRIST.

God by enduring the malediction even unto death, that by the atoning sacrifice thus offered he might accomplish the work of human redemption, which was the great object of his coming into the world. Had this struggle been much longer continued, it might possibly have proved fatal by exhaustion, but not within the period of three hours indicated in the sacred narrative, which moreover plainly proves by the occurrences preceding and following his death, that it was occasioned, not by weakness, but by violence. His energy of mind and body immediately before his death, was evinced by the most perfect self-possession, and by loud and fervent exclamations. The expressions used by the evangelists in describing his last moments, are, it is well known, emphatic.—" About the ninth hour,"—says Matthew,—" Jesus cried with a loud voice, Eli! Eli! lama sabachthani? that is, my God! my God! why hast thou forsaken me?"—Even in this mortal struggle his mind was neither paralyzed nor engrossed by his sufferings, but full of intelligence, piety, and love, engaged in earnest meditation on the prophecies of Scripture, and taking an active part in their completion. For it was chiefly on this account, and not merely to satisfy a natural want, which in such cases is exceedingly urgent, that for the first and only time he complained of thirst.—" Jesus, knowing that all things were now accomplished, that the Scripture might be fulfilled, said, I thirst."—Hereupon a sponge dipped in vinegar, probably mixed with water, was applied to his lips by one of the soldiers, and he soon afterward—" cried again with a loud voice, saying [All] is accomplished: Father! into thy hands I commit my spirit. Having thus spoken, he bowed his head and resigned his spirit."*—The energy

---

* Περὶ δὲ τὴν ἐννάτην ὥραν, ἀνεβόησεν ὁ ᾿Ιησοῦς φωνῇ μεγάλῃ, λέγων, etc. . . . Ὁ δὲ ᾿Ιησοῦς, πάλιν κράξας φωνῇ μεγάλῃ, ἀφῆκε τὸ πνεῦμα.

of mind and body thus displayed by the Saviour in the very act of dissolution, proves beyond all contradiction that his sudden death was the result, not of exhaustion, but of some latent and destructive agency. Such was the impression which it made on competent and unprejudiced spectators, the Roman officer on duty, and his soldiers; for we are told that—" when the centurion who stood opposite, and those who were with him guarding Jesus, observed the earthquake, and the [other] events, [and] that he expired with such a cry, they feared greatly, [and] gave glory to God, saying, Certainly this man was a Son of God."

Respecting the final exclamation of Christ, the younger Grüner has made an apposite remark, which is confirmed by other authors.—" It is common "—says he,—" for persons whose heart is oppressed by excessive congestion of blood, with anxiety and palpitation, and who are threatened with suffocation, to cry out with a loud voice."*— Assuming that the heart of Christ was ruptured the suddenness of his death implies a rapid and extensive rent, the natural result of violent action. That even during so brief an interval there would be sufficient time for his uttering the few words ascribed to him by the evangelists, appears from several recorded examples, among others, from a case mentioned by Mr. Griffiths, of Hereford, in the following terms.—" A stout man, forty-three years of age, fell from the height of about five feet on an iron spike, which wounded his left breast. Getting up without assistance, he staggered toward me, made one or two exclamations, and died in my arms about two minutes

---

Matt. chap. 27, v. 46, 50;—Luke, chap. 23, v. 46;—John, chap. 19, v. 28–30.

* Matt. chap. 27, v. 54;—Mark, chap. 15, v. 39;—Luke, chap. 23, v. 47;—Kuinoël, Comment. in Lib. Hist. Nov. Test., Matt. chap. 27, v.

after the accident. On examining the body, it was found that the sixth rib on the left side had been fractured, and that in penetrating the thoracic cavity, the iron spike had driven in the pericardium without tearing it, while the heart itself had been ruptured, and its bag completely filled with blood."—A similar instance is related by Christian Vater, in the German Ephemerides.—" I examined,"—says he,—" the body of a woman about thirty years of age, who, on the 9th of April, 1695, was struck on the chest, and killed by a carriage running over her. I observed that on the left side the upper ribs near the breastbone, together with the clavicle, were fractured, but scarcely depressed, while the pericardium was not at all injured. The right ventricle of the heart was, nevertheless, found ruptured to the extent of more than an inch not far from the apex, and the pericardium was fully distended with blood. Hence I concluded that the rupture had been occasioned, not so much by the fractured ribs as by the reaction of the blood, which, under the sudden concussion and compression of the chest, had yielded a proportionally greater resistance."—Another case is given by Ludwig, in his Adversaria.—" A robust young man, nineteen years of age, employed as a groom, received a violent kick on the breast from a furious horse, by which he was thrown backward on the ground. He speedily, however, got up, and evinced a feeling of indignation; but on hastening shortly after toward the stable, dropped down dead. On inspecting the body, the sternum was found fractured transversely, about four inches and a half above its point, the lower portion having been forced in so as, without injuring the pericardium, to occasion a rupture of the right auricle of the heart. The pericardium was so distended by a large quantity of transparent serum and coagulated blood, as to push the lungs upward. The yellowish serum contained in its cavity exceeded half a pound. The heart was encompassed by much clotted blood, which adhered to it on all sides, and was perceived to have escaped slowly through a fissure detected in the margin of the right auricle."—These cases afford a further proof that in such occurrences death is less attributable to the rupture of the heart, abstractedly considered, than to the extravasation of blood into the pericardial sac.*

SECTION III.

The flow of blood and water from the side of Christ, when pierced some time after his death by the soldier's spear, has been a source of difficulty and perplexity both to ancient and modern commentators. To account for so extraordinary a circumstance, many of the former had recourse to their favorite expedient of miraculous interposition, designed, as they imagined, to convey important symbolical instruction. Several of the latter, among whom the Bartholines and the Grüners are the most considerable, have on the contrary ascribed it to serous effusion, either into the pericardial or pleural sacs, naturally produced by that extreme debility which they suppose to have attended the Saviour's death. The two opinions are, it is evident, mutually destructive, and for the refutation of both, the arguments already proposed might perhaps be deemed sufficient, but others will here be added. In favor of miraculous agency for such a purpose, neither necessity nor proof can be alleged, and that which really occurred on this occasion was of a widely different character. It will now be shown that serous effusion into the pectoral cavities did not take place, and, if it had, would

---

* Miscellan. Acad. Curios. Naturæ; Dec. 3; Ann. 9 et 10; pp. 293, 294;—C. D. Ludwig, Adversaria Medico-Practica; 3 vols. 8vo, Lipsiæ, 1769; vol. i. pp. 136, 137.

not account for the fact; while rupture of the heart, which furnishes a complete solution of it, is distinctly intimated by all the circumstances. In order to explain the effusion of blood and water from the side of Christ, it is necessary to understand the nature of the wound inflicted on him, namely, that it was a stab to the heart. This appears from the prediction of Zechariah quoted by John,—"They shall look on him whom they pierced;"— for in this passage both the Hebrew and the Greek terms signify a fatal wound, and in the Old Testament the meaning of the former is almost always that of stabbing to the heart, a practice familiar to the ancient Israelites, on which account mention is so often made in that portion of Scripture of smiting under the fifth rib; so that the prediction might with perfect propriety have been rendered,—"They shall look on him whom they pierced to the heart." *—It appears also, from the circumstances of the case, and the evident intentions of the soldier in wounding the body of Christ; not, as some have supposed, through mere wantonness or insolence, but for a very reasonable and even necessary purpose, namely, to ascertain, or insure his death. For the soldiers had received a command from the Roman governor to dispatch the crucified persons, in order that their bodies might be removed and buried before sunset then rapidly approaching. After breaking the legs of the two malefactors they

---

* "דקר, to thrust through, to pierce, stab, as with a sword or spear." —Gesenius's Hebrew and English Lexicon;—"'Ἐκκεντέω, pungo, stimulo, transfigo, transverbero;—Νύττω, vel Νύσσω, pungo, punctim cœdo, vulnero, fodico;"—Schleusner's Lexicon of the Greek Test.—See also Numbers, chap. 25, v. 6-8;—Judges, chap. 9, v. 53, 54;—1 Sam. chap. 31, v. 3, 4;—2 Sam. chap. 2, v. 22, 23; chap. 3, v. 27; chap. 4, v. 5, 6; chap. 18, v. 14; chap. 20, v. 9, 10;—1 Chron. chap. 10, v. 3, 4;—Prov. chap. 12, v. 18;—Isaiah, chap. 13, v. 15;—Jerem. chap. 37, v. 9, 10; chap. 51, v. 4;—Lament. chap. 4, v. 9;—Zechar. chap. 12, v. 10;—John, chap. 19, v. 34, 37;—Revel. chap. 1, v. 7; etc.

came to Jesus, whom in appearance as well as in reality they found already dead. But the sudden death of a young and robust man, after a crucifixion of only six hours, was extraordinary, and to them unaccountable. Like the Grüners, and other modern authors, the soldiers might readily have suspected that he was not actually dead, but only in a fainting state, and they had good reason to make sure of the fact; for, if through carelessness or mistake they had suffered any of the crucified persons to escape, they would have been answerable for the neglect with their lives. An example of such severity occurs in Luke's account of the persecution of the early Christians at Jerusalem by Herod Agrippa I., who, having been disappointed in his designs against Peter, owing to the deliverance of the apostle from prison by miraculous interposition, ordered the guards, although perfectly innocent in the matter, to be put to death.

The Roman practice of dispatching, in some instances, crucified persons by breaking their legs, stabbing them with swords or spears, etc., is well known, and, as above noticed, has been fully described by Salmasius, Lipsius, Bosius, and others. When the soldier, therefore, pierced the side of Christ, he did nothing more than what was usual, and, having such an object in view, would naturally inflict a decisive wound, that is, a stab to the heart. This opinion has accordingly been adopted by a great number of theological writers, many of whom are cited by Thomas Bartholinus, a Danish physician, who, however, in an express treatise on the subject, follows the guidance of his father Caspar, and objects to this opinion for no better reason than that, when speaking of the wound, and of the scar which remained after Christ's resurrection, the evangelist John mentions the side only, and not the heart. As a faithful witness of the transaction, John of course relates only what he saw, but leaves his readers to draw a rational inference from the facts described, which can be none other than that here stated.* The subject is treated with considerable accuracy in the Pictorial Bible, from which the following is an extract:—" In the accounts of our Lord's crucifixion there are several circumstances which exhibit differences from the customary practice of the Romans, and which were in fact so many points of accommodation to the peculiar notions of the Jews, and operated rather favorably for the condemned persons. In the first place, the Romans usually left the crucified ones to linger on in their tortures till life became extinct, and this commonly did not happen till the third or fourth day, and some even lingered until the seventh. Soldiers were stationed to prevent interference or relief from friends, till they were dead, and a guard was even afterward maintained, that the bodies might not be stolen away and buried. For the Romans left the bodies to consume on the crosses, as formerly [happened] on gibbets in this country, by the natural progress of decay, or from the ravenings of birds, or, if the cross were low, beasts of prey. But, as such lingering deaths, as well as the continued exposure of the body, were most wisely and mercifully forbidden by the letter and spirit of the law of Moses, which directed that criminals—'hanged on a tree'—should be taken down before sunset, the Roman soldiers in Judea were directed to extinguish, on the approach of sunset, what remained of life in those upon the cross. We see that the two thieves were thus dispatched by their legs being broken, and the body of Christ would doubtless have been thus treated; but it had been foretold that not a bone of him should be broken, and he expired before this became necessary. The spear-thrust given him by

* Thomas Bartholinus, De Latere Christi aperto, etc., pp. 17-22, 45, etc.;—Idem. Epistola ad Hieron. Bardium, pp. 565-570;—Acts, chap. 12, v. 18, 19.

the soldier was doubtless to ascertain whether he were really dead or only in a swoon, and the resulting evidence that life had departed from him rendered further measures unnecessary; indeed, the wound then inflicted, being in the left side, piercing the pericardium, as evinced by the outflow of blood and lymph, would have been sufficient, and was no doubt intended to produce death, if Jesus had not been dead already. (See John, chap. 19, v. 33.) Piercing the side is said to have been one of the common methods of accelerating the death of crucified persons, as well as the breaking of their bones."*—Nearly similar is the view taken by Rambach.—" The indignity "—says he —" offered to our Saviour's body was this: a soldier with a spear stabbed it in the breast, or side. This was done, indeed, out of wantonness or insolence; or, perhaps, the soldier might at the same time have an intention of trying whether Jesus was really dead, or only in a swoon. He therefore stabs him with a spear near the heart, that he might see whether he had still any life in him; so that, by giving him a wound, he designed to dispatch him, in case any life remained in him. That it was no small wound which the spear made in the breast of our blessed Lord, but a large incision, appears from what he says to the incredulous Thomas after his resurrection,—'Reach hither thy hand, and thrust it into my side.'—What followed this injurious piercing of our Saviour's side is likewise mentioned by St. John in these words:—' And forthwith came thereout blood and water.'—This was undoubtedly an extraordinary event, since the providence of God directed the soldier's spear to make an incision in the place where these different humors were lodged, and at the same time hindered these two fluids from intermixing; for St. John, who stood by, could plainly distinguish both blood and water issuing from the wound."—On a subject of this

* Pictorial Bible: Note on Mark, chap. 15, v. 13.

DEATH OF CHRIST.

kind, the opinion of Dr. Priestley is not undeserving of notice.—"The death of Jesus"—he observes—"was so evident to the soldiers who attended the execution, and who, no doubt (being used to the business) were sufficient judges of the signs of death, that, concluding him to be actually dead, they did not break his bones, as they did those of the other persons who were executed along with him. One of them, however, did what was fully equivalent to it, for he thrust his spear into his side, so that blood and water evidently flowed out of the wound. Now, though we may be at a loss to account for the water, it was certainly impossible so to pierce the body as that blood should visibly and instantly flow from the wound, without piercing either the heart itself, or some large blood-vessel, the rupture of which would have been mortal."[*]—The views of the Grüners concerning this point are to the same effect, and, on account of the medical character of the authors, are perhaps still more entitled to attention.

Admitting therefore as a fact, that not long after the death of Christ his heart was pierced by a spear, the next inquiry relates to the blood and water which immediately flowed from the wound. On this subject two opinions have prevailed in modern times: the one, that the blood and water were mixed, and derived from one or both of the pleural sacs; the other, that they issued separately, the blood from the heart, the water from the pericardium. The former opinion was supported by the Bartholines, the latter by the Grüners. Before entering into this discussion, it may be proper to state for the information of readers not familiar with anatomical details, that as the heart is surrounded by the pericardium, so each lung is enveloped by a double membrane, or bag, called the

[*] Rambach, On the Sufferings of Christ, vol. iii. pp. 271, 272;—Dr. Priestley, On the Resurrection of Jesus, pp. 12, 13.

pleural sac, adhering by its outer surface to the lung and side, and enclosing between its layers a space, or cavity, which in health is merely bedewed with a little watery fluid or vapor, serving the purpose of lubrication; but in certain morbid states is capable of containing a considerable quantity of serous liquid, either pure or tinged with blood. In reference to the effusion of blood and water from the side of Christ, the Rev. Mr. Hewlett, a commentator of judgment and research, expresses himself in the following dubious manner.—" Medical writers afford numerous instances of a large effusion of bloody lymph into the cavities of the pleura, from diseases of the lungs, and in cases of violent death with long struggling. . . . A skilful and learned physician informed the editor that in cases of violent and painful death, there is usually an effusion of lymph, or of lymph mixed with blood, into the cavities of the chest and abdomen. . . . It is, however, reasonable to acquiesce with those who are of opinion that the evangelist here intended to express more than a pathological fact."—The physician meant in this passage was no doubt the late Dr. Willan, who—in his "History of the Ministry of Jesus Christ,"—makes a similar remark, equally indicative of doubt and uncertainty.—" We have instances of watery effusion into the cavities of the pleura to a considerable amount, in cases of violent death with long struggling. . . . The phenomenon here mentioned by the evangelist is generally looked on as miraculous." *

Hieronymus Bardus ascribes the blood to the heart, and the water to the pericardium, both of which he supposes were pierced by the soldier's spear; but is at a loss to understand how the two liquids could have issued

---

* Hewlett's Bible, etc.; Notes on John, chap. 19, v. 34, and Acts, chap. 1, v. 18; Dr. Willan, History of the Ministry of Jesus Christ, etc.; p. 195.—Mr. Hewlett also regards Luke, chap. 22, v. 43, 44, as of doubtful authority.

separately without a miracle, which to this extent he consequently admits. His correspondent Thomas Bartholinus judiciously rejects supernatural agency altogether, but his own view of the matter is equally inadmissible. He objects to the notion that the heart and pericardium were wounded, because in that case he imagines their contents would not have flowed out immediately nor completely, but that a part of them would have escaped into the bottom of the chest. He therefore prefers the explanation proposed by his father Caspar, and previously mentioned; namely, that the spear opened one of the pleural sacs, and discharged a collection of bloody serum, which he thinks would naturally have been formed there during the sufferings of crucifixion, especially in a person of delicate frame and feeble constitution, which, like Priestley and others, he improperly attributes to Christ. The Grüners, on the contrary, maintain the opinion of Bardus, with the addition of some erroneous notions of their own. Thus, in commenting on John, chap. 19, v. 34, the elder Grüner observes,—"It was doubtless the left side that was pierced by the soldier's spear. According to the testimony of John, immediately after the infliction of this wound there flowed out blood and water. Such an effusion could scarcely have taken place except from the left side, under which, besides the lung, lies the pericardium full of water when a person dies after extreme anxiety, as likewise the heart, connected with the arch of the aorta. The lung slightly wounded might have yielded a little blood, but certainly not water. That conjecture is therefore the most probable, and the most in accordance with forensic medicine, which derives the blood from the [left] ventricle of the heart, and the water from the pericardium." *—In a special treatise on the cross and crucifixion,

---

* Thomas Bartholinus, De Latere Christi aperto, etc., pp. 17-22, 45, 165;—Hieron. Bardus, Epist. ad Thom. Bartholinum, ibid. pp. 553-556;

Kipping draws the same conclusion, with the exception of regarding the water poured out on this occasion as naturally contained in the pericardium.—"The soldier"—he remarks,—"pierced with a spear the Redeemer's left side, not to try whether he was dead, but, supposing that he was in a dying state, to deprive him entirely of life, and put an end to his pains; also, that he might thus be [legally] removed from the cross, on which according to the Jewish law he could not be left. He transfixed the heart, for it was from thence that the blood flowed, and by the same stroke previously wounded the pericardium, which contains a quantity of water for the purpose of cooling the excessive heat of the heart."—This opinion has been adopted by Bishop Watson in his Apology for the Bible. —"John"—says he,—"tells us that he saw one of the soldiers pierce the side of Jesus with a spear, and that blood and water flowed through the wound; and lest any one should doubt of the fact from its not being mentioned by the other evangelists, he asserts it with peculiar earnestness;—'And he that saw it bare record, and his record is true, and he knoweth that he saith true, that ye might believe.'—John saw blood and water flowing from the wound; the blood is easily accounted for, but whence came the water? The anatomists tell us that it came from the pericardium. So consistent is evangelical testimony with the most curious researches into natural science."* This consistency is indeed perfectly admirable, and extends much further than the learned bishop could have imagined, but not exactly in the manner which he supposed: for in the ordinary state of things the quantity of water found in the pericardium after death is so

—Thom. Bartholinus, Epist. ad Hieron. Bard. rescripta, pp. 565–570;— Kuinoël, Comment. in Lib. Historic. Nov. Test., John, chap. 19, v. 34.

* M. H. Kipping, De Cruce et Cruciariis, pp. 187–195;—Bishop Watson, Apologies for Christianity, and the Bible, pp. 313, 314.

minute, that in a case like that under consideration it would have been absolutely imperceptible. Haller states that a small quantity of water, not exceeding a few drachms, has frequently been found in the pericardium of executed persons; but, except under very peculiar or morbid circumstances, the eminent anatomists John and Charles Bell deny the occurrence altogether.—" If,"— they observe,—" a person have labored under a continued weakness, or have been long diseased, if a person have lain long on his death-bed, if the body have been long kept after death, there is both a condensation of the natural halitus in all the parts of the body, and an exudation of thin lymph from every vessel, there is water found in every cavity from the ventricles of the brain to the cavity of the ankle-joint, and so in the pericardium among the rest. But, if you open a living animal, as a dog, or if you open suddenly the body of suicides, or if you have brought to the dissecting-room the body of a criminal who has just been hanged, there is not in the pericardium one single particle of water to be found. When such fluid is to be found, it is of the same nature with the dropsical fluids of other cavities. In the child and in young people, it is reddish, especially if the pericardium be inflamed; in older people it is pellucid, or of a light straw-color; in old age, and in the larger animals, it is thicker, and more directly resembles the liquor of a joint." —The slight discrepancy observable between writers on this subject may, as Klefeker has remarked, be referred to their having described the state of the pericardium under very different circumstances. Naturally it exhibits scarcely any thing which deserves the name of liquid; but after some forms of violent death, more especially when attended with obstructed circulation, it may contain a little serum, either pure or mixed with blood. An effusion of the latter kind is said to have been noticed in stags killed after a hard chase; and in some rare instances of sudden death occasioned by strong mental emotion, the pericardium has been found distended with blood, owing probably, as Morgagni suspected, to organic disease, and the rupture of vessels; but for the statement of the Grüners, that after death accompanied with anxiety the pericardium is full of water, there is no evidence.*

Whether, however, such conditions are of common occurrence or not, their occurrence at the death of Christ is disproved by the well-known facts of the case. Neither the period of three hours occupied by his peculiar mental sufferings, nor that of six hours which comprised the entire crucifixion, were sufficient to occasion in a young and vigorous person such an effusion of blood or serum into the pectoral cavities as is here supposed. Had it really happened within so short a space of time, it would have produced symptoms of debility and suffocation, quite incompatible with the intelligence, the presence of mind, and the loud and pious exclamations which immediately preceded his death; and the manner of that death, instead of being sudden and unexpected, would have been slow and progressive. Still less, if possible, would such an effusion have accorded with the discharge of blood and water from the side of Christ, when afterward pierced by the soldier's spear. As this remarkable fact was witnessed by the apostle John, a person of humble rank, destitute of medical or other learning, and at the time of observation probably removed to some distance from the cross, while the soldiers were occupied in dispatching the

---

* Haller, Element Physiolog. Corp. Human. vol. i. pp. 282, 283;—John and Charles Bell, Anatomy of the Human Body, vol. ii. pp. 53–55;—Johan Bohn, De Renunciatione Vulnerum, pp. 226, 227;—J. P. Klefeker, De Halitu Pericardii, pp. 25–28;—G. M. Zecchinelli, Sulla Angina del Petto, etc., vol. i. pp. 95, 96;—Morgagni, De Causis et Sedibus Morborum, vol. iii. pp. 462–467.

crucified persons, it is obvious that the discharge of blood and water must have been considerable, and the distinction between the two substances strongly marked. Bloody serum, whether originally effused in that state, or resulting from subsequent mixture, would not have presented this character; for it would neither have issued rapidly, nor in sufficient quantity, nor would its distinction from ordinary blood have been so striking as to have attracted the attention of an uninformed and somewhat distant spectator. Moreover, unless blood has been previously extravasated, little or none can by any kind of wound be extracted from a dead body, except by the action of gravity, the heart being usually empty, or, if otherwise, devoid of power to expel its contents. This important fact, overlooked by most other writers, was perceived and acknowledged by the Grüners, who nevertheless failed to discover the true explanation, and were induced to adopt the inadmissible opinion that Christ was not actually dead when pierced by the soldier's spear, but merely in a faint and languid condition, which allowed the heart to act feebly, and, on being wounded, to pour forth its blood preceded by the water, which they suppose had previously collected in the pericardium.— "Blood and water"—they remark,—"flowed from the wound together, and as it appears with force, which is the act not of a dead, but of a living body. Therefore, when Christ on the cross was stabbed by the soldier, he still retained a degree of life, although extremely feeble and ready to expire; but on receiving the wound in his breast, he must be regarded as having truly and suddenly died, for by this wound the fountain of life must have been exhausted, and its small remaining force entirely extinguished."—In confutation of this opinion it is sufficient to adduce, as has been already done, the testimony of the evangelists, that the condition of Christ immediately before his death was not that of debility, but of agony, and that he died some time before receiving the wound with the spear, and not of course, as the Grüners and others pretend, in consequence of that wound. The statement of John on this point is clear and decisive.—"So the soldiers came and broke the legs of the first and of the other who was crucified with Jesus; but on coming to him, as they perceived that he was already dead, they did not break his legs: one of the soldiers, however, pierced his side with a spear, and immediately there came forth blood and water."—But supposing, for the sake of argument, that Jesus was really although feebly alive at the time, there could have been little or no effusion of any kind, and certainly none of blood and water from his side when it was pierced with a spear; for in such cases there is little or no serous fluid in the pericardium, the blood does not separate into its constituents, and the heart is nearly empty, and scarcely able to maintain the slightest motion in its contents, much less to discharge them with force from the body; so that, after all, nothing is gained by this extravagant and antiscriptural supposition. The neglect or contradiction by these otherwise estimable authors of the narratives of the evangelists, as if they were not entitled to the fullest confidence, is much to be regretted, since it vitiates their reasonings on the subject, and leaves a painful impression that they were not entirely free from the lax and neological sentiments which they undertook to oppose.*

It will now be shown that the effusion of blood and water from the side of Christ, whereof no satisfactory solution can otherwise be given, is fully explained by the rupture of his heart; and that the exact and critical accordance of this presumed event with all the circumstances of

* Kuinoël, Comment. in Lib. Historic. Nov. Test., John, chap. 19, v. 31-34.

the case, taken in conjunction with the arguments previously adduced, **may justly be** regarded as completing the demonstration that it was the true and immediate **cause of his death.** It has been already proved **that in such cases rupture of the heart** is the result of **its own violent action, and** generally occurs in the **left, or principal ventricle.** Of such action the mental agony endured **by** Christ during the last three hours **of his crucifixion, and** which not long before forced from **him a bloody sweat,** was a real and **adequate cause; and the rapid manner of** his death **implies that the rent was large and sudden. Rapid as it was, the space of a minute or two would naturally however intervene, and this would afford a sufficient time for his uttering the two short sentences** ascribed to him by the evangelists,—["All] is accomplished : Father! into thy hands I commit my spirit;"—as likewise for a discharge of blood from the ruptured heart into its enclosing capsule. The excessive excitement which led to **this** catastrophe would occasion the words **to be pronounced with vehemence, and the previous accumulation in the heart and great vessels produced by such** excitement **would cause the effusion to be copious. From the** researches **of Lancisi, Ramazzini, Morgagni, and other anatomists,** it appears that a quart of blood, and sometimes much more, might thus be collected in the pericardium, where it would speedily separate **into its** solid and liquid constituents, technically called crassamentum **and serum, but in ordinary language,—" blood and** water." *—Several **instances have been** adduced of the common use of **such** language **even by** medical writers, and, as before observed, it **is not less** natural than common, since the cras-

---

* B. Ramazzini, Opera, p. 171;—J. M. Lancisi, Opera, vol. i., pp. 157-159, etc.;—Morgagni, De Causis et Sedibus Morborum, v. ii. pp. 296, 297; vol. iii. pp. 412, 413; vol. iv. p. 557.—See also Dr. Fischer's case, at pp. 97, 98.

samentum contains the greater part of the solid and more essential ingredients of the blood, while, with the exception of albumen, the serum consists chiefly of water. Accordingly, in the book of Exodus, the blood of the paschal lamb sprinkled at evening on the lintel and door-posts of the Israelitish dwellings in Egypt, is still termed blood when viewed by the destroying angel at midnight, although at that time nothing but the solid coagulum could have remained.* Other examples of a similar kind will be subjoined. It has also been shown that, as the object of the soldier in wounding the body of Christ must have been either to ascertain, or to insure his death, he would purposely aim at the heart, and therefore transfix the lower part of the left side, an act sufficiently intimated by the statement of the evangelist.—" They did not break his legs : one of the soldiers, however, pierced his side with a spear."—In so doing he would open the pericardium obliquely from below; and supposing that capsule to be distended with crassamentum and serum, and consequently pressed against the side, its contents would by the force of gravity be instantly and completely discharged through the wound, in a full stream of clear watery liquid intermixed with clotted blood, exactly corresponding to the remaining clause of the sacred narrative,—" and immediately there came forth blood and water."—The amount of such contents must of course vary with the circumstances, but may be very considerable, and therefore, when outwardly discharged, sufficiently conspicuous. In one of the instances on record it was—" about a quart of blood and water;"—in another,—" five or six pounds by weight;"—in a third,—" an immense quantity of coagulated blood;"—and in two cases of spontaneous rupture of the left ventricle of the heart described by Taxil St.

* Exodus, chap. 12, v. 21-23.

Vincent,—"an enormous collection of half-coagulated blood." *

It will next be shown that, while such an effusion would necessarily have followed rupture of the heart, it could not have occurred under any other conceivable circumstances; thus proving, by a sort of *experimentum crucis* which leaves no alternative, that the former was truly and exclusively the immediate cause of the Saviour's death. The laws which regulate the separation of the blood into its constituents are still involved in some degree of obscurity, partly because the process is connected with the mysterious principle of life, which the blood possesses in common with the solids of the body. In its perfect and living state the blood is a complex but uniform liquid, composed chiefly of water, albumen, and fibrine, holding in solution minute quantities of saline matters, and having diffused through it numerous organized particles, which, being the source of its color, are called the red globules. This constitution of the blood is maintained more or less completely as long as it remains within the vascular system, and during life; but on the failure of either of these conditions, it undergoes a remarkable change. In ordinary circumstances, the blood when discharged from its vessels soon loses its vitality, and not long after becomes dissevered. The fibrine spontaneously concretes into a soft spongy mass, within the interstices of which the red globules are entangled and detained. The other ingredients, namely, the water, albumen, and saline matter, continue liquid; and as the specific gravity of the two portions is different, they necessarily separate from each other, and there results a large quantity of transparent straw-colored liquid in which a smaller quantity of dark red coagulum sinks or swims, according as it is more or less firmly con-

---

* Journal Universel des Sciences médicales, vol. xix. pp. 257–260.

solidated. The blood retained in the vascular system after death often undergoes a somewhat similar change, but neither so rapidly, nor so completely. The coagulation of the fibrine takes place more slowly, the red globules are more uniformly diffused among the other ingredients, and the consequence is, that in the heart and vessels of dead bodies pale or red coagula often occur, but clear and colorless serum is very seldom found. If, however, at or before death blood is extravasated into the pericardium, or any of the other serous capsules, it suffers the same change as if it were removed from the body; that is to say, it speedily separates into serum and crassamentum.

In confirmation of these statements, some authorities and examples will now be cited. The influence of vital conditions in modifying the spontaneous decomposition of the blood is mentioned by several physiologists.—" In persons killed by lightning,"—says Mr. Mayo,—" by blows on the stomach, by the bite of venomous serpents, or through the influence of acrid vegetable poisons, or in persons dying from violent mental emotion, the blood is said to be found fluid, and the muscles do not become rigid." *—The principle was more fully expounded by the celebrated John Hunter, who writes as follows:—" In many diseases not inflammatory, namely, those called putrid, where the solids have a tendency to fall into those changes natural to animal matter deprived of its preserving principle, the blood has no disposition to coagulate. . . . . Many kinds of death, as well as putrid diseases, produce this effect on the blood, an instance of which was met with in a gentleman, who, being in perfect health, died instantaneously from passion; this having been so violent as to produce death in every part at once, and his

* Herbert Mayo, Outlines of Human Physiology, pp. 30, 31.

blood did not coagulate. A healthy woman was taken in labor of her fourth child. As the child was coming into the world, the woman died almost instantly. On opening the body next day, there appeared no cause for death whatever, every part being natural and sound; but the blood was in a fluid state, nor did it coagulate on being exposed. A soldier, a healthy young man, confined for desertion, received a blow on the pit of his stomach from one of his comrades, from which he dropped down, and died almost instantly. On opening the body no preternatural appearance was observed, but the blood was in a perfectly fluid state, and did not coagulate when taken out of the vessels, and exposed a considerable time. In animals struck dead by lightning the blood does not coagulate, nor [do] the muscles contract, both being killed at once. There are other instances. Two deer were hunted to death, in which case they acted till the very power of action ceased, and of course death ensued. On opening them the blood was fluid, only a little thickened, and the muscles were not rigid, as we find them where they are capable of acting from the stimulus of death. In both cases the life of the solids and of the blood was destroyed at the same time, and at once."*—These observations strongly support the conclusion already established, that the death of Christ was not the result of simple exhaustion, occasioned either by the ordinary sufferings of crucifixion, or by the influence of powerful passions, independently of rupture of the heart; since in the former case he could neither have exhibited for so long a time the signs of mental and bodily energy, nor could his blood after death have divided into its constituents; a process which the opposite state of agony must on the contrary, by exalting vital action, have tended to pro-

* John Hunter, Works, vol. i. pp. 238, 239.

mote. In mentioning the flow of blood and water from the side of Christ, it is most probable the apostle John was at first unacquainted with the nature and import of the fact which he related; but that by meditation and inquiry he subsequently became aware of the different conditions assumed by blood under different circumstances; and hence, in Revelation xvi. 3, when describing the visionary conversion of the sea into liquid blood, he says,—"Ἐγένετο αἷμα ὡς νεκροῦ; It became blood like that of a corpse."

The fact that clear serum is very rarely found within the heart and great vessels, and consequently that the blood of Christ, which actually separated into its constituents, must have been previously extravasated into some internal cavity where that change might have taken place, is proved by the most satisfactory evidence. Schwencke, one of the earlier writers on this subject, briefly remarks, —"In dead bodies the separation of the blood into its parts is not strictly observed, for within the vessels it is found mixed and fluid."—Mr. Paget, of St. Bartholomew's Hospital, who has witnessed several hundreds of dissections, and taken accurate notes of the condition of the blood found after death in nearly a hundred and fifty of the bodies which he examined, intimates in a published report, and still more explicitly in a letter to the author—"I have never found clear serum, such as I could suppose to be separated from the blood in its coagulation, collecting in any part of the body after death."—Dr. John Davy, whose practice as an army physician has been most extensive, was for many years accustomed in the examination of dead bodies to pay attention to the condition of the blood in the heart and great vessels, especially in reference to coagulation, and of about two hundred of these inspections he has published detailed accounts. The result is that, although he has found the blood either wholly solid, wholly liquid, or in various intermediate conditions, he met with only a single instance, and that under very peculiar circumstances, in which a portion of clear serum was detached from the crassamentum.* In his excellent work on Human Physiology, Dr. Carpenter remarks,—"Instances occasionally present themselves in which the blood does not coagulate after death, and in most of these there has been some sudden and violent shock to the nervous system, which has destroyed the vitality of solids and fluids alike. This is generally the case in men and animals killed by lightning, or by strong electric shocks, and in those poisoned by prussic acid, or whose life has been destroyed by a blow on the epigastrium. It has also been observed in some instances of rupture of the heart, or of a large aneurism near it, and a very interesting phenomenon then not unfrequently presents itself;—the coagulation of the blood which has been effused into the pericardium (the effusion having taken place during the last moments of life), while that in the vessels has remained fluid."†—The variable tendency of blood in dead bodies either to separate into its constituents or not, according as it is situated within or without the vascular system, and the occurrence of a complete division into crassamentum and colorless serum in extravasated blood only, are here stated so distinctly as almost to preclude the necessity of any further quotations; but for the sake of illustration a few examples will be annexed.

The Commentaries of the Academy of Bologna, for 1757, contain an account by Galeati of a man who, after having long enjoyed good health, and taken much eques-

---

* Thomas Schweneke, Hæmatologia, pp. 90, 91;—Dr. John Davy, Researches Physiological and Anatomical, vol. ii. pp. 190-213.

† Dr. W. B. Carpenter's Principles of Human Physiology, etc., pp. 475, 476.

trian and other exercise, adopted a sedentary mode of life, in consequence of which he labored for more than thirty years under various pains and ailments, and at length died suddenly. Besides several other lesions observed in the body, a small rupture was found in the left ventricle of the heart; and the pericardium was so distended as to occupy a third part of the cavity of the chest. On opening it, a large quantity of serum was discharged, and two pounds of clotted blood were seen adhering at the bottom. —In the London Medical Repository for 1814, Mr. Watson relates the case of a gentleman between fifty and sixty years of age, who died suddenly from the rupture of an aneurism of the aorta; and observes,—"The sac had burst by an aperture of nearly three-fourths of an inch in length into the pericardium, which, as well as the sac itself, was filled with coagula and serum, to the amount of about five pounds."—The London Medical and Physical Journal for May, 1822, reports from the Paris Athenæum of Medicine, an instance of spontaneous rupture of the heart in a gentleman aged about sixty-five years, of moderate habits, and in the full enjoyment of health. With the exception of the rupture, the heart was in every respect perfect, its substance being neither softer nor thinner than usual.—"The pericardium, which appeared much distended, had a bluish color, and presented an evident degree of fluctuation, contained a quantity of serum and coagulated blood."—The same Journal, for April, 1826, mentions a case, in which a small aneurism of the aorta burst by a minute orifice into the pericardial sac, and occasioned immediate death,—"On opening the body, the pericardium was found to be distended with blood; separated, however, into coagulum and serum."*—Wheeler's

---

* Comment. de Rebus in Scient. Nat. et Medicina gestis. 8vo, Lipsiæ, 1758: vol. vii. pp. 389, 390;—London Medical Repository, vol. i. pp. 99–102;—London Med. and Phys. Journal, vol. xlvii. pp. 432, 433; vol. lv. pp. 271–274.

Manchester Chronicle, for November 22, 1834, describes a diseased aorta, which had ruptured by a small aperture into the pericardium, and must have induced almost instantaneous death. On inspection the heart was found enlarged, and—"the pericardium"—says the surgeon, Mr. Ollier,—"contained about a quart of blood and water;"—which he afterward explains by saying,—"The blood was separated, although indistinctly, into serum and crassamentum."—Morgagni relates a similar case; also another, in which an aneurism of the aorta produced sudden death by bursting into the left pleura, which enclosed a large quantity of clear water and coagulated blood, while the blood in the heart and vessels was liquid and black. The late Sir David Barry died suddenly, owing to the bursting of an aneurism of the aorta into the right pleural sac, which contained a great quantity of clear serum, intermixed with large coagula of blood, the whole effusion amounting to full five pints. A parallel case is reported in the Edinburgh Medical and Surgical Journal for January, 1843, in which,—"the cavity of the right pleura was found to be almost filled with blood, which had separated into serum and crassamentum; the former amounted to three pints, and the coagulated portion, which was exceedingly firm, weighed about three pounds."—The Dublin Medical Transactions, for 1830, mention the case of a robust man who died suddenly from pulmonary hæmorrhage bursting into the left pleural sac, which on examination was found to contain—"about three quarts of blood, the serum supernatant to a great degree, as in blood allowed to stand after venesection, and the clot in considerable quantity, but very soft, occupying the most dependent portion of the cavity. . . . The heart was sound, and empty of blood, and the blood of the body generally was fluid."*

* Morgagni, De Caus. et Sed. Morb. vol. iii. pp. 116-118;—433-436.

The facts above stated are, it is presumed, sufficient to prove that the blood and water which flowed from the side of Christ, when pierced by the soldier's spear, were the result of a previous effusion into the pericardial sac of a quantity of blood, which had there separated into serum and crassamentum, and was derived from rupture of the heart. The only conceivable alternatives are simple hæmorrhage into the pericardium, and dilatation of one or more of the cardiac chambers; each of which conditions might, like rupture itself, be induced by violent action of the heart owing to agony of mind, and in each of which the blood might be found after death divided into its constituents. Of these alternatives the former is liable to the objection, that the few instances of the kind placed on record seem to have depended either on the rupture of a blood-vessel, or on some peculiar laxity of the pericardial capillaries, implying local debility or disease. But, as no defect of this or any other description could have existed in the body of Christ, which was perfect and vigorous, and when previously tested in the garden of Gethsemane had been proved to be free from such predisposition, this solution is inadmissible. Objections still stronger apply to the other alternative, namely, dilatation of one or more of the cardiac chambers, for in that case neither would the mode of death have been equally speedy and sudden, nor would the quantity of blood retained in the heart have exceeded a few ounces; and, as even of this small quantity the whole could scarcely have been discharged through the wound made by the spear, the consequent flow of blood and water would not have been sufficiently conspicuous to attract the attention of the evangelist John, and induce him to insert it in his narrative. A weightier ob-

—Medico-Chirurg. Review for 1836, vol. xxiv. pp. 298–300;—Edin. Med. and Surg. Journal; vol. lix. pp. 115–117;—Dublin Med. Trans. New Series, vol. i. part i. pp. 11–16.

jection is suggested by the different time required for the coagulation of blood, according as it is situated within or without the vascular system. When effused into the pericardium, owing to a rupture of the heart which proves almost immediately fatal, its mode of concretion cannot materially differ from that which occurs when it is drawn from the body during life. In the latter case it happens, generally speaking, in a few minutes, and the complete separation of the serum and crassamentum in an hour; the process being more rapid when the original temperature of the blood is maintained, than when it is allowed to cool.* From a great number of accurate dissections, Mr. Paget has ascertained that this change takes place much more slowly in blood remaining after death within the heart and great vessels, than in that which has been removed from them.—" In the majority of cases "—he observes,—" the blood does not coagulate in the body for the first four hours after its rest has commenced, and in many it remains fluid for six, eight, or more hours, and yet coagulates within a few minutes of its being let out of the vessels." †—This important fact, not hitherto generally known, is decisive of the point now under consideration. For the death of Christ happened at the ninth hour, that is, about three o'clock in the afternoon, on Friday, the first day of the paschal festival, which as is well known was celebrated at the vernal equinox; and his body was embalmed and laid in the tomb before six the same evening, when the sun set, and the Jewish sabbath began. Between the time of his death and that when his side was

* Hewson on the Blood, pp. 1, 5, 25, 26, 120;—Hey, pp. 37, 38;—Hunter, pp. 19, 21, 22;—Wilson, pp. 28-31;—Thackrah, pp. 33, 34, 67, 91.

† James Paget, Esq., On the Coagulation of the Blood after Death; in the London Medical Gazette for 1840;—New Series, vol. i. pp. 613-618.

pierced by the soldier, the longest interval which can with any probability be assigned is two hours; an interval which, although abundantly sufficient for the separation of extravasated blood into its constituents, more especially in the pericardium of a body still warm, and fixed in an erect posture on a cross, was, as it now appears, far too short for the coagulation of blood still remaining in the heart.

In conclusion, it may therefore with certainty be affirmed that, between the agony of mind which the Saviour endured in the garden of Gethsemane, and the profuse sweat mixed with clotted blood, which so rapidly followed it, violent palpitation of the heart must necessarily have intervened; this being the only known condition which could have been at once the effect of the former occurrence, and the cause of the latter. In like manner, when on the cross this agony was renewed, and by the addition of bodily suffering was increased to the utmost intensity, no other known condition could have formed the connecting link between that mental anguish and his sudden death, preceded by loud exclamations, and followed by an effusion of blood and water from his side when afterward pierced with a spear, than the aggravation even to rupture of the same violent action of the heart, of which the previous palpitation and bloody sweat were but a lower degree, and a natural prelude. If, while every other explanation hitherto offered has been shown to be untenable, the cause now assigned for the death of Christ, namely, RUPTURE OF THE HEART FROM AGONY OF MIND, has been proved to be the result of an actual power in Nature, fully adequate to the effect, really present without counteraction, minutely agreeing with all the facts of the case, and necessarily implied by them, this cause must, according to the principles of inductive reasoning, be regarded as demonstrated.

PART II.

ELUCIDATION OF SCRIPTURAL TRUTH BY THE FOREGOING EXPLANATION.

CHAPTER I.

ON THE DOCTRINE OF ATONEMENT IN RELATION TO THE DEATH OF CHRIST.

IF the view above taken of the immediate cause of the death of Christ is correct, it ought to be in perfect harmony with all the representations made on the subject in Scripture, whether in the form of types, prophecies, narratives, symbols, doctrines, or precepts. To show that this is really the case, and that it not only agrees with all the inspired statements, but also affords them new and valuable illustration, thereby acquiring, if that were necessary, additional evidence for itself, is the object of the remaining part of this treatise.

Had it pleased God to proclaim atonement by the blood of Christ as a matter of simple revelation, it would have been the duty of mankind to accept the testimony without further inquiry. Since, however, he has chosen that it shall be not only declared as a doctrine, but also demonstrated as a fact, it becomes at once their duty and their privilege to examine with devout attention the evidence whereby he proves that he pardons sin without clearing the guilty, and—"is just even in justifying him that believeth in Jesus."*—That sinful beings could not be thus justified by an arbitrary act of grace, but only through the medium of an atonement, that is, by a competent victim suffering in their stead the penalty due to their sins, is the dictate both of reason and of revelation. The laws of God, like the divine essence itself, are immutable, and constantly in action. Their claims are imperative and inviolable. To pardon transgression without demanding compensation would render the judge an accomplice with the criminal; and in no other way can the bolt of vengeance be averted from the head of the guilty, than by falling on that of a suitable substitute. Yet, it may naturally be asked, How can these things be? The penalty due to sin is nothing less than the divine malediction. Was it either just or possible that this malediction should fall on the beloved Son of God, in whom the Father was ever well pleased, and never more so than when he was thus achieving by his death the salvation of mankind? To elucidate in some degree this point, without pretending to fathom all the depths of a subject which in its full comprehension exceeds the capacity of the human mind, it may be observed that the primitive character both of sin and of its punishment is negative. In violating moral principle the sinner abandons God, and, by a necessary reaction, God, who is as it were moral principle personified, abandons him; not indeed totally, for that would be annihilation, but to the precise extent prescribed by consummate equity and wisdom. His outward suppport he withdraws in part, the enjoyment of his friendship and the sanctifying influence of his Spirit he withdraws entirely; but still retains the prerogative of providing an atonement in harmony with all his attri-

---

* Exodus, chap. 34, v. 5-7;—Rom. chap. 3, v. 23-26.

butes, and of thereby restoring the sinner, otherwise without hope and without God in the world, to grace and succor, and consequently to rectitude and happiness. The misery inseparable from sin depends primarily on loss of the divine favor and protection, and not on any positive infliction from that adorable Being whose work is perfect, whose nature is love, and who cannot be directly the author of evil, either physical or moral. It depends more immediately on bereavement of the conditions necessary to happiness; on disorder internal and external, producing anguish, disease, and death; and on exposure to the assaults of other depraved beings, more especially Satan and his angels. In sustaining the divine malediction, the impenitent sinner is distressed by those evils only which are its remote result. In reference to God, his desperate enmity prompts him to say,—"Depart from me, for I desire not the knowledge of thy ways;"—but, could such an infliction befall a pure and perfect human being, his language would be,—"Cast me not away from thy presence, and take not thy Holy Spirit from me."*— As such a being could not, however, thus suffer on his own account, but only as the substitute of others, it will here be proper to inquire what are the conditions requisite to constitute an atoning victim, capable of propitiating divine justice, and of making reconciliation for transgressors.

The Scriptures, which in such an inquiry must be our principal guide, represent the atonement as having regard not only to the intrinsic nature of God, but also to his relative character, as the moral governor of the universe. Hence it was necessary that it should be both adequate and exemplary, for an insufficient and clandestine transaction, under the name of an atonement, would have been

---

* Job, chap. 21, v. 14, 15;—Psalm 51, v. 11.

rather an insult than a satisfaction. In a work planned and executed by the Deity, it might be expected that the three sacred persons would perform their respective and appropriate offices; and they are accordingly found harmoniously coöperating in every step of the process. To constitute a suitable mediator between God and man, it was requisite that the two natures should be intimately associated, and that the human nature thus adopted, although derived from a fallen race, should be pure and perfect. Hence the necessity for that special interposition of the Holy Spirit in the conception of Christ, which is so plainly described in Luke's gospel. By means of this mysterious union, the sufferings and death which the human nature alone could sustain, were invested with that transcendent dignity and value which the divine nature alone could impart.* To render an atonement for human guilt, it was necessary that the victim thus provided should endure the penalty incurred, namely, the divine malediction, which in such a case could assume no other outward form than that of a public execution, wherein all parties concerned should in some measure concur in acknowledging the innocence of Christ, and at the same time in subjecting him to a cruel and ignominious death, such as that of crucifixion. It was further necessary to show that he died not merely as a martyr, but as a victim. For this purpose the ordinary sufferings of the cross would not have been sufficient, but those which he actually endured were conclusive, by exhibiting the awful spectacle of an innocent human being dying of grief under the divine malediction. The discharge of such an office was an act which, although requiring the sanction of the Deity, could not even by the Deity be commanded, but

---

* Matt. chap. 1, v. 18-25;—Luke, chap. 1, v. 26-38;—1 Tim. chap. 2, v. 5, 6;—Heb. chap. 2, v. 9-18; chap. 4, v. 14-16; chap. 7, v. 13-17, 23-28; chap. 9, v. 11-15.

must have been **purely** voluntary; implying a virtual **compact between the** parties, securing to the meritorious sufferer a commensurate reward, namely, the salvation **of all** who should embrace the atonement which **he thus accomplished.** The well-known statement of prophecy is,— "**It pleased** the Lord to bruise him; he hath **put him to** grief. When thou shalt make his soul an offering for **sin, he shall see his seed, he shall prolong his days, and the** pleasure of the Lord shall prosper in his hand. He shall see of the travail **of his soul, and shall be satisfied. By his knowledge shall my righteous servant justify many, for he shall bear their iniquities."***—To such a being the **divine malediction must have been productive of the severest mental anguish; and, although from a** regard to the **object in view** this infliction would be sustained with the most dutiful submission, yet in reference to his own personal feelings it must have been endured with the greatest horror and repugnance. This conflict of opposite motives, far from indicating, as some have imagined, **any defect of character or** of cordiality, **implied on the contrary the highest moral excellence; since the strong aversion of Christ to incur the malediction, and his still stronger** resolution to bear it **with all its consequences, were alike** expressive of the most exalted **piety** and benevolence. **With** the utmost reluctance to lose his habitual enjoyment **of the** divine communion, **he nevertheless** submitted to abandonment in compliance with the gracious purposes **of God toward** mankind, which could no otherwise have **been fulfilled. The** natural effect of such a struggle on the **body of Christ** must have been, not a simple extinction of vitality, as might have happened from mere sorrow or consternation, but violent excitement and excessive palpitation, occasioning in the first degree bloody sweat,

* Isaiah, chap. 53, v. 10-12;—Luke, chap. 24, v. 25-27;—Heb. chap. 12, v. 1-3;—1 Peter, chap. 1, v. 10-12.

and in the second sudden death from rupture of the heart.* That the Saviour's death was actually thus induced, has already it is presumed been demonstrated; it now appears that such a mode of death was not only in full accordance with the principle of atonement, but also its necessary expression and result; and it will next be shown, rather more distinctly than before, that the agony which ruptured the heart of Christ was really occasioned by his pious endurance of the divine malediction due to human depravity.

To render this atonement complete and effectual, it was indispensable that it should be both real and public; in other words, that the malediction should be borne truly, in order to satisfy the claims of divine justice, and conspicuously, in order to produce on the human race, and perhaps also on other classes of intelligent beings, a salutary and indelible impression. In accomplishing this design, notwithstanding difficulties seemingly almost insuperable, the wisdom, power, and goodness of the Deity were strikingly displayed.—"This thing"—said the apostle Paul,—"was not done in a corner."—On the contrary, nothing was omitted which could attract attention to the crucifixion of Christ, and mark it as an event unparalleled in the history of the world. The place, the time, the season, the agents, the circumstances, were all admirably adapted to the purpose. The place was Jerusalem, then in the perfection of its strength and beauty, the centre of revealed religion, the city of the living God, and the only spot on earth where sacrifice could be lawfully offered;—the time, the latter period of the Mosaic dispensation, shortly about to be superseded by the new and better covenant, a period long before predicted, when Judah, deprived of his sceptre, had become tributary to

* Matt. chap. 26, v. 36–44, 53, 54;—Mark, chap. 14, v. 32–39;—Luke, chap. 22, v. 39–41;—Heb. chap. 5, v. 5–10.

the Roman empire, then in the zenith of its power;* the season, the passover, that solemn festival, typical of human redemption, to which millions of worshippers from all quarters of the world zealously resorted;—the principal agents, the Israelitish nation, once the favored people of God, but now in a low and degenerate state, and evidently laboring under his displeasure; seconded in their hostility to Christ by their Roman masters, but headed by their own civil and ecclesiastical rulers, who throughout the whole transaction took a prominent and official part;—the circumstances, the crucifixion of a holy and mysterious person charged with the most atrocious crimes, but whom all parties virtually acquitted, and who died on the cross suddenly and prematurely, after first complaining of abandonment by the Deity, and finally claiming his acceptance. To render this extraordinary person an object of universal attention, divine providence employed all possible and suitable means. After a long succession of types, prophecies, and other preparatory measures, he appeared in the world as the heir of David and of the throne of Israel. His birth, which occurred in a supernatural manner at Bethlehem, the city of David, had been announced by a star or meteor; his claim to be the Messiah had been recognized by the usurper Herod, who commanded an indiscriminate massacre of all the male children in Bethlehem below a certain age, in the vain hope of destroying among their number the new-born king of the Jews.† After passing thirty years in humble and laborious privacy, Christ at length shone forth as a sacred person, introduced by John the Baptist, the greatest of preceding prophets, raised up for the express purpose of proclaiming his title, and preparing his way. During his

---

* Genesis, chap. 49, v. 8-10;—Daniel, chap. 2, v. 40-45;—Acts, chap. 26, v. 21-26.

† Matt. chap. 1, 2;—Luke, chap. 1, v. 26-38; chap. 2, v. 1-38.

own ministry of three years in the capital and provinces of Palestine, he exercised the prophetical office with equal dignity and meekness, speaking as never man spake, and doing works which no other man ever did, teaching the sublimest truths of morality and religion with original authority, and confirming them by numerous and splendid miracles of beneficence. So unexampled a display of goodness and power excited the admiration, if it did not win the affections of the people of Israel, and his name was celebrated not only throughout his native land, but also in the neighboring countries, whence many—" came to hear him, and to be healed of their diseases." Far from courting retirement, he showed himself freely to the world, delivered discourses and performed miracles—" in synagogues, and in the temple, where all the Jews assembled," *—addressed vast multitudes in the open air, disputed publicly with the scribes, Pharisees, and priests, and became still more conspicuous by the very opposition which they raised against him, as well as by the marvellous wisdom with which, until his hour was come, he defeated all their efforts to subvert or destroy him. As that hour approached, his celebrity rapidly increased, and attained its highest development within a few days of his death on the cross, whereby, as before stated, the necessary conditions of atonement, namely, a real and public endurance of the divine malediction, were fulfilled.

The malediction borne by Christ consisted, as has been suggested, in a partial loss of God's protection, and a temporary loss of his communion, voluntarily sustained by an innocent human being, as the just retribution of human guilt. Up to this time he had constantly enjoyed both those blessings, but now began to be deprived of them, and consequently to be abandoned to the power of his

* Matt. chap. 4, v. 23-25;—Luke, chap. 6, v. 17-19;—John, chap. 1, v. 28-36; chap. 18, v. 19, 20.

malignant enemies, the chief of whom, it is lamentable to reflect, were the Jewish hierarchy. Enjoying the highest religious privileges, these priests ought to have been the most pious and virtuous of mankind; but their extensive degeneracy, and more especially their inveterate hatred to Christ and the gospel, practically demonstrated the desperate nature of human depravity; while this very character, in conjunction with their sacred office, peculiarly qualified them to take a principal, although an unconscious part, in accomplishing the atoning sacrifice, which, on account of that depravity, he was about to render.* Had they declared in his favor, the intended sacrifice could not have been properly effected, and it might with some plausibility have been alleged that it was not necessary; since mankind were not so completely fallen as had been supposed, and did not therefore stand in need of so costly and transcendent a remedy for their restoration. The Jewish hierarchy were, moreover, the only earthly tribunal competent to try the cause now at issue, namely, whether Jesus of Nazareth was or was not the predicted Messiah; and, if he were condemned, to pronounce against him the divine malediction, as a false pretender to so sublime and sacred a character. The result proved that with all their superior religious advantages, with the Scriptures in their hands, and with a perfect knowledge of the facts concerned, they were destitute of true piety, alienated from the life of God, and bitterly opposed to his plan of salvation. Slaves to their passions, and idolaters of wealth and power, they despised the claims of a lowly and suffering Messiah, and openly declared that they would not have such a man to reign over them. Abhorring the gospel, which they soon perceived tended to the overthrow of their own temporary institution, they were anxious to crush at one blow both the person of Jesus and his cause;

* John, chap. 15, v. 18-25; chap. 18, v. 33-35.

and therefore resolved that his death should be the result of a judicial sentence from the Sanhedrim, the supreme council of the nation, condemning him as a blasphemer and an impostor. In the execution of this project they had, however, great difficulties to encounter. Deprived by their political condition of the authority to inflict capital punishment, they had no other means of obtaining the fulfilment of their sentence than, either by soliciting the consent of the Roman procurator, or, as in the case of Stephen, the first martyr, by instigating the people to an act of lawless and sanguinary violence.* The former of these expedients was humiliating, the latter was dangerous, and both were uncertain. During the preceding visit of Jesus to Jerusalem, about three months before, the people were, indeed, so far influenced by their rulers that they twice attempted to stone him in the very courts of the temple; and nothing less than an exertion of supernatural power, and a speedy retreat from the capital, was sufficient to preserve his life. So confident, in consequence, were the Sanhedrim of their success on the next occasion, that they issued an edict for his apprehension whenever he should again appear in the city.† But in this expectation they were completely disappointed; for, by seasonably interposing the miracle of raising Lazarus from the dead, a miracle which Christ himself stated was performed to promote his own glory, the tide of popularity was entirely turned in his favor; and, instead of being seized and arraigned as a criminal, he entered Jerusalem a few days before the passover in peaceful triumph, amid the plaudits of his dis-

* The reduction of Judea several years before to a Roman province under the government of a procurator, without whose sanction capital punishment could not be inflicted, is accurately described by the Jewish historian.—Whiston's Josephus, vol. iii. pp. 55, 56, 373. John, chap. 11, v. 47–53; chap. 18, v. 28–32; chap. 19, v. 8–11.

† John, chap. 8, v. 59; chap. 10, v. 31–33, 39; chap. 11, v. 55–57.

ciples, and the acclamations of the multitude, who hailed him with hosannas as the son of David, and the King of Israel. Instead of hiding himself in obscurity, he boldly encountered his powerful enemies on their own ground, in the courts and porticos of the temple, where he freely exposed their ignorance, reproved their vices, baffled all their attempts either to take him by force, or to lower him in public estimation, and displayed the true dignity and authority of a prophet, by healing the sick, instructing the people, and for the second time expelling the traders in victims from the sacred precincts. No better means could have been devised to raise the celebrity of Christ, to attract attention to his person, and to render him an object of universal interest and admiration. Accordingly, on his arrival—" the whole city was moved, saying, Who is this? The multitudes replied, This is Jesus, the prophet from Nazareth in Galilee."—Early every morning they thronged to the temple to hear his discourses, and seemed to hang on his words. Even Greek proselytes, who had come up to worship at the festival, expressed a desire to see him ; and the two disciples, travelling to Emmaus on the day of his resurrection, thought it incredible that there should be a single stranger in Jerusalem who had not heard of—" the prophet mighty in word and deed before God and all the people."—The Sanhedrim were now sorely perplexed. They had a little before asked themselves the question,—" What are we doing? for this man worketh many miracles. If we let him thus alone, all men will believe on him, and the Romans will come and destroy both our place and nation."—They observed with dismay that this prediction seemed to be on the point of fulfilment, and with undissembled vexation said to each other,—" Do ye see that your efforts are unavailing? Behold! the [whole] world is gone after him."*—Fully aware of the evils of

* Matt. chap. 21, v. 10, 11 ;—Luke, chap. 19, v. 47, 48 ; chap. 21,

delay, they still more apprehended the perils of precipitation. They were sensible that the cause of Christ must rapidly advance, if they suffered the passover to terminate without carrying into effect their loudly-proclaimed threatenings against him, and permitted the great body of Israelites, assembled at Jerusalem from all parts of the world, to return to their homes with the intelligence of his triumph, and of their defeat; yet on the other hand they feared that, in the actual state of affairs, any attempt to seize him publicly and bring him to trial, might provoke resistance and insurrection. Only two days before the passover they consequently held a special council, and came to the resolution that it was expedient to postpone the execution of their design to a more convenient season. They said—" Not during the festival, lest there be a tumult among the people." *—Of the danger to be dreaded from such tumults they were sufficiently apprised. From an estimate taken by the chief priests, at the request of Cestius Gallus during the reign of Nero, it appears that the number of persons of both sexes who celebrated the passover was at one particular time nearly three millions. Supposing only half that number to have been males, the presence in Jerusalem of more than a million of zealous Israelites, conscious of their own strength and animated by civil and religious enthusiasm, furnished a sufficient ground of anxiety and apprehension both to the Jewish and the Roman governors; and it was but a few years before that, on occasions like the present, the most

v. 37, 38; chap. 24, v. 17-19;—John, chap. 11, v. 45-48; chap. 12, v. 17-23.

* Matt. chap. 26, v. 1-5;—Mark, chap. 14, v. 1, 2. The expression in the authorized version,—" Not on the feast-*day*,"—is incorrect; since the original terms,—" Μὴ ἐν τῇ ἑορτῇ,"—are not restricted to the paschal day, but equally include the seven following days of the feast of unleavened bread, during the whole of which the same danger was to be dreaded.

appalling scenes of bloodshed and devastation had been witnessed. At the commencement of the reign of Archelaus a sedition broke out during the passover, and was not suppressed until three thousand of the people had been slain by the royal troops, many of whom likewise were stoned in the first assault. Soon afterward, owing to the avarice and audacity of Sabinus, a procurator of Augustus, another sedition arose during the pentecost, wherein a great number both of Jews and Romans perished, and a considerable portion of the outer colonnades of the temple was destroyed by fire.* Whatever might be the result of a popular insurrection at the moment, the more prudent and intelligent among the Jews were well persuaded that the Roman domination must ultimately be promoted by such outrages, and were therefore more disposed to pursue a pacific and temporizing policy, than to provoke the exertion of a hostile force which they felt themselves unable permanently to resist. In pursuance of this policy, the chief priests and the other members of the Sanhedrim determined to postpone their designs against the life of Jesus; but a higher power, which looked down with supreme contempt on all their projects, had otherwise ordained.

It is one of the peculiar prerogatives of the Deity, by an administration of inscrutable wisdom, to render the motives and actions of depraved beings subservient to his own purposes, without in the slightest degree restricting their freedom, diminishing their responsibility, or participating in their crimes. The evil passions and culpable delusions of the Jewish hierarchy were thus overruled, in a manner which they neither intended nor understood, to accomplish the great atoning sacrifice which God had announced from the beginning, and by which their typical

---

* Whiston's Josephus, vol. iii. pp. 33, 34, 39, 40; vol. iv. pp. 231, 232.

and temporary priesthood was shortly to be abolished. The Scripture had long before declared of them, and of their Gentile allies,—"He that sitteth in the heavens shall laugh, the Lord shall have them in derision."—It was through such a secret, yet effective interposition of providence that, at the very moment when they were on the point of abandoning their prosecution of Christ, Judas Iscariot was thrown in their way.* Without stopping to analyze the character or circumstances of this wretched apostate, whose treachery had been predicted more than a thousand years before, it is obvious that, with the opportunities and facilities which as one of the apostles and companions of Jesus he enjoyed, it was completely in his power, under divine permission, to fulfil the promise which he now made them, to deliver him into their hands without tumult, and in the absence of the multitude. Overjoyed at so gratifying and unexpected a proposal, of which they at once perceived the practicability and advantage, the Sanhedrim instantly reversed their previous decision, and closed with the offer; but, doubting perhaps whether Judas would really accomplish so infamous an undertaking, they at first agreed to give him no higher a reward than thirty shekels, the price of a slave, until by his fidelity and success he should have proved himself worthy of their further patronage and liberality.

They now saw their way clear, and their plan of operation was soon fixed. Having been foiled in all their attempts to excite the people against Christ, they deter-

* The resolution of Judas Iscariot to betray his master was evidently formed at Bethany on the preceding Saturday evening; but, by the unexpected popularity of Christ, its execution was providentially restrained until four days afterward. Matt. chap. 26, v. 1-16;—Mark, chap. 14, v. 1-11;—Luke, chap. 22, v. 1-6;—John, chap. 12, v. 1-8;—Psalm 2, v. 1-4.

mined to convert his popularity into a crime, and to denounce him to Pontius Pilate as a dangerous demagogue whom it was expedient to arrest without delay, in order to prevent a general insurrection of the nation against the Roman government, to which at this juncture they affected to be warmly attached. Although such an application is not described by the evangelists, it is evidently implied, since without the consent of the governor the aid of the garrison could not have been obtained. Were Jesus once a prisoner in their hands, and branded with their official censure, the Jewish rulers easily foresaw that the multitude, disappointed in their expectations of him as a temporal Messiah, would speedily exchange their admiration for abhorrence, and zealously join with themselves in demanding his crucifixion as an impostor. The great point was to make themselves quietly masters of his person, and the means of doing this seemed to be now within their reach. To prevent suspicion, and avoid unnecessary danger, Jesus was in the habit of retiring from Jerusalem every evening, and of passing the night either at Bethany, or on some part of the Mount of Olives. Without the assistance of a partisan, his enemies found it difficult to discover his place of retreat. They were also uncertain what auxiliaries he might have at command, and fearful of provoking public indignation by openly pursuing him with a civil or military force. Besides which, to whatever source they might choose to ascribe his miraculous powers, they were firmly convinced of their reality, and apprehensive that by their means he might, as on former occasions, escape from their view, and elude their pursuit. But they had now, as they supposed, an unexpected opportunity of surmounting all these difficulties at once. By the help of a disciple who had voluntarily abandoned his master's cause, they calculated that they should be able to surprise him in his retirement at a short distance from Jerusalem, a little before midnight, during the approaching paschal festival, when the whole Jewish people would either be engaged in that solemnity, or retired to rest. All this they probably represented to Pilate, with a view to prejudice his judgment, and gain his concurrence, at the same time requesting that, in order to be provided against every chance of resistance, he would on this occasion grant them the aid of the Roman cohort. Such at least was their mode of proceeding on the following day, when they were anxious that the tomb containing the body of Christ should be effectually secured.* From the conduct of Pilate throughout the whole affair, it may be inferred that he regarded Jesus as a harmless and benevolent enthusiast, whose popularity excited the envy of the Jewish priests, but was not of a nature to occasion the slightest alarm to himself. But although such might be his private opinion on the subject, he could not with propriety refuse the application of so dignified a body as the Sanhedrim, more especially when they merely urged him to sanction a precautionary measure, the neglect of which might have been dangerous, while its execution would, as he imagined, be free from inconvenience, and leave him at perfect liberty to dispose of the case afterward as he might think proper. He therefore gave the necessary orders, and at the appointed hour of the night the assembled force, guided by the traitor Judas, and furnished with lanterns and torches, apparently on account of the darkness caused by the lunar eclipse then in progress, silently issued from Jerusalem for the purpose of seizing Jesus in the garden of Gethsemane.

Of the number and strength of this force it is probable that, owing to the brevity and simplicity of the evangelical narrative, few persons have an adequate notion. From

* Matt. chap. 27, v. 62–66.

that narrative it may, however, be collected that it was extremely numerous, and consisted of a Jewish and a Gentile party. The Jewish party, chiefly described by Luke, comprised a large body of the officers attendant on the Sanhedrim, supported by several members of the supreme council itself, as well as by some of the leaders of the temple guard, and followed by many of their servants or slaves.* The Gentile party which, although intimated by the other evangelists, is expressly named by John only, was the Roman cohort, under the orders of its prefect, or commander. These were armed with swords, and if they were merely an ordinary legionary cohort, their number must have been from four to six hundred; but if, as has been suggested by Biscoe and others, an independent body, they amounted to a thousand men. It is by no means unlikely that some of the guards of Herod Antipas, the tetrarch of Galilee, who had come up to Jerusalem to keep the passover, and took a conspicuous part in the proceedings of the following day, were likewise added, with a view to obviate any difficulty which might have arisen from the circumstance of Jesus being a subject of that government, and more especially to suppress any resistance which might have been apprehended from his Galilean followers.† Well, therefore, might the apostles, when they afterward reflected on this marvellous transaction, thus acknowledge in their prayer to God its minute and accurate fulfilment of ancient prophecy:—"Lord! thou art God, who madest heaven and earth, and the sea,

* Matt. chap. 26, v. 47;—Mark, chap. 14, v. 43;—Luke, chap. 22, v. 47-53;—John, chap. 18, v. 1-3, 10-12.

† Biscoe, Sermons on the Acts of the Apostles, vol. i. pp. 328, 329, 335;—Whiston's Josephus, vol. iv. p. 8;—Luke, chap. 23, v. 5-12. The statement of John, chap. 18, v. 12, is, ἡ σπεῖρα, καὶ ὁ χιλίαρχος, καὶ οἱ ὑπηρέται τῶν Ἰουδαίων: that of Matt. chap. 26, v. 47, and of Mark, chap. 14, v. 43, is ὄχλος πολὺς.

and all that is in them; who by the mouth of thy servant David saidst,—'Why did the Gentiles rage, and the people project vain things? The kings of the earth came forth, and the rulers were assembled in a common purpose against the Lord, and against his Christ.'—For in truth against thy holy Son Jesus, whom thou hast anointed, both Herod and Pontius Pilate, with the Gentiles, and the people of Israel, were assembled in this city, to accomplish the things which thy hand and thy counsel had foreappointed to take place."—The final sufferings of Christ, which terminated the next day in his death on the cross, had now commenced. For the first time in his life the protection of Providence was withdrawn from him. The Scriptural promise which had always hitherto been realized,—"He shall give his angels charge over thee, to keep thee in all thy ways," etc.,—no longer applied to him; for he was delivered into the hands of his enemies, including not only evil men, but evil spirits, as appears from his previous intimation,—"The prince of this world cometh, and hath nothing in me;"—and from his remark to the chief priests, elders, etc., who came forth to seize him,— "This is your hour and the power of darkness."*

The explanation of this change is easy and obvious. His public ministry had now closed, and he was about to offer the atoning sacrifice which had been so long predicted, and of which the essential conditions were, that a pure and perfect human being should, by his own free will and consent, suffer the divine malediction due to the sins of mankind. It is a most remarkable circumstance, that the innocence of Christ was attested by the same parties who were concerned in his death. The Deity had more than once proclaimed by a voice from heaven,—"This is my beloved

---

* Psalm 2, v. 1–3; Psalm 91, v. 9–12;—Matt. chap. 4, v. 5, 6;—Luke, chap. 22, v. 52, 53;—John, chap. 14, v. 30, 31;—Acts, chap. 4, v. 23–28.—ἐν τῇ πόλει ταύτῃ, added by Griesbach, in v. 27.

Son, in whom I am well pleased."—Satan had often acknowledged by the mouth of demoniacs,—" I know who thou art, the holy one of God;"—His wretched agent, Judas Iscariot, had scarcely completed the treachery which he had been bribed to commit, when he was overwhelmed with remorse and despair; and having thrown back to the priests in the temple the thirty shekels, with the spontaneous confession,—" I have sinned by betraying innocent blood,"—went away and hanged himself;—Pontius Pilate, although a cruel and unprincipled man, was by his conversation with Christ impressed with such a respect for his character, that he repeatedly declared him to be guiltless, earnestly pleaded his cause, made strong efforts for his release, and did not pronounce sentence against him till his own life seemed to be endangered by his refusal. Then, in the presence of the assembled people he took water, according to the custom of the Jews and other Eastern nations, and washed his hands, saying,— "I am innocent of the blood of this righteous man: See ye to it."—Herod Antipas, in whose dominions Jesus had passed the greater part of his life, ridiculed his claim to a kingdom which was not of this world, but tacitly agreed with Pilate in acquitting him of all blame.*—The penitent malefactor crucified with him confessed his own delinquencies, and those of his accomplice, but affirmed of Jesus without contradiction,—"This man never did any thing amiss."—The centurion who attended at the crucifixion, struck with astonishment on beholding the manner of his death, and the prodigies by which it was accompanied, exclaimed—" Certainly this man was a Son of God;" and even the multitude, who had recently clamored for

---

* Deuteron. chap. 21, v. 1-9;—Psalm 26, v. 6;—Matt. chap. 3, v. 16, 17; chap. 27, v. 3-5, 24, 25;—Mark, chap. 1, v. 23, 24, 34; chap. 3, v. 9-12; chap. 5, v. 6-8;—Luke, chap. 8, v. 27-29; chap. 9, v. 34, 35; chap. 23, v. 6-15;—2 Peter, chap. 1, v. 16-18.

his destruction, were seized with compunction, and retired from the scene smiting their breasts.*

Lastly, his inveterate enemies, the Jewish hierarchy, bore unintentionally a similar testimony. Had they been well disposed, all of them would at once have adopted the language of Nicodemus, one of their number;—" Rabbi! we know that thou art a teacher come from God, for no one can do these miracles which thou doest unless God be with him;"—and, in fact, but a few days before his death, they publicly addressed him in language nearly equivalent,—" Rabbi! we know that thou speakest and teachest rightly, and dost not accept persons, but teachest the way of God truly."—Nevertheless, so bitterly opposed were they to this way of God which they affected to approve, that on his raising Lazarus from the dead, and thereby gaining many proselytes, they held a council; and at the suggestion of Caiaphas their president, resolved that, for the safety of the nation, it was expedient as soon as possible to put Jesus to death. To term such an act expedient, was in effect to acknowledge it to be unjust. By the evangelist John, who alone records the transaction, it is intimated that, however unworthy of such an honor, Caiaphas, as high-priest, spoke on this occasion under a divine impulse, when he predicted that Christ would die for the Israelitish people;—" and not for that people only," —adds the evangelist,--" but also that he might gather together in one [body] the children of God who were scattered abroad."—On their own admission, the death of Christ was therefore regarded by the Jewish hierarchy as a public sacrifice, and they unintentionally proceeded to accomplish it in a manner exactly corresponding to this view. Before offering any victim at the altar, it was their duty as priests carefully to examine it, in order to ascer-

* Matt. chap. 27, v. 54;—Mark, chap. 15, v. 39;—Luke, chap. 23, v. 39–41, 47, 48.

tain that it was pure and perfect. Thus, during the last few days of the life of Jesus, they subjected him to every possible trial; being indeed provoked to do their worst by his severe, yet merited denunciations against themselves; but with all their efforts, were unable to detect in him the slightest fault. When at length he was delivered into their hands, and placed at their bar, they could not, even with the aid of false witnesses, convict him of any offence; and to effect their purpose had no other resource than, by a previous and arbitrary compact among themselves, to pronounce him guilty of blasphemy, and deserving of death, merely for declaring himself to be the Christ; although by an overwhelming display of miraculous and other evidence, which they could neither refute nor deny, he had fully established his claim to that character.* By so doing, they virtually proclaimed what was actually the case; namely, that he was an innocent victim, who for the benefit of others was unjustly treated as a malefactor, and devoted to a cruel and ignominious death. They at the same time exhibited in their own persons the desperate nature of human depravity, the insufficiency of all the means hitherto employed for its correction, and the consequent necessity of that atoning sacrifice which they were now unconsciously laboring to fulfil.

It was requisite, however, to show that, on the part of Christ, this sacrifice was spontaneous and intentional; and that, although abandoned for a while to the power of his enemies, he was neither surprised by fraud, nor subdued by force, but voluntarily submitted to a violent death, which, had he been disposed, he might at any moment have declined. In proof of this, he publicly declared at Jerusalem a few months before,—"Therefore doth my

---

* Matt. chap. 26, v. 62–66;—Mark, chap. 14, v. 60–64;—Luke, chap. 20, v. 19–22;—John, chap. 3, v. 1, 2; chap. 11, v. 47–53; chap. 15, v. 22–25; chap. 18, v. 12–14.

Father love me, because I lay down my life to take it again. No one taketh it from me, but I lay it down of my own accord. I have authority to lay it down, and authority to take it again. This commandment I have received from my Father."*—He had also repeatedly predicted to his disciples all the particulars of his capture, crucifixion, death, and resurrection; and, by his recent institution of the Lord's Supper, distinctly apprised them that he was about to offer himself as an atoning sacrifice for the sins of mankind, and to ratify by his blood a new covenant of reconciliation with God, whereof that sacrifice was to be the basis. Having soon afterward intimated to Judas Iscariot that he was aware of his intended treachery, he dismissed him from the table, with an injunction to execute speedily what he had undertaken. But a more complete and public proof of his self-dedication was given a little later at Gethsemane, where he had scarcely recovered from his deadly agony, and resumed his usual energy and composure, when the formidable band above described, conducted by Judas, came forth to apprehend him. To prevent, as they supposed, any mistake or disappointment, they halted at the entrance of the garden, while their infamous guide went forward, and executed the preconcerted signal by which, amid the darkness and confusion of the night, the person of Christ was to be made known to his pursuers. But in this case artifice and violence were alike superfluous; for Jesus, as is stated by the evangelist John,—" knowing all that was about to befall him,"—was fully prepared to surrender himself into their hands. To the salutation of his treacherous disciple he therefore calmly replied,—" Companion! for what purpose art thou come? Judas! dost thou betray the Son of Man by a kiss?"—Then advancing with consummate dignity toward the armed band, who stood waiting for

* John, chap. 10, v. 17, 18.

his appearance, he asked them whom they sought; and on their answering—"Jesus of Nazareth,"—replied—"I am he."—These few and simple words were accompanied with a supernatural influence which, like a shock of earthquake, prostrated the whole adverse party to the ground, whence, but for the permission of him whom they regarded as their victim, they would never again have risen.* As, however, he came into the world, not to destroy men's lives but to save them, they were merely admonished, not injured by a miraculous interposition, which in extent and moral value exceeded that displayed by the prophet Elijah who, on a somewhat similar occasion, had called down fire from heaven against his assailants. Elated by this achievement, and imagining that nothing more was requisite for his master's deliverance from his adversaries than a suitable exhibition of zeal and courage on the part of his friends, the apostle Peter, ever foremost both in word and deed, drew his sword, and wounded one of the hostile band, who happened to be a slave of the high-priest. Far from rendering any service, this rash and unwarrantable act seriously endangered his own life, as well as the cause which he meant to sustain; but, by a wise and energetic interference, Christ at once protected his disciple, and vindicated his own character. He severely reproved the offence, healed the wounded slave, disclaimed all recourse to violence, and stated that his surrender to the constituted authorities was voluntary and predetermined. Remonstrating with Peter without naming him, he asked,—"The cup which the Father hath given me, shall I not drink it? Thinkest thou that I cannot even now request my father, and he would send to my aid more than twelve legions of angels? [but] how then would the Scriptures be fulfilled, [which declare]

---

* Matt. chap. 26, v. 47-50;—Luke, chap. 22, v. 47, 48;—John, chap. 13, v. 1-3; chap. 18, v. 1-6.

that thus it must be?"*—Then turning toward his Jewish opponents, he strongly exposed their injustice in attacking him by night with a military force, designed to intimate that he was the chief of a political faction; whereas, had there been any real ground for apprehending him, he was during several preceding days completely in their power, while preaching the gospel in the courts and porticos of the temple. By this touching and unanswerable appeal, he drew the attention of all the Jews present to the accomplishment of the ancient prophecy concerning him, which announced that, although he had done no violence, neither was any deceit in his mouth, he was ranked with transgressors.† Having thus demonstrated that he was an innocent and willing victim, led as a lamb to the slaughter, and about to lay down his life, the just for the unjust, to fulfil the divine purpose, he resigned himself into the hands of his obdurate enemies, while his terrified apostles, concluding that all was lost, forsook him and fled.

After a long and anxious struggle, the Sanhedrim seemed at length to have gained a triumph over Christ, by which they were enabled on the following day to bring him to an ignominious death, tending, as far as human influence could avail, to brand with perpetual infamy both his character and his cause. For, although his death was executed by Gentiles, who were then the political masters of Judea, it was virtually the act of the Israelitish people, headed by their civil and ecclesiastical rulers. The consent of Pilate, necessary for the attainment of their wishes, was so manifestly extorted from him by importunity and intimidation that he loudly protested

---

* 2 Kings, chap. 1, v. 1-15;—Matt. chap. 26, v. 51-54;—Luke, chap. 9, v. 51-56;—John, chap. 18, v. 10, 11.

† Isaiah, chap. 53, v. 9, 12;—Mark, chap. 15, v. 28;—Luke, chap. 22, v. 37.

against the injustice of the sentence which he was in a measure compelled to pronounce. Abandoned to the malice of his enemies, Christ was now subjected to every kind of cruelty and outrage. By the multitude, who had previously favored him, in the hope that he would shortly appear as their temporal sovereign and deliverer, he was pursued with a savage animosity, expressive of their bitter disappointment and mortification. By the Jewish hierarchy, the highest religious authority on earth, he was condemned for blasphemy; by the Roman government, the highest temporal authority, for sedition. Excommunicated by the one, degraded by the other, and rejected by all, he was mocked, and buffeted, and scourged, and finally led forth, laden with the cross, to suffer without the walls of Jerusalem the death of a miscreant and a slave. Stripped as a criminal, and crowned with thorns as an impostor, he was crucified between two malefactors, in the room of their leader Barabbas, who, although guilty of sedition and murder, was by the special request of the Jewish people rescued from deserved punishment, in order that Jesus, the model of every virtue, might be numbered with transgressors.* Nor was the malignity of his adversaries yet satisfied. While he hung on the cross, a spectacle to men and angels, and an object, it might have been supposed, of commiseration even to the most hostile of his persecutors, they barbarously continued to revile and insult him. Approaching in quick succession, Jews and Gentiles, priests and soldiers, rulers and populace, down to the hardened criminal crucified by his side, vied with each other in deriding his pretensions,

---

* In the provinces of the Roman empire crucifixion was the punishment usually inflicted on robbers, murderers, and persons guilty of sedition or rebellion against the government. For example, see Whiston's Josephus, vol. iii. pp. 45, 120, 169, 172, 173, 367, 368; vol. iv. pp. 171, 172.

and exulting in his disgrace. Forgetful of their rank and station, many even of the chief priests, scribes, and elders, joined with the multitude in swelling the note of execration. While thus unwittingly fulfilling the prophecies of Scripture by rejecting their own Messiah, and avowing themselves in their official character the principal authors of his death, they proved how incapable they were of contriving or conceiving the sublime plan of human redemption; and, although esteemed the holiest of mankind, how absolutely, and even more than others, they stood in need of its succor. Not less blind, however, than depraved, they remarked with peculiar satisfaction that Christ was now evidently abandoned by God, of whom he had proclaimed himself the beloved and only-begotten Son, and triumphantly appealed to the divine rejection of him, as justifying and confirming their own.—" He saved others, [but] cannot save himself. If he is the Christ, the chosen of God, the king of Israel, let him now come down from the cross, that we may see and believe. He trusted in God, let [God] now deliver him, if he will have him, for he said, I am the Son of God."*

But, their inference was as fallacious as their conduct was execrable. The outward dispensations of God's providence are no certain tests of his estimation; and thus far all the load of suffering accumulated on the head of Jesus, grievous as it was, yet being the result of malignity and violence, and entirely opposite to his desert, was neither sufficient to overwhelm his spirit, nor to prove him the object of divine malediction. On the contrary, he had himself taught his disciples,—" Happy are they who are persecuted for righteousness' sake, for theirs is the kingdom of heaven. Happy are ye, when for my sake men shall hate you, and excommunicate you, and re-

* Matt. chap. 27, v. 41–43;—Mark, chap. 15, v. 31, 32;—Luke, chap. 23, v. 35.

proach you, and persecute you, and utter all manner of calumny against you. Rejoice and exult in that day, for behold! great is your reward in heaven, for in like manner did their fathers to the prophets who [came] before you."—The apostles and their associates seconded this doctrine, both by precept and example. In his address to the Sanhedrim, Stephen the first martyr indignantly exclaimed,—" Ye stiff-necked, and uncircumcised in heart and ears! ye always resist the Holy Spirit. As your fathers [did], so do ye. Which of the prophets did your fathers forbear to persecute and slay? even those who foretold the coming of that righteous person, of whom ye have now been the betrayers and murderers." *—Paul assured both the Jewish and Gentile churches that their persecutions, like his own, far from implying God's displeasure against them, were a proof of his confidence and favor, and secured to them an eternal reward so infinitely outweighing their temporal sufferings, that it was their privilege not merely to endure, but even to glory in tribulations. The language of Peter is precisely similar:— " If any one suffer as a Christian, let him not be ashamed, but [rather] glorify God on that account: . . . . Let those who suffer by the will of God commit their souls to him in well-doing, as to a faithful creator." †—The whole deportment of Christ under his outward sufferings served to show that, considered in themselves alone, he regarded them without dismay, and endured them without distress. That the captain of salvation should have evinced less courage than many of his humble followers, or failed to exemplify his own precepts, would be an incredible supposition. The annals of most nations afford numerous in-

---

* Matt. chap. 5, v. 10-12;—Luke, chap. 6, v. 22, 23;—Acts, chap. 7, v. 51, 52.

† Romans, chap. 5, v. 1-5; chap. 8, v. 16-18;—Philipp. chap. 1, v. 27-30;—2 Thess. chap. 1, v. 3-7;—1 Peter, chap. 4, v. 12-19.

stances in which torments still greater than those of crucifixion have been borne, even by youths and women, with the most invincible constancy and patience. Several have been already mentioned; and, were it necessary, others to an almost unlimited extent might be adduced. It may be sufficient to quote the account given by Josephus of the fortitude of the Essenes, who, in addition to the Pharisees and the Sadducees, constituted the third religious sect among the Jews.—"They contemn,"—says that historian,—"the miseries of life, and are above pain by the generosity of their mind. And as for death, if it will be for their glory, they esteem it better than living always. And, indeed, our war with the Romans gave abundant evidence what great souls they had in their trials; wherein, although they were tortured and distorted, burnt and torn to pieces, and went through all kinds of instruments of torment, that they might be forced either to blaspheme their legislator, or to eat what was forbidden them, yet could they not be made to do either, no, nor once to flatter their tormentors, nor to shed a tear; but they smiled in their very pains, and laughed those to scorn who inflicted the torments upon them, and resigned up their souls with great alacrity, as expecting to receive them again."

The evangelical narrative accordingly shows that, on the very evening when Christ was betrayed, instead of brooding in solitary apprehension over the doom which awaited him, and of which he had the most distinct anticipation, he affectionately joined his apostles at the paschal supper, which he superintended as the head of the family, and employed several of the few remaining hours of his life in consoling, instructing, and praying for them. —"Jesus, knowing before the feast of the passover that his hour to depart from this world to the Father was arrived, having [hitherto] loved his disciples who were in the world, continued to show his love for them to the end." *—The calm and dignified manner in which he surrendered himself to his enemies at Gethsemane, after giving them sufficient proof that, had he been disposed, he possessed abundant power to deliver himself from their hands, has been noticed. Both before the Sanhedrim, and at the tribunal of Pilate, he displayed similar firmness, made the noble profession recommended by the apostle Paul to the imitation of Timothy, and of course of all other Christians subjected to persecution, and declined the repeated opportunities offered him by the Roman governor, to save his life by lowering his pretensions. When on his way to Golgotha his fate was bewailed by a number of compassionate Jewish women, he turned toward them, and replied with the majesty of a prophet, and the benevolence of a martyr,—"Daughters of Jerusalem! weep not for me, but weep for yourselves and for your children."—In like manner, while suffering the very act of crucifixion, he prayed for his executioners,—"Father! forgive them, for they know not what they are doing;" assured the penitent malefactor,—"I tell thee truly, this day thou shalt be with me in Paradise;"—and with kind and provident consideration for his afflicted mother, committed her to the care of his beloved apostle John. He refused the cup of medicated wine, usually taken by crucified persons in order to mitigate their bodily sufferings; and, in uttering the only complaint of this kind which fell from his lips, the same apostle intimates that it was not so much with a view to his own relief, as to the accomplishment of prophecy that he exclaimed,—"I thirst."—

* The authorized version of this passage is ambiguous, and tends to countenance the error committed by Lightfoot and other commentators, that Christ either did not partake of the paschal supper at all, or not at the same time with the Israelitish people generally. John, chap. 13, v. 1;—Whiston's Josephus, vol. iii. pp. 377, 378.

A similar representation is given by Paul, when encouraging the persecuted Hebrew Christians of his time to imitate the fortitude and perseverance of their divine master:—"Let us run with patience the race set before us, fixing our attention on Jesus, who in the [conflict of] faith led and overcame; who for the sake of the joy proposed to him endured [the] cross, despising [the] shame, and has [in consequence] sat down at the right hand of the throne of God."*—In this passage it is remarkable that the apostle alludes only to "the shame" of the cross, as if, under ordinary circumstances, that was the only part of the punishment capable of distressing a mind of superior dignity; and as if the mere bodily pains of crucifixion, on which some authors have so profusely descanted, were scarcely deserving of notice.

Thus far, therefore, it is impossible to trace in the sufferings of Christ any evidence of the divine malediction under which it was necessary that he should die, both really, in order to make an adequate atonement for the sins of the world, and manifestly, in order to demonstrate to all intelligent beings that in the work of human salvation the justice of God was not less glorified than his mercy. Thus far, Christ appeared only as a martyr to the cause which he had undertaken; and had this been, all, would doubtless have maintained to the end the same calmness and patience which he had evinced from the beginning; nor would the manner of his death have varied in any material respect from that of many of the early Christian martyrs, who, when condemned to the cross or the stake, employed themselves as long as breath and strength remained, either in acts of devotion to God, or in religious exhortations to the surrounding multitude. But a different scene now claims our attention. He who sus-

* Luke, chap. 23, v. 27–34, 39–43;—John, chap. 19, v. 28;—1 Tim. chap. 6, v. 12–14;—Heb. chap. 12, v. 1–3;—Revel. chap. 3, v. 21.

tained every other suffering with unshaken firmness, was destined to endure an infliction of overwhelming severity, in which the very perfection of his nature was to prove the principal source of his distress. To advance the divine glory, to magnify the law and make it honorable, and to accomplish the redemption of mankind, Christ voluntarily consented to bear in his own person the retribution due to human depravity, and in that capacity to lose for a time all sense of God's friendship, and all enjoyment of his communion, although conscious that the misery thence arising would occasion his death. From this internal and actual abandonment, all the outward manifestations of malediction to which he was exposed derived their significancy and effect. The Jewish Sanhedrim, including the hierarchy, who by virtue of their sacred office were really invested with the power of blessing and cursing, had judicially condemned him to death on a charge of blasphemy. The punishment of this offence, according to the law of Moses, was stoning by the people without the city, followed by the suspension of the corpse on a gibbet, or tree.—"The Hebrews,"—says Kipping,—"first put to death, either by strangling or stoning, those criminals whom they hanged. The dead bodies were afterward exposed to view, suspended from a tree, not by the neck, but by the arms; and this kind of suspension was not so much a punishment itself, as a consequence of punishment. The Rabbi Solomon Jarchi cites as a common rule among the Hebrews,—"All those who are stoned are [subsequently] hanged."—Salmasius gives a similar account, and adds from the rabbinical writings, that only blasphemers and idolaters were wont to be thus suspended.* Had the people of Israel at that time pos-

---

* Kipping, De Cruce, et Cruciariis, pp. 18, 19 (freely translated).—Salmasius, De Cruce, etc., pp. 620, 621.—Poole, Synopsis Criticorum, etc., Note on Luke, chap. 23, v. 33.

sessed political independence, this would have been the punishment inflicted on Christ, but as they were subjects of the Roman empire, it was commuted for that of crucifixion. In this change they acquiesced the more readily because, together with an equal, or even a greater share of ignominy, and torture, the Roman punishment bore, like their own, the stamp of divine malediction, agreeably to the declaration of the Old Testament quoted by the apostle Paul,—" Cursed [is] every one that hangeth on a tree;"—and it was in accordance with the same law that they were so anxious for the dispatch and removal of the crucified persons before sunset. On the occasion of an act of blasphemy having been committed by one of the mixed multitude, soon after the departure of the Israelites out of Egypt,—"the Lord spake unto Moses, saying; Bring forth him that hath cursed without the camp, and let all that heard [him] lay their hands upon his head, and let all the congregation stone him. And thou shalt speak unto the children of Israel, saying, Whosoever curseth his God shall bear his sin; and he that blasphemeth the name of the Lord shall surely be put to death, [and] all the congregation shall certainly stone him."—It was further commanded,—" If a man have committed a sin worthy of death, and he be to be put to death, and thou hang him on a tree, his body shall not remain all night upon the tree, but thou shalt in any wise bury him that day (for he that is hanged [is] accursed of God), that thy land be not defiled, which the Lord thy God giveth thee [for] an inheritance." *—Among other outward signs of malediction were the earthquake, which at the same time rent the rocks; and the extraordinary darkness, owing perhaps, as already suggested, to a shower of volcanic ashes, which for three hours during the middle of the day obscured the

* Levit. chap. 24, v. 10-16 ;—Deut. chap. 21, v. 22, 23 ;—Joshua, chap. 8, v. 28, 29 ; chap. 10, v. 26, 27 ;—Galat. chap. 3, v. 13.

sun and the air, and overspread the whole of Palestine. To discuss the subject at large in this place would be unsuitable, but both reason and Scripture seem to intimate that, during the present period of the world, these terrific convulsions of Nature are results of the primeval curse which the fall of man entailed on the earth, exhibiting a partial return toward the original chaos whence it was produced by the Deity, when he beheld every thing which he had made, and declared it to be very good; and affording a fearful presage of the general conflagration, preparatory to a new and happier arrangement, which it is ultimately destined to undergo. In all other parts of the sacred writings, when volcanic movements are noticed, they are represented as tokens of God's displeasure, and there is therefore the less ground to doubt that they were intended to have the same import on this solemn occasion.

The external signs of divine malediction which accompanied the death of Christ were necessary for the purpose of public impression, a purpose which has ever since been fully accomplished; although, owing to the perverseness of the human mind, too often with an unfavorable effect.—" The doctrine of the cross "—says the apostle Paul,—" is to them that perish foolishness, but to us who are saved it is the power of God; .... for the Jews require signs, and the Greeks seek after wisdom, but we preach Christ crucified, to the Jews an offence, to the Gentiles foolishness, but to them that are called, both Jews and Greeks, Christ the power of God, and the wisdom of God."—The apostle Peter, writing concerning the Saviour to the Jewish converts of Asia Minor, remarks in like manner,—"To you that believe [he is] precious, but to them that are disobedient the stone which the builders disallowed has [nevertheless] become the corner-stone, and [at the same time] a stone of stumbling, and a rock of offence." *—The extreme repugnance of unconverted Israelites, for the reason here stated, to the doctrine of the cross, is well displayed in the interesting conference, whether real or imaginary, between Justin Martyr and Trypho the Jew. Toward the conclusion of the discussion the latter observes,—" Respecting the ignominious crucifixion of Christ we hesitate, for the law declares that a crucified person is accursed, and of this point I cannot, therefore, easily be persuaded. That Christ is doomed to suffer, the Holy Scriptures plainly announce; but whether to suffer in a manner which by the law is connected with a curse, we wish, if you have any proof, to learn [from you]. . . . That he is to suffer, and to be led as a sheep [to the slaughter] we know; but show us whether he is also to be crucified, and to die in so base and ignominious a manner, under a punishment which by the law is devoted to malediction; for of such an indignity we cannot even entertain the thought." †—To expect salvation from one who suffered the death of the cross, attended with every circumstance of infamy and contempt, has always appeared to the unbelieving Gentile the height of folly, and to the unbelieving Jew not only absurd, but impious, in consequence of the death of the cross being by the law of Moses indelibly stamped with the divine malediction; and yet it is to this very malediction, really but vicariously endured, that it owes all its efficacy and glory.

The nature of those mental sufferings of Christ which depended on this cause has been much misrepresented, both by the adversaries and the advocates of the gospel. By some of the former they have been ascribed to the disappointment and despair of a deluded enthusiast, con-

---

* Rom. chap. 9, v. 30–33;—1 Corinth. chap. 1, v. 17-25;—Galat. chap. 5, v. 11;—1 Peter, chap. 2, v. 6-8.

† Justinus (Martyr), cum Tryphone Judæo Dialogus, pp. 271, 272;— Bosius, Crux triumphans, etc., p. 47.

vinced too late of the folly of his expectations, and the vanity of his pretensions; by some of the latter they have been either exaggerated, as denoting an infliction of divine wrath identical with that which is supposed to attend final condemnation; or underrated, as not exceeding the natural and moderate sorrow which might be felt by any virtuous and benevolent man, on contemplating the painful spectacle of human vice and misery, more especially if persecuted to death, on account of his well-meant but unsuccessful endeavors to promote reformation and happiness. Of hostile sentiments, thinly covered by a veil of affected candor, a striking instance occurs in the celebrated work of Gibbon, from which the following are extracts.—"The familiar companions of Jesus of Nazareth conversed with their friend and countryman, who, in all the actions of rational and animal life, appeared of the same species with themselves. His progress from infancy to youth and manhood was marked by a regular increase in stature and wisdom; and after a painful agony of mind and body, he expired on the cross. He lived and died for the service of mankind, but the life and death of Socrates had likewise been devoted to the cause of religion and justice; and although the stoic or the hero may disdain the humble virtues of Jesus, the tears which he shed over his friend and country may be esteemed the purest evidence of his humanity. . . . The heretics abused the passionate exclamations of—'My God! my God! why hast thou *forsaken* me?'—Rousseau, who has drawn an eloquent but indecent parallel between Christ and Socrates, forgets that not a word of impatience or despair escaped from the mouth of the dying philosopher. In the Messiah such sentiments could be only apparent, and such ill-sounding words are properly explained as the application of a psalm and prophecy."* More chargeable with

---

* Gibbon; Decline and Fall of the Roman Empire, vol. viii. pp. 261, 262, 270, 271.

forgetfulness than Rousseau, Gibbon omits to mention that these ill-sounding words, as he terms them, were followed by others of a more auspicious nature, and that immediately before his death Christ triumphantly exclaimed,—["All] is accomplished : Father! into thy hands I commit my spirit."—Even such disparaging remarks may, however, have their use, by deterring better-disposed persons from inadvertently following a similar course, and making injudicious attempts to extenuate the Saviour's mental sufferings, as if they implied despondency or pusillanimity, and tended to throw discredit on his character and cause. It is remarkable that, owing no doubt to want of due consideration, several pious and learned authors, and even reverend prelates, have fallen into this error, of which the subjoined passage from Bishop Horne's excellent Commentary on the Psalms furnishes an example:—"In the language of this divine book"—he remarks,—"the prayers and praises of the church have been offered up to the throne of grace from age to age. And it appears to have been the manual of the Son of God in the days of his flesh, who, at the conclusion of his last supper, is generally supposed, and that upon good grounds, to have sung a hymn taken from it (Psalms 113 to 118, inclusive), who pronounced on the cross the beginning of the twenty-second psalm,—'My God! my God! why hast thou forsaken me?'—and expired with a part of the thirty-first psalm in his mouth,—'Into thy hands I commend my spirit.'—Thus he who had not the Spirit by measure, in whom were hidden all the treasures of wisdom and knowledge, and who spake as never man spake, yet chose to conclude his life, to solace himself in his greatest agony, and at last to breathe out his soul, in the Psalmist's form of words rather than his own. No tongue of man or angel, as Dr. Hammond justly observes, can convey a higher idea of any book, and of their felicity who use it aright." *—This style of exposition is singularly defective and objectionable. More importance is apparently attached to the prophecy than to its fulfilment. It seems to be forgotten that the psalms were not mere human compositions, but indited by the same Holy Spirit which was bestowed on Christ without measure, and he is improperly represented as solacing himself by citations from them when, in reality, he was giving expression to the spontaneous and overpowering emotions of a heart bursting with grief. The remarks of Paley on the same subject, in his valuable work on the evidences of Christianity, are liable to similar censure.—" Our Saviour "—he observes,—" uttered no impassioned devotion. There was no heat in his piety, or in the language in which he expressed it, no vehement or rapturous ejaculations, no violent urgency in his prayers. The Lord's prayer is a model of calm devotion. His words in the garden are unaffected expressions of a deep, indeed, but sober piety. He never appears to have been worked up into any thing like that elation, or that emotion of spirits, which is occasionally observed in most of those to whom the name of enthusiast can in any degree be applied."—Under the influence of such sentiments, it is not remarkable that Paley should have disliked the term *agony* employed by Luke, and have endeavored to explain it away.—" The three first evangelists"—says he,—" record what is called our Saviour's agony, i. e., his devotion in the garden, immediately before he was apprehended."—The best refutation of such lowering statements is furnished by the words of the sacred writers themselves. Luke's description of the awful scene at Géthsemane is,—" And there appeared to him an angel from heaven, strengthening him. Then, falling into an agony, he prayed most earnestly, and his

* Bishop Horne; Commentary on the Book of Psalms; vol. i. Preface, pp. 3, 4.

sweat became as it were clots of blood dropping to the ground."—The apostle Paul in like manner declares, that —"in the days of his flesh [the Saviour] offered prayers and supplications, [accompanied] with tears and loud cries, to him who was able to save him from death, and was heard on account of [his] pious fear; [and that thus], although he was a son, he learned obedience from his sufferings." *—That his language and conduct were perfectly rational and unaffected, is undoubtedly true; but if the narrative of which this is a part does not describe the most vehement and impassioned devotion; if a state of mental distress which threatened to destroy his life, and brought an angel to his aid, does not employ strong emotion; if agony and bloody sweat did not exhibit heat in piety; and if earnest and reiterated supplications, attended with tears and cries, did not express urgency in prayer, it is difficult to imagine what can. The palpable contradiction of Scripture in this instance, by so acute and talented an author, plainly shows that his views on the subject, like those of many others, were erroneous, and that further explanation was required.

There is a different class of theologians who readily admit that on this occasion Christ suffered profound grief, but are willing to ascribe it to natural and ordinary causes, such as his abhorrence of the depravity and compassion for the misery of mankind, more particularly of his countrymen the Jews, his foreknowledge of the awful doom which awaited them, his dejection on account of their almost universal opposition to himself, and his dissatisfaction at the ill success of his laborious efforts for their conversion and salvation. But these and similar causes which have been alleged, supposing them to have been real, which is not always the case, are quite inade-

* Paley, View of the Evidences of Christianity, vol. ii. pp. 59, 60, 118; —Luke, chap. 22, v. 39-44;—Heb. chap. 5, v. 5-10.

quate to explain the sorrows of Gethsemane and Calvary, which lasted but a few hours, and were evidently of a very peculiar and personal nature. The influence of such causes, whatever might have been its amount, was not limited to those periods, but must have operated more or less uniformly throughout the whole course of his life, or at least of his ministry; and yet, as will presently be shown, his habitual state of mind was far from being unhappy. Any sufferings of this kind to which he was liable must have been greatly alleviated by his complete knowledge of the divine purposes, and his cordial acquiescence in them, by the satisfaction which he derived from pursuits of active usefulness and benevolence, by the soothing intercourse of friends and disciples, and by the spontaneous tendency of eminent piety and virtue to produce serenity and joy. It should also be remembered that the humanity which he assumed was perfect in all points, and therefore not less endued with energy and courage than with kindness and humility. In this and other respects the apostle Paul closely imitated his divine master, and, as before remarked, recommended the persecuted Hebrew Christians of his time to follow the example of him—"who for the sake of the joy proposed to him endured [the] cross (as well as the contradiction of sinners against himself), despising [the] shame, and had [in consequence] sat down at the right hand of the throne of God."—With all his meekness and compassion, Christ could on proper occasions severely rebuke the vices of men, and predict their punishment. He exhorted his followers to bear persecutions and afflictions not only with patience, but with exultation, as proofs of the divine confidence, and pledges of future reward; and his addresses to his apostles at the last supper, a few hours only before his death, were full of consolation and encouragement.— "Peace I impart to you, my peace I give to you: not as the world giveth give I to you. Let not your heart be troubled, neither let it be afraid. . . . These things I have spoken to you that my joy in you may continue, that your joy may be complete, . . . [and] that in me ye may have peace. In the world ye have affliction, but be of good cheer, I have overcome the world."*

The sorrow which caused his sudden death, must consequently have had a deeper source than that here suggested; but, in avoiding one error, some caution is necessary to avoid falling into the opposite one. By an improper use or interpretation of figurative language, some of the older theological writers represent Christ as having suffered a positive infliction of divine wrath. Thus the celebrated President Edwards observes:—" Christ never so eminently appeared *for* divine justice, and yet never suffered so much *from* divine justice, as when he offered up himself a sacrifice for our sins. In Christ's great sufferings did his infinite regard to the honor of God's justice distinguishingly appear, for it was from regard to *that*, that he thus humbled himself; and yet, in these sufferings Christ was the mark of the vindictive expressions of that very justice of God. Revenging justice then spent all its force upon him, on account of our guilt. . . . And this was the way and means by which Christ stood up for the honor of God's justice, viz., by thus suffering its terrible executions: for when he had undertaken for sinners, and had substituted himself in their room, divine justice could have its due honor no other way than by his suffering its revenges." †—The erroneousness, not to say the absurdity of such views, has been exposed by several judicious authors, among others by Dr. Moses Stuart, in his Com-

---

* John, chap. 14, v. 27; chap. 15, v. 11; chap. 16, v. 33;—Hebrews, chap. 12, v. 1-3;—See also the Treatises of Moore, and Harwood, on the agony of Christ.

† President Edwards, Works, vol. vi. pp. 413, 414.

mentary on the Epistle to the Hebrews, whose words are as follows:—" The sentiment of the clause [Heb. ix. 28] clearly is, that Jesus by his death (which could take place but once) endured the penalty that our sins deserved, or bore the sorrows due to us. But this general expression is not to be understood as if the writer meant to say with philosophical precision, that the sufferings of Jesus were in *all* respects, and considered in *every* point of view, an exact and specific *quid pro quo*, as it regards the penalty threatened against sin. A *guilty conscience* the Saviour had not; *eternal punishment* he did not suffer; *despair of deliverance* he did not entertain. It is altogether unnecessary to suppose that the writer meant to be understood here with metaphysical exactness. But that *vicarious* suffering is here designated seems to be an unavoidable conclusion, as well from the *usus loquendi* of the Scriptures, as from the nature of the argument through the whole of chapters ix. and x."*—A similar view of the matter is taken by Outram, Whitby, Doddridge, Dr. Pye Smith, and other commentators. So far, indeed, was Christ on the cross from having been the object of God's wrath that, as he himself often declared, he was on that very account the object of his highest approbation and complacency.—" Therefore "—said he,—" doth my Father love me, because I lay down my life to take it again."

How, then, it may be asked, did Christ suffer the divine malediction, not in appearance only but in reality, in order to make atonement for the sins of the world? In order to answer this question, it is necessary to consider the absolute perfection of his human nature, and his constant and beatific communion with the Father, up to the period immediately preceding his death; for to suppose that his whole life was one continued scene of sorrow and

---

* Dr. Moses Stuart; Commentary on the Epistle to the Hebrews, vol. ii. pp. 445–447; John, chap. 10, v. 17, 18.

distress is a great, although not an uncommon mistake. It is true that he stripped himself of his primeval glory, assumed the form of a servant, submitted to poverty, opposition, and contempt, and was painfully affected by contemplating the depravity and misery of mankind; but all this was compensated by that happy and intimate friendship with God which he uninterruptedly enjoyed, in a degree of which the most pious and virtuous of men cannot form any adequate conception. That such was the fact might reasonably be presumed from the dignity of his person, the superlative excellence of his character, and his peculiar relation to the Deity; but it is also fully stated in Scripture, and abundantly proved by his own declarations, his frequent acts of private and public devotion, his unexampled power of performing miracles, and the remarkable tokens of divine protection and distinction which he repeatedly received. Even as a child, it is recorded of him that—"he became strong in spirit, being filled with wisdom, and that the grace of God was upon him."—When at the age of twelve years he first went up to the paschal festival at Jerusalem, he was unexpectedly found in the temple, which he claimed as his Father's house, discoursing with the doctors of the law, and astonishing them by his early proficiency in religious knowledge. After his return to Nazareth, he continued—"to grow in wisdom, and in stature, and in favor with God and man."—At the age of thirty years he was baptized by his precursor John, and at the same time installed into his own prophetical office. On this important occasion he received the most distinguished attestation which the Deity could bestow, for the Holy Spirit descended on him in a visible form like a dove, and a voice from heaven proclaimed,—"Thou at my beloved Son: in thee I am well pleased." *—A similar recognition took place about

* Luke, chap. 2, v. 40-52; chap. 3, v. 21-23.

three years afterward at his transfiguration, when, says the apostle Peter, one of the three select witnesses of that august scene,—" he received from God the Father honor and glory, when there came such a voice to him from the majestic glory, This is my beloved Son, in whom I am well pleased."—Both on his first and last official visits to Jerusalem he was evidently sustained by supernatural influence, when amid the immense multitudes assembled at the passover, and notwithstanding the formidable hostility of the civil and ecclesiastical rulers, he went boldly into the temple, and expelled from its outer courts those who, by establishing therein a market for victims, had rendered the sacred place a scene of extortionate and unhallowed gain, or as he emphatically termed it,—" a den of thieves."—Throughout the whole of his brief ministry he was under the special care of divine providence; and the prediction quoted by Satan, during the severe temptation with which immediately after his baptism he was permitted to assail him, was not on that account the less applicable,—" He will give his angels charge concerning thee to guard thee thoroughly, and they will support thee on their hands, lest thou shouldst strike thy foot against a stone."—Agreeably to this prediction, holy angels, who had doubtless been unseen spectators of the temptation, appeared at the end of it, and ministered to him. In the garden of Gethsemane an angel was dispatched to strengthen him, when in danger of sinking under consternation and grief; and, had it been compatible with the great object which he was pursuing, he could at that or at any time have summoned more than twelve legions of those mighty spirits to his aid.* When on his first evan-

---

* Psalm 91, v. 9–12;—Matt. chap. 4, v. 5, 6, 11; chap. 26, v. 51–54; —Mark, chap. 1, v. 12, 13; chap. 11, v. 15–18;—Luke, chap. 4, v. 9–11, 28–30; chap. 9, v. 28–36; chap. 22, v. 43;—John, chap. 2, 13–17; chap. 7, v. 30; chap. 8, v. 20, 59; chap. 10, v. 31, 39;—Acts, chap. 10, v. 37, 38;—2 Peter, chap. 1, v. 16–18.

gelical visit to Nazareth his life was in imminent peril from the rage of its inhabitants, who were hurrying him to the brink of a precipice, with the intention of casting him down headlong, it was manifestly by divine assistance that,—" passing through the midst of them, he went his way."—In a similar manner he was repeatedly preserved from the violence of his enemies at Jerusalem, particularly in one instance when, on the multitude proceeding to stone him, he was suddenly concealed from their sight,—"and, going through the midst of them, passed by."—The evangelist John, who alone records these latter interpositions, also furnishes their explanation, namely, that—"his hour was not yet come;"—in other words that, until the hour of his final suffering arrived, he was under the peculiar protection of Providence.

The unlimited amount of miraculous power with which Christ was invested, more especially when viewed in connection with the attendant circumstances, affords conclusive evidence of his having possessed in the highest degree the friendship of his heavenly Father.—" God "—says the apostle Peter,—" anointed Jesus of Nazareth with the Holy Spirit, and with power, who went about doing good, and healing all who were oppressed by the devil, for God was with him."—To this decisive test of divine coöperation, he himself often appealed. Thus, on defending himself from the prosecution of the Sanhedrim, for restoring on a sabbath-day the infirm man at the pool of Bethesda, he said—" My Father worketh thus far, and I work. . . . The Father loveth the Son, and showeth him all things which he himself doeth, and will show him greater works than these, to your astonishment; for, as the Father raiseth and reviveth the dead, so likewise the Son reviveth whomsoever he chooseth;"—a miracle beyond all others stupendous, and which he afterward repeatedly displayed. Both to his enemies and to his disciples he addressed the cogent argument,—"If I do not the works of my Father, believe me not; but if do [them], although ye believe not me, believe the works, that ye may know and believe that the Father is in me, and I in him."—When at the last supper the apostle Philip inconsiderately requested,—"Lord, show us the Father, and it sufficeth us,"—he replied with some warmth,—"Have I been so long with you, and yet hast thou not known me, Philip? He that hath seen me hath seen the Father. How [then] sayest thou, Show us the Father? Believest thou not that I am in the Father, and [that] the Father is in me? The words which I speak to you I speak not of myself, but the Father who dwelleth in me doeth the works;"—and the unanswerable charge which he brought against his adversaries was,—"If I had not come and spoken to them, they would not have had sin; but now they have no excuse for their sin. He that hateth me, hateth my Father also. If I had not done among them such works as no one else ever did, they would not have had sin; but now they have both seen and hated both me and my Father."* His constant and intimate friendship with God was further proved by his repeated declarations, and his frequent acts of devotion both private and public. During his ministry in Galilee he often retired from the multitude, and even from the society of his relatives and disciples, to some solitary place, where he might more freely and uninterruptedly pour forth his adorations and thanksgivings; and previously to the election of the twelve apostles, ascended a mountain near Capernaum, and passed a whole night in secret prayer. To his public devotions he twice subjoined the assurance, —"All things are delivered to me by my Father, and no one knoweth the Son but the Father, neither knoweth any one the Father but the Son, and [he] to whom the Son will

---

* John, chap. 5, v. 17-21, 36; chap. 10, v. 37, 38; chap. 12, v. 44, 45; chap. 14, v. 8-11; chap. 15, v. 22-24.

reveal [him]."—Immediately before raising Lazarus from the dead,—"he lifted up his eyes and said, Father! I thank thee that thou hast heard me. I know, indeed, that thou hearest me always, but because of the multitude who stand by I said [it], that they may believe that thou hast sent me;"—and after another public address to the Father, during his last visit to Jerusalem, was answered by a voice from heaven. His predecessor, John the Baptist, testified of him,—"He whom God hath sent speaketh the words of God, for the Father giveth [him] the Spirit without measure. The Father loveth the Son, and hath given all things into his hand."—Christ, in like manner, said of himself to his disciples,—"My food is to do the will of him that sent me, and to finish his work;"—and to his adversaries,—"He that sent me is with me. The Father hath not left me alone, because I always do the things which please him."* Expressions of this kind abound, as might be expected, in his discourses to the apostles at the last supper, and in his sublime prayer at the end of it. The following are specimens:—"As the Father hath loved me so have I loved you: continue in my love. If ye keep my commandments ye shall continue in my love, even as I have kept my Father's commandments, and continue in his love."—In his final address to God, which is a model of fervent devotion, he says of himself,—"I have glorified thee on the earth. I have finished the work which thou gavest me to do; and now, Father! glorify me in thy presence with the glory which I there enjoyed before the world existed;"—and of his apostles,—"The glory which thou gavest me I have given them, that they may be one even as we are one: I in them, and thou in me, that they may

---

* Matt. chap. 11, v. 25-27;—Mark, chap. 1, v. 35;—Luke, chap. 5, v. 16; chap. 6, v. 12, 13; chap. 10, v. 21, 22;—John, chap. 3, v. 34, 35; chap. 4, v. 31-34; chap. 8, v. 16, 29; chap. 11, v. 41, 42; chap. 12, v. 27-30

be perfected in one, and that the world may know that thou hast sent me, and hast loved them as thou hast loved me;"—and concludes with the important statement,—" I have declared to them thy name, and will declare [it], that the love wherewith thou hast loved me may be in them, and I in them."*

The preceding quotations may suffice to illustrate the close and endearing friendship with the Father which Christ must necessarily have enjoyed during the whole of his life on earth, down to its final scene, a friendship which enabled him to bear outward trials and troubles with patience and serenity, and yielded him a constant supply of the purest and most elevated happiness. Of the intensity of this friendship it is impossible for any human being to form an adequate conception, but it must evidently have included the following conditions;—a vivid sense of the presence and favor of God, an ardent admiration of his character and works, a perfect conformity to his mind and will, an implicit confidence in his plans and arrangements, and a cordial devotedness to his service and glory. This is in fact a brief description of true religion, as suggested both by reason and revelation, a state of mind which may be realized to a considerable extent on earth, but of which the full attainment constitutes the peculiar felicity of heaven. By profane persons it is regarded with incredulity and contempt, as a fallacy or a fraud; but since they are confessedly ignorant of the qualification which they presume to deny, their objections are entitled to no greater respect than would be those of persons born blind or deaf to the alleged capacity of others to perceive beautiful sights or melodious sounds. Religion, or friendship with God, is nevertheless the indispensable basis of human happiness. To promote it, both by precept and example, is the grand object of the Scriptures, wherein it is

* John, chap. 15, v. 9, 10; chap. 17, v. 4, 5, 22, 23, 26.

accordingly depicted in the most splendid colors, and represented by the most attractive images, sometimes by the conjugal relation in its highest perfection, sometimes by a fountain of living water springing up in the human heart, as an inexhaustible source of joy and satisfaction, extinguishing its morbid thirst for inferior gratifications, and flowing onward to eternal life. Of the emphatic language in which its blessings are celebrated by those who have experienced them, the following are well-known specimens,—" How excellent [is] thy loving-kindness, O God! therefore the children of men put their trust under the shadow of thy wings. They shall be abundantly satisfied with the fatness of thy house, and thou shalt make them drink of the river of thy pleasures. For, with thee [is] the fountain of life; in thy light shall we see light. . . . [There are] many that say, Who will show us [any] good? Lord! lift thou up the light of thy countenance upon us. Thou hast put gladness in my heart, more than in the time [when] their corn and their wine increased. . . . Because thy loving-kindness [is] better than life, my lips shall praise thee. . . . I [am] continually with thee; thou hast holden [me] by my right hand. Thou shalt guide with thy counsel, and afterward receive me [to] glory. Whom have I in heaven [but thee]? And [there is] none upon earth [that] I desire besides thee. My flesh and my heart fail, [but] God [is] the strength of my heart, and my portion forever. . . . Thou wilt show me the path of life. In thy presence [is] fulness of joy. At thy right hand [are] pleasures for evermore." *—Not less energetic, on the other hand, is the language in which pious persons are represented in Scripture as bewailing their loss of the light of God's countenance, and expressing the intolerable anguish and desolation of heart occasioned by a sense of

---

* Psalm 4, v. 6–8; Psalm 16, v. 11; Psalm 36, v. 7–9; Psalm 63, v. 3; Psalm 73, v. 23–26.

his abandonment. Thus the Psalmist complains,—" Unto thee will I cry, O Lord, my rock! Be not silent to me, lest, [if] thou be silent to me, I become like them that go down into the pit. . . . Thou has laid me in the lowest pit, in darkness, in the deeps. Thy wrath lieth hard upon me, and thou hast afflicted [me] with all thy waves. . . . Lord! why castest thou off my soul, [why] hidest thou thy face from me? I [am] afflicted and ready to die from [my] youth up: [while] I suffer thy terrors, I am distracted. Thy fierce wrath goeth over me: thy terrors have cut me off."—Thus Job laments,—" Oh that I knew where I might find him, [that] I might come [even] to his seat! . . . . Behold, I go forward, but he [is] not [there], and backward, but I cannot perceive him; on the left hand where he doth work, but I cannot behold [him]; he hideth himself on the right hand that I cannot see [him]. . . . Oh that my grief were thoroughly weighed, and my calamity laid in the balances together! for now it would be heavier than the sand of the sea, therefore my words are swallowed up; for the arrows of the Almighty [are] within me, the poison whereof drinketh up my spirit: the terrors of God do set themselves in array against me." *

 The happiness derived from the friendship of God, and the misery occasioned by its privation, are thus powerfully felt by pious persons, and by them alone; but even such persons cannot suitably appreciate the intensity of these emotions, as they were experienced by the pure and perfect humanity of Christ. Hence the difficulty of conceiving, in a manner at all adequate to the dignity of the subject, the mental sufferings which he endured from the temporary, but complete interruption of his hallowed communion with the Father; a privation which, attended as it was with a partial loss of protection, and with all the

---

* Job, chap. 6, v. 1–4; chap. 23, v. 3, 8, 9;—Psalm 28, v. 1; Psalm 88, v. 6, 7, 14–16.

subordinate manifestations and inflictions thereon depending, constituted the divine malediction which he had undertaken vicariously to sustain. The nature of these sufferings, as distinguished from all others, is indicated by their limitation with respect to time, place, and circumstances, by their extraordinary intensity and fatality, and by his own explicit declarations. His earliest anticipation of them seems to have occurred at the conclusion of his ministry in Jerusalem, when he publicly acknowledged,— " Now is my soul troubled, and what shall I say ? Father! save me from this hour ? Yet, for this [purpose] am I come to this hour. Father, glorify thy name!"—This was, however, merely an anticipation, and not the reality; for a voice from heaven immediately replied,—"I have both glorified [it], and will glorify [it] again;" and he remarked to the surrounding multitude,—"This voice came not for my sake, but for yours."—His peculiar mental sufferings commenced in the garden of Gethsemane, and were renewed and completed at Calvary. Their identity on the two occasions was proved by their proceeding from the same cause, and producing similar effects ; by the abruptness of their commencement and conclusion, and the shortness of their continuance ; by the similar language which he applied to each, and by his comparative calmness and composure during the intervening period. A transition more sudden or violent than that which took place from the seraphic discourses and devotions of Christ after the paschal supper, to the horrors of Gethsemane, can scarcely be conceived. That he was about to suffer from the immediate hand of God, is implied by his prediction to the apostles on the way. In the absence of all external infliction, the cup of trembling which was then presented to him by the Father, and which he so earnestly petitioned might if possible be withdrawn, could have been none other than the cup of the wrath of God,—" the poison whereof drinketh up the spirit."*—It was piety which prompted his reluctance to receive this cup, and piety which urged him to drain it to the dregs; and the deadly struggle between these powerful and opposite emotions occasioned that agony and bloody sweat, the natural prelude to rupture of the heart, which, without the interposition of miraculous aid, would apparently have realized his own previous declaration,—"My soul is exceedingly sorrowful, even unto death."—In reference to the dependence of these physical effects on mental causes, it is rather singular that while, as was formerly shown, a majority of the older theological writers proposed explanations which are unsatisfactory and inadmissible, a few of them adopted views which, with the exception of some extravagant expressions and errors of detail, nearly resemble those above stated. Thus Gisbert Voetius, about the middle of the seventeenth century, speaking of Christ's bloody sweat, observes,—"Like the flow of blood and water from his side, I regard it as natural in reference to its proximate cause, although marvellous, a miracle of Nature, and even supernatural, if we regard the efficient, remote, and final causes. The proximate cause is, I think, to be found in the passions and their conflict, that is, partly in the passions of grief and fear, which draw the blood and animal spirits from the external parts toward the heart, and partly in those of love, desire, and zeal, which propel the blood and spirits from the heart toward the external parts. Hence it happened that the blood, driven backward and forward, like the sea in the straits of Euripus, and thereby attenuated, burst forth from the veins in conjunction with serous liquid, through

---

* Job, chap. 6, v. 4;—Isaiah, chap. 51, v. 17;—Zechar. chap. 13, v. 7;—Matt. chap. 26, v. 30-42;—Mark, chap. 14, v. 26-36;—Luke, chap. 22, v. 39-44;—John, chap. 12, v. 23-33; chap. 18, v. 11;—Heb. chap. 5, v. 5-10;—Rev. chap. 14, v. 10; chap. 16, v. 19.

the skin. That such a circumstance may actually take place, especially when the texture of the body and skin is thin and porous, is testified by philosophers and physicians, suggested by reason, and taught by experience." *— Bartholomew à Medina, after remarking that Christ was young and vigorous, gives a similar explanation of his bloody sweat.—" For,"—says he,—" through the fervor of his prayer, and his fear and horror of death, his blood at first collected about the heart; but afterward, his strong love and ardent desire of accomplishing his Father's will, and of redeeming mankind, intervening like a mighty force, overcame his fear and sensitive affection, and drove the blood powerfully outward. Hence, owing to the sudden violence occasioned by this glorious victory, blood mixed with common sweat burst forth abundantly through all the pores of the skin, dilated by the excessive effort, and flowed to the ground."—On experiencing at Gethsemane for the first time the terrors of divine abandonment, Christ appears to have been seized with such consternation and distress, as threatened to destroy him by the simple extinction of vital power. Falling prostrate on the earth—"he prayed that, if it were possible, the hour might pass from him;"—meaning by that expression, not as the above and other authors have supposed, the ordinary sufferings and death of the cross then comparatively distant, but the peculiar mental sufferings of the hour which he was now encountering.† The favor so earnestly solicited could not, however, be granted. To his reiterated supplications no direct answer was returned; but, after a fearful interval, an angel was dispatched to restore his sinking strength, and thereby to save him from

---

* Kipping, De Cruce, et Cruciariis, pp. 199, 200 ;—Matt. chap. 26, v. 38 ;—Mark, chap. 14, v. 34.

† Julius Cæsar Baricelli, De Hydronosa Natura, etc., pp. 156-158 ;— Mark, chap. 14, v. 35.

immediate death. This partial relief supplied by a subordinate agent was itself a humiliation, and proved that the principal source of comfort, the light of God's countenance, was still withheld. He accordingly availed himself of his renovated energy to pray with increased importunity, till the violent effort forced a bloody sweat from his body, a natural sign and result of the corresponding conflict of his soul. At length—"he was heard on account of [his] pious fear."—The hour of preliminary malediction came to an end, and when the hostile band drew near to apprehend him, it was evident from his conversation and conduct that he had recovered all his usual dignity and self-possession. That he should again enjoy a sense of the divine friendship, at the very time when—"all the disciples forsook him and fled,"—he had himself not long before predicted, when he said to them—"Do ye now believe? Behold the hour cometh, and is now come, when ye will be dispersed each one to his own [home], and will leave me alone; and yet I am not alone, because the Father is with me."*—That God was really with him appeared, among other indications, by his renewed exercise of miraculous power, both in overthrowing the party that went forth against him, and in healing the slave wounded by Peter; and until the hour of noon on the following day, the internal support which he thus enjoyed enabled him to bear with firmness all the sufferings of mind and body which the powerful and malignant enemies into whose hands he was delivered were permitted to inflict. These ordinary sufferings were, however, only the outward manifestations and effects of that divine malediction, which he was now again actually to endure.

The second period of Christ's abandonment, like the former one, began and ended abruptly. During the first

---

* Matt. chap. 26, v. 56;—Luke, chap. 22, v. 43, 44;—John, chap. 16, v. 31, 32;—Heb. chap. 5, v. 7–9.

three hours of his crucifixion he had calmly conversed with those around him, and by his benevolent concern for the penitent malefactor, for his afflicted mother, and even for his ferocious executioners, as likewise a little before for the women who bewailed his fate, and for his fellow-countrymen generally, had shown himself more attentive to the feelings and interests of others than to his own. But at noon a sudden change occurred, accompanied by a preternatural darkness, expressive of a second hiding of God's countenance, which overspread Jerusalem and the whole land for three successive hours. During the interval no intercourse took place between Christ and the bystanders, and a solemn pause in the evangelical narrative concurs with other circumstances, to intimate that he was again enduring the peculiar sufferings of Gethsemane, which not even inspired writers felt themselves competent to describe. The following remarks of the excellent Rambach are perhaps as suitable as any which merely human faculties could suggest.—"With regard to our blessed Lord himself, this outward darkness was an emblem of the inward darkness in which his sacred soul was then involved. For, as the light of the natural sun was then withdrawn from the inhabitants of the earth, so the light of the divine consolation and inward joy was at that time withdrawn from the soul of Jesus Christ; and, as cold and darkness then prevailed throughout the whole region of the air, so the soul of our blessed Saviour was to experience something of the terrors of eternal darkness, which now overwhelmed his conscience from a sense of the imputation of all the sins of the whole world, and threw it into the utmost anguish and consternation. . . . The only begotten Son of the Father here laments that he is forsaken of God, and this not in mere idea but in reality. For as Christ had taken our sins upon him, and become a curse for us, so was he forsaken by God, not only outwardly, by withdrawing his protection from him and giving him up to his enemies, but likewise inwardly, the Deity suspending his blissful operations on his understanding, will, conscience, and affections, and permitting all the power of the devil and the agonies of death jointly to assault him. As in quality of our surety he was to feel our pains, to bear our griefs, and carry our sorrows, so was is soul to be deprived for a while of the brightness of God's countenance, and the enjoyment of the supreme good, by which the inward sensation of the pain would have been very much abated, if not totally extinguished. On the other hand, he was to suffer all the floods of the divine wrath to pass over him; which would have overwhelmed our Saviour's human nature, had not the divinity within him supported it in this terrible trial." *—On this occasion his demeanor was widely different from that at Gethsemane. He uttered neither prayers nor lamentations, which would now have been not only unavailing, but in the presence of an immense and hostile multitude unsuitable, and liable to misinterpretation. Having, as it were, learned to suffer, and become acquainted with grief, he was not as before overwhelmed with consternation. His outward sufferings, abstractedly considered, were not indeed difficult to support; and yet, regarded as intimations of the divine abandonment on account of human depravity, appreciated by a mind of exquisite moral sensibility, they no doubt contributed to his distress. But the principal and immediate cause of his sorrow was the abandonment itself. His human, and perhaps also his spiritual enemies, had done their worst, and having exhausted every torment which malice could suggest, or cruelty execute, were reduced to sullen inaction. He had been despised, rejected, insulted, scourged, and crucified, and had borne all this with patience and fortitude; but the sufferings of malediction,

* Rambach, on the Sufferings of Christ, vol. iii. pp. 183, 184, 187, 188.

now superadded, were of a different nature, and occupied a distinct period of time. Lacerated in body, and still more wounded in spirit, he hung for three hours longer on the cross, enveloped in darkness, deprived of divine communion, and destitute of comfort from any other source. Nothing less than his unspeakable love to God and man induced and enabled him thus to endure from both an infliction, alike tremendous and undeserved, and to persist till the last moment in fulfilling the fatal task, which he had undertaken without compulsion, and might have declined without reproach. If one hour of such suffering at Gethsemane had nearly been destructive to him, its renewal for three hours at Golgotha might well prove actually so, more especially as he had now no prospect of relief except from a violent death, and this only to be effected by draining the cup of malediction to the dregs. —"Christ" says the apostle Paul,—"hath redeemed us from the curse of the law, by being cursed on our behalf; for it is written, Cursed [is] every one that hangeth on a tree. . . . [God] made him who knew not sin to be sin for us, that we might become the righteousness of God by him."*—The natural and necessary result at length took place. For three hours he sustained unutterable agony, in a deadly and incessant struggle between two opposite passions, each indicative of the most ardent piety, and the most consummate moral excellence;—an intense desire to recover that divine communion which was essential to his existence, and a still stronger desire, by resigning it at the expense of his life, to fulfil the gracious purposes of God toward mankind. The latter ultimately prevailed, but the mental conflict, the continuance of which depended every moment on his own voluntary yet reluctant concurrence, occasioned the rupture of his heart; a little before which he publicly revealed the

* 2 Corinth. chap. 5, v. 20, 21;—Galat. chap. 3, v. 13.

true cause of his sufferings, by uttering the loud and bitter cry,—"My God! my God! why hast thou forsaken me?" —Here, however, his sufferings ended, and his sorrow was turned into joy. The victory for which he had so energetically contended was won, in proof of which the preternatural darkness cleared away, the evening sun shone forth with renewed splendor, and the Saviour's dying words were those of exultation and triumph;—["All] is accomplished! Father! into thy hands I commit my spirit."

The sudden occurrence, the peculiar manner, and all the affecting circumstances of Christ's death, point to one only conclusion, and admit of no other explanation, than that it was the death of an atoning victim vicariously enduring the divine malediction, for which purpose no other mode of death would have been adapted. An incompetent or sinful being would have perished by some of the remote consequences of this malediction; but an adequate and innocent victim must have been destroyed by the malediction itself, and in the manner here represented. It was the only death worthy of him to suffer, who was— "the lamb of God, that taketh away the sin of the world," —and of him to accept, who had intimated,—"The sacrifices of God are a broken and contrite heart."—It was the death of a pure and perfect human being sustaining and discharging the penalty due to human depravity, and thereby acquiring an equitable claim to—"see of the travail of his soul and to be satisfied,"—by becoming the author of eternal salvation to all that obey him.* If in this inquiry the mysterious association of the divine with the human nature of Christ, which is so plainly revealed in Scripture, has hitherto received little notice, it has been for the obvious reason that with the Saviour's sufferings and death his human nature alone was directly concerned.

* Psalm 51, v. 16, 17;—Isaiah, chap. 53, v. 10, 11;—John, chap. 1, v. 29. 35, 36;—Heb. chap. 5, v. 9.

It may now, however, be appropriately remarked, that the happiness which he enjoyed from divine communion, and the misery which he endured from its loss, must both have been unspeakably augmented by this association, which moreover imparted an infinite dignity and value to his atoning sacrifice. The demonstration of the immediate or physical cause of the death of Christ which has now been given serves, therefore, to illustrate and confirm the scriptural doctrine of atonement; which, when rightly understood, is evidently worthy of universal acceptance, demanding alike the homage of the understanding, and the adoration of the heart.

CHAPTER II.

ON THE TYPES AND PROPHECIES OF THE OLD TESTAMENT IN RELATION TO THE DEATH OF CHRIST.

EVANGELICAL religion, the remedy which God has provided for the restoration of human nature from its fallen and degenerate state to his favor and friendship, although revealed with more or less clearness at different periods of the world, has always been essentially one and the same. Previously to the advent of the Saviour, it could scarcely be represented otherwise than through the medium of types and prophecies, with which both the patriarchal and the Mosaic dispensations were therefore duly provided. In the preceding chapter it was shown that the peculiar cause and manner of the death of Christ, now presumed to have been demonstrated, furnish a new and powerful illustration of the principle of atonement, the fundamental doctrine of the gospel. In the present one it will be shown that the same fact throws a remarkable light on the types and prophecies of the Old Testament relative to the same subject, and that some of them could not by any other means have been explained or fulfilled.

Of scriptural prophecies, or divine predictions respecting coming events, it seems to be a necessary rule that, until the time of their accomplishment, they are to a certain extent mysterious and obscure; for it is obvious that an unreserved disclosure of futurity to the human race would in general be incompatible with their actual condition, as well as with the regular accomplishment of the events predicted. It is indeed the dictate of revelation, as well as of reason,—"that no prophecy of Scripture furnishes its own interpretation;"—and the very circumstance, that precisely such an amount of information is in this manner afforded as tends to do good, without being liable to abuse, is in itself a strong proof of divine superintendence.* Another, and not less striking proof of the same kind is suggested by the connection of these prophecies with appropriate types; that is, with familiar illustrations of important facts or principles by sensible and similar objects. Owing to the happy combination of these two modes of instruction, the one supplying certainty, the other clearness, those cardinal truths of Christianity which are necessary for salvation were from the earliest times sufficiently declared and inculcated for practical purposes. No sooner had the first parents of mankind fallen from their original state of innocence and happiness, than it pleased God to give them a prediction, and a type of restoration. The prediction, remarkable for its sententious brevity, assured them that one of their descendants, who should be in a peculiar sense—"the seed of the woman"—would crush the head of Satan, the infernal serpent by whom they had been beguiled into sin; and that the victor himself would be wounded in the conflict.† The type consisted in the rite of animal sacrifice, appointed at the same time as the basis of acceptable worship, plainly intimating that for the reconciliation of sinners to God, the violent death of a suitable victim, offered to him as their substitute, was absolutely necessary. Hence originated

* 2 Peter, chap. 1, v. 19-21. Τοῦτο πρῶτον γινώσκοντες, ὅτι πᾶσα προφητεία γραφῆς ἰδίας ἐπιλύσεως οὐ γίνεται.
† Gen. chap. 3, v. 14, 15;—2 Corinth. chap. 11, v. 3;—1 Tim. chap. 2, v. 13, 14;—Heb. chap. 2, v. 14, 15;—Revel. chap. 12, v. 9; chap. 20, v. 1, 2.

the use of skins for vesture, which by his command they then adopted, and by which he practically taught them that, although in the dignity of their native innocence they had no need of clothing, they could not as fallen creatures be permitted to enter his presence, except in the garb of atonement. The prediction conjoined with the type conveyed to them therefore the important information, that the future Saviour would be one of their race, yet descended from a female parent only; and, as such an event implies divine interposition, and every work of God is perfect, would possess a pure and immaculate human nature, wherein by the sacrifice of himself he would render an atonement for the sins of mankind, and deliver them from the tyranny of Satan, who by instigating his death would unwittingly contribute to the destruction of his own power. Thus, by the divine prerogative of regarding the future as the past, Christ was "the lamb slain from the foundation of the world, ... whom God"—says the apostle Paul,—"foreappointed [to be] a propitiatory [sacrifice] through faith in his blood, to demonstrate his justice, because of the seeming impunity of previous sins through the forbearance of God, to demonstrate his justice at the present time, [and to show] that he is just even in justifying him that believeth in Jesus;"—a passage of the greatest value, and, with the exception of a somewhat similar one in the first epistle of Peter, almost unique. It is highly probable that, owing to their peculiar position, as well as to their superior knowledge derived from former intercourse with the Deity, these comparatively brief declarations were sufficient for the spiritual instruction and guidance of the primeval pair, and through them of their antediluvian descendants. At that early period, however, as in later times, the gracious plan of salvation, although cordially embraced by a few, was by the majority of men rejected to their own perdition.

It was, for example,—" by faith that Abel offered to God a more complete sacrifice than Cain, and on that account is recorded [in Scripture] as a just person, God [himself] testifying concerning his gifts;"—while Cain, who presuming on the sufficiency of mere natural religion repudiated the atonement, was disapproved, and still persisting in the same evil course, incurred the guilt of fratricide, and the penalty of malediction.* By this solemn transaction it was plainly proved that animal oblations, representing the sacrifice of Christ, were divinely instituted from the beginning; and this simple but expressive rite was ever afterward employed for the same purpose till, as the shadow gives place to the substance, the type was at length superseded by the reality.

Still further to designate the purity and beneficence of the future Saviour, a distinction was also established between clean and unclean animals, those only being accepted for sacrifice which exhibit a mild and gentle nature, subsist on vegetable food, and are friendly and serviceable to mankind. Thus—" Abel brought of the firstlings of his flock, and of the fat thereof,"—as an offering to the Lord; and after escaping from the deluge,—" Noah built an altar to the Lord, and took of every clean beast, and of every clean fowl, and offered burnt-offerings on the altar."—The animals which Abraham was directed to sacrifice, on his admission into the Israelitish covenant, were the heifer, the goat, the sheep, the dove, and the pigeon; but, when at a later period he was commanded to present his only son Isaac as a burnt-offering on Mount

---

* "Ὃν προέθετο ὁ θεὸς ἱλαστήριον διὰ τῆς πίστεως ἐν τῷ αὐτοῦ αἵματι, εἰς ἔνδειξιν τῆς δικαιοσύνης αὐτοῦ, διὰ τὴν πάρεσιν τῶν προγεγονότων ἁμαρτημάτων ἐν τῇ ἀνοχῇ τοῦ θεοῦ, πρὸς ἔνδειξιν τῆς δικαιοσύνης αὐτοῦ ἐν τῷ νῦν καιρῷ, εἰς τὸ εἶναι αὐτὸν δίκαιον, καὶ δικαιοῦντα τὸν ἐκ πίστεως Ἰησοῦ.— Romans, chap. 3, v. 23-26;—Gen. chap. 4, v. 1-12;—Heb. chap. 11, v. 4;—1 Peter, chap. 1, v. 18-21;—Rev. chap. 13, v. 8.

Moriah, he received a significant intimation, that the lamb provided by God as the true atoning victim for the sins of the world would be, like Isaac, a human being, and an only and well-beloved son.* As a recompense of his faith and obedience, Abraham now received a renewed promise, accompanied with an oath, that in his seed all the families of the earth should be blessed; and anticipated with joy the day of Christ, which he was thus enabled to see afar off. His pious successors—"Isaac and Jacob, joint-heirs with him of the same promise,"—publicly professed their faith and hope in the future Redeemer, through the same divinely-appointed rite of animal sacrifice.† The suitableness and significancy of this rite, in reference to the purpose which it was designed to answer, cannot be better expressed than in the words of Dr. Pye Smith, in his work on the priesthood of Christ.—"A sacrifice, properly so called,"—observes this excellent author,—"is the solemn infliction of death on a living creature, generally by effusion of its blood, in a way of religious worship; and the presenting of this act to the Deity, as a supplication for the pardon of sin, and a supposed means of compensation for the insult and injury thereby offered to his majesty and government. . . . Let us in imagination view the striking scenery of a patriarchal or Levitical sacrifice. A victim is selected, the best of the flock or the herd, without blemish or defect. It is brought before the altar of the Lord, its owner lays his hand upon its head, its life-blood flows upon the ground, it is divided and burned with fire; while the conscious sinner sees his own desert, and prays,—'Now, O Lord! I have sinned, I have committed iniquity, I have rebelled, thus and thus have I

---

* Gen. chap. 4, v. 3; chap. 7, v. 1, 2, 7–9; chap. 8, v. 20, 21; chap. 15, v. 8, 9; chap. 22, v. 1, 2;—Levit. chap. 1, v. 1–3, 10, 14.

† Gen. chap. 15; chap. 22, v. 1–18; chap. 26, v. 23–25; chap. 33, v. 18–20;—John, chap. 8, v. 56;—Heb. chap. 11, v. 8–10.

done; but I return in repentance to thy presence, and be this my expiation!' .... In this solemn and affecting manner was it declared to ages and generations, that—'God is the righteous judge, of purer eyes than to behold evil, and who cannot countenance iniquity, that his wrath is revealed from heaven against all ungodliness and unrighteousness of men, that the wages of sin is death, that there is forgiveness with the Lord and plenteous redemption, but that without the shedding of blood there is no remission.'* .... The ancient sacrifices were originally designed as symbols, emblems, and representations of the great work, for the effecting of which the Messiah was promised to fallen man. In support of this proposition, our first article of evidence is deduced from explicit declarations of the Old Testament.—'Sacrifice and offering thou wouldst not. A body hast thou prepared for me. Burnt-offering and sin-offering thou requirest not. Then said I, Lo I come! In the volume of the book it is written of me, I delight to do thy will, O God! yea, thy law is within my heart.'—The authority of the New Testament decides the application of this passage to the Messiah. The language of rejection applied to the legal offerings can be understood only as a strong denial of any intrinsic value or efficacy in them; for the command to offer those sacrifices was unquestionably binding upon the Hebrew nation, so long as the Levitical covenant continued in force. The leading idea in this distinguished passage manifestly is, that the Messiah should supersede all the sacrificial observances by actually performing *that very requisite*, that good pleasure of Jehovah, which they were totally unable to accomplish. Now, their known and avowed intention was—'to make an atonement before the Lord for the soul that had sinned, that it might be for-

* Psalm 7, v. 11; Psalm 130, v. 4, 7;—Habak. chap. 1, v. 12, 13;—Rom. chap. 1, v. 18; chap. 6, v. 22, 23;—Heb. chap. 9, v. 27, 28.

given him for all that he had done. . . . The blood I have given to you [to be offered] upon the altar, to make atonement for your souls, because it is the blood which maketh atonement for the soul.'—But to this point they could never attain. For this, as considered separately from their declarative intention, he that commanded them had no delight in them. *This*, therefore, must have been the object in which the divine complacency rested, this the grand purpose for which in due time the Messiah should be manifested,—'to put away sin by the sacrifice of himself.'" *

When the descendants of the patriarchs had grown into a nation, and after being delivered from their bondage in Egypt, were conducted by Moses and Aaron to the foot of Mount Sinai, and there brought into covenant with God as his chosen and peculiar people, the system of types and prophecies respecting Christ was more fully developed. From that time till his entrance into the world,—" the law was our schoolmaster to bring us to Christ, [and] a shadow of good things to come;"—in other words, it was one of the chief objects of the Mosaic institution to announce and illustrate the great facts connected with his person and office, and more especially to show that he would become the Saviour of mankind, by suffering in their stead the divine malediction due to their sins.† Hence, under the Israelitish dispensation, the principle of atonement was typically represented on the largest scale. One of their tribes was wholly consecrated to religious offices, and the rest of the nation was commanded

---

* Dr. J. P. Smith, On the Sacrifice and Priesthood of Jesus Christ, etc., pp. 3, 4, 14–17, 19–21 ;—Levit. chap. 6, v. 1–7 ; chap. 17, v. 10–12 ;—Psalm 40, v. 6–8 ; Psalm 110, v. 4 ;—Heb. chap. 9, v. 24–26 ; chap. 10, v. 1–10.

† Galat. chap. 3, v. 21–26 ;—Coloss. chap. 2, v. 16, 17 ;—Heb. chap. 8, v. 1–6 ; chap. 10, v. 1–10.

to provide for its maintenance, and to reverence its authority. To intimate the constant presence of God with his people as their benefactor and protector, he commanded that a splendid tent, afterward exchanged for a still more magnificent temple, should be erected in the midst of them, like a royal palace, where he would statedly dispense his favors, and receive their homage and adoration. But none could enjoy these privileges except through the medium of a figurative atonement, which was, therefore, continually exhibited in a most distinct and impressive manner. With the exception of the sacred tribe, the worshippers were never admitted into the temple itself, but only into its outer court, where twice every day animal sacrifices were offered on a spacious brazen altar. At each of these times, while some of the priests were thus engaged, others within the sanctuary burnt incense on a smaller golden altar, whence a cloud of fragrance, ascending before the most holy place which symbolized the divine presence, signified that, in virtue of the atoning sacrifice wherein they had just participated, the prayers and thanksgivings of the people were accepted by God. Besides these constant and ordinary rites, others still more specific and expressive were occasionally interposed, by which this figurative mode of representation was rendered complete. It was, moreover, supported throughout by a corresponding series of predictions, delivered by prophets raised up from time to time, and qualified by superior wisdom and virtue, as well as by an extraordinary endowment of the Holy Spirit, to be the religious instructors of the Israelitish nation, to write their annals, and to foretell future events, particularly those which related to the promised Messiah. With a view to prevent interference and abuse on the part of profane persons, while communicating sufficient information for the benefit of the pious and well-disposed, these predictions are, with a few remarkable exceptions, brief, partial, and intermixed with other matters. Their separate impression is hereby somewhat weakened; but when collected and arranged, they are found to be so copious, distinct, and precise, as to resemble history rather than prophecy. Retrospectively considered, it seems indeed wonderful that previously to their accomplishment they were not recognized and opposed, and that no Celsus or Porphyry should have subsequently arisen, to denounce them as the forgeries of a later age. The consummate skill displayed in this administration of the prophecies concerning Christ, as likewise in their conjunction with types and ceremonies, which silently presented the same testimony in a form adapted to all capacities, affords a strong proof of the truth and divine origin of the Scriptures of the Old Testament.

A still stronger proof, if possible, is furnished by the event itself; since it involved conditions so singular, complex, and apparently incompatible, that, as formerly remarked, by no wisdom or power less than those of the Deity could they have been either anticipated or fulfilled. That the death of Christ should exactly agree with all the types and prophecies by which it had been previously announced, was obviously necessary; and in various parts of the New Testament this necessity is accordingly affirmed with a degree of earnestness and solemnity, well calculated to rebuke the licentious practice which is sometimes adopted, of suppressing or evading positive predictions of Scripture, merely because it is difficult to conceive how they could be realized. Thus, when Christ on the day of his resurrection conversed with the two disciples travelling to Emmaus,—" he began from Moses, and [proceeding through] all the prophets, explained to them throughout the Scriptures the things respecting himself;"—and immediately before his ascension said to the apostles— " These [are] the words which I spake to you while [I was] yet with you, that all which was written concerning me in the law of Moses, in the prophets, and in the psalms, must be fulfilled. Then he opened their minds to understand the Scriptures, and said to them, Thus it is written, and thus it was necessary that Christ should suffer, and rise from the dead on the third day, and that repentance and discharge of sins should be proclaimed in his name to all the Gentiles, beginning from Jerusalem."*—In like manner Peter, when addressing the vast multitude in that city on the miraculous cure of the man who had been lame from his birth, after reproaching them with—" killing the prince of life,"—observed,—" Now I know, brethren, that ye did [this] in ignorance, as [did] also your rulers, but the sufferings which by the mouth of all his prophets God had before declared that Christ should undergo, he hath thus accomplished;"—and, after quoting a suitable passage from the writings of Moses, added,—" Yea, and all the prophets who have spoken, from Samuel downward, have also announced these days."—So, in his first epistle to the Corinthian Christians, Paul reminds them,—" I delivered to you at the beginning [the same gospel] which I received [namely], that Christ died on account of our sins, according to the Scriptures, and that he was buried, and rose again on the third day according to the Scriptures." —His discourse at the synagogue of Antioch, in Pisidia, commenced with these words,—" Brethren of the race of Abraham! and [all others] among you who fear God, to you is the message of this salvation sent. For they that dwell at Jerusalem, and their rulers, having neither recognized [Christ], nor [understood] the words of the prophets which are read every sabbath-day, fulfilled [them] by condemning [him]. Although they did not find [in him] any offence deserving of death, they requested Pilate that he might be slain; and, when they had accomplished all that

* Luke, chap. 24, v. 25–27, 44–47.

was written concerning him, they took [him] down from the tree, [and] laid [him] in a tomb; but God raised him from the dead."* Finally, in his celebrated defence before Agrippa, the same apostle said of himself,—"Having received help from God I continue to this day, bearing witness to small and great, [yet] without stating any thing more than both the prophets and Moses predicted [namely], that Christ should suffer [death], [be] the first to rise from the dead, [and] show light to the people [of Israel], and to the Gentiles."

From these and other scriptural explanations it is evident that almost all the types of Christ under the Mosaic dispensation, such as the daily sacrifice, the paschal lamb, the scape-goat, the sin-offering, etc., intimated that his death would be that of an atoning victim, vicariously suffered for the expiation of human guilt; agreeably to which his forerunner, John the Baptist, publicly proclaimed him to be—" the lamb of God, that taketh away the sin of the world."—The predictions of the Old Testament relative to this momentous subject give a similar representation, strengthened by the superior fulness, perspicuity, and authority derived from written language. With the types and prophecies thus interpreted, the facts of Christ's death, as recorded in the New Testament, exactly and exclusively correspond; and the internal evidence of truth furnished by a connected view of the whole is like—" a threefold cord, which is not quickly broken." †—In the following remarks, the principal particulars of this evidence will be produced and illustrated. To make atonement for the sins of the world, it was necessary that Christ should possess a pure and perfect human nature,

---

* Acts, chap. 3, v. 13-18; 22-24; chap. 13, v. 26-30;—1 Corinth chap. 15, v. 3, 4.

† Eccles. chap. 4, v. 9-12;—John, chap. 1, v. 29, 36;—Acts, chap 26, v. 22, 23.

and in that nature voluntarily suffer the malediction due to human depravity. It has been shown that in his case the divine malediction consisted in a partial loss of God's protection and a temporary loss of his communion, the former constituting its outward manifestation, the latter its intrinsic reality; and that the result of this infliction was intense mental agony, terminating in sudden death by rupture of the heart, attended with a copious effusion of the heart's blood into its containing capsule, and a subsequent separation of that blood into its solid and liquid ingredients. Marvellous and unparalleled as was this combination of circumstances, it is depicted with almost equal clearness in the types and prophecies of the Old Testament, as in the narratives of the evangelists. In reference to its outward manifestation, the malediction was necessarily confined to the channel of divine institution. It could not have been legitimately pronounced except by the Jewish hierarchy, nor fully sustained except by a member of the Mosaic covenant. Hence Christ was—"born under the law, that he might redeem those [who are] under the law;"—and thereby became subject to the authority of its priesthood, who, while professing to expect the promised Messiah, were devoted to worldly affections, and predetermined not to acknowledge any one in that capacity, unless he were a powerful and magnificent prince. The lowly and indigent Jesus of Nazareth was therefore the object of their aversion and contempt; and they firmly persuaded themselves that, should the nation be induced by his discourses or his miracles to accept him as their leader, the result would be ruinous to their prosperity, and perhaps fatal to their existence.* They had, however, little ground of apprehension, for in their rejection of his claims, and their hostility to his person, they were zealously seconded by the great body of Israel-

* John, chap, 11, v. 45-50;—Galat. chap. 4, v. 4, 5.

ites assembled at the paschal and other festivals in Jerusalem; and it was thus demonstrated that, in spite of their superior religious advantages, both priests and people thoroughly participated in the general depravity of mankind, and were in consequence abandoned to judicial blindness, and to the most culpable and pernicious delusions.

When Jesus was arraigned before the Sanhedrim, he was accordingly declared guilty of blasphemy, and deserving of death, merely for avowing his true character as the Messiah, which had not only been proclaimed by John the Baptist, but also publicly and repeatedly acknowledged by the Deity himself. Had they possessed civil power as well as sacerdotal authority, they would on that occasion, in conformity with the directions of the law of Moses respecting such offences, have dispatched him by stoning; and his dead body, after having been suspended or crucified, would have been cast the same day before sunset into some common and dishonored grave. The law in question is thus cited by Josephus:—"He that blasphemeth God, let him be stoned, and let him hang upon a tree all that day, and then let him be buried in an ignominious and obscure manner."—To the same effect he remarks in another part of his works:—"The Jews used to take so much care of the burial of men, that they took down those that were condemned and crucified, and buried them before the going down of the sun." But such a mode of death, involving the semblance only of malediction, not its reality, would have been unfit for the purpose; and in order to fulfil the conditions of atonement, it was necessary that he should be crucified alive. Hence, as this cruel and infamous punishment was not in use among the Israelitish people when governed by their own laws, they were at that critical period placed by divine Providence under the dominion of the Romans, by whom it was habitually practised.* But the Roman procurator was neither obliged nor disposed to execute the sentence of death pronounced against Jesus by the Jewish Sanhedrim on the ground of blasphemy, and they were therefore under the necessity of transforming that accusation into one of sedition against the state, before they could obtain a corresponding sentence from the civil tribunal. Of the falsehood of this latter charge the governor, after due inquiry, was fully convinced. In a private conference Christ explained to him, as he had formerly done to his own countrymen, that, although he was truly a king, and in a certain sense the king of the Jews, yet his kingdom was purely spiritual, and totally unconnected with the politics of the present world. On hearing this, Pilate, who probably regarded such a kingdom as the delusion of a visionary mind, acquitted him of all blame, and earnestly labored to release him; but having been guilty of great abuses in his government, fearful of being accused to the emperor as a favorer of usurpation, and alarmed by the growing violence of the multitude, he was at length induced to comply with their demands, by ordering the crucifixion of their innocent victim. Nothing could, however, be more evident than that in so doing he was merely the instrument of the Jewish priesthood and people, who, by their outrageous conduct before the judgment-seat, and their savage triumph at the place of execution, openly avowed that they were the principal, although not the immediate agents in the death of Jesus, and that their chief object in accomplishing it was to deny on behalf of

---

* The crucifixion of eight hundred Jewish prisoners at Jerusalem by their king Alexander Jannæus, forms no exception to this statement; since that prince was a usurper and a tyrant, who violated the laws of Moses, as well as those of justice and humanity. Levit. chap. 24, v. 10–16;—Deuteron. chap. 21, v. 22, 23;—Whiston's Josephus, vol. i. p. 188; vol. ii. pp. 243, 244; vol. iv. p. 87.

the nation at large his claim to be the predicted Messiah, and as they supposed effectually to defeat it. Hence, the apostles and their associates soon afterward charged them, in the most direct manner, with being the authors of this judicial murder. Speaking of Christ to the people assembled at Jerusalem on the subsequent day of Pentecost, Peter boldly affirmed,—" This man, having been delivered up by the determinate council and foreknowledge of God, ye took, [and] by the hands of wicked men crucified and slew." *—The language which they addressed on this subject to the Sanhedrim was equally strong, as appears from the following speech of the same apostle, when first arraigned before them :—"Rulers of the people, and elders of Israel! If we are this day examined concerning the benefit [conferred] on the lame man, [and] the means by which he has been healed, be it known to you all, and to all the people of Israel, that by the name of Jesus Christ of Nazareth, whom ye crucified, [but] whom God raised from the dead, [even] by him does this man stand before you whole. This is the stone which was set at naught by you builders, [but] which has become the [head] stone of the corner." †—The prominent part taken by the Jewish people and their rulers in this transaction did not, however, exculpate Pontius Pilate and Herod Antipas, the legitimate governors of the nation, from their share in its guilt. They were well aware of the innocence of Christ, and, humanly speaking, it was not less in their power than it was their duty to have protected him ; yet, through fear or indifference, they basely abandoned him to his enemies, and thereby rendered themselves equally responsible for the crime of his crucifixion.

Such were the principal external circumstances which

* Acts, chap. 2, v. 22, 23.
† Psalm 118, v. 22, 23 ;—Matt. chap. 21, v. 42-44 ;—Acts, chap. 3, v. 13-15 ; chap. 4, v. 8-12 ; chap. 5, v. 29-31 ; chap. 7. v. 51, 52.

attended this awful event; and it will now be shown how exactly they were intimated long before, more especially in reference to the peculiar mode and cause of the death of Jesus, by the types and prophecies of the Mosaic dispensation. That all the animal sacrifices under the law were types of the one great sacrifice offered by Christ, is plainly declared by the apostle Paul, in his epistle to the Hebrews. It is also intimated in numerous other passages both of the New and Old Testaments, particularly in the very remarkable one quoted by the same apostle from the fortieth psalm:—" On coming into the world [Christ] said,—Sacrifice and offering thou desiredst not, but a body hast thou prepared for me. In whole burnt-offerings and [sacrifices] for sin thou hadst no pleasure; then I said, Lo, I come! (In a chapter of the book it is written of me), to do thy will, O God!"*—In these few words several important truths are announced; namely, that the Levitical sacrifices, although divinely appointed, were incapable of rendering a real atonement for sin, and therefore merely prefigured the perfect and satisfactory sacrifice of Christ; that he came into the world to accomplish by his vicarious death the gracious designs of the Father, who prepared for him a body specially adapted for the purpose; but that his acceptance of this office was purely voluntary, and the result of his own free and benevolent choice. Among the many statements of the New Testament to this effect, the following may be cited as specimens. The apostle John says of Christ:—" Ye know that he was manifested to take away our sins, and that in him there is no sin."— Referring to himself and the other apostles, Paul remarks: —" We are ambassadors for Christ, as if God entreated you through us, we beseech [you] in Christ's stead, be ye reconciled to God; for he hath made him who knew not sin to be sin for us, that we might become the righteous-

* Psalm 40, v. 6-8;—Heb. chap. 10, v. 1-10.

ness of God by him. . . . We have not a high-priest who cannot sympathize with our infirmities, but was in all respects tried as we are, [yet] without sin; . . . . for it was fit that we should have such a high-priest [as is] holy, harmless, undefiled, separate from sinners, and made higher than the heavens. . . . . As beloved children, be ye therefore imitators of God, and walk in love, as Christ also loved us, and presented himself to God on our behalf, as a sweet-smelling oblation and sacrifice."—In a manner precisely similar Peter observes, in his first epistle to the Christian Jews of Asia Minor:—" Christ suffered once on account of sins, the just for the unjust, that he might bring us to God; . . . . for it was not by perishable things, [such as] silver or gold, that ye were redeemed from your unprofitable [religious] course derived by tradition from the fathers, but by the precious blood of Christ, as of a lamb without blemish, and without spot; . . . . who did no sin, neither was deceit found in his mouth; who when reviled did not revile in return, when he suffered did not threaten, but committed [himself] to him that judgeth righteously; who himself bore our sins in his own body on the tree, that we being delivered from sins should live unto righteousness, by whose stripes ye were healed; for ye were as sheep going astray, but have now returned to the shepherd and bishop of your souls." *—In the sentence last quoted, and in some other parts of the New Testament, the well-known and marvellous prophecy which occupies the fifty-third chapter of Isaiah, is clearly represented as having been fulfilled in Christ.—" Surely he hath borne our griefs, and carried our sorrows, yet we did esteem him stricken, smitten of God, and afflicted; but he [was] wounded for our transgressions, [he was] bruised

* 2 Corinth. chap. 5, v. 20, 21;—Ephes. chap. 5, v. 1, 2;—Heb. chap. 4, v. 14-16; chap. 7, v. 26; chap. 9, v. 13, 14;—1 Peter, chap. 1, v. 18 -21;—chap. 2, v. 21-25; chap. 3, v. 18;—1 John, chap. 3, v. 5.

for our iniquities, the chastisement of our peace [was] upon him, and with his stripes we are healed. All we like sheep have gone astray, we have turned every one to his own way, and the Lord hath laid on him the iniquity of us all. He was oppressed and he was afflicted, yet he opened not his mouth: he is brought as a lamb to the slaughter, and as a sheep before her shearers is dumb, so he openeth not his mouth."—The language of prophecy respecting the death of Christ, delivered more than seven hundred years before its occurrence, was therefore sufficiently explicit; and the typical indications of the same event, furnished by the Mosaic institution at a still earlier period, were not less so. Besides many other expiatory sacrifices presented on various occasions, two were celebrated in the court of the tabernacle or temple every day, such being the divine direction.—" This [is] the offering made by fire, which ye shall offer unto the Lord; two lambs of the first year without spot, day by day, [for] a continual burnt-offering; the one lamb shalt thou offer in the morning, and the other lamb shalt thou offer at even."

Types and prophecies thus concurred in announcing that the true lamb of God, who by a public and violent death would ultimately make atonement for the sins of the world, was to be perfect in body and mind, the demand of the law respecting every such victim being,—" It shall be perfect to be accepted: there shall be no blemish therein." —Agreeably to this requirement, as well as to the intrinsic exigency of the case, the human nature of Christ was, as he himself declared, specially provided by the Deity:— " A body hast thou prepared for me;"—and it is obvious that a body so provided could not have been otherwise than perfect. Hence, both the prophet and the apostle describe him as God's—" elect and righteous servant, in whom his soul delighted, who did no violence, neither [was any] deceit in his mouth."—In the primeval promise also, the future deliverer of mankind, who was to bruise the serpent's head, is significantly styled—" the seed of the woman;"—a term evidently implying supernatural interposition, by which alone the prediction could have been realized. The corresponding fact is appropriately supplied by Luke,—" the beloved physician,"—who intimates on angelic authority, that the Saviour's body was formed by the Holy Spirit in the womb of a pious Hebrew virgin, whereby he was entirely preserved from the hereditary corruption of fallen humanity, which he must otherwise have participated.* Among the numerous proofs of Christ's immaculate sanctity, it will be sufficient to refer to the testimony of the Deity himself, communicated more than once by a voice from heaven. The first declaration of this kind occurred at his baptism, when the Holy Spirit, descending in a visible form, conferred on him without measure the extraordinary and miraculous powers necessary for the discharge of his prophetical office, which then commenced, and also distinctly marked him out as the atoning victim of the new covenant; in allusion to which the Baptist thenceforth proclaimed him to be—" the lamb of God, that taketh away the sin of the world."—It was no doubt to this divine testimony that Christ alluded at a later period, when in the synagogue at Capernaum he said to the multitude whom he had recently fed:—" Labor not for the food which perisheth, but for that which endureth to eternal life, which the Son of Man will give you, for him hath God the Father sealed."†—It appears from the

* Gen. chap. 3, v. 14, 15;—Levit. chap. 22. v. 17-25;—Numb. chap. 28, v. 1-8;—Isaiah, chap. 28, v. 16; chap. 42, v. 1; chap. 53, v. 4-7, 9-11;—Luke, chap. 1, v. 34, 35;—Acts, chap. 8, v. 30-35;—Galat. chap. 4, v. 4, 5;—1 Peter, chap. 1, v. 18-20; chap. 2, v. 3-7, 21-23; chap. 3, v. 18;—2 Peter, chap. 1, v. 16-18.

† John, chap. 1, v. 29-39; chap. 3, v. 34; chap. 6, v. 27;—Acts,

rabbinical writings that, before a victim of this description was presented at the altar, it was most carefully examined within and without by the priests; and if found in the slightest degree faulty or defective, was rejected as inadmissible. That a similar practice prevailed among the ancient Egyptians is stated by Herodotus; who, after minutely describing the details of the process, observes,— "If in all these instances the bull appears to be unblemished, the priest fastens the byblus round his horns; he then applies a preparation of earth which receives the impression of his seal, and the animal is led away. This seal is of so great importance, that to sacrifice a beast which has it not, is deemed a capital offence."*—Although not positively mentioned in Scripture, it can scarcely be doubted that among the Jews also, approved victims were in like manner sealed by the priests; and it is, therefore, more than probable that when the Saviour said of himself, "Him hath God the Father sealed,"—he alluded to his public designation by divine authority as the true atoning victim, who was to give his flesh and blood for the life of the world.

This office was accordingly prefigured by all the animal sacrifices under the Mosaic law, but especially by those offered on the great day of expiation in the seventh month. On this solemn occasion a bullock and a goat were slaughtered as sin-offerings, the former for the priesthood, the latter for the people. A portion of their blood, accompanied with the fumes of incense, was presented to God by the high-priest in the inner sanctuary, and their bodies were consumed with fire without the camp or city, where the tabernacle or temple was situated. Another goat, ceremonially charged with the collective sins of the

chap. 10, v. 34-38;—2 Corinth. chap. 1, v. 21, 22;—Ephes. chap. 1, v. 12-14; chap. 4, v. 30.

* Beloe's Herodotus, vol. i. pp. 357, 358;—Job, chap. 38, v. 14.

nation, was at the same time conducted to a desert, and there abandoned. Deliverance from sin and its consequences by the intervention of an approved substitute, taking on himself the guilt of the transgressor, and suffering in his stead the punishment due to his offences, was by these rites plainly indicated; but to render the figure still more expressive, the animals thus devoted, although clean by nature, were regarded as polluted by the transaction, so that the priests and others who touched them became legally defiled, and were obliged to wash both their persons and their clothes. It is evident, however, that all this was representation only, not reality; a shadow of good things to come, not the substance. In the former point of view nothing could be more significant: in the latter, nothing could be more absurd; and the very grossness of the absurdity seemed to be an effectual security against any misapprehension or abuse. The following remarks from a treatise on the atonement, by the late Mr. Hey, of Leeds, may serve to elucidate this subject.—
" The true notion of a sacrifice for sin . . . . is that of something devoted to death, as the means of expiating guilt, or removing the obligation to punishment from the offender. . . . Both the goats appointed for a sin-offering are spoken of as making atonement, Lev. chap. 16, v. 5. They were both likewise made ceremonially accursed, and equally defiled the persons who touched them; for neither the man who led the scape-goat into the wilderness, nor he that carried out the flesh of the goat slain, could return into the camp, until he had washed his clothes, and bathed his flesh in water; from all which it is probable that the two goats were intended to point out the same thing in different respects: the one by its death, the *means* of pardon; the other by its removal into the wilderness, the *certainty* of it."—In another passage of the same work, the author judiciously observes,—" There is no necessity to

suppose that each circumstance of every institution which was designed to typify the method of our redemption by Christ, should have something corresponding to it in the antitype; because many, if not all of those institutions had other purposes to answer, besides that of being types of our redemption. The propitiatory sacrifices, as I have already observed, were branches of a political law, and had an immediate reference to crimes committed against God as civil governor. Various circumstances belonging to them might be needful in this respect, which were not intended to be typical. The same may be said with regard to the passover, and other types of Christ. Besides, so many things were to be prefigured concerning our Redeemer, that no one institution could exhibit them all, and, therefore, it was necessary that different types should be appointed. The whole ceremonial law did but afford an imperfect resemblance of the things which are typified; it was but the shadow of good things to come, and not the very image of the things."*—These rites were in fact merely types of the true atonement ultimately accomplished by Christ, and are thus explained by the apostle Paul in his epistle to the Hebrews;—"for, of those animals"—says he—"whose blood is brought as a sin-offering by the high-priest into the most holy place, the bodies are burned without the camp; on which account Jesus also, that he might consecrate the people with his own blood, suffered without the gate [of Jerusalem]; wherefore let us go forth to him without the camp, bearing his reproach."—The fact of his having been put to death without the camp was obscurely predicted by Christ himself a few days previously to the event, when in the parable of the proprietor and his husbandmen, he represented the latter as casting the heir out of the vineyard,

* W. Hey, Short Defence of the Doctrine of Atonement, pp. 57, 71, 76;—Levit. chap. 16, passim; chap. 23, v. 26–32.

and slaying him; but is more clearly stated by the beloved disciple.—" Bearing his cross,—says [John], Jesus " went forth to the place named after a skull, and in Hebrew called Golgotha, where they crucified him, and with him two others, one on each side, and Jesus in the midst;"— and, after describing his death, subjoins,—" Now in the place where he had been crucified was a garden, and in the garden a new tomb," etc.—These circumstances are decisive; for neither gardens, tombs, nor public executions were permitted within the walls of Jerusalem. The same fact is implied, although not quite so distinctly, by the other evangelists; among whom Matthew, when mentioning the report of Christ's resurrection carried to the chief priests by the soldiers who guarded the tomb, says, they—" came to the city;"—signifying, of course, that they had previously been out of it.* The passage last quoted from the epistle to the Hebrews is of great value and importance, for it proves that the death of Christ on the cross was in the divine estimation a real sacrifice, and the antitype of the various sin-offerings appointed by the Mosaic law. This was, indeed, the only mode in which such a sacrifice could have taken place, since by the same law, as well as by the law of nature, the formal immolation of human beings was absolutely prohibited; and one of the many charges brought against the ancient Israelites in their own Scriptures is, that—" they shed innocent blood, [even] the blood of their sons and of their daughters, whom they sacrificed unto the idols of Canaan, and the

---

* It is remarkable that Josephus often calls the Israelitish camp in the wilderness the city, and the tabernacle the temple; while in this part of the epistle to the Hebrews the apostle Paul adopts the opposite practice. See Whiston's Josephus, vol. i. pp. 146-148;—Matt. chap. 21, v. 36-39; chap. 27, v. 31-34; chap. 28, v. 11;—Mark, chap. 15, v. 20- 22;—Luke, chap. 20, 13-15; chap. 23, v. 26, 33;—John, chap. 19, v. 16-20, 41, 42;—Heb. chap. 13, v. 10-14.

land was polluted with blood."*—All the essential conditions of a sacrifice were, however, realized in the Saviour's crucifixion; for he was virtually offered up by the legitimate authorities, the Jewish priesthood, who with the other members of the Sanhedrim appeared on the occasion as principals, and of whom the Roman governor was merely the reluctant instrument. Yet, with all their power and malice, they were unable to deny the miracles which proved his mission, or to convict him of the smallest offence; but, on the contrary, were compelled indirectly to acknowledge that he was an innocent victim sacrificed, as they supposed, for the safety of the nation.

The crucifixion of Christ was thus prefigured in a lively manner by the Levitical sacrifices, wherein the violent death of a pure and perfect animal, and its oblation to God on account of sin in the presence of his assembled people, closely resembled the public execution of an innocent human victim. With these typical representations addressed to the senses, the special prophecies of the Old Testament on the same subject strikingly agree; particularly those contained in the fifty-third chapter of Isaiah, and the twenty-second psalm. That Christ died as an atoning sacrifice for the sins of his people, could not be more clearly stated than in the well-known words of the evangelical prophet, who by the privilege of inspiration describes the future as if it were already past.—" He [was] wounded for our transgressions, [he was] bruised for our iniquities, the chastisement of our peace [was] upon him, and with his stripes we are healed."—A little after the Deity himself is represented as declaring,—" He shall see of the travail of his soul, [and] shall be satisfied. By his knowledge shall my righteous servant justify many, for he shall bear their iniquities."—That his death should

* Psalm 106, v. 31-38;—Isaiah, chap. 57, v. 4, 5;—Ezek. chap. 16, v. 20, 21.

take place by a public execution, the result of a judicial sentence, is expressed in the following terms:—"He was taken from prison and from judgment, and who shall declare his generation? for he was cut off out of the land of the living, for the transgression of my people was he stricken."—The psalmist is still more explicit, and plainly intimates the specific mode of execution, namely, by crucifixion, the principal circumstances of which are detailed with a degree of minuteness, belonging to history rather than to prophecy. The derision of Christ by the priesthood and the people is thus anticipated.—"All they that see me laugh me to scorn, they shoot out the lip, they shake the head [saying], He trusted on the Lord [that] he would deliver him. Let him deliver him, seeing he delighted in him. . . . Many bulls have compassed me, strong [bulls] of Bashan have beset me round. They gaped upon me [with] their mouths, [as] a ravening and a roaring lion."—The narrative of the evangelists is precisely similar, and in some parts identical.—"Those who passed by reviled him, shaking their heads and saying, Aha! thou that destroyest the temple, and rebuildest [it] in three days, save thyself. If thou art the Son of God, come down from the cross. In like manner the chief priests also, jesting among themselves with the scribes and elders, said, he saved others, [but] cannot save himself. If he is the Christ, the chosen of God, the king of Israel, let him now come down from the cross, that we may see and believe. He trusted in God; let [God] now deliver him if he will have him; for he said, I am the Son of God."*—But, as before observed, the crucifixion of living persons, although common among some other nations, was not practised by the people of Israel: and hence, in language familiar to the Jews, who were in the

* Psalm 22, v. 7, 8, 12, 13;—Isaiah, chap. 53, v. 5, 8, 11;—Matt. chap. 27, v. 39-43;—Mark, chap. 15, v. 29-32;—Luke, chap. 23, v. 35.

habit of styling Gentiles—"dogs, the wicked, the profane," etc.,—the psalm proceeds to mark that peculiarity in the death of Christ.—"Dogs have compassed me, the assembly of the wicked have enclosed me, they pierced my hands and my feet. I may tell all my bones. They look [and] stare upon me : they part my garments among them, and cast lots upon my vesture."—The account given by the evangelists is the exact counterpart of this description.—" When the [Roman] soldiers had crucified Jesus, they took his outer garments, and divided them into four parts, for each soldier a part, as likewise his vest. Now the vest was without seam, woven from the top throughout; so they said one to another, Let us not rend it, but cast lots for it, [to settle] whose it shall be; in fulfilment of the Scripture which saith,—They parted my garments among them, and for my vesture they cast lots. Thus accordingly the soldiers did; for after parting his outer garments, they cast lots for them, [to settle] what each man should take. It was the third hour when they crucified him; and they sat down and guarded him there, while the people stood looking on."—A remark formerly made may here be repeated; namely, that the prophecies of Scripture are usually clear or obscure, in proportion as there was more or less danger that the information afforded by them might be abused by human interference. In the present instance, those which relate to the Jewish priesthood and people are so full and distinct that, had not their minds been thoroughly blinded by prejudice and passion, in consequence of which they did not understand the words of the prophets read in their synagogues every sabbath-day, it is difficult to conceive how they could have fulfilled them by condemning and persecuting Christ. With respect to the Roman soldiers no such danger was to be apprehended, and their proceedings on this occasion are therefore still more plainly predicted. After crucifying their prisoner, they were to take possession of his clothing, dividing for that purpose his outer garments into portions, but disposing of his vesture without rending it, by lot. The design and use of this minute intimation, in itself of no importance, are sufficiently obvious; namely, to identify Jesus of Nazareth as the Saviour of the world, by showing that in him alone all the numerous and extraordinary circumstances ascribed to the Messiah in the Old Testament actually concurred. A similar remark may be made on the prediction of Isaiah, that, although by the enemies of Christ his grave was appointed among the wicked, his tomb should be with a rich man; or, as it is accurately rendered by Dr. Henderson:

> "They had also assigned him his grave with the wicked,
> But he was with the rich after his death."

This prediction, than which few things could at the time have appeared more improbable, was wonderfully accomplished when it might least have been expected, by the pious zeal of Joseph of Arimathea, a rich man, and a member of the Sanhedrim, who, having promptly obtained the necessary permission from Pontius Pilate, rescued the body of Jesus from the hands of those who would otherwise have speedily thrown it, together with those of the malefactors, into some ignominious pit; and having with the aid of Nicodemus embalmed it according to the Jewish manner, gave it an honorable interment in his own new tomb, hewn out of the native rock in the immediate vicinity of the place of crucifixion, and wherein no one had previously been deposited.*

---

* Dr. Henderson's Isaiah, p. 384;—Psalm 22, v. 16-18;—Isaiah chap. 53, v. 9;—Matt. chap. 27, v. 35, 36, 57-60;—Mark, chap. 15, v 24, 42-46;—Luke, chap. 23, v. 33-36, 50-54;—John, chap. 19, v. 23 24, 38-42;—Acts, chap. 2, v. 22, 23.

The singular combination of Jews and Gentiles, notwithstanding their mutual enmity, in opposing Christ, is likewise noticed in the second Psalm, which was quoted and explained in this sense by the twelve apostles shortly after the day of Pentecost:—"Why do the heathen rage, and the people imagine a vain thing? The kings of the earth set themselves, and the rulers take council together against the Lord, and against his anointed [saying], Let us break their bands asunder, and cast away their cords from us."—In another part of the prophetical Scriptures,—the book of Daniel,—the particular Gentile nation which would be engaged in this transaction is clearly indicated, as—"the fourth kingdom upon earth," —that is, the Roman empire, under which crucifixion was a common punishment more especially for political offences, and in the eastern provinces. In this sublime book, the Roman empire, like its predecessors, the Babylonian, Persian, and Grecian, is depicted by the emblem of a ferocious wild beast; and its character is drawn too graphically to be mistaken.—"The fourth beast shall be the fourth kingdom upon earth, which shall be diverse from all kingdoms, and shall devour the whole earth, and shall tread it down, and break it in pieces. . . . The fourth kingdom shall be strong as iron. Forasmuch as iron breaketh in pieces and subdueth all [things]; and as iron that breaketh all these, shall it break in pieces and bruise."—That the kingdom of God, that is, the gospel dispensation, portrayed by a stone cut out of a mountain without hands, and becoming itself a great mountain which fills the whole earth, should spring up under the Roman Empire, and ultimately overthrow it, is thus plainly announced:—"And in the days of these kings, shall the God of heaven set up a kingdom which shall never be destroyed; and the kingdom shall not be left to other people, [but] it shall break in pieces and consume all these kingdoms, and it shall stand forever."—The manner in which the incipient fulfilment of this prophecy is intimated by the evangelist Luke, is at once simple and effective.—" Now in those days there went forth a decree from Augustus Cæsar, that the whole empire should be registered. . . . In the fifteenth year of the reign of Tiberius Cæsar, Pontius Pilate being governor of Judea, etc., . . . a message from God came to John the son of Zachariah, in the wilderness. . . . In those days "—adds Matthew,—" appeared John the Baptist, preaching in the wilderness of Judea, and saying Repent, for the kingdom of heaven is at hand."*—Among the minor types or illustrations of crucifixion, may be reckoned the brazen serpent which by divine command Moses erected in the wilderness, when the Israelites on account of their murmurings against God were plagued with serpents, whereby many of them were destroyed; but, on looking toward the brazen serpent, all who had been bitten and survived, recovered. The aged Simeon may be supposed to have had this type in view, when he said of the infant Jesus to Mary his mother:—" Behold! this [child] is set for the fall and rising again of many in Israel, and for a sign which shall be spoken against (yea, a sword shall pierce through thine own soul also), that the thoughts of many hearts may be revealed."—But the principal ground for this opinion is that Christ himself, in his conference with Nicodemus, made a similar application of the fact:—" As Moses lifted up the serpent in the wilderness, even so must the Son of Man be lifted up; that whosoever believeth in him should not perish, but have eternal life;"—and on two other occasions remarked, that, when he had been thus lifted up or crucified, he would draw all men to

---

* Psalm 2, v. 1-3 ;—Daniel, chap. 2, v. 31-45 ; chap. 7, v. 7, 23-27 ; —Matt. chap. 3, v. 1, 2 ;—Luke, chap. 2, v. 1; chap. 3, v. 1, 2 ;—Acts chap. 4, v. 23-28.

himself; and that his Jewish adversaries, in spite of their inveterate repugnance to the doctrine of the cross, would then at length discover his true character and office.*

The indications respecting the Saviour's death, furnished by the types and prophecies of the Old Testament, are not, however, confined to its outward circumstances, but extend to its intrinsic nature, and show that it was, not in appearance only, but in reality, the death of an atoning victim suffering the divine malediction due to human transgression. The Gentile punishment of crucifixion alive was the only one whereby these indications could have been suitably accomplished, because it was the only one in which the sign and the reality of malediction could be effectually united. Hence both the punishment and the agents by whom it was to be executed were so plainly designated in the ancient Scriptures; and, as it was not in use among the Jews, they were at that critical period placed by divine providence under the dominion of the Romans, among whom it was familiar. The period may well be termed critical; for in Daniel's celebrated prophecy of the seventy weeks it had been accurately defined, and no other period before or after would either have corresponded in point of time, or have supplied the necessary conditions. As in the atoning sacrifice which he offered Christ was the priest as well as the victim, it was necessary, according to the law of Moses, that at the time of his death he should not be less than thirty years of age. Had it occurred under the reign of Jewish princes, either twenty-three years earlier, when Archelaus was ethnarch of Judea, or eight years later, when Herod Agrippa was king of Palestine, it would not have been the death of the

* Numb. chap. 21, v. 4–9;—Isaiah, chap. 45, v. 20–25;—Zech. chap. 12, v. 10;—Luke, chap. 2, v. 34, 35; chap. 13, v. 22–30;—John, chap. 3, v. 14–17; chap. 8, v. 28; chap. 12, v. 30–31.

cross; and in the former case he would have been too young for the office. That he should be crucified alive by the hands of Romans, was not, however, sufficient; for, had he died on the cross in the ordinary manner, his death would have been that of a martyr only, not that of an atoning victim. To signify that he would not die in this manner, it was therefore ordained by the Mosaic law, which in such matters was wisely respected by the Roman governors of Judea, that those who were suspended on a tree should before sunset the same day be taken down and buried; and as crucified persons, if left to themselves, might continue alive on the cross for two or three days, the command implied that the death of Christ would be accelerated by some additional agency. The method usually employed for this purpose was that of breaking the legs, but the same law intimated that in his case there should be no such infliction; for concerning the paschal lamb, one of the principal types of Christ, it positively commanded,—" Ye shall not break a bone thereof: "—a prohibition which is accordingly thus applied by the apostle John.*

But the indications of prophecy on this point are not negative only, they also distinctly describe the agency by which the effect was to be produced; namely, agony of mind, under a sense of divine abandonment piously endured to expiate human guilt, and terminating in rupture of the heart, with effusion of the life's blood, and consequently premature and sudden death. The language of the evangelical prophet on these points is strong and unequivocal.—" All we like sheep have gone astray, we have turned every one to his own way, and the Lord hath laid on him the iniquity of us all. . . . It pleased the Lord to bruise him, he hath put [him] to grief. When thou shalt

* Exod. chap. 12, v. 43-46;—Numb. chap. 4, v. 1-3; chap. 9, v. 9-12;—John, chap. 19, v. 30-37;—1 Corinth. chap. 5, v. 7.

make his soul an offering for sin, he shall see [his] seed, he shall prolong [his] days, and the pleasure of the Lord shall prosper in his hand. He shall see of the travail of his soul, [and] shall be satisfied; by his knowledge shall my righteous servant justify many, for he shall bear their iniquities."—The mental agony of the Saviour could not be more forcibly depicted than by the expression,—"the travail of his soul;"—and this is declared to have been occasioned by divine infliction, in consequence of his becoming the righteous substitute of sinners, and bearing the iniquities of mankind. In the corresponding prophecy of Zechariah, the Deity is in like manner represented as saying,—" Awake, O sword! against my shepherd, and against the man [that is] my fellow, saith the Lord of hosts: smite the shepherd, and the sheep shall be scattered;"—a passage of which the import and application cannot be mistaken, since it is thus appropriated by Christ himself. In the twenty-second psalm, the very words in which he expressed his bitter sense of divine abandonment are accurately predicted:—"My God! my God! why hast thou forsaken me? [Why art thou so] far from helping me, [and from] the words of my roaring? O my God! I cry in the daytime, but thou hearest not, and in the night season, and am not silent."—A distinct reference seems here to be made to his mental sufferings both at Gethsemane, and at Golgotha, of which the former occurred during the night, and the latter during the day; as likewise to the loud cries which on each occasion were their natural, and almost necessary consequence. A little later, allusion is made to the other physical effects proceeding from the same cause, including bloody sweat, intense thirst, and ultimately rupture of the heart.—" I am poured out like water, and all my bones are out of joint; my heart is like wax, it is melted in the midst of my bowels. My strength is dried up like a potsherd, and my tongue cleaveth to my jaws, and thou hast brought me into the dust of death."*—Isaiah goes a step farther, and intimates that the Saviour's death was more immediately induced by a copious and rapid effusion of blood; but in order to perceive the full force of this intimation, it is necessary to modify in a slight degree the authorized English version of the passage, and to adopt that proposed by several eminent biblical critics of modern times; a version the more entitled to confidence because, although it strongly confirms the views here advocated, it was made without any knowledge of them. Of these versions, borrowed from Dr. Pye Smith's excellent work on the sacrifice and priesthood of Christ, the first is by the distinguished scholar, Sir J. D. Michaelis, professor at Göttingen, who died in 1791; the second by the celebrated professor of divinity in the University of Erlangen, Dr. G. F. Seiler, who died in 1807. The translation of Isaiah, chap. 53, v. 12, furnished by Michaelis is,—"Therefore will I give him a share of booty with the great ones, and he shall have the mighty ones for his spoil, since he hath poured out his life's-blood unto death, and was reckoned among malefactors; but he bare the sins of many, and will pray for the transgressors."—The version of Dr. Seiler is,—"Therefore I assign to him many for his booty, and he himself shall as his booty distribute the mighty; because he poured out his life's-blood unto death, because he was reckoned among the transgressors, because he hath borne the sins of many, and hath prayed for the transgressors."—When it is considered that the Hebrew term corresponding to soul is not unfrequently used in the sense of life, or life's-blood, and that in this passage the prophet is describing Christ as a sin-offering, a lamb led

---

* Psalm 22, v. 1, 2, 14, 15;—Isaiah, chap. 53, v. 6, 10, 11;—Zechar. chap. 13, v. 7;—Matt. chap. 26, v. 31;—Mark, chap. 14, v. 27;—Heb. chap. 5, v. 5-10.

to the slaughter to expiate the transgressions of many, there can be little doubt that he is alluding to the sacrificial effusion of his blood, typified by that of ordinary victims both under the patriarchal and the Mosaic dispensations, wherein the life's-blood of animals was by divine appointment made the ostensible means of purification, ransom, and atonement; and hence, in order to mark and maintain its ritual sanctity, its use as an article of food was prohibited on pain of death. In the strongest possible language the Deity is thus represented as declaring,—" Whatsoever man [there be] of the house of Israel, or of the strangers that sojourn among you, that eateth any manner of blood, I will even set my face against that soul that eateth blood, and will cut him off from among his people: for the life of the flesh [is] in the blood, and I have given it to you upon the altar to make an atonement for your souls; for it [is] the blood [that] maketh an atonement for the soul;"—and again,—" Be sure that thou eat not the blood, for the blood [is] the life, and thou mayest not eat the life with the flesh. Thou shalt not eat it, thou shalt pour it upon the earth as water. Thou shalt not eat it, that it may go well with thee, and with thy children after thee, when thou shalt do [that which is] right in the sight of the Lord."—The comment of the Jewish historian on these laws is remarkable.—" Moses " —says Josephus,—" entirely forbade us the use of blood for food, and esteemed it to contain the soul and spirit." *
—In order the more exactly to fulfil the divine directions in this respect, it was the practice of the Hebrew priests when slaughtering a victim, rapidly to divide all the large vessels of the neck, as well as the windpipe, with a sharp

---

* Whiston's Josephus, vol. i. p. 146;—Dr. J. P. Smith, On the Sacrifice and Priesthood of Jesus Christ, pp. 284-288, 294;—Gen. chap. 9, v. 2-5; —Levit. chap. 3, v. 17; chap. 7, v. 22-27; chap. 17, v. 10-14;—Deut. chap. 12, v. 15, 16, 23-27; chap. 15, v. 22, 23.

two-edged sword driven nearly to the backbone, so as to destroy the animal's life by the sudden effusion of the greater part of its blood, which was afterward solemnly sprinkled or poured out, as the symbol of atonement and propitiation. The process is well described by Outram in his treatise on sacrifices, who further remarks:—"The most sacred of all rites was the sprinkling of blood, whereby the life or soul of the victim was supposed to be offered to God, as the supreme lord of life and death; for, as in these religious acts whatsoever was laid on the altar of God was thought to be offered to him, so with the blood, as the vehicle of the life and soul, and sometimes even termed the life itself, the life and soul were supposed to be thus offered. Hence may be understood the passage in the Revelation of St. John,—'I saw under the altar the souls of those who had been slain on account of the word of God, and of the testimony which they had given;'— for the souls of whom he here speaks were, as the words themselves show, the souls of those who, like so many sacred victims, had shed their blood."[*]—That the blood of inferior victims represented that of Christ is declared in many parts of the New Testament, more especially by the apostle Paul in his epistle to the Hebrews, who observes,—"According to the law almost all things are purified by blood, and without effusion of blood there is no discharge [of sins. It was] therefore necessary that the types of heavenly things should be thus purified, but the heavenly things themselves by better sacrifices than these."—This view of the subject is well expressed by Rambach, who remarks that, under the Mosaic law,—"the atonement for sin was not made till all the blood of the animal was drained off and poured at the foot of the altar.

[*] Outram, De Sacrificiis, pp. 164–169;—Rambach, On the Sufferings of Christ, vol. iii. pp. 281, 282, 289–292;—Heb. chap. 4, v. 12;—Revel. chap. i. v. 16; chap. 6, v. 9–11.

Hence St. Paul says, that—'without shedding of blood there is no remission.'—The pouring forth the blood of the sacrifice at the foot of the altar represents with regard to Christ the abundant shedding of his blood on the cross, till the absolute separation of his body and soul. For it is said of Christ,—'He hath poured out his soul unto death;'—and consequently he poured out his blood with the utmost willingness and overflowing zeal for the honor of God, and the unspeakable good of mankind."*—But here a formidable difficulty presents itself. The ordinary death of the cross did not furnish the requisite condition. Instead of occurring suddenly by the effusion of the life's-blood, it was effected by slow exhaustion, and protracted torture. The scanty drainings of blood from the transfixed extremities could not satisfy the demands of the Levitical law; and if under that dispensation one of the inferior animals had been thus slain, it could not have been accepted as a victim at the altar. The stab with the soldier's spear might, in appearance at least, have answered the purpose, had it been given during life, but Jesus was already dead when it took place. The fatal hæmorrhage foretold in Scripture is moreover represented as the result, not of external violence but of inward grief, and in a certain sense as his own act;—"He poured out his life's-blood unto death."—During a long succession of ages the types and prophecies of Scripture announced that Christ would suffer the death of malediction, and of the cross; not, however, in the usual manner, nor yet by the fracture of his limbs, but by some extraordinary process connected with—"the travail of his soul,"—and terminating on the very day of his crucifixion in the effusion of his life's-blood, the indispensable medium of atonement. The key to this enigma has already been supplied. By voluntary suffering the divine malediction, of which the

---

* Rambach, as above cited;—Heb. chap. 9, v. 11-15, 19-23.

cross was the appointed emblem, Christ endured a degree of mental agony which, after previously forcing from him a bloody sweat, at length occasioned sudden rupture of the heart, attended with an internal discharge of blood proving instantly fatal. In order that there might be a public demonstration of this event, which otherwise would not have been perceived, it was further predicted,— "They shall look on him whom they pierced."—This actually happened some time after his death, and the immediate flow of blood and water, which followed the wound made in his side by the soldier's spear, proved that it had been preceded by rupture of the heart, which was likewise predicted in express terms:—"My heart is like wax, it is melted in the midst of my bowels."—Thus, as was intimated at the beginning, the peculiar cause of the death of Christ, which by a regular induction from the evangelical narrative has been ascertained as a fact, remarkably illustrates the entire series of types and prophecies relating to that solemn event, which could not indeed in any other manner have been completely fulfilled. These in turn, by their minute and perfect correspondence with the circumstances, afford, if that were necessary, an additional confirmation of the fact itself, and the whole transaction demonstrates with irresistible evidence the special interposition and superintendence of the Deity.

CHAPTER III.

ON THE NARRATIVES AND SYMBOLS OF THE NEW TESTAMENT IN RELATION TO THE DEATH OF CHRIST.

In the Scriptures of the New Testament, composed directly or indirectly by the apostles under the guidance of the Holy Spirit, the death of Christ occupies a prominent place, as the common centre or foundation of the entire system of evangelical truth therein delivered. Hence, if the explanation of the event which has now been offered is correct, it may be expected to elucidate and confirm all the representations given of it in that portion of the sacred volume, whether in the form of narratives and symbols by which the fact is described, or in that of doctrines and precepts by which it is applied to important purposes.

The four gospels are brief but graphic memoirs of the life of Christ on earth. Those of Matthew and John were composed by the apostles whose names they bear, those of Mark and Luke by eminent disciples under the superintendence of apostles, particularly Peter and Paul. They are all, however, similar in their origin, and equal in their authority, consisting of reports furnished by eyewitnesses and attendants of Christ, selected by himself as his ambassadors to the world, qualified for their office by the extraordinary influence of the Holy Spirit, and accredited by their personal character, their successful ministry, and their miraculous powers. All the gospels were published within a few years after the ascension of Christ, while the events which they commemorate were still recent, and the greater part of them well known to the inhabitants of the country where they occurred. The genuineness of these narratives was attested by the contemporary churches to whose care they were committed; and, with the exception of slight and immaterial variations, unavoidable when manuscripts are repeatedly copied, they have been transmitted unaltered to the present day. The earliest gospel was probably that of Luke, addressed to converted Greeks; the second that of Matthew, addressed to converted Jews. The third, that of Mark, is chiefly a harmonized epitome of the two preceding ones, omitting the preliminary transactions, and most of the longer discourses; and the last, that of John, is a supplemental gospel, furnishing many interesting particulars concerning the opposition made to Christ by the Jewish rulers and people, which could not have been conveniently related at an earlier period, and which this apostle was peculiarly qualified to describe.

In the narratives of the four evangelists, more especially when harmonized and combined, the outward circumstances connected with the sufferings of Christ are so admirably depicted, that by their aid the attentive reader is, after the lapse of eighteen centuries, rendered almost a spectator of the scene. While, however, the inspired writers faithfully record all that was seen and heard on the occasion, it is not probable that they understood, and it is certain that they do not explain the immediate cause of the Saviour's death. On the contrary, their accounts of it, although bearing all the marks of fidelity, appear at first sight so strange and mysterious, that some persons have deemed them incredible. Yet, when carefully examined, they are found to be perfectly natural and consistent, and while excluding every other interpretation, actually suggest that which has been so often repeated, and may now be regarded as demonstrated. The satisfactory solution which it affords of every difficulty, and its critical accordance with four independent reports, neither entirely similar, nor equally complete, are interesting facts, which strongly confirm the truth both of the narratives and of the explanation. After celebrating the paschal supper, and instituting his own, the evangelists state that Christ devoted a considerable time to the instruction and consolation of his apostles, and concluded the sacred engagement by a prayer to God, remarkable for its ardent and elevated piety. In reference to his human nature, he was now in the flower of his age, full of health and vigor, and perfect in body and mind; yet, on retiring with his disciples from the upper chamber in Jerusalem to the garden of Gethsemane, they represent him as suddenly falling into a state of consternation and distress so intense that, had he not been relieved by divine interposition, it would probably within the short space of an hour have terminated his life. Having, however, prayed to him who had the power to save him from death, he received supernatural aid, which enabled him to subdue the dreadful emotions by which he had been at first almost overwhelmed. Matthew and Mark express these emotions with corresponding emphasis, employing for the purpose the strongest terms which the Greek language could supply. They describe him as saying,—"My soul is exceedingly sorrowful, even unto death;"—and having thrown himself on the ground, as praying that, if possible, the hour might pass from him. Luke alone mentions that an angel was sent to strengthen him; on which, says the sacred historian,—"falling into an agony he prayed most earnestly, and his sweat became as it were clots of blood dropping to the ground."—John, the latest of the evangelists, takes no notice of the sufferings of

Christ at Gethsemane, evidently implying by his silence that the account given of them by his predecessors was accurate and complete. At the conclusion of this fearful hour, the Saviour resumed with astonishing rapidity his accustomed energy and composure. Although perfectly aware of all that was to befall him, he intrepidly went forth to meet the formidable party who were advancing to apprehend him; and before surrendering himself into their hands showed them that, had it been compatible with the object of his mission, he could easily have delivered himself from their power. He asked them whom they sought: they answered, Jesus of Nazareth; and, on his replying—"I am he, they drew backward, and fell to the ground."*—From that moment he maintained the same firm and dignified demeanor throughout the harassing scenes of his trials by the Sanhedrim, and by Pilate, as well as during the first three hours of his crucifixion; proving that there was nothing in the ordinary sufferings connected with that punishment which he could not have borne with fortitude. But another astonishing change now took place. At the moment of noon the peculiar sufferings of Gethsemane were renewed, although, conformably to the difference of circumstances, with less of outward manifestation than before. During three additional hours he hung on the cross in silent agony, aptly represented by the supernatural darkness which simultaneously covered the land. At the end of that time, Matthew and Mark relate that he complained of divine abandonment; John states that he declared all to be accomplished; and Luke that he commended his spirit to the care of his heavenly Father. All the evangelists describe his death as happening suddenly, and much earlier than could have been expected, while uttering in a remarkably

---

* Matt. chap. 26, v. 36-39;—Mark, chap. 14, v. 32-36;—Luke, chap. 22, v. 39-44;—John, chap. 18, v. 1-6.

loud voice these solemn and devout exclamations. Mark alone mentions the surprise of the Roman governor on hearing of so unexampled an occurrence, and John that, an hour or two later, one of the soldiers sent to dispatch the crucified persons found him dead; but from anxiety, as may justly be presumed, to make sure of the fact which he might otherwise have reasonably doubted, pierced the side of Christ with a spear, on which there immediately flowed out blood and water.

Now it is evident that each of these accounts is marvellous, and the combination of them all still more so. Yet, the latter alone furnishes the materials of the solution above given, the only one which perfectly agrees with each of the evangelical narratives taken separately, and with the whole united, but which none of them singly supply. For the extreme consternation of Jesus on entering the garden of Gethsemane, as particularly described by Matthew and Mark, an adequate cause is assigned by his then experiencing for the first time the terrors of divine abandonment, which occasioned him to fall prostrate on the ground, and almost destroyed him by the simple exhaustion of vital power. His agony and bloody sweat, mentioned by Luke alone, who as a physician was more likely than others to notice the occurrence, implied renovated strength, which the same evangelist accordingly ascribes to angelic agency. This enabled him to sustain a severe conflict between two opposite, but equally virtuous emotions; the desire of recovering his habitual communion with God, in which his happiness consisted, and the desire, by resigning that communion, of making an atonement for the sins of the world, which could by no other means have been accomplished. Of such a conflict, excessive action of the heart and bloody sweat were the natural consequences and exponents. The subsequent return of his ordinary firmness and tranquillity is satisfactorily accounted for by the temporary suspension, as predicted by himself a little before, of this peculiar mode of suffering; and the horror and distress which characterized the last three hours of its crucifixion by its renewal; although, owing to its having been previously experienced, it was now attended with less consternation than at first. The cause of this distress was plainly avowed by himself in the affecting words recorded by Matthew and Mark,—"My God! my God! why hast thou forsaken me?"—The first mentioned by John, and the loud exclamation described by all the evangelists, as well as by the apostle Paul, are the usual concomitants of overaction of the heart; and the sudden death of Christ in the midst of these exclamations is fully explained by the final rupture of that organ. To render the demonstration complete, John alone, who by standing near the cross had superior opportunities of observation, notices the subsequent piercing of his side with a spear by one of the soldiers, an act immediately followed by an effusion of blood and water, the necessary result of previous rupture of the heart, but which could not have occurred under any other circumstances. The critical accordance of the four gospels on this and other occasions with singular and complex realities, capable of being independently verified, but which there is every reason to believe the authors themselves did not at the time thoroughly comprehend, affords a striking proof that they were written from actual observation, and under the superintendence of the Holy Spirit, who thus as it were affixed his seal to the evangelical narrative.

That the death of Christ was the death of an atoning victim, and his blood that of the new covenant, is sufficiently demonstrated by the types, prophecies, and narratives of Scripture already adduced; but on account of the immense importance of the subject, and the necessity of impressing it in the strongest possible manner on the human mind, it pleased God to provide two significant symbols, as additional testimonies to the fact, the former on his own part, the latter on that of Christian churches. These were the rending of the veil in the temple, and the Lord's supper. Whatever view might have been taken of the death of Christ either by his enemies or his friends, it was between himself and his heavenly Father a transaction of the most sublime and momentous character. Through the eternal Spirit he offered himself a spotless sacrifice to God, by whom the atonement was accepted as perfectly satisfactory, and available to all the purposes for which it was designed. Of the divine acceptance it was most desirable that there should be at the time a direct and decisive proof; and this was furnished by the supernatural rending of the veil in the temple, a remarkable occurrence, which had been in some degree intimated by one of the later prophets of the Old Testament. The second temple at Jerusalem, erected by the comparatively small and feeble body of Israelites, who at the termination of the Babylonish captivity returned to their native land, and were there reorganized as the chosen people of God, was, as might have been expected, very inferior in beauty and magnificence to its celebrated predecessor, the temple of Solomon; and hence, at its foundation, while the younger part of the assembly shouted for joy, the aged men who had seen the first temple wept aloud. The fact is thus reported by Ezra the priest, an eye-witness of the scene.—"When the builders laid the foundation of the temple of the Lord [the high-priest and his attendants], set the priests in their apparel with trumpets, and the Levites the sons of Asaph with cymbals, to praise the Lord, after the ordinance of David, king of Israel. And they sang together by course, in praising and giving thanks unto the Lord, because [he is] good, for his mercy [endureth] forever toward **Israel.** And all the people shouted with a great **shout when** they praised the Lord, because the foundation **of the** house of the Lord was laid. But many of the priests, and Levites, and chief of the fathers [who were] ancient men that had **seen the first house, when** the foundation of this house was laid before **their** eyes, wept with a loud voice, and many shouted aloud for joy, so that the people could not discern the noise of the shout of joy from the noise of the weeping **of the people;** for the people shouted with a loud **shout, and the noise was heard afar off.**"*—This interesting circumstance was noticed by the Deity himself, and through the medium of the prophet Haggai made the subject of the following comment.—" Speak now to Zerubbabel the son of Shealtiel, **governor of Judah,** and to Joshua the son of Josedech, **the high-priest,** and to the residue of the people, saying,—Who [is] left among you that saw this house in her first glory? And how do ye see it now? [Is it] not in your eyes in comparison of it as **nothing?** Yet now be strong, O Zerubbabel! saith **the Lord, and be strong,** O Joshua son of Josedech, the high-priest! **and be strong, all ye people of the land!** saith the Lord, and work, **for I** [am] with you, saith **the Lord of hosts.** [According to] the word that I covenanted with **you when ye came out of Egypt,** so my Spirit remaineth **among you.** Fear ye not; for thus saith the Lord of hosts, Yet once it [is] a little while, and I will shake the heavens, and the earth, and the sea, and the dry [land]; and I will shake all nations, and the **desire of** all nations shall come, and I will fill this house **with** glory, saith the Lord of hosts. The silver [is] mine, and the gold [is] mine, saith the Lord of **hosts.** The glory of this latter house shall be greater than [that] of the former, saith the Lord of hosts, and in this place will I give peace, saith the Lord of hosts."—

* Ezra, chap. 3, v. 8-13.

The frequent repetition of the epithet,—"the Lord of hosts,"—seems designed to suggest that, however great might be the effect to be produced, or the difficulties to be overcome, he who made the promise was able to accomplish it. The substance of this remarkable prediction is concentrated in the last verse, which was partially fulfilled a few years before the Christian era, when, as related by Josephus, the temple was taken down to its foundation, and rebuilt with the utmost splendor by the first Herod.

Of its extraordinary magnificence some notion may be obtained from the descriptions of the Jewish historian, who flourished during its most perfect state, and as a priest must have been intimately acquainted with every part of the edifice. After giving an account of the massy foundations by which the mount of the temple was covered and enclosed, he proceeds:—"Now, for the works that were above, ... these were not unworthy of such foundations, for all the cloisters [or colonnades] were double, and the pillars to them belonging were twenty-five cubits in height, and supported by cloisters. These pillars were of one entire stone each of them, and that stone was white marble, and the roofs were adorned with cedar curiously graven. The natural magnificence and excellent polish, and the harmony of the joints in these cloisters, afforded a prospect that was very remarkable. The cloisters [of the outmost court] were in breadth thirty cubits, while the entire compass of it was by measure six furlongs, including the tower of Antonia."—After stating that the wall of the inner court or sanctuary, which was four square, had ten gates, he observes,—"Nine of these gates were on every side covered over with gold and silver, as were the jambs of their doors and their lintels; but there was one gate, that was without the [inward court of the] holy house, which was of Corinthian brass, and greatly excelled those that were only covered over with silver and gold. Each gate had two doors, whose height was severally thirty cubits, and their breadth fifteen."—Of the temple itself, properly so called, the same historian writes,—" Now, the outward face of the temple, in its front, wanted nothing that was likely to surprise either men's minds, or their eyes; for it was covered all over with plates of gold of great weight, and at the first rising of the sun reflected back a very fiery splendor, and made those who forced themselves to look upon it to turn their eyes away, just as they would have done at the sun's own rays. But this temple appeared to strangers, when they were coming to it at a distance, like a mountain covered with snow; for as to those parts of it that were not gilt, they were exceedingly white."—Thus literally and completely was the ancient prophecy fulfilled:—"The silver [is] mine, and the gold [is] mine, saith the Lord of hosts. The glory of this latter house shall be greater than [that] of the former, saith the Lord of hosts; and in this place will I give peace, saith the Lord of hosts."—And it was most suitable and wise that when the great atoning sacrifice, which the temple had been divinely appointed to typify and attest, was about to be offered, it should thus recover all its primitive magnificence, so as to attract universal attention; and that, when after the lapse of about eighty years this important purpose had been fully accomplished, it should be finally destroyed.*

Herod was, it is true, unworthy of sustaining such an office, but the sanctity of the renovated building was, nevertheless, acknowledged by Christ at his coming; for, although he came to establish a pure and spiritual religion, independent of forms and ceremonies, yet, as a faithful member of the Mosaic covenant, he always paid the strictest attention, as did likewise his apostles, to its

* Whiston's Josephus, vol. ii. pp. 369-376; vol. iv. pp. 141-148;— Haggai, chap. 2, v. 1-9.

ritual, as well as its moral requirements. It was in the temple, thus restored to its original opulence and beauty that, when an infant, he was solemnly presented to God, as the long promised seed of the woman, the first-born son of a virgin mother, and the illustrious heir of the house of David. There, when about twelve years of age, he was found conversing on religious subjects with the doctors of the law; and, when gently reproved by Joseph and Mary for leaving them without stating whither he was going, replied—"Knew ye not that I must be in my Father's house?"*—Twice afterward, at the beginning and the end of his public ministry, he expelled from its outer courts the dealers in victims, and the money-changers, who there pursued a profane and extortionate trade; saying to them, —"Make not my Father's house a place of merchandise." —On the last of these occasions, a little before the passover, he further honored the temple by performing there several miraculous cures; and, although generally slighted by its older inhabitants, was, agreeably to an ancient prediction, welcomed by their children with shouts of—"Hosanna to the Son of David!"—At the same time he may be supposed to have mentally devoted himself, on the very day appointed by the law of Moses, to his sacrificial office, as the true paschal lamb by whose blood, just about to be shed, his faithful followers were to obtain eternal redemption.†—Several other declarations of the later prophets were thus realized, particularly that of Malachi,—"Behold! I will send my messenger, and he shall prepare the way before me, and the Lord whom ye seek shall suddenly come to his temple, even the messenger of the covenant

---

* Οὐκ ᾔδειτε ὅτι ἐν τοῖς τοῦ πατρός μου δεῖ εἶναί με;—Luke, chap. 2, v. 49.

† Exodus, chap. 12, v. 1-13;—Matt. chap. 21, v. 12-16;—Mark, chap. 11, v. 11-17;—Luke, chap. 2, v. 21-38; chap. 19, v. 45, 46;—John, chap. 2, v. 13-17;—1 Corinth. chap. 5, v. 6-8;—Heb. chap. 9, v. 11, 12.

whom ye delight in. Behold! he shall come, saith the Lord of hosts;"—and that of Zechariah—"Behold! the man whose name [is] the Branch, he shall grow up out of his place, and he shall build the temple of the Lord, even he shall build the temple of the Lord; and he shall bear the glory, and shall sit and rule upon his throne, and the counsel of peace shall be between them both."—In conformity with this statement, Christ on his first official visit to Jerusalem, referred to his body as the true temple; and in reply to the demand of his antagonists for a sign, said—"Destroy this temple, and within three days I will raise it up."—In a similar sense, the Christian church universal is in the New Testament represented as a holy temple,—"built on the foundation of the apostles and prophets, Jesus Christ himself being the chief cornerstone;"—and in the heavenly world there will be no temple,—"for the Lord God Almighty and the Lamb are the temple thereof."*

But the prediction of Haggai was destined to receive a still closer and more important accomplishment, for the proper understanding of which it is necessary to revert to some of the ceremonial arrangements of the Mosaic dispensation. The temple at Jerusalem, like the tabernacle in the wilderness, was designed to represent the residence of the Deity in the midst of the Israelitish nation, as their sovereign and protector. Independently of the portico or entrance, which was closed by a veil, it consisted of two apartments, whereof the larger and exterior, called the sanctuary, was as it were the antechamber, and the inner, termed the most holy place, was the presence-chamber of the great king. Between the two was a door-way, closed by a second veil which completely concealed the interior

---

* Zechar. chap. 6, v. 9-13;—Malachi, chap. 3, v. 1;—John, chap. 2, v. 18-21;—Ephes. chap. 2, v. 19-22;—1 Peter, chap. 2, v. 4-6;—Revel. chap. 21, v. 22.

from view. Into the sanctuary the priests only, as the chosen ministers of God, were daily admitted, and there performed their sacred functions, while the people worshipped in the outer court. Into the most holy place none was allowed to enter but the high-priest, and that only once a year, on the day of atonement, when he there presented the blood of victims, together with a censer of incense, which having been kindled at the brazen altar without the sanctuary, was laid on the golden altar within. The whole was intended to show in a lively and impressive manner, that the Deity can neither hold communion with sinful men, nor receive their worship, except through the medium of an interceding priest, and an atoning sacrifice, both provided by himself. In his omniscient view, Christ was from the beginning the great high-priest consecrated forever after the order of Melchisedec, and the lamb of God which taketh away the sin of the world; but during the preparatory period of the Levitical economy that priesthood and sacrifice were prefigured by various types, which, although intrinsically of no value, effectively represented the future reality. At length, however, the shadows gave place to the substance, and the important transition was announced by a suitable symbolical attestation. Immediately before he expired on the cross, Christ proclaimed with a loud voice,—"[All] is accomplished;"—and, in accordance with this declaration, at the very moment of his death, the mysterious veil, which for so many ages had hung before the most holy place, was supernaturally rent asunder from the top to the bottom, affording a plain intimation that God had now received that long-predicted and perfect atonement, by means of which all who are willing to embrace the covenant thus ratified have free access to his presence, and are restored to his friendship and favor. This explanation is ably illustrated in Rambach's treatise on the sufferings of Christ.—"In the temple"—

says this judicious author,—" were two veils, one of which hung before the door leading into the sanctuary, and the other before the door or opening into the holy of holies; and these were made of azure, purple, and scarlet silk threads, curiously interwoven, and embroidered with the most beautiful flowers and cherubims. But the latter only of these veils is here spoken of. If one considers that, according to the testimony even of the Jews themselves, this veil was of a most curious and strong texture like tapestry, and was thirty ells in length, and four fingers thick, that it was no old tattered curtain, but a masterly piece of art lately woven (for a new veil was made and hung up in the temple every year), and lastly, that this strong veil hung in a place where it could not be damaged by the weather, the hand of God must necessarily be acknowledged to have been concerned in the rending of it. What a terror must this sudden and unexpected rent have struck into the priests, who probably were performing the service in the sanctuary, lighting the lamps of the golden candlestick, and burning incense; for it was about the time of evening sacrifice! . . . . But to the faithful this rending of the veil is a joyful type, representing that an entrance was then opened to them into the sanctuary which is not made with hands. Hitherto the flesh of Jesus Christ, by the imputation of our sins to him, had hung before it as a veil; but when this veil was rent at the separation of his soul and body by death, and Jesus Christ the true highpriest had himself with his own blood entered into the holy place, i. e., into heaven, the way to the throne of grace is cleared of all obstacles, heaven is laid open, and the covering which hung before the mysteries of the Levitical worship is removed."—This exposition rests, however, on a better foundation than any merely human opinion; for the apostle Paul expressly declares in his epistle to the Hebrews, that the inner veil of the temple signified the body of Christ, and that by the rending of that body, and the effusion of his blood as an atoning sacrifice, he entered as mediator of the new covenant, and high-priest of future blessings, into the heavenly sanctuary, whereof the most holy place in the Jewish temple was but a type, having thus obtained eternal salvation for all his faithful followers.* The symbolical attestation of this event, by the supernatural rending of the veil in the temple at the very moment of his death, was, therefore, most appropriate and significant; since it certified by divine authority the nature of the transaction, as well as the true character and mutual relation of the Mosaic and the Christian covenants. The agreement of this testimony with the explanation which has now been given of the Saviour's death is complete. The two circumstances peculiar to that explanation, namely, the sudden rupture of his heart, and the effusion of his life's blood, were thus actually pointed out in the most striking manner by the Deity himself, as the essential conditions of the great atonement which he had provided, and which could in no other way have been properly accomplished or represented. Thus were fulfilled the ancient prophecy, that in the second temple God would give peace, and the apostolical declaration that Christ made peace by the blood of his cross.

The miraculous appearance may be regarded as the second of the three principal testimonies,—the water, the blood, and the Spirit,—which, as stated by the apostle John, God gave to his Son; namely, at his baptism, when he entered on his prophetical office; at his death, when as the high-priest of his church he completed the atonement; and at the subsequent feast of pentecost, when, having commenced his kingdom, he sent forth his apostles to

---

* Rambach, On the Sufferings of Christ, vol. iii. pp. 236-240;—Whiston's Josephus, vol. i. pp. 126, 127; vol. iv. pp. 144, 145;—Heb. chap. 6, v. 16-20: chap. 9, v. 1-14; chap. 10, v. 19-22.

preach the gospel to the world at large. The passage has long been disfigured, as is well known, by interpolations, apart from which it reads as follows:—"Who is he that overcometh the world but he who believeth that Jesus is the Son of God? This is he who came with water and blood [even] Jesus Christ, not with water only, but with water and blood, and it is the Spirit that beareth witness, because the Spirit is the truth; for there are three that bear witness, the Spirit, and the water, and the blood, and these three agree in one. If we receive the testimony of men, the testimony of God is greater, for this is the testimony of God which he hath given concerning his Son. He that believeth on the Son of God hath the testimony in himself; he that believeth not God hath made him a liar, because he believeth not the testimony which God hath given concerning his Son: and the testimony is this, that God hath given to us eternal life, and [that] this life is in his Son. He that hath the Son hath life, and he that hath not the Son of God hath not life."—That the doctrine of the Trinity is involved in this passage is true, but not in the direct manner commonly supposed. The three sacred persons repeatedly concurred in bearing witness to Christ, not however in heaven, where such testimony would have been superfluous, but on earth, where it was strongly required. The first of these testimonies occurred at the baptism of Christ, when the Holy Spirit descended on him in visible form like a dove, and a voice from heaven proclaimed—"Thou art my beloved Son: in thee I am well pleased." *—The third took place on the memorable day of pentecost, when the apostles were endued with those miraculous gifts of the Holy Spirit, which at once stamped their mission with divine authority, and qualified them for its effective discharge. On that occa-

* Matt. chap. 3, v. 16, 17;—Mark, chap. 1, v. 9-11;—Luke, chap. 3, v. 21-23;—John, chap. 1, v. 29-34;—1 John, chap. 5, v. 5-12.

sion Peter, speaking of Christ, said to the multitude,—
"This man, having been delivered up by the determinate
counsel and foreknowledge of God, ye took, [and] by the
hands of wicked men crucified and slew. . . . This Jesus
God raised [from the dead], whereof we all are witnesses.
Having therefore been exalted to the right hand of God,
and having received from the Father the promised [gift]
of the Holy Spirit, he hath shed forth that which ye now
see and hear."—The second testimony was that now under consideration, given at the crucifixion of Christ, when
he poured forth his life's blood unto death, and through
the eternal Spirit offered himself as a spotless victim of
God; and when by the earthquake, the revival of many
pious persons long deceased, and above all by the rending
of the veil in the temple, the Father publicly signified his
acceptance of the atoning sacrifice thus accomplished.*

Of the two symbols connected with the gospel dispensation, the first was therefore a testimony respecting the
nature and design of the death of Christ rendered by the
Deity; the second was a similar testimony rendered by
Christians in their collective capacity, as religious societies or churches. The Lord's supper, instituted by the
Saviour himself, is a simple but significant rite, whereby he
directed that his atoning death should be commemorated,
and in a certain sense represented, as the foundation and
bond of the new covenant. It was probably in reference
to this rite that the apostle Paul, in his epistle to the
Galatians, reminds them that Jesus Christ, who suffered
the death of malediction, had been visibly exhibited to
them as a crucified victim. Until his death actually took
place, the Christian covenant which had been virtually introduced immediately after the fall, and a second time at
the call of Abraham, was neither ratified, nor fully devel-

* Matt. chap. 27, v. 50-54;—Mark, chap. 15, v. 37-39;—Luke, chap.
23, v. 44-47;—Acts, chap. 2, v. 1-4, 22-24, 32-36

oped; for, as the same apostle remarks,—" A covenant has no force while the covenant-victim remains alive."— In this point of view, although really prior, it was apparently posterior to the Mosaic covenant; on which account, and with regard more especially to the Israelitish nation, as the depositaries of revelation and the peculiar people of God, it is termed in both volumes of Scripture,—"the new covenant."*—Thus, in his epistle to the Hebrews, Paul quotes a remarkable passage from the book of Jeremiah, where it is thus described. Christ, observes the apostle,—"hath obtained a more exalted ministry [than that of Aaron] inasmuch as he is [the] mediator of a better covenant, which was established on better promises. For if the first [covenant] had been faultless, no place would have been sought for a second. Nevertheless, when rebuking [the people], it is said [in the Scripture], Behold the days come, saith the Lord, when I will make a new covenant with the house of Israel, and with the house of Judah, not according to the covenant which I made with their fathers in the day when I took them by the hand to lead them out of the land of Egypt, because they forsook my covenant, and I disregarded them, saith the Lord; for this [is] the covenant which I will make with the house of Israel after those days, saith the Lord, I will put my laws into their minds, and will write them on their hearts, and will be to them a God, and they shall be to me a people, and they shall not teach every one his neighbor, and every one his brother, saying, Know the Lord, for they shall all know me, from the least of them to the greatest; for I will be merciful to their iniquities, and their sins and transgressions I will remember no more."—With similar

---

* Διαθήκη γὰρ ἐπὶ νεκροῖς βεβαία, ἐπεὶ μήποτε ἰσχύει ὅτε ζῇ ὁ διαθέμενος: Heb. chap. 9, v. 15-17; chap. 11, v. 4;—Rom. chap. 4, v. 9-13; —1 Corinth. chap. 11, v. 23-26;—2 Corinth. chap. 3, v. 5, 6;—Galat. chap. 3, v. 1-9.

views, Peter congratulates the Jewish Christians of Asia Minor on having actually made this happy transition; —" Ye [are] a chosen race, a royal priesthood, a holy nation, a favored people, and should therefore show forth the praises of him who hath called you out of darkness into his marvellous light; who formerly [were] not a people, but [are] now the people of God, who [had] not obtained mercy, but now [have] obtained mercy." *—At the ratification of the first covenant, says Paul,—" when every commandment of the law had been recited to all the people by Moses, he took the blood of calves and goats, with water and scarlet wool, and hyssop, and sprinkled both the book and all the people saying, This [is] the blood of the covenant which God hath appointed for you." —At the institution of the Lord's Supper, which immediately followed the last passover celebrated by Christ with his apostles, it is stated that,—" as they were eating, Jesus took bread, and after offering thanks brake, and gave [it] to the disciples, and said, Take, eat, this is my body which is broken for you. Do this in remembrance of me. In like manner also, after offering thanks, he gave to them the cup after supper, saying, Drink ye all of it. And they did so. And he said to them, This cup [is] the new covenant by my blood which [is] shed for you [and] for many for the discharge of sins. Do this, whenever ye drink [of it] in remembrance of me. I tell you that I will not henceforth drink of this fruit of the vine, till the day when I shall drink it new with you in my Father's kingdom." †— The meaning and design of this rite, as well as the super-

* Jerem. chap. 31, v. 31-34;—Heb. chap. 8, passim;—1 Peter, chap. 2, v. 9, 10.

† Exod. chap. 24, v. 4-8;—Matt. chap. 26, v. 26-29;—Mark, chap. 14, v. 22-25;—Luke chap. 22, v. 17-20;—1 Corinth. chap. 11, v. 23-26; —Heb. chap. 9, v. 16-23. By the book, in the latter passage, is meant the book or roll of that national covenant, in its more detailed or extended form, which God made with the Israelitish people at Mount Sinai.

natural rending of the veil in the temple, are strongly illustrated by the explanation here given, which in its turn is confirmed and dignified by the association. This symbol, like the former one, overlooks the minor circumstances of the crucifixion; and singling out the two essential conditions which proved it to be an atoning sacrifice, namely, the rending of the Saviour's body,—in other words, the rupture of his heart, and the consequent effusion of his life's blood,—assigns to them that prominence and importance in the plan of redemption, to which they are justly entitled. By these symbols the seal of divine authority was affixed to the transaction now explained; since with all the weight of that authority they demand attention to two cardinal facts in the death of Christ, which admit of no other interpretation. In this manner only could his body have been broken, or his life's blood poured out, as an atonement for the sins of mankind. By these symbols, therefore, the two parties to the new covenant, the Deity on the one side, and Christian churches on the other, appropriately signified their concurrence in the mediatorial sacrifice by which alone that covenant could have been ratified.

Nor was this their only use; for they also powerfully contributed to mark the important distinction between the two covenants, which by many persons, more especially at the commencement of the gospel dispensation, were apt to be confounded. In reference to religion, the whole human race was at that time divided into four classes of very unequal extent; namely, Christian Jews, Christian Gentiles, and those who, whether Jews or Gentiles, had not embraced the gospel. For acceptance with God unbelieving Jews relied on the old covenant, Christians of both sections on the new, and unbelieving Gentiles, who had no covenant at all, on their self-imposed and idolatrous worship. In repudiating open idolatry

Christians and unbelieving Jews were agreed, but respecting the nature and import of the two covenants they widely differed. Both covenants were in fact of divine origin, but the Mosaic was merely a national and external covenant, introductory to the Christian, which it typified and predicted. During the apostolical period of nearly forty years both dispensations were coexistent; and, while Christian Gentiles had no connection with the old covenant, and unbelieving Israelites rejected the new, Christian Jews were consistent members of both. To prevent as far as possible the confusion which was liable to arise from so extraordinary a state of things, it pleased God to ordain that Christianity, like Judaism, should have its initiatory and commemorative rites, whereby the true relation, as well as distinction between the two covenants might be clearly displayed. The initiatory rite of Judaism intimated that impurity of conduct was incompatible with a divine alliance; that of Christianity represented the special influence of the Holy Spirit, which purifies and consecrates the heart. The commemorative rite of Judaism intimated that an adequate atoning sacrifice was necessary for salvation; that of Christianity represented this sacrifice as actually accomplished. By observing the Christian rites, both Jews and Gentiles professed that they sought the favor of God, not through the works of the law, but through faith in Christ. Both parties, however, evinced a proper reverence for the Mosaic institution, which, although temporary and subordinate, was nevertheless divinely appointed, and highly important; the former by a cheerful compliance with all its requirements, until by the interposition of its supreme author it was finally abolished; the latter by abstaining from blood as an article of food, so long as by its sacrificial employment at the temple in Jerusalem it typified the blood of Christ. Nothing could be better adapted than these symbols to show that, although both religions came from God, Judaism was merely the scaffolding, and Christianity the finished edifice. By adopting them, the Jewish convert publicly professed that he renounced all dependence on the old covenant for the salvation of the soul; and, in common with the Gentile convert, sought reconciliation with God exclusively from the new. By refusing them, the unconverted Jew made it manifest that he preferred the shadow to the substance, rejected the counsel of God against himself; and, in his idolatry of the temple and its ceremonies, was guilty, like the unconverted Gentile, of worshipping the creature more than the Creator.*

The distinctive character and mutual relation of the two covenants were, however, chiefly intimated by their commemorative rites. In order to make a powerful and vivid impression on the human mind during the many ages which preceded the coming of Christ, it was expedient that his sacrificial death should be represented by that of animals. The rupture of his heart owing to mental agony could not indeed be thus expressed; but the effusion of his life's blood was plainly foreshown by the manner in which victims were slain, namely, by the rapid division of the large vessels of the neck, which necessarily occasioned a copious and fatal discharge of blood, derived almost directly from the heart. Yet, from the intrinsic worthlessness of these sacrifices, and from their perpetual repetition, as well as from the continued suspension of the veil before the inner sanctuary of the tabernacle, or temple, notwithstanding their oblation, it might reasonably

---

* This charge seems to be preferred by the apostle Paul against unbelieving Jews, in Philipp. chap. 3, v. 2, 3;—Heb. chap. 8, v. 3, 5; chap. 9, v. 11-14; and chap. 13, v. 10; as against unbelieving Gentiles in Rom. chap. 1, v. 21-25. See also John, chap. 4, v. 19-24;—Acts, chap. 15, v. 19, 20, 28, 29; chap. 21, v. 17-26.

have been inferred that they were merely outward and temporary signs of some great future reality. The same conclusion might have been deduced from the circumstance, that the semblance of atonement which they displayed was palpably, and it may be said designedly imperfect. On some occasions, it is true, they presented, in accordance with the common feelings and usages of mankind, the aspect of a friendly repast, wherein the parties to the covenant solemnly united; the blood and fat of the victims, accompanied with flour, unleavened bread, wine, oil, and especially with salt, the emblem of friendship, being offered on the altar, while their flesh was eaten by the worshippers and the priests. Yet, even on these occasions, the incomplete and shadowy character of the transaction was strongly marked; for the use of blood and fat as articles of food was universally prohibited on pain of death, as was likewise the flesh of all victims peculiarly significant of propitiation, such as those offered on the day of atonement; which, as if really defiled by imputed sin, were commanded, after being slaughtered in the usual manner, to be wholly consumed by fire without the walls of the city.* The commemorative rite of Christianity testified, on the contrary, that by means of a propitiatory sacrifice of infinite value recently offered, the types and shadows of the preceding institution had been realized, and a full reconciliation with God procured for all who are willing to embrace it. The perfection of the sacrifice was denoted by the breaking of bread, and the pouring out of wine, representing the rupture of the Saviour's heart, and the effusion of his blood, the two essential conditions of his atoning death on the cross, which

---

* Levit. chap. 2; chap. 3, v, 16-19; chap. 6, v. 14-30; chap. 7, v. 22-27; chap. 16; chap. 17, v. 10-14;—Numb. chap. 15, v. 1-12; chap. 18, v. 19; chaps. 28, 29;—Deut. chap. 12, v. 15, 16, 23-27;—2 Chron. chap. 13, v. 4, 5;—Ezra, chap. 6, v. 8-10.

proved that the malediction due to human depravity had been actually sustained and exhausted. The completeness of the reconciliation was denoted by Christians partaking together of the bread and wine, thus broken and poured out in token of their being voluntarily identified with that atoning sacrifice of which the Deity himself had publicly signified his acceptance, and of their consequent restoration to his favor and communion. In reference to the solemn import of the sign, the apostle Paul puts the question to the Corinthians,—" The cup of blessing [over] which we give thanks, is it not a participation of the blood of Christ? The bread which we break, is it not a participation of the body of Christ? For we, [however] many, are one bread, [that is] one body, because we all partake of that one bread. Behold Israel after the flesh. Are not those who eat of the sacrifices partakers with the altar?"—In conformity with this view, the apostle subsequently declares,—" Whosoever shall eat the bread, or drink the cup of the Lord unworthily, will be guilty of [an offence against] the body and blood of the Lord; therefore let a man examine himself, and so let him eat of the bread, and drink of the cup."—In reference to the importance of the spiritual reality thereby signified, Christ himself assured the Jews,— " Unless ye eat the flesh of the Son of man, and drink his blood, ye have no life in you. He that eateth my flesh, and drinketh my blood, hath eternal life, and I will raise him up at the last day; for my flesh is meat indeed, and my blood is drink indeed. He that eateth my flesh, and drinketh my blood, abideth in me, and I [abide] in him. As the living Father hath sent me, and I live by the Father, even so he that eateth me shall live by me. This is the bread that came down from heaven; not as your fathers ate the manna and are dead, he that eateth this bread shall live for ever."—As if for the express purpose of preventing the misapplication of these figurative terms in a literal sense, which has since so lamentably prevailed, he afterward added,—" Doth this offend you ? What and if ye shall see the Son of man ascend where he was before ? It is the Spirit which giveth life : the flesh availeth nothing. The words which I speak to you are spirit and life."—Yet, although such expressions cannot prove, what is evidently impossible, the presence of the Saviour's body and blood in the sacramental elements, they most undoubtedly imply the rupture of his heart, and the effusion of his blood, as the consummation of his atoning sacrifice on the cross; in reference to which they are not stronger than the nature of the subject requires, but would otherwise be extravagant, or unmeaning.* To express by suitable ceremonies the participation of human beings in such a sacrifice, and its resulting benefits, two methods were appointed in Scripture, the one connected with the exterior of the body, the other with its interior. Thus, under the patriarchal and Mosaic dispensations, dedication to the service of God was represented by pouring oil or water on the head ; worshippers partook in certain cases of the flesh of victims, or walked between their severed halves, and the first parents of mankind were even clothed in their skins. These two modes were equally adopted in the Christian rites of baptism and the Lord's supper; the former denoting the purifying influence of the Holy Spirit, descending on converts like dew from heaven, and consecrating them to the divine service ; the latter the efficacy of the body and blood of Christ symbolically eaten and drunk, in other words, of his atoning sacrifice cordially embraced by them, as the source of their spiritual life and energy, and the pledge of their friendship with God. The rites thus attached to both dispensations exhibited, like

* John, chap. 6, v. 53-63 ;—1 Corinth. chap. 10, v. 15-18; chap. 11 v. 27, 28.

the dispensations themselves, characteristic features of similitude and diversity. The Mosaic rites represented the objects in view, as was desirable before the reality had taken place, in a more lively and expressive manner, but at the same time in a manner less suited for general and permanent use. The blood of victims was daily poured out at the foot of the altar. Their flesh was sometimes eaten by the worshippers, but on the most solemn occasions was wholly consumed by fire without the camp; and the baptismal water was mingled either with their ashes, or their blood. The Christian rites, more simple and more easily practised, were thereby better adapted to a spiritual and universal dispensation, following instead of preceding the reality, and accompanied with a larger measure of Scriptural instruction. Under this dispensation the baptismal water was pure and clean, and the sacred repast, open to all sincere converts, consisted of unleavened bread and red wine. The apostle Paul accordingly invites such converts to approach the throne of grace, having their hearts purified by sprinkling from an evil conscience, and their bodies washed with *pure* water. As the Lord's supper was originally instituted during the paschal festival, the bread used in it on that occasion was necessarily unleavened; and, as pointed allusions to red wine occur in several parts of Scripture, and much of the wine made in Palestine was, and still is, of that color, it may reasonably be presumed that the wine employed to typify the blood of Christ was red.* That these changes in the sacramental ordinances were predicted in some passages of the Old Testament may the more confidently be

---

* Exod. chap. 24, v. 3-8;—Levit. chap. 14;—Numb. chap. 19;—Psalm 75, v. 8; Psalm 133;—Prov. chap. 23, v. 31;—Isa. chap. 27, v. 2; chap. 63, v. 1-3;—1 Corinth. chap. 5, v. 6-8;—Heb. chap. 9, v. 8-14, 18-21; chap. 10, v. 19-22;—Rev. chap. 14, v. 17-20; chap. 19, v. 11-15.

inferred, because language precisely similar is applied to corresponding evangelical subjects in the New. Thus, after inquiring,—"What shall I render unto the Lord [for] all his benefits toward me?"—the psalmist replies,—"I will take the cup of salvation, and call upon the name of the Lord;"—and, in a remarkable prophecy of Ezekiel concerning the future restoration and conversion of the people of Israel, a passage strikingly analogous to that previously quoted from the book of Jeremiah, God is represented as saying,—"Then will I sprinkle *clean* water upon you, and ye shall be clean: from all your filthiness, and from all your idols will I cleanse you. A new heart also will I give you, and a new spirit will I put within you, and I will take away the stony heart out of your flesh, and will give you a heart of flesh: and I will put my Spirit within you, and cause you to walk in my statutes, and ye shall keep my judgments and do [them.]"

The simultaneous observance by divine authority both of the Jewish and the Christian rites, during the apostolical age, served to distinguish the shadow from the substance, the type from the antitype; and to show that, valuable as was the Mosaic covenant for many external and national objects, personal reconciliation and friendship with God are attainable by that covenant only which, although instituted from the beginning, is in a relative sense, and in reference to its actual ratification, termed new. While, therefore, the explanation of the death of Christ now given strongly illustrates the import and design of the two symbols connected with it, the divine appointment of those symbols implies and confirms the explanation.*

* Psalm 16, v. 4, 5; Psalm 116, v. 12, 13;—Isa. chap. 52, v. 13-15; —Jer. chap. 31, v. 31-34;—Ezek. chap. 36, v. 22-28;—Acts, chap. 9, v. 13, 14, 20, 21; chap. 22, v. 16;—Rom. chap. 10, v. 4-13;—1 Corinth. chap. 1, v. 1, 2; chap. 10, v. 15-21; 2 Tim. chap. 2, v. 22;—Heb. chap. 8, v. 6-13 chap. 10, v. 15-22;—1 Peter, chap. 1, v. 1, 2.

CHAPTER IV.

ON THE DOCTRINES AND PRECEPTS OF CHRISTIANITY IN RELATION TO THE DEATH OF CHRIST.

THE systematic theology of the New Testament, both doctrinal and practical, is chiefly contained in the epistles, or pastoral letters, addressed to particular churches or individual Christians by some of the apostles; and it is a remarkable fact, that almost all the expositions of evangelical truth furnished by these inspired writers, as well as all their applications of it to the improvement of character and conduct, are expressly grounded on the death of Christ, and distinctly refer to its two principal features above pointed out, namely, as constituting a propitiatory sacrifice, and as occasioned by the effusion of his blood. In the following discussion, this fact will first be proved by quotations from the apostolical writings, and afterward illustrated by showing its significancy and importance.

The plan of human salvation is described in Scripture as commencing with a covenant of reconciliation between God and men, founded on the atoning sacrifice of Christ. To atone for sin, the vicarious death of a suitable victim by the effusion of its life's blood was indispensable. For this purpose the life's blood of the victims offered under the patriarchal and Mosaic dispensations was totally inadequate, but that of Christ was perfectly sufficient; and it was through the oblation of this blood on the cross that he became at once the mediator, priest, and victim of the new covenant, whereby those who embrace it are spiritually united to him, to each other, and to God. This arrangement is most clearly and copiously described by the apostle Paul, in his epistle to the Hebrew Christians of Palestine. After alluding to the structure and furniture of the tabernacle, or temple, and particularly to the veil which concealed the inner sanctuary from view, he proceeds as follows,—" These things being thus arranged, the priests enter at all times into the first sanctuary to perform the sacred services; but into the second the highpriest alone [enters] once a year, not without blood, which he offers for his own sins, and for those of the people. The Holy Spirit herein signified that the way into the most holy place was not yet made manifest, while the first tabernacle retained [its] institutions; which [is only] a figure [referring] to the present time, whereby both gifts and sacrifices are offered which cannot make the worshipper perfect as regards the conscience, [being] merely rites of outward purification by meats, and drinks, and various washings, reserved for a time of reformation. But Christ having arrived, [as] high-priest of the blessings to come, by the greater and more perfect tabernacle not made with hands, that is, not of this institution, neither by the blood of goats and calves, but *by his own blood*, entered once for all into the most holy place, having achieved an everlasting redemption. For, if the blood of bulls and goats, and the ashes of a heifer, sprinkled on those who are unclean, sanctify to the purification of the flesh, how much more will *the blood of Christ*, who through the eternal Spirit offered himself [as a] spotless [sacrifice] to God, purify your consciences from dead works to worship the living God? And for this end he is [the] mediator of [the] new covenant; that, [in consequence of] a death having taken place as a ransom for the transgressions [committed] under the first covenant, those who are called might attain the promised [gift] of the eternal inheritance. For, where [there is] a covenant, the death of the covenant-victim must necessarily take place; for a covenant [is] ratified over dead [victims], not having any force while the victim remains alive. On which account, neither was the first [covenant] solemnized without blood; for, when every commandment of the law had been recited to all the people by Moses, he took the blood of calves and goats, with water, and scarlet-wool, and hyssop, and sprinkled both the book and all the people, saying, This [is] the blood of the covenant which God hath appointed for you. And in like manner he sprinkled with the blood both the tabernacle, and all the implements of the sacred service; and [indeed], according to the law, almost all things are purified by blood, and without effusion of blood there is no discharge [of sins. It was] therefore necessary that the types of heavenly things should be thus purified, but the heavenly things themselves by better sacrifices than these; for Christ has not entered into the most holy place made with hands, the figure of the true [sanctuary], but into heaven itself, now to appear in the presence of God on our behalf.*. . . For the law, presenting a shadow [only] of the future blessings, [and] not their very substance, can never by the same sacrifices which they offer year by year render those who attend them henceforth perfect; for [otherwise,] would they not have ceased to be offered? since the worshippers, once purified, would have had no further consciousness of sins. But by these [sacrifices] a fresh commemoration of sins [is made] every year; for [it is] impossible that the blood of bulls and goats should take away sins. Wherefore, on coming into the world [Christ] said, Sacrifice and offering thou desir-

---

* Heb. chap. 9, v. 6–24. With a view to show the frequency and force of the allusions made in the epistles to the blood of Christ, the corresponding words are throughout this chapter printed in Italics.

edst not, but a body hast thou prepared for me. In whole burnt-offerings and [sacrifices] for sin thou hast no pleasure, then I said, Lo, I come (in a chapter of the book it is written of me), to do thy will, O God! [When, after] previously saying, Sacrifice, and offering, and whole burnt-offerings, and [sacrifices] for sin thou desiredst not, neither hadst pleasure [therein], which are offered according to the law, he adds, Lo, I come to do thy will! he taketh away the first, that he may establish the second; by which will we are sanctified through the offering of the body of Jesus Christ once for all. . . . Having then, brethren, liberty to enter into the most holy place *by the blood of Jesus*, that newly-opened and living way which he hath consecrated for us through the veil, that is, his flesh, and [having] a high-priest over the house of God, let us draw near with a sincere heart in full assurance of faith, having our hearts purified by sprinkling from an evil conscience, and our bodies washed with pure water."*

Nor was this, as some may have supposed, merely a figurative mode of speaking adopted to conciliate Jews; for the apostle uses precisely similar language when addressing Gentile Christians, as appears from the following passages in his epistles to the Ephesians and Colossians. —"Remember"—says he to the former,—"that ye who were once Gentiles in flesh, and called uncircumcision by those who derive their name from the circumcision made by hands in the flesh, were at that time without Christ, aliens from the commonwealth of Israel, and strangers to the covenants of promise, without hope, and without God in the world; but that now, by Christ Jesus, ye who once were far off have *by the blood of Christ* been brought nigh. For he is our peace, who hath united the two [parties], destroyed the middle wall of separation, and abolished

* Heb. chap. 10, v. 1–10, 19–22; chap. 13, v. 10–14.

by his flesh the enmity [namely], the law of commandment in [the form of] decrees, that by [thus] making peace he might combine in himself the two [parties] into one new man, and reconcile both in one body to God through the cross, having slain the enmity thereby ; and came and proclaimed peace to you who [were] far off, and to them [who were] nigh ; for through him we both have access by one Spirit to the Father."—To the Colossians the apostle remarks,—" It pleased [the Father] that in him the whole church should dwell; having made peace *through the blood of his cross*, by him to reconcile all to himself, by him [alike], whether those on earth, or those in heaven;"—that is, whether Jews or Gentiles. That the new covenant like the old was ratified by the life's blood of its victim, is, moreover, declared by Christ himself, who said on instituting the Lord's supper—" This cup [is] the new covenant *by my blood*, which [is] shed for you [and] for many, for the discharge of sins ; "—and the same meaning is evidently attached by the apostles Peter and Paul to the same term, whether they mention the blood of the covenant or the blood of sprinkling. When congratulating the Hebrew Christians on their conversion, the latter observes that they had come—" to Jesus, [the] mediator of [the] new covenant, and to [the] *blood of sprinkling*, which speaketh better things than [that of] Abel ; "—and in another place styles Christ,—" the great shepherd of the sheep, *by the blood of* [the] *everlasting covenant*." *—In the administration of this covenant the three divine persons manifestly concurred : planned and executed by the

* "Ὅτι ἐν αὐτῷ εὐδόκησε πᾶν τὸ πλήρωμα κατοικῆσαι· Coloss. chap. 1, v. 19, 20 ;—Ephes. chap. 2, v. 11-18 ;—Heb. chap. 10, v. 28, 29 ; chap. 12, v. 22-24 ; chap. 13, v. 20, 21. Whether the epistle which bears the name of the Ephesians was addressed to the Gentile Christians of Ephesus, or, as is more probable, to those of Laodicea, does not affect the present argument.

Father, it was ratified by the blood of Christ, and published to the world by his chosen ambassadors, whose testimony was supported by that of the Holy Spirit. To demonstrate the truth of this covenant, to explain its nature, and to press it with authority on the acceptance of mankind, was the peculiar office of the apostles; an office partly discharged during their lives by preaching, but which by means of their inspired writings they will continue to exercise till the end of time.—"How shall we escape,"—says one of their number,—"if we neglect so great a salvation? which began to be spoken by the Lord, [and] was confirmed to us by those who heard [him]; God [also] subjoining his testimony by signs, and wonders, and various miraculous powers and gifts of the Holy Spirit, dispensed according to his own will."—On another occasion he remarks,—"The whole [proceeds] from God, who hath reconciled us to himself through Jesus Christ, and hath given to us the ministry of reconciliation. . . . We are, therefore, ambassadors for Christ; [and], as if God entreated [you] through us, we beseech [you] in Christ's stead,—Be ye reconciled to God: for he hath made him who knew not sin to be sin for us, that we might become [the] righteousness of God by him." *

The covenant of reconciliation, thus attested and recommended, may be regarded as an act of amnesty granted by the gracious sovereign of the universe to his rebellious subjects of the human race, and during a certain period lying open for the benefit of all who are willing to embrace it; the Scripture declaring that—"God would have all men to be saved, and to come to an acknowledgment of the truth,"—and proclaiming with some of its latest words,—"Whosoever will, let him take the water of life freely."—By the same inspired authority the blood of Christ is represented, not only as the bond of this cove-

* 2 Corinth. chap. 5, v. 18-21;—Heb. chap. 2 v. 1-4.

nant, but also as the medium of all the benefits thence resulting, namely, spiritual knowledge, and a complete deliverance from the guilt, the power, and the penal consequences of sin; or, to use the emphatic language of the apostle Paul,—"Christ is by God made to us wisdom, and justification, sanctification, and redemption."—The wisdom which is from above, or evangelical instruction, necessarily lies at the root of the process. Thus, after stating that under this dispensation—"Whosoever calls on the name of the Lord shall be saved,"—the apostle asks,—"How then shall they call [on him] in whom they have not believed, and how shall they believe [in him] of whom they have not heard, and how shall they hear without a preacher, and how shall they preach unless they are sent?" —justly concluding—"So then faith [cometh] by preaching, and preaching by the command of God."*—In this process the Deity shows a due regard to the nature of man, who, although fallen and depraved, is still a rational and moral agent, and cannot be rendered wise, virtuous, or happy, without his own consent and coöperation. The message of the gospel having been authenticated and explained, he is invited to believe and accept it; and on so doing, is reconciled to God, and entitled to all the blessings of salvation. Evangelical faith is not, however, a mere belief in the message, or a vague and general trust in the divine mercy, but a cordial and practical adhesion to the new covenant, on an adequate understanding of its nature. Hereupon the convert becomes spiritually united, and as it were identified with the mediator, by virtue of whose atoning sacrifice he is justified by God, as the moral governor of the world; or, in other words, is legally absolved from guilt, and regarded as an innocent and upright per-

* Κύριε, τίs ἐπίστευσε τῇ ἀκοῇ ἡμῶν; Ἄρα, ἡ πίστις ἐξ ἀκοῆς, ἡ δὲ ἀκοὴ διὰ ῥήματος Θεοῦ· Rom. chap. 10, v. 13-17 ;—1 Corinth. chap. 1, v. 30, 31 ;—1 Tim. chap. 2, v. 1-4 ;—Revel. chap. 22, v. 17.

son. This unspeakable benefit is in Scripture distinctly ascribed to the blood of Christ, who, on instituting the Lord's supper, presented a cup of wine to his apostles, in token of their embracing the new covenant about to be ratified *by his blood*, and thereby obtaining the discharge of their sins. . . . "That he might consecrate the people *with his own blood*,"—says the apostle Paul,—" Jesus suffered without the gate [of Jerusalem];"—and hence, —" we have redemption *through his blood*, [even] the discharge of sins, according to the munificence of his grace . . . . for all have sinned, and fallen short of the glory of God, being justified freely by his grace, through the redemption which [is] in Christ Jesus; whom God foreappointed [to be] a propitiatory [sacrifice], *through faith in his blood*, to demonstrate his justice,—because of the seeming impunity of previous sins through the forbearance of God,—to demonstrate his justice at the present time, [and to show] that he is just even in justifying him that believeth in Jesus.* . . . God displays his love toward us, in that while we were yet sinners Christ died for us. Much more, therefore, being now *justified by his blood*, shall we be saved from wrath by him; for if when we were enemies we were reconciled to God through the death of his Son, much more being reconciled shall we be saved by his life."

The blessings of salvation are so intimately and inseparably connected, that the existence of any one of them necessarily implies that of all the rest, agreeably to the statement of the same apostle:—" We know that to

* The term πάρεσις ἁμαρτημάτων, which occurs in no other part of the New Testament, and, on account of the difficulty of expressing its meaning by any single English word, is here rendered—"seeming impunity,"—probably signifies the apparent discharge of sins without an adequate ransom, as for example by the Levitical sacrifices.—Matt. chap. 26, v. 26-29;—Luke, chap. 22, v. 17-20;—Rom. chap. 3, v. 23-26;— Ephes. chap. 1, v. 4-7;—Heb. chap. 13, v. 10-12.

those who love God, who are called according to [his] purpose, all things work together for good. For whom he foreknew them he also predestined [to be] conformed to the image of his Son, that he might be the first-born among many brethren; and whom he predestined them he also called, and whom he called them he also justified, and whom he justified them he also glorified."*—In reference to human agency, these blessings commence at the moment of conversion, when justification by faith and reconciliation with God are immediately attained; but sanctification and redemption are slow and gradual processes, the former not being completed till death, nor the latter till the resurrection of the just. By the message of the gospel addressed to the understanding, in conjunction with the influence of the Holy Spirit applied to the affections, men are invited to embrace the Christian covenant. If they do so, they are regenerated, that is, become in the highest sense of the term children of God, who accepts them graciously, loves them freely, translates them from the kingdom of Satan into the kingdom of his beloved Son, and places them under the tuition and guidance of his Spirit, the author and finisher of this new creation. John accordingly remarks—"To as many as received him [Christ] granted the privilege of being children of God, [even] to those who believed on his name." —A genuine filial affection toward their heavenly Father, resembling in kind that of Christ himself, and grounded on his atoning sacrifice, is at the same time formed in their hearts; a principle at first feeble and rudimental, like a vegetable or animal germ, but which is progressively nurtured and increased till, on becoming fully developed and matured, it transforms the whole character into the divine image. This is the process of sanctification, wherein the convert himself performs a subordinate

* Rom. chap. 5, v. 8–10; chap. 6, v. 22, 23; chap. 8, v. 28–30.

but important part; since throughout his subsequent life it is powerfully opposed, although with continually decreasing effect, by the remains of a corrupt and fallen nature.* Redemption, or deliverance from sin in consequence of the payment of the requisite ransom, comprehends in a large sense the entire process of salvation; but, while justification is a deliverance from the guilt of sin, and sanctification a deliverance from its power, redemption is more properly a deliverance from its penal consequences. This is partially effected in the present life, the troubles and sorrows of which are to a Christian either mitigated, or overruled for good; but death, the common lot of fallen men, cannot be avoided. At the moment of dissolution, however, the ransomed spirit, clothed with some ethereal vehicle, specially provided by the Deity, and admirably adapted to its intermediate stage of existence, passes at once into the blissful presence of God; and at the resurrection of the just, when the work of redemption will be completed, the body also, raised from the earth in a refined and glorified state, will be reunited to the spirit, and thenceforth be its inseparable companion through a happy eternity. These latter blessings, like the former ones, are in Scripture ascribed to the blood of Christ, as their procuring and meritorious cause; but, owing to their mutual connection, two or more of them are sometimes included under the same general expression, on which account, when a separate proof of each is required, the repeated quotation of such passages can scarcely be declined. By those, for example, which mention the blood of Christ as sprinkling, washing, purifying, etc., it is probably represented as the medium of sanctification no less than of justification. Thus Peter

* John, chap. 1, v. 11-13;—Galat. chap. 4, v. 19, 20;—Ephes. chap. 5, v. 1, 2;—Coloss. chap. 1, v. 12, 13, 27;—2 Peter, chap. 2, v. 1-4;—1 John, chap. 3, v. 7-9.

salutes the Christian Jews of Asia Minor as—"elect according to the foreknowledge of God the Father, by sanctification of the Spirit, unto obedience, and *sprinkling of the blood of Jesus Christ;*"—and reminds them—"that they had been redeemed from their unprofitable [religious] course, derived by tradition from the fathers, not by perishable things, [such as] silver or gold, but *by the precious blood of Christ*, as of a lamb without blemish and without spot."*—After assuring those of Palestine that, not—"by the blood of goats and calves, but *by his own blood*, [Christ] entered once for all into the most holy place, having achieved an everlasting redemption,"— Paul asks—"How much more will *the blood of Christ*, who through the eternal Spirit offered himself [as a] spotless [sacrifice] to God, purify your consciences from dead works to worship the living God?"—and denounces a fearful doom to the apostate,—"who had trampled on the Son of God, regarded *the blood of the covenant* by which he was purified as destitute of sanctity, and insulted the Spirit of grace."—In his epistle to the Ephesians he speaks of the Father, as—"having by the good pleasure of his will predestined us to be his adopted children through Jesus Christ, to the glory of his grace, which he hath bestowed on us in the beloved one, by whom we have redemption *through his blood*, [even] the discharge of sins, according to the munificence of his grace;"—a passage which corresponds with his parting injunction to the elders of the Ephesian church:—"Take heed to yourselves, and to all the flock wherein the Holy Spirit hath made you pastors, to tend the church of the Lord which he hath purchased *with his own blood;*"—and is more fully explained in his epistle to the Colossians, where he mentions himself as—"giving thanks to the Father, who

* 1 Corinth. chap. 15, v. 42-57;—2 Corinth. chap. 5. v. 1-8;—1 Peter, chap. 1, v. 1, 2, 18, 19.

hath qualified us to share in the inheritance of the saints in light, who hath delivered us from the dominion of darkness, and translated us into the kingdom of his beloved Son, by whom we have redemption, [even] the discharge of sins.*... If,"—says the apostle John,—"we say that we have fellowship with [God], and walk in darkness, we lie and do not the truth; but if we walk in the light, [even] as he is in the light, we have fellowship with each other, and *the blood of his Son Jesus Christ* cleanseth us from all sin."—At the commencement of the Apocalypse he breaks forth into the sublime doxology,—"To him that loveth us, and hath washed us from our sins *in his own blood*, and hath made us kings and priests to his God and Father, to him [be ascribed] glory and power throughout endless ages. Amen."—The glorified Saviour appears on the celestial throne, as—"a lamb that had been slain."—Of the souls of the early martyrs in heaven it is said,—"These are they who have come out of the great persecution, and have washed their robes, and made them white *in the blood of the Lamb*."—It was—"because of *the blood of the Lamb*, and of the word of their testimony, that they overcame [Satan], and withheld not their lives from death;"—and lastly, the glorified spirits around the throne are described as addressing the Saviour in a new hymn of praise, "Thou art worthy to take the book [of prophecy], and to open its seals, because thou wast slain [as a sacrifice], and hast redeemed us to God *by thy blood* out of every tribe, and language, and people, and nation." †

It has thus been shown that, in many parts of the apostolical writings, the blood of Christ is emphatically de-

---

* Acts, chap. 20, v. 28;—Ephes. chap. 1, v. 3–7;—Coloss. chap. 1, v. 12–14;—Heb. chap. 9, v. 11–15; chap. 10, v. 28, 29.

† 1 John, chap. 1, v. 5–7; Revel. chap. 1, v. 5, 6; chap. 5, v. 6–10; chap. 7, v. 13, 14; chap. 12, v. 10, 11.

clared to be the bond of the new covenant, the price of human redemption, and the medium whereby men are enlightened, justified, sanctified, and finally saved. On their first proposal such statements are liable to the objections formerly suggested; namely, that the death of the cross is not naturally attended with the requisite effusion of blood, and that blood abstractedly considered, even the blood of Christ itself, does not possess the requisite value. The explanation already given under the first of these heads is equally applicable to all the rest. The life's blood of Christ was actually poured out, owing to the rupture of his heart, occasioned by his pious endurance of the divine malediction due to human depravity, of which malediction suspension on a tree was the appointed sign. Hence, this blood publicly displayed after his death, is the natural proof and expression of his atoning sacrifice, and the central fact wherein all the other conditions of the plan of salvation visibly unite. It is accordingly always in reference to the atonement thereby accomplished that the blood of Christ is mentioned in Scripture, and from its relation to that stupendous transaction it derives all its significancy and importance. For such a purpose a fatal effusion of blood was necessary, no other blood than that of Christ on the cross would have sufficed, and in no other manner could the cross have furnished the blood so required. Taken in this connection, the blood of Christ aptly represents the satisfaction which he made to divine justice, whereby God is enabled, consistently with all his attributes, to enter into a covenant of reconciliation with sinful men; as likewise the ransom whereby they are lawfully redeemed from the dominion of Satan, translated into the kingdom of Christ, and placed under the influence of the Holy Spirit, in order to their immediate regeneration, and ultimate perfection. In the first and last steps of the process the subjects of it are comparatively passive; but in the two intermediate stages of justification and sanctification they actively cooperate, and in both of them the blood of Christ, regarded as the sign of his atoning sacrifice, is an important agent. For, the Christian covenant is not like the Mosaic, national and external, but personal and spiritual. No one can enter it except by his own free-will, and with a full understanding and approval of its terms and conditions. This is no slight or easy act, implying merely assent to a doctrine, or compliance with a ceremony, but one which involves on the part of the convert a deep conviction of his sin and danger, genuine repentance toward God, an earnest desire to be restored to his favor, and a cordial concurrence in the plan which he has provided for that end. With reverential gratitude and affection he therefore embraces Christ, as the mediator of the new covenant, lays his hand as it were on the head of the bleeding victim, appropriates to himself the atoning sacrifice by which alone he can be rescued from merited malediction, and thus performs his humble but indispensable part in the solemn compact. With such explanation, it is not difficult to understand the scriptural statement, that, on doing this, he is for Christ's sake absolved from all iniquity, and admitted as if he were a pure and innocent being to the friendship and favor of God; in other words, that he is freely justified by faith through the blood of the cross, and consequently has peace with God. On the same principle, the influence ascribed to the blood of Christ in the work of sanctification is easily explained. When a convert embraces the Saviour as his substitute, he also embraces him as his model, and becomes identified with him in all possible respects. Hence, in Scripture he is said to put on Christ, to be one spirit, and, in a certain sense, one body with him, and Christ is said to be formed and to dwell in his heart, as the hope of glory. Thus, the apostle Paul exhorts the Romans—"to put on the Lord Jesus Christ;"—asks the Corinthians,—"Know ye not that your bodies are members of Christ?"—assures them,—"He that is joined to the Lord is one spirit;"—declares to the Ephesians,—"We are members of his body, of his flesh, and of his bones;"—and prays—"that, through faith, Christ may dwell in their hearts;"—reminds the Galatians,—"As many of you as have been baptized into Christ have put on Christ;"—and, apprehensive lest by adopting Judaism they had fallen from a state of grace, affectionately addresses them,—"My little children, with whom I again travail in birth until Christ is formed within you." *

But the character preëminently displayed by Christ is that of filial piety and devotedness to God, carried to such an unbounded extent, that in order to promote his glory he voluntarily endured his malediction. A character similar in kind, although inferior in degree, is impressed by the Holy Spirit on the hearts of all who enter into the Christian covenant. By that act they become in the highest sense of the term sons of God, and thenceforth, like beloved children, imitate the perfections of their heavenly Father, in whatever manner those perfections are displayed, but more especially as they are exhibited in the person and office of Christ. In common with the apostle of the Gentiles they are enabled to say,—"The [same] God who commanded light to shine out of darkness hath shined into our hearts, enlightening [us] with a knowledge of the glory of God in the face of Jesus Christ;"—and therefore,—"while diffusing with unveiled face the glory of the Lord, we are transformed into the same image, from glory to glory, even as by the Spirit of the Lord."—Their

---

* John, chap. 17, v. 26;—Rom. chap. 13, v. 14;—1 Corinth. chap. 6, v. 15-17;—Galat. chap. 3, v. 26, 27; chap. 4, v. 19, 20;—Ephes. chap. 3, v. 14-19; chap. 5, v. 29, 30;—Coloss. chap. 1, v. 26, 27.

filial affection toward God is moreover combined with profound gratitude for their personal salvation, a cordial approval of the principles and means by which it is accomplished, and a zealous desire to serve and please their divine benefactor.—" It was fit "—says St. Paul,—" that he for whom are all things, and through whom are all things, in conducting many sons to glory, should make the leader of their salvation perfect through sufferings: for he who sanctifieth and they who are sanctified [are] all [children] of one [father]; wherefore [Christ] is not ashamed to call them brethren, saying, I will declare thy name to my brethren, in the midst of the church I will sing praise to thee.* . . . As beloved children, be ye therefore imitators of God, and walk in love, as Christ also loved us, and presented himself to God on our behalf as a sweet-smelling oblation and sacrifice. . . . I beseech you, brethren, by the mercies of God, to present your bodies [as] a living sacrifice, holy [and] well-pleasing to God, [which is] your reasonable service; and be not conformed to this world, but be transformed by the renewing of your mind, that ye may prove what is the good, and acceptable, and perfect will of God."—Treading in the footsteps of their Saviour, they adopt, and, as far as possible, copy all his proceedings on their behalf. Like him, they die to sin, rise again to a new and holy life, and, by a well-grounded anticipation of future glory, virtually sit down with him in the heavenly regions.—" What then " —asks the same apostle,—" shall we say? Shall we continue in sin that grace may abound? Certainly not. How shall we who have died to sin live any longer therein? Know ye not that as many of us as have been baptized into Christ Jesus have been baptized into his death? We have therefore been buried with him by this baptism into death; so that, as Christ was raised from the dead by the

---

* 2 Corinth. chap. 3, v. 18; chap. 4, v. 6;—Heb. chap. 2, v. 10-12.

glorious power of the Father, we also have walked in newness of life. For, if we have been planted together in the likeness of his death, we shall be also [in the likeness] of his resurrection; knowing this, that our old man hath been crucified with [Christ], that the body of sin might be mortified, that we should no longer be the slaves of sin, for he that is dead is freed from sin." *—When admonishing the Colossians to avoid Judaical errors, he tells them,—" Ye are complete in [Christ], who is the head of all principality and power, by whom also ye have been circumcised with a circumcision not made by hands, in putting off the body of the flesh by the circumcision of Christ; having in baptism been buried with him, by whom also ye have been raised together [with him], through that faith [which is produced] by the operation of God who raised him from the dead;"—and therefore exhorts them, —" If, then, ye have been raised with Christ, seek those things which are above, where Christ sitteth at the right hand of God. Set your affections on things above, not on things on the earth, for ye are dead, and your life is hid with Christ in God. When Christ [who is] our life shall appear, ye also shall appear with him in glory." †— But their progress is slow and difficult, owing to the opposition of a fallen and depraved nature with which, as it cannot be instantaneously destroyed, they are appointed during the remainder of their days unceasingly to contend. At the commencement of their course this nature, which, like a corrupt tree, yields only evil fruit, is strong and vigorous; while the regenerate nature, like a germ of heavenly origin, engrafted on it, is feeble and rudimental. These two principles are mutually counteractive; and, in proportion as either of them flourishes and pre-

---

* Rom. chap. 6, v. 1-7; chap. 12, v. 1, 2;—Ephes. chap. 2, v. 1-6; chap. v. 1, 2;—Philipp. chap. 3, v. 7-14.

† Coloss. chap. 2, v. 8-12; chap. 3, v. 1-4.

vails, the other is enfeebled and subdued. The conflict between them is sometimes illustrated by the imaginary conjunction in one person of two men,—the old, and the new,—each struggling for the mastery; and according to either illustration, if the new nature is assiduously cultivated, it becomes strong and advances to maturity, while, by means of an intrinsic antagonism, the old nature gradually decays and dies. Thus, in the well-known account of his religious experience, the apostle Paul sorrowfully acknowledges,—" I find a law, that when I would do good evil besets me : for I delight in the law of God according to the inward man, but see another law in my members warring against the law of my mind, and bringing me into captivity to the law of sin which is in my members. Wretched man that I am! Who will deliver me from this dead body? I thank God, through Jesus Christ our Lord."—He accordingly admonishes the Galatians,— " Walk in the Spirit, and ye will not fulfil the lust of the flesh; for the flesh lusteth against the Spirit, and the Spirit against the flesh, and these are at war with each other, so as to prevent your doing the things that ye would;"—charges the Ephesians—" to put off in reference to their former mode of life the old man which is corrupt according to the deceitful lusts, and to be renewed in the spirit of their mind and to put on the new [man], which, according to God, is renewed in righteousness and true holiness;"—and reminds the Colossians—" that they had put off the old man with his deeds, and had put on the new [man], which is renewed unto knowledge according to the image of his Creator." *

In this, as in all the other parts of the plan of salvation, the conduct of the Deity is not less distinguished by wisdom, than by benevolence and power. Had men re-

* Rom. chap. 7, v. 21–25; chap. 8, v. 12–17;—Galat. chap. 5, v. 16, 17;—Ephes. chap. 4, v. 20–21;—Coloss. chap. 3, v. 9, 10.

tained their original innocence, the ordinary manifestations of his attributes in the course of nature and providence would have been sufficient to excite them to piety and virtue; but, since in consequence of their depravity this is not the case, he has been pleased to interpose for their recovery by an extraordinary manifestation of the same attributes, directed to this special object, and accompanied with a corresponding supply of renovating influence. Yet, although the agency employed for this purpose is chiefly supernatural, the mode of action is strictly natural. The laws of the human mind are neither violated, nor superseded. The most effective means are applied to enlighten the understandings of men with moral and religious truth, to awaken their consciences, and to purify their affections; but after all, the result must depend on their own choice. As has been already remarked, they cannot be made holy or happy by mere external agency, without their own consent and concurrence. Life and death, a blessing and a curse, are set before them; but they are at liberty either to reject the counsel of God against themselves, or to accept it. If they cordially embrace his covenant of reconciliation, he admits them at once into his family as beloved children, gives them the paternal injunction,—" Be ye holy, for I am holy,"—and offers them the aid of his Spirit, to enable them to carry this command into effect. But, in order that their obedience may be genuine and liberal, the result of conviction and approval, and alike exempt from the compulsion of fear and the pretension of merit, they are first freely justified through faith in the blood of Christ, and afterward sanctified through the same faith working by love. Sanctification is therefore merely the progressive development of conversion, the same principles and motives operating in both.

This important truth is clearly stated in many parts

of the New Testament, particularly in Paul's epistle to Titus:—"The saving grace of God"—says the apostle,—"hath appeared to all men, teaching us that, renouncing ungodliness and worldly lusts, we should live rationally, justly, and piously in the present world, looking forward to the blessed hope, and the glorious appearing of our great God and Saviour, Jesus Christ, who gave himself for us that he might redeem us from all iniquity, and purify [us] to himself, [as] a superior people zealous of good works. . . . When the kindness and benevolence of God our Saviour toward men appeared, [it was] not by works of righteousness which he had done, but according to his mercy that he saved us, through [the] washing of regeneration, and [the] renewing of the Holy Spirit, which he shed on us abundantly through Jesus Christ our Saviour, that, having been justified by his grace, we might become heirs according to the hope of eternal life. [It is] a true saying, and on these [points] I wish thee to insist, that they who have believed on God should set their hearts on excelling in good works."—The Christian is enjoined to add to his faith virtue, and to work out his salvation, which here means his sanctification, with fear and trembling, because it is God who of his own good pleasure works in him both to will and to do, but who does this only on condition of his faithful and cordial coöperation.* Although found in a fallen and degraded state, he is wisely treated as a rational and moral agent, who in accepting and fulfilling the plan provided for his restoration must exert his own intelligence, energy, and free-will. By daily employing his faculties for this purpose, vigorously practising self-denial, resisting temptation, enduring affliction, and cultivating right principles and affections, in conjunc-

---

* Philipp. chap. 2, v. 12, 13 ;—Titus, chap. 2, v. 11-14 ; chap. 3, v. 4-8 ;—1 Peter, chap. 1, v. 14-16 ;—2 Peter, chap. 1, v. 5-11 ; chap. 2, v. 20-22.

tion with a diligent use of outward ordinances, and an humble dependence on the influence of the Holy Spirit, he daily grows in grace, and continually approaches nearer to that standard of perfection, which in the present stage of existence he does not expect fully to attain. All this is in strict accordance with the laws of the human mind. Active powers are strengthened by exercise, ardent affections are nurtured by long and devoted attention to their objects, and principles are tested and invigorated by overcoming obstacles, whether pleasing or painful. But, to maintain a conflict so arduous strong motives are required. These are in part supplied by gracious promises of realizing the divine friendship and favor during the life which now is, and in a still higher degree at its termination, when the purified spirit will pass at once into the blissful presence of its father and its God, where there is fulness of joy, and where there are pleasures for evermore. Such promises frequently occur in the messages sent by Christ to the seven Asian churches; as for example, in the concluding passage.—" Behold! I stand at the door and knock. If any one hear my voice, and open the door, I will come in to him, and sup with him, and he [shall sup] with me. To him that overcometh I will give the privilege of sitting with me on my throne, as I also overcame, and am seated with my Father on his throne. He that hath an ear, let him hear what the Spirit saith to the churches."—In Eastern courts, when the sovereign invites himself to sup with any of his courtiers, his invitation is regarded as a command, and the favored subject, far from presuming to sit at table with his royal guest, waits on him as a servant. But, such is the superiority of divine condescension to any thing witnessed among men, that Christ stands at the door of the heart, and knocks; and, when freely admitted, obliges his host to sup with him.*

* The effect is well illustrated by the conversion of Zaccheus, Luke,

The apostle John, through whom these messages were transmitted, remarks in his first epistle,—"Beloved, we are now the children of God, and it doth not yet appear what we shall be, but we know that when he shall appear we shall be like him, for we shall see him as he is; and every one who hath this hope in him purifieth himself even as he is pure."—The apostle Peter likewise reminds the Christian Jews of Asia Minor, that they had received from Christ—"exceedingly great and precious promises, in order that by them ye might become partakers of the divine nature, having escaped from the corruption which is in the world through lust; wherefore, giving all diligence, add to your faith virtue," etc.;—and lastly, Paul tells the Corinthian Christians,—"Ye are the temple of the living God, as God hath said, I will dwell in them, and walk [in them], and will be their God, and they shall be my people. Wherefore, come out from among them and be separate, saith the Lord, and touch not that which is unclean, and I will receive you, and will be your father, and ye shall be my sons and daughters, saith the Lord Almighty. Having then such promises, beloved, let us cleanse ourselves from every defilement of flesh and spirit, and perfect holiness in the fear of God." *

But, although other influences may legitimately cooperate in exciting the Christian to perform his part in the work of sanctification with diligence and fidelity, the most powerful of all is that derived from a grateful and affectionate contemplation of the atoning sacrifice of Christ, as represented by his blood, which is therefore said to be applied by the Holy Spirit to the heart. The peculiar efficacy of this motive has often been noticed in treatises

---

chap. 19, v. 1–10. See also chap. 12, v. 35–37; chap. 22, v. 24–30;—Revel. chap. 3, v. 20–22.

* 2 Corinth. chap. 6, v. 16–18; chap. 7, v, 1;—2 Peter, chap. 1, v. 3–5;—1 John, chap. 3, v. 1–3.

on practical religion, but has seldom, perhaps, been better expressed than in those published several years since by Thomas Erskine, Esq., of the Scottish bar.—"The sacrifice of Christ"—says this excellent author,—"has associated sin with the blood of a benefactor, as well as with our own personal sufferings; and obedience with the dying entreaty of a friend breathing out a tortured life for us, as well as with our own unending glory in his blessed society. . . . The same God, that he might declare his abhorrence of sin in the very form and substance of his plan of mercy, sent forth his Son to make a propitiation *through his blood*. This is the God with whom we have to do: this is his character, the just God, and yet the Saviour. . . . The same truth, with regard to the character of God and the condition of man, which is so fully developed in the New Testament, is exhibited also in the Old, through an obscurer medium of types, and shadows, and prophecy. . . . This belief is inseparably connected with a belief of the reality of Christ's sufferings; and, if Christ's sufferings were not real, we may give up the Bible. . . . And when we see a system such as Christianity asserting to itself a divine original, tending most distinctly to the eradication of moral evil, harmonizing so beautifully with the most enlightened views of the character of God, and adapted so wonderfully to the capacities of man, does not the probability amount to an assurance that God has indeed made a movement toward man, and that such an antidote is, indeed, contained in the truth of the gospel?* . . . . Thus it appears that the heart of man, the Bible, and the course of Providence, have a mutual adaptation to each other; and hence we may conclude that they proceed from the same source,—we may conclude that the same God who made man, and encompassed him with the

---

* Thomas Erskine, Esq., Remarks on the Internal Evidence for the Truth of Revealed Religion, pp. 73, 104, 130, 149, 164, 165.

trials of life, gave the Bible to instruct him how these trials might be made subservient to his eternal happiness. . . . . The death of Christ, in which all the facts of the gospel meet as in their centre, is described as an atonement for the sins of the world, required by infinite holiness, provided by infinite love. He, by the grace of God, tasted death for every man: he, the one, bare the sins of the many. This marks God's judgment of human guilt: the punishment inflicted on the representative measures the deservings of those whose place he filled. It was an act of justice.—'Christ died under the sentence of sin.'— This is an address to the conscience, to the sense of right and wrong; and it is only through the information of the conscience that we can comprehend it. It was an act of generous love, of self-sacrifice.—'Herein is love, not that we loved God, but that he loved us, and sent his Son to be the propitiation for our sins.' . . . The unmeasured love which provided the lamb for the burnt-offering, the pure and awful holiness which required the atonement, the eternal identity of a departure from God and a departure from happiness, of a return to God and a return to happiness,—this is the lesson of the cross.* . . . Joy in the atonement, merely as the means of escape from misery, is blessed by the Spirit of God to bring forth the fruit of holy love, to the praise of the glory of his grace, in the hardest and the foulest heart. The joy of a free deliverance softens and expands the heart: it is thus prepared to look at the blood which was its ransom with tenderness and gratitude, and thus it is led to rejoice in the love of him whose blood was shed. . . . And, when the affections are attracted, think, what it is which attracts them: it is not a kindness merely, it is a high and holy kindness, it is a

---

* Thomas Erskine, Esq., Remarks on the Internal Evidence for the Truth of Revealed Religion; pp. 175, 176, 186;—Essay on Faith, pp. 49, 51.

wise kindness, it is an eternal kindness: it is the perfection of moral beauty, an uncreated loveliness, which, while it expands the affections, purifies and tranquillizes them. In like manner self-love, or the prudential principle, finds its object and its repose in the atonement. . . . Any one of the doctrines of the atonement which can make us fearless or careless of sinning must be a wrong view, because it is not good nor profitable to men. That blessed doctrine declares sin pardoned, not because it is overlooked or winked at, but because the weight of its condemnation has been sustained on our behalf by our elder brother and representative: this makes sin hateful, by connecting it with the blood of our best friend. . . . We may without faith in Christ regard the consequences of sin with dislike and apprehension, and we may even feel it to be a pollution to the dignity of our nature; but our hearts can never loathe it for its own sake until we see it connected with the blood of him who loved us, and gave himself for us. . . . The more freely grace is proclaimed, the more deeply sin is condemned; and it is the belief of having much forgiven that compels the heart to love much.* . . . Who, it may be asked, is this God whom we are called on thus to love? It is that God who hath so hated sin, and so loved the world, that he gave his only-begotten Son to the death, to condemn sin, and to save the world. . . . That blood branded sin: it removed every obstacle that barred the approach of the sinner to God, or of God to the sinner: and it gave a pledge and a specimen of the richness and the holiness of divine love. This revelation is the instrument by which the Spirit of God writes the law upon the heart, in fulfilment of the promise made through Jeremiah. (Chap. 31, v. 13.) It was given that men might see God as he is, and learn to love him as he ought

* Thomas Erskine, Esq., *Essay on Faith*, pp. 75, 100, 112, 113, 118, 119.

to be loved."*—Such love when perfect fulfils the moral law. That law merely demands from intelligent beings a cordial and universal regard to the relations in which they are placed; and nothing can be so effectual in producing this regard, the deficiency of which constitutes depravity, as a filial love to God, founded on a grateful acceptance of the salvation which he freely offers through the atoning blood of Christ. Such love implies unbounded admiration for the perfections of the Deity, and profound reverence for his laws and arrangements, the excellence and necessity of which are so strikingly displayed in that wondrous transaction. This, therefore, is the true principle of evangelical sanctification, the fundamental motive by which all the moral precepts of the New Testament are ultimately enforced. Thus, in one place, after establishing the doctrine of justification by faith, the apostle Paul remarks,—" But, if while seeking to be justified by Christ we ourselves are found sinners, [is] Christ on that account a minister of sin? By no means. For, if I rebuild the things which I destroyed, I prove myself a transgressor: for I through the law have become dead to the law, that I might live unto God. I am crucified with Christ, yet I live, nevertheless not I, but Christ liveth in me; and the life which I now live in the flesh I live by faith in the Son of God, who loved me and gave himself for me."—In a similar style he observes on another occasion,—"The love of Christ constraineth us, since we thus judge, that if one died for all, all were [virtually] dead; and that he died for all, that they who live should no longer live to themselves, but to him who for their sake died and rose again. Henceforth therefore we know no one according to the flesh; yea, if we have even known Christ according to the flesh, we now know him so no more.

* Thomas Erskine, Esq., *Three Essays on the Unconditional Freeness of the Gospel*, p. 54.

Hence, if any one [is] in Christ, [he is] a new creature: old things have passed away, behold all things have become new." *

It thus appears that the explanation here given of the cause and mode of the Saviour's death, not only perfectly harmonizes with all the doctrines and precepts of the New Testament, but also powerfully illustrates and confirms them; a circumstance which affords additional proof of its truth and utility. Yet, as this explanation is discoverable by reason, and the knowledge of it is not absolutely necessary for the purposes of practical religion, it accords with the general character of revelation that it should not be formally stated, but merely suggested by the Scriptures. They therefore simply declare that the blood of Christ, poured forth at his death on the cross, rendered an atonement to divine justice for human depravity, and was consequently the source of all the blessings of salvation, the medium by which those who come to God through him are justified, sanctified, and finally redeemed. Such statements, abstractedly considered, are attended with some degree of obscurity which the explanation now proposed satisfactorily removes, and thereby furnishes a new elucidation of the gospel plan, calculated under the divine blessing to produce a salutary effect, both on the understanding and on the heart.

* 2 Corinth. chap. 5, v. 14-17;—Galat. chap. 2, v. 17-20; chap. 5, v. 24;—Philipp. chap. 2, v. 5-8;—Heb. chap. 12, v. 1-3;—1 Peter, chap. 4, v. 1, 2.

CHAPTER V.

ON THE PECULIAR EVIDENCE OF THE TRUTH OF CHRISTIANITY, FURNISHED BY THE FOREGOING EXPLANATION OF THE DEATH OF CHRIST.

It has been the object of the former parts of this treatise to demonstrate the immediate cause and mode of the death of Christ; and the proof has chiefly consisted in showing that the explanation proposed is in exact accordance both with the laws of Nature, and with all the representations made on the subject in Scripture. The design of the present section is, on the other hand, to show that the representations thus made and explained, furnish new and peculiar evidence of the truth of the Scripture, and consequently of the religion which it reveals. These representations include a circumstance, which, although undoubtedly implied, is nevertheless so latent and extraordinary, that it has never yet been fully recognized; namely, that the death of Christ on the cross was induced, not as is commonly imagined, by the usual sufferings of crucifixion, but by the rupture of his heart, and the effusion of his life's blood, occasioned by his pious endurance of the divine malediction due to human depravity. This circumstance, which manifestly bears a most intimate relation to the whole circle of Christian doctrines, is found to be not only in perfect accordance, but also in necessary connection, with all the other circumstances of the case. On many passages of Scripture it casts a new and unexpected light; and to some, which, without its aid, appear inexplicable, or are liable to be misunderstood, it supplies a satisfactory and useful elucidation. The argument now maintained is, that this minute and universal agreement is incompatible with delusion, imposture, or casual coincidence, and admits of no other solution than the truth of the religion to which it appertains. The several particulars of this agreement, in reference to the laws of the human body and mind, the fundamental principle of atonement, the types and prophecies of the Old Testament, and the narratives, symbols, doctrines, and precepts of the New, have already been considered at some length; but a brief recapitulation of them will here be given, in order to show their special application to the present purpose, and the irresistible evidence which results from the harmonious concurrence of the whole.

In the first place,—Mental agony, or a violent conflict between opposite and distressing emotions, naturally occasions palpitation; and, when rapidly raised to the highest degree, produces either bloody sweat, or sudden death by rupture of the heart, an event usually attended with loud cries. In the latter case, although scarcely in any other, the blood inwardly effused separates after death into its solid and liquid parts, so as to present when exposed, the appearance commonly termed blood and water. Such is precisely the view which, in the simplest form of narrative, and without note or comment, the Scripture gives of the death of Christ. In the garden of Gethsemane he was subjected for the first time to mental sufferings of overwhelming severity, which rendered his—" soul exceedingly sorrowful, even unto death;"—and, had he not received angelic succor, would apparently, without the aid of any external infliction, have proved fatal on the spot; but, having been thus seasonably counteracted, proceeded no further than to induce a bloody sweat.—" His sweat

became as it were clots of blood dropping to the ground."
—After a respite of some hours, during which he evinced the greatest fortitude and self-possession, these peculiar sufferings were renewed on the cross, where they again attained their highest intensity, and on this occasion were unattended with any intermission or relief. The consequence was that, after silently enduring them for three hours, he suddenly expired amid loud and fervent exclamations, long before the outward punishment could have proved fatal; and, on his side having been afterward pierced by a spear,—" immediately there came forth blood and water,"—implying that his heart had been previously ruptured. The correspondence of the several occurrences here related to the natural order of things is sufficiently obvious; and, as amid the wide range of possibilities many other causes and effects might have been assigned, although none of them would have possessed this necessary character, so exact and critical a correspondence between the statement and the reality, and that in reference to a transaction so singular and uncommon, must undoubtedly be regarded as a strong internal evidence of truth.

Secondly,—The doctrine of atonement, abstractedly considered, involves conditions seemingly discordant and almost incompatible, but by the scriptural account of the death of Christ is fully verified and explained. In order to reconcile the conflicting demands of justice and mercy, the malediction due to human depravity was to be diverted from its proper objects, by falling on the head of a suitable substitute. That substitute must therefore have possessed a pure and perfect human nature. The divine malediction falling on such a being must have assumed the form of a partial and temporary abandonment, and have occasioned intense mental agony, ending in rupture of the heart, the extreme limit of meritorious endurance. All this is accordingly represented in Scripture, which not only affirms the general principle of atonement, but also exhibits its fulfilment. Had the Scripture announced pardon for sin without providing satisfaction to divine justice, it would, by violating the moral law, have forfeited its title to inspiration; but, by realizing all the conditions of atonement, fully establishes its claim. Several elements of the process, being spiritual and invisible, could be ascertained only by competent testimony, or by external signs and results; and both are therefore liberally supplied. The purity of Christ's human nature was announced by an angel before his conception, and ascribed to its only possible cause, the special interposition of the Holy Spirit; but it was also practically demonstrated by his surmounting every trial and temptation to which he could be exposed, and was either directly or indirectly acknowledged both by his enemies and by the Deity. That he voluntarily submitted to divine abandonment in order to make atonement for the sins of the world, was distinctly predicted by the prophets, and declared by himself; but it was also proved, as has now been shown, by the natural and destructive effects of the malediction on his body and mind, namely, by his agony and bloody sweat at Gethsemane, by his premature and sudden death on the cross, and by the effusion of blood and water which ensued on his side being afterward pierced with a spear. The prominence thus given to the principle of atonement, and the critical agreement with that principle of the physical facts described as its results, furnish therefore a peculiar and incontestable evidence of the veracity and divine origin of the Scriptures.

Thirdly,—The numerous types and prophecies of Scripture relating to this momentous event, when separately contemplated, present difficulties and obscurities so great, and seemingly so insurmountable, that nothing but truth can account for their original introduction and ultimate fulfilment. Of this transaction, all preceding religious ceremonies were merely shadows and representations. A covenant of reconciliation freely granted by God to fallen man, and ratified by an atoning sacrifice, was the common object which they attested and prefigured, but could not realize. The insufficiency of the ancient sacrifices for their professed purpose was proved by their intrinsic worthlessness, and obvious inability to purify the conscience, and hence by their endless repetition. They served, however, to maintain a perpetual record of the demerit of sin, to intimate the need of expiation, and to define the singular and almost inconceivable combination of circumstances required in the one great and perfect sacrifice, by which they were at length to be forever superseded. A true atoning sacrifice implied that the divine malediction due to sin was vicariously endured by a suitable victim. As endured by Christ, it necessarily produced rupture of the heart, and effusion of the life's blood. To indicate this reality, the life's blood of animal victims was from the earliest period made an indispensable condition of ceremonial atonement; and it was distinctly announced that—"the sacrifices of God are a broken and a contrite heart."—For the same reason it was ordained that Christ should die the death of the cross, decreed by the Jewish Sanhedrim, but executed by a Gentile magistrate; and yet that, contrary to the usual custom in Judea, none of his bones should be broken, an exception which implied his premature dissolution on the same day; because, under all the circumstances of the case, this was the only mode of death which combined the appearance with the reality of that malediction, whereof suspension on a tree was the appointed emblem, and the Jewish hierarchy were the authorized ministers. But the punishment of crucifixion during life was not in use among the people of Israel; and it was therefore predicted that at the time of the Saviour's death the tribe of Judah, of which he was a member, should be subject to the Roman empire. The power of blessing and cursing was placed exclusively in the hands of the Aaronic priesthood; and it was consequently foretold that in accomplishing the death of Christ they would, although such an alliance was repugnant to their national customs and prejudices, be associated with Gentiles. His death was, however, occasioned not by the ordinary sufferings of the cross, but by the divine malediction itself, through the medium of agony of mind, and rupture of the heart. A slow and lingering punishment was therefore selected, as the only one suitable for the purpose, and it was predicted that he would pour forth his life's blood unto death. This announcement determined the precise mode in which his life was to be sacrificed; since in no other mode could the punishment of the cross, which conventionally denoted malediction, have furnished that effusion of life's blood which in this case was its natural result, and without which the Scripture declared there could be no discharge of sin. It was, moreover, requisite that this result should be publicly demonstrated; and it was accordingly predicted,—"They shall look on him whom they pierced;"—a prophecy literally acomplished by the spear of the Roman soldier after the death of Christ, but virtually by the sin of the world, which in this very manner had proved its cause. The effusion of blood and water which followed the wound formed an essential part of the demonstration, and was therefore prefigured by the employment of blood and water as the outward seal of the first covenant; wherein the life's blood of a clean and unoffending animal, mixed with pure and running water, faintly portrayed the stupendous reality which constituted the seal of the second. The extreme complication and singularity of these conditions, which it is evident could never occur more than once, and which it seemed almost impossible should ever occur at all, their express prediction so many ages before the event, and their exact accomplishment when the proper time arrived, triumphantly prove the truth and divine origin of the religious dispensation whereof they form a part; a dispensation as much beyond the wisdom of men to contrive, as it was beyond their power either to execute or to prevent.

Fourthly,—A similar conclusion results from the fact, that the same explanation of the death of Christ which is thus shown to be in perfect harmony with the laws of the human body and mind, with the fundamental doctrine of atonement, and with the types and prophecies of the Old Testament, is also suggested by the evangelical narratives of the New, although unnoticed, and seemingly unperceived by the evangelists themselves. Until this explanation is applied, their account of the event appears strange and mysterious. That a person in the prime of life and vigor should have died in six hours, under a punishment which rarely proved fatal in less than three days, that he should have previously sweated blood, and that, on his side being afterward pierced by a spear, there should immediately have issued blood and water, are circumstances which savor of the marvellous, and which those inclined to cavil at revelation might reject as incredible. This very narrative is, nevertheless, found on inquiry to contain the elements of an explanation which, although entirely satisfactory, is yet so latent, that it has never hitherto been generally acknowledged, and which it is manifest the sacred writers had neither the disposition nor the capacity to invent. Although doubtless endued with good natural abilities, they were, with one exception, uneducated men, selected from the lower classes of society to be witnesses of occurrences, some of which they were unable at the time fully to comprehend. Luke, as a physician, had in this respect an advantage over his brethren, and it was perhaps owing to this peculiarity that he alone mentions the bloody sweat of Christ in the garden of Gethsemane; but, in his brief account of the Saviour's death there is no sign of his having discerned its immediate cause, and the subsequent effusion of blood and water, which was not less deserving of notice, he totally omits. At that period, indeed, physiological science was not sufficiently advanced to enable him to form a correct judgment on the subject; yet the same science, in its more improved state at the present day, recognizes in these simple reports the distinct but unobtrusive traces of natural actions, remarkable for the singularity of their character and the rarity of their occurrence, by means of which every difficulty is removed, and the whole transaction is completely elucidated. That amid a multitude of possible alternatives, the narratives of the four evangelists, although differing from each other on several minor points, should exactly agree in supplying the materials of such an explanation, which it is probable the writers themselves did not clearly understand, is a most extraordinary coincidence, which admits of no other solution than the truth of the narratives, and the reality of the events which they describe.

But, besides their characteristic reports of the death of Christ, three of the evangelists give similar accounts of two symbolical actions intimately connected with that event, namely, the institution of the Lord's Supper, and the miraculous rending of the veil in the temple during the crucifixion. These actions seem to have been expressly designed by the Deity to form a congenial supplement to the types and prophecies of the Old Testament, and to prove that the whole emblematical system exhibited in the Scripture had the same divine author, and the same ultimate object. The two essential circumstances in the death of Christ which rendered it effectual as an atoning sacrifice, were the rupture of his heart, and the effusion of his life's blood; and these were precisely the circumstances which he commanded his disciples symbolically to represent, when occasionally commemorating that sacrifice by a sacred and social repast, consisting of bread broken, and of wine poured out. The peculiar importance of these circumstances was clearly expressed by him, when founding this simple but significant rite after celebrating the paschal supper with the apostles, on the evening immediately preceding his death; for, on giving them the bread he said,—"Take, eat, this is my body which is broken for you. Do this in remembrance of me;"—and, on presenting the wine,—" This cup [is] the new covenant by my blood, which [is] shed for you [and] for many, for the discharge of sins. Do this, whenever ye drink of it, in remembrance of me."—The same circumstances were publicly signalized in the same sense on the following day by a remarkable interposition of the Deity himself. The incompetency of the annual sin-offering, as well as of all the other sacrifices under the Mosaic law, to accomplish their ostensible purpose of atonement, was intimated by the mysterious veil, which during the whole of that dispensation excluded its members on pain of death from the inner sanctuary of the tabernacle, or temple, representing the beatific presence of God. But the efficacy of the blood of Christ to procure complete reconciliation was practically acknowledged, at the very moment when owing to the rupture of his heart it was actually poured out, by the supernatural rending of the veil in the temple from the top to the bottom, implying that a living or acceptable way of access to the divine presence was then for the first time opened, to all who are willing to avail themselves of so inestimable a benefit. The testimony respecting the immediate cause and mode of the death of Christ which by means of these two symbols is thus attributed to the Saviour, and to the Deity, is so direct and specific, so exactly in harmony with all the other alleged facts of the case, as well as with the explanation deducible from them, and so utterly incompatible with chance or imposture, that it cannot fail to be regarded as a distinct and decisive proof of the truth and divine origin of those Scriptures whereof it forms so remarkable a feature.

Fifthly,—In the doctrinal parts of the New Testament, Christ is represented as having suffered the death of the cross, and at the same time all the blessings of salvation are ascribed to his blood.—" He became obedient to death, even the death of the cross, ... made peace by the blood of his cross, ... and redeemed us from the curse of the law, by being cursed on our behalf; for it is written, Cursed is every one that hangeth on a tree."—Statements of this kind frequently repeated, and strongly enforced, are at first sight not free from obscurity; for the ordinary death of the cross does not furnish the requisite effusion of blood, neither does blood abstractedly considered possess the requisite value. But for practical purposes a general comprehension of the subject is sufficient; and, therefore, in most of these cases the connection between the means and the end is assumed by the Scripture, and not improperly admitted by the majority of Christians. Yet, a clear explanation, besides being manifestly conformable to the divine intentions, is highly desirable, not only to remove objections, but also because it may reasonably be expected that evangelical doctrines will be more efficacious in proportion as they are better understood. The demonstration now given of the immediate cause and mode of the death of Christ answers this purpose, and shows that the remarkable statements made in Scripture respecting that cardinal event, instead of being referable, as some have supposed, to poetical or figurative language, are strictly accurate and true, and that the more closely they are scrutinized the more weighty and affecting do they appear. As the natural expression and result of superlative moral excellence, perfect obedience toward God, unbounded benevolence toward man, and voluntary endurance of the malediction due to human depravity, the life's blood of Christ flowing from a heart ruptured by an agony of pious grief, was at once the blood of atonement, and the blood of the cross. Viewed in this connection, it is evidently well adapted to fulfil all the important functions assigned to it. As the blood of propitiation, it renders satisfaction to divine justice, and expiates the sins of the world. As the blood of the new covenant, it is the medium whereby God reconciles mankind to himself, not imputing to them their transgressions. As the blood of sprinkling, it purifies the conscience from dead works, to serve the living God. As the blood of redemption, it ransoms those who claim its protection from the primeval curse, and the consequent bondage of Satan, sin, and death, and exalts them to the glorious liberty of the children of God. The blood of Christ is thus perceived to be the only effectual instrument of conversion and sanctification. Had mankind retained their original innocence, the ordinary manifestations of the character of God, in his works of nature and providence, would have been sufficient to maintain them in an undeviating course of piety and virtue; but, after they had fallen from their integrity, a far more impressive display of the divine character became necessary for their moral regeneration; and this is supplied by the plan of salvation revealed in Scripture, and of which the blood of Christ is the natural emblem and expression. Ordained by the Father, provided by the Son, and applied by the Spirit, this blood exhibits the triune Deity engaged in the work of human restoration.

Wisdom and power make the necessary arrangements, and, without violating in the slightest degree the laws of rectitude and order, overcome difficulties apparently invincible, and realize conditions which might have been supposed unattainable. Mercy and justice combine to prove that God is just, even in justifying the guilty, on their cordially embracing the covenant of reconciliation. Transfused as it were from the heart of Christ to that of the convert, this blood dissolves its enmity, heals its barrenness, and imbues it with those filial sentiments of veneration, gratitude, and love toward a reconciled God and father, which constitute the germ of the regenerate character, and the root of evangelical religion. A method of instruction which provides ample information of a general nature for all, but at the same time reserves for those who more deeply investigate the subject the means of obtaining still clearer views of the fundamental truths of the gospel, by which their reality and mutual relation are rendered more manifest and more impressive, bears unequivocal marks of divine origin and design. The natural connection which is thus discovered to exist between the death of Christ on the cross, and its various applications in Scripture to doctrinal and practical purposes, presents a minute consistency, an adaptation of means to ends, and a conformity with the principles of morality, and the constitution of the human mind, which furnish a peculiar and undeniable evidence of truth. And, if either of the evidences here adduced would separately be sufficient for the purpose of demonstration, the conclusion resulting from the harmonious concurrence of the whole of them to the same end can be none other than that expressed in the words of the apostle Paul,—" It is an infallible declaration, and worthy of universal acceptance, that Jesus Christ came into the world to save sinners, and to cancel sin, by the sacrifice of himself."

CONCLUSION.

As the principal object of this treatise is to demonstrate and explain a fundamental fact in Christianity, many of its readers may be disposed to think that it should here terminate, and that any attempt at practical application, especially on the part of one who has no regular call to such an office, would be superfluous and obtrusive. Yet, on the other hand, it seems scarcely proper to quit so solemn a subject without making an effort to secure some of the beneficial effects which it is calculated to produce; and the author will therefore venture to address a few remarks of this kind, both to professed Christians and to those by whom the gospel, although sufficiently known, has never yet been cordially embraced.

Among the many who belong to the latter class, no reasonable person will, it is presumed, question the possibility of a revelation from heaven, the expediency of its publication in the written form, or the duty incumbent on all who are apprised of the existence of such a document, to give it a careful and candid examination; in order that, if spurious, it may be rejected, and if genuine, it may be acknowledged and obeyed. Such is confessedly the duty of subjects with regard to the alleged proclamations of their human governors; and the duty must be still more cogent in reference to proclamations which profess to emanate from the sovereign of the universe; for, when the reality of a message from God is under consideration, indifference and neglect are scarcely less criminal than blind credulity, or wilful unbelief. Except, therefore, a document of this kind is discredited by some glaring falsehood or deficiency, it demands immediate and impartial investigation, and the proper course to be pursued is to inquire at once for positive evidences of truth; since, whether these are discovered or found wanting, the principal question will thus be promptly resolved; and, if it is answered in the affirmative, there will be time enough afterward for the examination of difficulties and obscurities, inseparable from such subjects, but which in the case here supposed cannot be of material importance. To commence with the latter process is manifestly wrong; since it is well known that researches of this kind are usually unsatisfactory, and often interminable. After the most persevering and laborious study, no higher conclusion can result from them than the negative one above mentioned; and in the mean while, decisive proofs, admitting of easy and rapid attainment, may have been entirely neglected.

Of the divine origin of the Scriptures relating to the Mosaic and Christian covenants, which although distinct are intimately connected, many demonstrations have been given; and another of a somewhat novel description is now added, to which the serious attention of those who are still unconvinced is earnestly entreated. To such persons the author would respectfully say;—Examine strictly, but fairly, the evidence here presented, and ask yourselves whether it is chargeable with any fallacy or defect. Would a fable, whether cunningly or grossly devised, endure so minute and searching a scrutiny without being detected? Can a system of religious doctrine, which under such a scrutiny becomes only so much the clearer and the more confirmed, be otherwise than true? Consider the force which this demonstration derives from its physical character, whereby all the tangibleness and reality belonging to that branch of knowledge is extended to spiritual topics of the most refined and elevated nature;—from its latency, whereby it plainly appears not to be artificially contrived, but essentially connected with the subject;—and from its perfect harmony, when at length developed, with all previous evidences to the same effect. If, on doing this, you find that you can neither deny the facts, refute the reasoning, nor disprove the conclusion, you have no alternative but to acknowledge the Scriptures, thus and otherwise demonstrated, and more especially the gospel, which it is their principal object to proclaim, as a genuine revelation from God.

But the matter does not end here. The gospel is not merely a message to be believed, but an offer to be accepted, and that offer nothing less than the divine friendship, which on certain conditions you are graciously invited to embrace, with a view to your present and eternal happiness, thus only to be secured. These conditions are repentance toward God, faith in the Lord Jesus Christ, and coöperation with the Holy Spirit in the work of personal sanctification; implying on your part a consciousness of depravity, a desire of salvation, and a willingness to adopt the plan divinely provided for that purpose. To refuse this plan, or to substitute another in its place, would manifestly be the height of impiety and presumption. Whatever may be the ultimate fate of those who have never heard of a Saviour, little reflection is required to answer the questions proposed by the two principal apostles;—"How shall we escape, if we neglect so great a salvation?"—and—"What [will be] the end of those who obey not the gospel of God?"*—This plan com-

---

* Heb. chap. 2, v. 1–4;—1 Peter, chap. 4, v. 17, 18.

mends itself to the approbation of all well-disposed and intelligent minds, by its exact conformity to natural facts and principles. It is obvious, even to ordinary reason, that God can neither transgress his own laws nor suffer them to be transgressed with impunity by others, hence the necessity of atonement;—that depraved beings cannot be reclaimed and elevated by their own unassisted efforts, hence the necessity of the Holy Spirit's influence; and that free agents, when thus depraved, cannot be made virtuous and happy without their own concurrence, hence the vast amount of religious and moral instruction communicated by the Scriptures, and their numerous and urgent exhortations to repentance and self-culture.

Depravity, or deficiency of moral principle, is the mental malady of all mankind in their present stage of existence. Under many varieties of mode and degree, it adheres more or less to every human being without exception, prevails in all times and places; and, if left to itself, shows no tendency to amendment. The explanation of this state of things may be difficult, but the fact is certain, being as fully attested by experience as by revelation. From this negative yet prolific source are derived the various defects and derelictions of duty which, although less appalling than positive transgressions, involve so large an amount of evil; as well as the more flagrant crimes which, with all their aggravation, are merely the result of unbridled appetites and passions, neither hurtful nor sinful in themselves, but liable to become inordinate and destructive when not controlled by higher motives. The supremacy of moral principle in rational beings, that is, of a cordial and inviolable regard to the relations in which they are placed, is, on the other hand, the original law of their nature, indispensable to their complete enjoyment of the divine friendship, and consequently to their happiness. The demands of this principle are represented in Scripture by the two cardinal commandments,—"Thou shalt love the Lord thy God with all thy heart, with all thy mind, with all thy soul, and with all thy strength;"—and—"Thou shalt love thy neighbor as thyself."—The means of recovering this principle, when lost, are supplied by the gospel alone, which not merely exhibits in theory the conditions required for the purpose, but has also been found practically efficacious by men of all classes, and under all circumstances. Whether high or low, young or old, refined or ignorant,—"Greek or Jew, Barbarian, Scythian, bond, or free,"—all who ever gave it a fair trial have experienced that—"it is the power of God unto salvation to every one that believeth."*—Under the gospel dispensation, the Deity does not command mankind to make an atonement for their sins, and by their own efforts to reëstablish the authority of the moral principle over their hearts; but graciously offers to bestow on them both these inestimable blessings, on the sole condition of their grateful and willing coöperation.

Unless, however, men are conscious of their mental disease, anxious for its removal, confident in the means appointed for their recovery and resolute in applying them, the remedy is provided in vain. Rational conviction is, accordingly, the first step toward conversion. It is on this account that so many demonstrations of the truth of Christianity, and so many expositions of its nature and design, have been collected. It is for this purpose that the present treatise has been composed. Once more, therefore, would the author say to all who on this momentous subject have hitherto been skeptical or indifferent,—Examine attentively the foundation on which you are invited to build, and convince yourselves of its firmness and security, as likewise of the guilt and danger of rejecting it. Having

---

* Matt. chap. 22, v. 34–40;—Mark, chap. 12, v, 28–31;—Rom. chap. 1, v. 14–16;—Coloss. chap. 3, v. 10, 11.

done this, break off delay, resist the evil influences which would oppose a right decision, and engage with energy in the course enjoined by your benevolent Creator. Life, the only opportunity granted for this purpose, is short and uncertain. Death can never be far distant. The prize to be lost or won is nothing less than the friendship of God, and eternal happiness. Compared with such a prize, no exertions can be too great, no sacrifices or sufferings too severe; and yet it is offered to you as a free gift, demanding only your cordial and active concurrence. Resolve, then, to close at once with the gracious invitation. You cannot decide too soon. To-morrow may be too late—" Behold! now is the accepted time; behold! now is the day of salvation."*

To Christian readers the foregoing treatise cannot be expected to communicate much information; but may, nevertheless, be of some service, either by presenting old truths in a new light, or by suggesting useful applications. Thus, it may perhaps induce them to maintain with increased earnestness the supreme authority of the Scriptures, rationally interpreted, as the sole and sufficient code of revealed religion, to the total exclusion of human opinions and traditions. But, as these Scriptures were composed in ancient times, and foreign languages, they require to be translated and explained; and, in order that the meaning and spirit of the original may be fully and faithfully represented, such translation and exposition must be founded on fixed and demonstrative principles, and sustained by the aids of sound and scientific learning. To a considerable extent this has been already accomplished; so that, notwithstanding the impediments occasioned by the number and variety of existing languages, almost all nations are now enabled to read the word of God in their own tongues. There still remain, however,

* 2 Corinth. chap. 6, v. 1, 2;—Heb. chap. 3, v. 7-15.

difficulties and obscurities connected with scriptural subjects, which, although not of vital consequence, are neither uninteresting nor unimportant. To elucidate them, as far as may be practicable, recourse must be had to the same method of critical investigation which is employed to illustrate human writings; namely, an accurate analysis and application of all the facts and principles concerned, including the laws of mind and speech, to which must be added a due regard to the effects of divine interposition, whether providential or miraculous. This is indeed the only method which exists for the attainment of knowledge on such subjects, and the only one capable of yielding rigorous demonstration. Nothing, therefore, can be substituted in its place; and the mere opinions and traditions of men, even of the wisest and best, cannot of themselves furnish sufficient ground for assent. On the other hand, when a scriptural demonstration has once been established, it becomes a permanent and universal acquisition, independent of authority, incapable of refutation, and available to all mankind. The treatise now completed has been constructed throughout in accordance with these views; and if the efforts of the author have proved in any degree successful, they may give encouragement to others to do likewise.

It may also suggest to Christians of different denominations additional motives to unity and brotherly kindness; by reminding them that, in spite of their lamentable dissensions on religious subjects, the points wherein they agree are far more numerous and important than those on which they differ. By all who make a credible profession of the gospel, the divine authority of the Scriptures, for example, is fully admitted, and by a large proportion of them the scriptural system of facts, doctrines, and precepts, which has been cited in this treatise, is firmly maintained. Might they not hence infer, even independently of other arguments, that this system comprises the essentials of Christianity, and was intended by its adorable author to be the basis on which his followers should universally combine? If such is the case, ought they not on this very ground to esteem all other religious tenets and observances, even when correct and useful, as non-essential; to regard all their fellow-Christians, notwithstanding minor differences of opinion and infirmities of character, with cordial affection, as members of the same spiritual family; and to join them as freely as possible in friendly communion, with a view to their mutual improvement, and the benefit of the world at large? That during the long period of eighteen centuries Christian churches should have pursued a course so opposite, should have committed so many crimes and errors, and at the end of that period should still continue in a state so defective and discordant, is a deplorable fact, which strongly illustrates the force of human depravity, and the obstinate resistance which it opposes, even in persons professedly pious, to the only remedy which God has provided for its correction. In order to prevent similar evils in time to come, and to hasten the final triumph of the gospel, every Christian should remember that, whatever may be his predilection for the particular church with which he is connected, nothing can justify him in countenancing its abuses, or release him from his responsibility to obey all the commands of God, without exception or reserve, especially the great command so distinctly stated by the apostle John,—" that we should believe on the name of his Son Jesus Christ, and love one another, as he gave us commandment."—And lest there should be any doubt respecting the proper objects of this brotherly love, the same apostle shortly afterward adds,—" Whosoever believeth that Jesus is the Christ is born of God, and whosoever loveth him that begat loveth him also [that is] begotten by him."*—Every

* 1 John, chap. 3, v. 21–23; chap. 4, v. 19–21; chap. 5, v. 1–3.

Christian who means to comply with this command must, therefore, faithfully maintain the system of evangelical truth exhibited in the sacred volume, and zealously cultivate the holy and benevolent dispositions which it is the principal design of that system to produce. If he does this, he will be infallibly led to esteem as his fellow-Christians all who sincerely love the Lord Jesus Christ, to delight in their society, and, as opportunity permits, to coöperate with them for the advancement of their common cause. An absolute uniformity on all points of religious opinion and practice is neither possible, nor perhaps desirable; but such a degree of unanimity as is here advocated would answer every useful purpose, and might easily be attained by all who really desire it, and who for this end are resolved, at whatever sacrifice, to obey God rather than man.

Lastly, this treatise may furnish Christians with additional motives to engage with energy in missionary exertions, both at home and abroad. For the office of pastor, or superintendent of a church, few of them comparatively have either call or qualification; but to be a missionary, on a larger or smaller scale, is the duty and privilege of every Christian. In a remarkable passage of Paul's epistle to the Ephesians, it is expressly affirmed that one of the principal objects of the higher offices divinely established in the Christian church is to train its members to ministerial work, for the edification of the body of Christ; and the apostle therefore subjoins the appropriate exhortation,—"Let us be no longer children, ... but, holding the truth in love, let us in all things grow up unto him who is the head, [even] Christ, by whom the whole body is organized and compacted, and through the active coöperation of every member, according to the due proportion of each, increaseth unto the edification of itself in love." *—On this plan the primitive

* Ephes. chap. 4, v. 7–16;—Coloss. chap. 2, v. 16–19.

Christians constantly acted. So when, after the martyrdom of Stephen, the infant church at Jerusalem was severely persecuted by the Jewish authorities, all its members, with the exception of the apostles, fled from the capital, and dispersing themselves through the regions of Judea and Samaria, went everywhere preaching the gospel. Some of them even proceeded to Phœnicia and Cyprus; and, as soon as by the conversion of Cornelius and his friends the door of faith had been opened to the Gentiles, preached at Antioch to the idolatrous Greeks, with the happy result mentioned by the evangelist Luke, namely, that—"the hand of the Lord was with them, and a great number believed, [and] turned to the Lord."*— To this plan, under the divine blessing, Christianity owed much of its wonderful successes at the commencement of its career; and to the same plan, too generally neglected in later times, it must again be indebted, if that success is ever to be renewed. At present it scarcely keeps pace with the progress of population; but, were every Christian to do his duty in this respect, its converts would probably multiply with accelerating rapidity till they filled the earth. For the effective discharge of the missionary office, nothing more is required than a faithful application of the principles already described. The divine authority and sufficiency of the Scriptures must be strongly inculcated. From these sacred records the system of evangelical truth must be simply and clearly deduced, without addition, subtraction, or alteration. Nothing must be represented as essential to it which is not therein declared to be so; and the doctrines taught must be illustrated by suitable conduct on the part of the teacher, and more especially by the genuine manifestations of piety and integrity, of brotherly kindness toward all fellow-Christians, and of benevolence toward all mankind.

* Acts, chap. 8, v. 1-4; chap. 11, v. 18-21; chap. 15, v. 7-9, 13, 14.

The inducements to pursue this course are many and great; since it is evidently most acceptable to the Deity, necessary for the welfare of the human race, both in this world and in the next, beneficial to the agents themselves, and comparatively easy of execution. It is stated on the highest authority that—"all have sinned, and fallen short of the glory of God, [and are] justified freely by his grace, through the redemption which is in Christ Jesus; . . . . that God would have all men to be saved, and come to an acknowledgment of the truth; for [there is] one God, and one mediator between God and men, the man Christ Jesus, who gave himself a ransom for all, to be testified in due time; . . . . that there is no salvation in any other, for there is no other name under heaven, given among men, whereby we must be saved; . . . . that whoso reclaimeth a sinner from the error of his way, will save a soul from death, and cover a multitude of sins;"—and finally that . . . . "the teachers [of piety] shall shine as the brightness of the firmament, and they who turn many to righteousness as the stars for ever and ever."*—This is therefore the only method of salvation which God has provided, the only one which Christians are authorized to proclaim. It is not their office to judge other men, especially those to whom the message has never been addressed, nor to pronounce concerning their future destiny. It is not their province to convert the heart to God, a work far beyond the reach of human power, and to effect which is the peculiar prerogative of the Holy Spirit; but the work of ordinary instruction and persuasion which is really assigned to them, although humble and subordinate, is not the less necessary. That blessed agent declines the task of preliminary cultivation; but,

* Dan. chap. 12, v. 2, 3;—Acts, chap. 4, v. 8-12;—Rom. chap. 3, v. 23, 24;—1 Tim. chap. 2, v. 3-6;—James, chap. 5, v. 19, 20;—2 Peter, chap. 3, v. 9.

when the ground has been duly prepared, and the seed liberally sown, it is he alone who can impart the vital principle of genuine religion, and afterward advance it to perfection. Their simple but honorable duty is to disseminate the Scriptures as widely as possible, to make known the gospel therein revealed by their words, and to recommend it by their actions. But, as conversion is founded on conviction, and as miraculous proof is not now afforded, they must have recourse to rational and demonstrative evidence. To assist in furnishing such evidence is the object of the treatise now brought to a close; and, if it has accomplished this object, and shall in consequence contribute, however feebly, to the diffusion and beneficial influence of divine truth in the world, it seeks no other reward.

NOTES AND ILLUSTRATIONS.

NOTE I., PAGES 60–69.

ON THE ERRONEOUS READINGS OF THE VATICAN MANUSCRIPT.

THE Vatican manuscript omits the verses in Luke's gospel which describe the agony and bloody sweat of Christ in the garden of Gethsemane, and inserts a new clause in Matthew's gospel which virtually attributes the death of Christ on the cross to the wound inflicted by the soldier's spear. These variations, which were zealously advocated by the late Mr. Granville Penn, are by no means of a trifling nature, but involve very serious consequences. If they are correct, the view taken of the atonement, not only in this treatise, but also throughout the Scripture, is erroneous; if false, the Vatican manuscript, hitherto esteemed of great value, is convicted of corrupting the sacred text, at least in the New Testament, and must therefore lose much of its authority. These variations are however negatived, as has been already shown, by the strongest evidence, external and internal. In addition to the arguments previously employed for this purpose, the opposite testimony of some of the earliest biblical versions, namely, the Old Italic, the Vulgate, and the Peshito Syriac, will here be adduced; as likewise a few further remarks on the statements of Chrysostom, who is cited with so much confidence by Mr. Penn in support of his own opinions, and of the preëminent superiority of the Vatican manuscript. The Italic version of the passages in question is copied from the splendid work of Bianchini; the Vulgate from the folio Paris edition of 1549; and of the Peshito a literal English translation is given, which has been kindly furnished to the author by the Rev. Dr. Henderson.

NOTES AND ILLUSTRATIONS.

Luke, chap. 22, v. 43, 44.

VERCELLI MANUSCRIPT.

V. 43. Apparuit autem illi angelus de cœlo, confortans eum. Et factus est in agonia, et prolixius oravit. V. 44. Et factus est sudor illius quasi guttæ sanguinis decurrentis super terram.

VERONA MANUSCRIPT.

V. 43. Apparuit autem illi angelus de cœlo, confortans eum. Et factus est in agonia, et prolixius oravit. V. 44. Et factus est sudor ejus sicut guttæ sanguinis decurrentes in terram.

VULGATE.

V. 43. Apparuit autem illi angelus de cœlo, confortans eum. Et factus in agonia prolixius orabat. V. 44. Et factus est sudor ejus sicut guttæ sanguinis decurrentis in terram.

PESHITO.

And there appeared to him an angel from heaven, who strengthened him. And when he was in fear he prayed earnestly, and his sweat was as drops of blood, and it fell upon the ground.

Matthew, chap. 27, v. 47–50.

VERCELLI MANUSCRIPT.

V. 47. Quidam autem illic stantes et audientes dicebant, Heliam vocat iste. V. 48. Et continuo currens unus ex eis, accepta spongia, implevit aceto, et imposuit in harundine, et dabat ei bibere. V. 49. Ceteri vero dixerunt, Sine, videamus si venit Helias et liberavit eum. V. 50. Jesus autem, iterum clamans voce magna, emisit spiritum.

VERONA MANUSCRIPT.

V. 47. Quidam autem illic stantes et audientes dicebant, Heliam vocat iste. V. 48. Et continuo currens unus ex eis accepta spongia, implevit aceto, et imposuit in harundine, et dabat ei bibere. V. 49. Ceteri vero dixerunt, Sine, videamus si venit Helias et liberavit eum. V. 50. Jesus autem, iterum clamans voce magna, emisit spiritum.

VULGATE.

V. 47. Quidam autem illic stantes et audientes dicebant, Eliam vocat iste. V. 48. Et continuo currens unus ex eis acceptam spongiam implevit aceto, et imposuit arundini, et dabat ei bibere. V. 49. Cæteri vero dicebant, Sine, videamus an veniat Elias liberans eum. V. 50. Jesus autem, iterum clamans voce magna, emisit spiritum.

PESHITO.

Now certain men of them that stood there, when they heard said, This person calleth Elias. And immediately one of them ran, and took up a sponge, and filled it with vinegar, and placed it on a reed, and gave him to drink. But the rest said, Desist! we shall see whether Elias will come to deliver him. And Jesus cried again with a loud voice, and resigned his spirit.

John, chap. 19, v. 32–34.

VERCELLI MANUSCRIPT.

V. 32. Venerunt ergo milites, et primi quidem crura fregerunt, et alterius similiter qui simul crucifixus erat. V. 33. Ad Jesum autem cum venissent, et viderunt eum jam mortuum, non fraegerunt crura ejus. V. 34. Sed unus ex militibus lancia latus ejus percussit, et exiit confestim sanguis et aqua.

VERONA MANUSCRIPT.

V. 32. Venerunt ergo milites, et illius quidem primi fregerunt crura, et alterius qui simul crucifixus erat cum eo. V. 33. Ad Jesum autem cum venissent, ut viderunt eum jam mortuum, non fregerunt crura ejus. V. 34. Sed unus militum lancea latus ejus pupugit, et exivit continuo sanguis et aqua.

VULGATE.

V. 32. Venerunt ergo milites, et primi quidem fregerunt crura, et alterius qui crucifixus est cum eo. V. 33. Ad Jesum autem cum venissent, ut viderunt eum jam mortuum, non fregerunt ejus crura; V. 34. sed unus militum lancea latus ejus aperuit, et continuo exivit sanguis et aqua.

PESHITO.

And the soldiers came and brake the legs of the first, and of the other who was crucified with him; but when they came to Jesus, they saw that he was already dead, and brake not his legs; but one of the soldiers smote him in his side with a lance, and immediately there came out blood and water.

NOTES AND ILLUSTRATIONS.

It thus appears that these venerable and justly esteemed versions, which are probably more ancient than any Greek manuscript of the New Testament now extant, confirm the common readings of the two passages under discussion, and contradict those of the Vatican manuscript. To the omission by this manuscript of the former passage, which describes the agony and bloody sweat of Christ, the authority of Chrysostom, quoted by Mr. Penn, is not less opposed than these versions, as will be evident from the following paragraph, of which a translation has already been given in the text. In commenting on Matt. chap. 26, v. 36–38, this writer remarks:—" Ὁ δὲ ἐκτένως εὔχεται· καὶ, ἵνα μὴ δόξῃ ὑπόκρισις εἶναι τὸ πρᾶγμα, καὶ ἱδρῶτες ἐπιρρέουσι διὰ τὴν αἰτίαν πάλιν τὴν αὐτήν· καὶ, ἵνα μὴ τοῦτο εἴπωσιν αἱρετικοὶ, ὅτι ὑποκρίνεται τὴν ἀγωνίαν, διὰ τοῦτο καὶ ἱδρῶτες ὡς θρόμβοι αἵματος, καὶ ἄγγελος ἐνισχύων αὐτὸν ἐφάνη, καὶ μυρία φόβου τεκμήρια, ἵνα μὴ τις εἴπῃ τὰ ῥήματα πεπλασμένα εἶναι." *—Chrysostom here supposes that one principal object of recording in Scripture this narrative of the agony and bloody sweat of Christ, was to refute the error of those heretics who denied the reality of his mental sufferings; and it is in singular accordance with such a supposition, that the subtraction of this narrative from Luke's gospel is by competent judges attributed either to heretics, or to rash and injudicious critics, who did not well understand it.

How far Chrysostom approved of the new clause respecting the manner of Christ's death, inserted by the Vatican manuscript in Matthew's gospel, will be seen by another paragraph from his writings, wherein he comments as follows on Matt. chap. 27, v. 48, 49.—" Καὶ εὐθέως ἐπότισαν αὐτὸν ὄξος· ἕτερος δὲ προσελθὼν λόγχῃ αὐτοῦ τὴν πλευρὰν ἤνοιξε. Τί γένοιτ' ἂν τούτων παρανομώτερον, τί δὲ θηριωδέστερον; οἱ μέχρι τοσούτου τὴν ἑαυτῶν μανίαν ἐξέτειναν, καὶ εἰς νεκρὸν σῶμα λοιπὸν ὑβρίζοντες. Σὺ δέ μοι σκόπει, πῶς ταῖς παρανομίαις αὐτῶν εἰς ἡμετέραν κέχρηται σωτηρίαν· μετὰ γὰρ τὴν πληγὴν, αἱ πηγαὶ τῆς σωτηρίας ἡμῶν ἐκεῖθεν ἀνέβλυσαν. Ὁ δὲ Ἰησοῦς, κράξας φωνῇ μεγάλῃ, ἀφῆκε τὸ πνεῦμα. Τοῦτό ἐστιν ὃ ἔλεγεν· Ἐξουσίαν ἔχω θεῖναι τὴν ψυχήν μου, καὶ ἐξουσίαν ἔχω πάλιν λαβεῖν αὐτὴν, καὶ ἐγὼ τίθημι αὐτὴν ἀπ' ἐμαυτοῦ. Διὰ γὰρ τοῦτο καὶ φωνῇ ἐκραύγασεν, ἵνα δειχθῇ ὅτι καθ' ἐξουσίαν τὸ πρᾶγμα ἐγένετο. Ὁ γοῦν Μάρκος φησὶν ὅτι ἐθαύμασεν ὁ Πιλᾶτος εἰ ἤδη τέθνηκε, καὶ ὅτι ὁ κεντυρίων διὰ τοῦτο μάλιστα ἐπίστευσεν, ὅτι μετ' ἐξουσίας ἀπέθανεν." †—This passage relates to the

---

* Chrysostomus, Opera, vol. viii. p. 791. On account of its seeming to favor his own interpretation, Mr. Penn adopts a various reading of this passage, introduced by Morel;—" ὡς καὶ εἰς νεκρὸν σῶμα λοιπὸν ὑβρίζοντες "—but this reading, disapproved by Montfaucon, in his magnificent edition of Chrysostom, and at variance with the context, is evidently a corruption.

† Chrysostomus, Opera, vol. vii. p. 825.

treatment of Christ by the soldiers, after he had uttered the cry, Eloi! Eloi! lama sabachthani? and may be freely rendered thus.—"They immediately gave him vinegar to drink; but another of them coming up, with a spear pierced his side. What can be conceived more lawless, or more brutal than the conduct of these men, who indulged their rage to such an extent as even to insult a dead body? But observe how he employed their lawlessness for our salvation; for from the wound thus made the fountains of our salvation sprang forth. And Jesus, having cried with a loud voice, resigned his spirit. This fulfilled what he had previously said:—I have authority to lay down my life, and authority to take it again, and I lay it down of my own accord.—For it was to show that the act was voluntary, that he cried with a loud voice. Mark, accordingly says that Pilate wondered if he were already dead; and that the centurion believed on this account chiefly, because he died of his own accord."—Now, although Chrysostom here adopts the same order of narration as the editor of the Vatican manuscript, the diversity of their expressions renders it doubtful whether in so doing he followed his guidance. The words of the manuscript are,—"ἄλλος δὲ, λαβὼν λόγχην, ἔνυξεν αὐτοῦ τὴν πλευράν, καὶ ἐξῆλθεν ὕδωρ καὶ αἷμα:"—those of the commentator,—"ἕτερος δὲ προσελθὼν, λόγχῃ αὐτοῦ τὴν πλευρὰν ἤνοιξε."— It is far more probable that he borrowed the clause directly from John's gospel, for the purpose of describing in a single paragraph all the proceedings of the soldiers on this occasion; and it is certain that he did not draw from it those conclusions which have been so zealously embraced by Mr. Penn, since he ascribes the death of Christ, not to the wound inflicted by the soldier's spear, but to his own voluntary and supernatural agency, and represents that wound as a brutal insult offered to his dead body. On the whole, it must be evident that the objections which have been alleged against the various readings of the Vatican manuscript in these two important passages of the evangelical narrative, are not weakened, but on the contrary fully confirmed, by an appeal to the authority of Chrysostom.

NOTE II., PAGES 51–63.

ON CRUCIFIXION.

The treatise of Salmasius on the cross, composed with great judgment and perspicuity, and evidently founded on careful and extensive research, is a good specimen of the class of writings to which it belongs, and of the scholarship of the seventeenth century. The following passages are particularly deserving of attention, and their insertion will render it unnecessary to add other quotations of the same kind.—" Medium .... crucis lignum, quod eminebat ex antioriore parte, equi vice fuit lignei, quod inscendebat et inequitabat cruciarius. Corpus itaque ejus illo portabatur et sustentabatur. Unde et ἐποχεῖσθαι eo dixit crucifixum Justinus, in Tryphonis dialogo ;—'καὶ τὸ ἐν τῷ μέσῳ πηγνύμενον ὡς κέρας, καὶ αὐτὸ ἐξέχον ἐστὶν, ἐφ' ᾧ ἐποχοῦνται οἱ σταυρούμενοι. Et quod in medio impactum est instar cornu, et ipsum eminet, cui inequitant, et quo vectantur qui cruci affiguntur.'—De suppedaneo hæc accipi non posse certo certius est. E medio crucis stipite extabat hoc lignum, in ipso stipite infixum et impactum. Eo vectatum dicit crucifixum. Ergo interfemina hoc habebat, eique quasi inequitabat, quod est ἐποχεῖσθαι. Nam de equo dicitur cui eques insidet, ἔποχον γίνεσθαι, et ἐποχεῖσθαι. Eustathius, in loco superius citato, εἰς τὸν ἵππον ἀνάγειν, καὶ ἔποχον ποιεῖν. In eo ligno veluti subsidebant, toto corpore sustentati, quia illud natibus premebant, cruribus hinc inde pendulis. Hinc explicanda sunt illa Mæcenatis, quæ et alibi emendavimus, quibus præoptare se dicit, vel vitam in cruce retinere quam mori.—' Hanc mihi vel acuta subsidem cruce sustine'—Subsidere se mavult in cruce vivum et videntem, quam extra crucem lumine cassum esse. Subsidem dixit propter illud medium lignum, in quo quasi equitantes subsidebant. **Hominis ita subsidentis brachia, utrimque expansa, ad duas latitudinis partes extremas deligabantur, clavis** etiam affixæ: **pedes in ima extremitate longitudinis vinciebantur, et clavis configebantur: caput reclinatum habebatur ad extremitatem longitudinis summam, nec is pedibus insistebat suppedaneo, ut falso imaginati sunt. In medio igitur crucifixus requiescebat ligno, cui et insidebat ea parte quæ sedes in homine ex eo dicitur.** Idque clare Irenæus explicat, lib. II. adversus Hæreses, cap. 46.—' Ipse habitus crucis '—inquit,—' fines et summitates habet quinque, duos in longitudine, et duos in latitudine, et unum in medio, ubi requiescit qui clavis affigitur.'—Unum illum in medio stipitis crucis finem, sive extremitatem, τὸ ἄκρον in Græco fuit; Tertullianus, in libro II. adversus Nationes, sedilis excessum appellat his verbis :—' Pars crucis, et quidem major, est omne robur quod erecta statione defigitur. Sed nobis tota crux imputatur, cum antemna scilicet sua et cum illo sedilis excessu.'—Sedile est in quo sedetur, non quod pedibus subjicitur. Non potest itaque accipi de suppedaneo. Excessum vocat sedilis, quia excedens illud et eminens in medio crucis lignum pro sedili fuit, ad sustinendum cruciarium ei insidentem. Τὸ ἐξέχον ἐν μέσῳ πῆγμα appellat Justinus. Πῆγμα est id omne quod ex duobus lignis componitur. Lignum igitur illud eminens e medio stipite crucis, quod ipso stipiti infixum et impactum foret, πῆγμα appellatur. Idem Tertullianus, in libro adversus Judæos, cap. 10, unicornis cornui comparat palum illum e medio stipitis crucis exeuntem, sustentando corpori cruci affixi :—"Nam et antemna navis, quæ crucis pars est, hoc extremitates ejus vocantur; unicornis autem in medio stipite palus.'—Sic legendus ille locus ex veteribus libris." *

"Bene ait [Augustinus] corpus videri stare crucifixi in ea longitudine crucis quæ a transverso ligno pertinet ad solum usque, id est, ad eam partem quæ desinit esse conspicua, et in terram demersa occultatur. Nam, quamvis in ea parte sederet crucifixus, ligno e medio stipite longitudinis extante sustentatus, stare tamen potius videbatur quam sedere. Palus quippe fuit inter femina cruciarii positus, cui tanquam equuleo sic insidebat ut stantis statum præberet. Non enim prohibebat recta extendi femora et genua, pedesque in imo conjungi, ubi et clavis confixi tenebantur ad ipsum lignum arrectarium. Sic stabat simul et sedebat cruciarius. Stabat, quia directum et extentum corpus ejus stantis formam præferebat. Sedebat autem, quia ea parte qua sedetur in palo, qui sedilis instar, erat requiescebat. Mala tamen ea sessio fuit, et ad hoc tantum instituta, ut diutius persistere in cruce posset ac durare corpus cruciarii. Cum enim ad exemplum edendum, ut alia omnia supplicia, ita istud præcipue inventum esset, ea de causa longo tempore in cruce detinebantur qui hoc supplicio affecti fuerant. Necessaria itaque plane fuit hæc pali in media cruce defixio, ad sustentandum corpus patientis, quo in hoc statu diutius posset pendens conservari. Manus enim confixæ clavis, aut brachia funibus religata, vix potuissent molem corporis suo pondere deorsum ruentis sustinere, ubi tabo diffluere ac dissolvi ex mora longiore cœpisset. Quod enim de suppedaneo aiunt, cui et pedes innixos quasi scabello volunt requievisse, nemo est sensus communis vel mediocriter particeps quin videat, ruentis pondere suo deorsum corporis mortui onerosum truncum non posse pedibus, quamvis in ligno vinctis et constrictis, portari et sustentari." †

"Cum satis constet cruciarios suam crucem ipsosmet portasse, non tam magnam aut altam fuisse oportet quin hominis unius onus esse potuerit. Alta admodum crux, cum sua antemna, et cum palo qui e medio stipite eminebat, non fuisset ferendo, uni præsertim homini, et per aliquantum itineris spatium, ut sæpe locus supplicii extra urbem satis longe distabat a carceris loco e quo educebatur nocens plectendus. Præterea, cum elogium, sive titulus, ad caput crucifixi poneretur, omnibus legendus expositus, si nimis alta crux fuisset, de plano non potuisset legi. Nam λευκώματα non solebant grandioribus literis exarari, quam quæ possent non nimium excelso loco positæ a prætereuntibus facile cognosci. Pos-

* Salmasius, De Cruce, pp. 229-232.   † Ibid., pp. 251, 252.

tremo, certum est, **nulla scala admota,** impositos fuisse cruciarios illi sedili quod in media cruce depactum erat. Denique, de plano etiam cruciariis crura frangebant carnifices. Miles deinde ille qui lancea transfodit latus **Domini in** cruce pendentis, non alte suspensum fuisse indicat. Nam lancea, sive hasta Romana, quamvis aliquantum excesserit staturam hominis, tamen miles qui transverberasse ea dicitur Christi latus, non ex imo in altum debuit hastam infigere, sed ictum dirigere paululum ea allevata. . . . Crura, ut jam dixi, frangebantur cruciariis, et de plano quidem, a carnificibus vel militibus. Quod et historia Christi ostendit apud Johannem, ubi narratur petiisse a Pilato Judæos ut Christo, et **latronibus cum eo crucifixis, crura frangi juberet, et de cruce eorum corpora tolli.—** ' Venerunt ergo milites, **et prioris quidem latronis fregerunt crura, et alterius qui cum eo crucifixus est, Ad Jesum autem cum venissent, ut viderunt cum jam mortuum, non fregerunt ejus crura.**'—[Joann. cap. 19, v. 32, 33.] Ex quibus verbis non obscure liquet de plano frangi potuisse, et fracta vulgo esse crura cruciariis, absque ulla scalarum ope, aut scamni. Tres igitur, aut ad summum quatuor pedes a terra elatus videtur fuisse locus crucis in quo pedes cruciarii erant suffixi, ut a milite vel carnifice, stante in pedibus suis, crura ejus frangi facile possent. Unde etiam colligi potest, minima adjutum longitudine, aliquem protensa manu potuisse os in cruce pendentis attingere. Manum, inquam, aliquis extendens, et in manu habens vel pedalis longitudinis aut bipedalis bacillum vel virgam, ad os cruciarii in humerum **puta inclinatum caput habentis,** potuit **pervenire.**" *

With slight exceptions, a more graphic or correct account of crucifixion than is here furnished by Salmasius can scarcely be conceived. Among other points, he fully proves the existence and utility of a material part of the cross which, although described by several ancient authors, has been almost entirely overlooked in modern times; namely, the short horizontal bar which projected forward from the middle of the upright post, and whereon the crucified persons sat astride; while, in consequence of his legs being extended, and his feet nailed to the lower part of the post, he at the same time appeared to stand. Owing to this arrangement, the punishment was less excruciating and more protracted than is commonly imagined; in proof of which examples are above given of persons who, having been taken from the cross within a moderate time, and consigned to medical care, recovered and survived. The following are additional instances of the same kind:—The first is the case of **Matthew Lovat,** an Italian lunatic, laboring under that peculiar form of insanity which prompts to suicide, who from this cause inflicted various

* Salmasius, De Cruce, pp. 283, 284, 316, 317.

injuries on himself, repeated at intervals during several years. In the month of July, 1802, he committed an act of self-mutilation; and on the 21st of September, 1803, attempted to crucify himself, but was prevented from accomplishing his purpose by several people, who came upon him just as he was driving the nail into his left foot. He was more successful in a second attempt of this kind, which took place at Venice on the 19th of July, 1805, when he was forty-six years of age. About eight o'clock in the morning of that day he was observed by the people who passed in the street fixed to a cross, with the exception of his right hand, which hung loosely by his side. The cross was enclosed in a net of small cords, and suspended by ropes from a beam in his chamber, out of the window of which, having a low parapet, he had contrived, after nailing himself to the cross, to throw the whole apparatus. He had also crowned himself with thorns, two or three of which pierced the skin of his forehead; had transfixed his hands and feet with three long and sharp nails, and inflicted two inches below the left hypochondrium a wound with a cobbler's knife, which did not, however, injure any of the internal parts. As soon as he was perceived, some humane people ran up-stairs, disengaged him from the cross, and put him to bed. In the course of the day he was removed to an hospital, where he was carefully treated, and early in August all his wounds were completely cured. He was afterward transferred to a lunatic asylum, and on the 8th of April, 1806, died of exhaustion, induced partly by long and repeated abstinence from food, and partly by pectoral disorder.*—Several other cases of voluntary crucifixion are mentioned in the Correspondence of the Baron de Grimm, as having occurred at the French metropolis during the years 1759 and 1760, among the fanatical followers of the Abbé Paris, who, in consequence of the irregular nervous and muscular actions which they displayed, obtained the name of *Convulsionnaires*. All the parties were females of humble condition, and regarded as nuns, or religious devotees, acting under the guidance of an ecclesiastical director. They were liable to fits of nervous agitation, or weakness, which was said to be relieved by bodily inflictions, administered at their own request by the director or others. Four women are particularly described as having with this view undergone crucifixion, one of them twice, and another three times, and as having remained on the cross for different periods, varying from half an hour to nearly four hours; yet they uttered no cries, did not lose any considerable quantity of blood, and all speedily recovered. These facts appear to have been minutely

---

* Cesare Ruggieri, M. D., Narrative of the Crucifixion of Matthew Lovat, etc., in the Pamphleteer, vol. iii. pp. 361–375.

observed by numerous spectators, and to have been immediately committed to writing from notes taken at the time. Like similar facts previously mentioned, they serve to show that the death of the cross, when not accelerated by extraneous agency, is peculiarly slow and lingering, and that the bodily sufferings with which it is attended are by no means so intolerable as is usually supposed.*

Of the fortitude with which such sufferings, and even much greater ones, have been encountered and endured, numerous examples might be added to the few here subjoined, several of which are borrowed from Wanley's extensive collection of anecdotes illustrative of human character.—" Asdrubal managed the war of the Carthaginians in Spain, and by force and fraud had made himself the master of most of it; but having slain a certain nobleman of Spain, a servant of his, a Frenchman [Gaul] by birth, highly resented it, and determined with himself to revenge the death of his lord, though at the price of his own life. Whereupon he assaulted Asdrubal and slew him. He was taken in the fact, tormented, and fastened to a cross; but, in the midst of all his pains, he bore a countenance that showed more of joy than grief, as one that was well satisfied in his revenge."—The description of this occurrence by Valerius Maximus is equally concise and forcible.—" Servus barbarus Asdrubalem, quod dominum suum occidisset graviter ferens, subito aggressus interemit. Cumque comprehensus omni modo cruciaretur, lætitiam tamen quam ex vindicta ceperat in ore constantissime retinuit."—" Theodorus being threatened with death by Lysimachus;—Speak in this manner—said he,—to thy purple minions, for to Theodorus it is all one whether he putrefy under ground, or on a cross above it."—" Andronicus Commenus fell alive into the hands of his enemy; who, having loaded him with injuries, abandoned the miserable emperor to the people, for the punishment of his perfidiousness [and during several days he was consequently subjected to every kind of cruelty and indignity]. All these, and greater inhumanities, the aged emperor underwent with that invincible patience, that he was heard to say no other thing than,—Lord have mercy upon me;—and—Why do ye break a bruised reed?"—" When they would have fastened Polycarp to the stake, the brave bishop cried out to let him alone as he was; for that God, who had enabled him to endure the fire, would enable him also, without any chains of theirs, to stand unmoved in the midst of the flames; so, with his hands behind him, unstirred he took his crown." †—Josephus gives an account

---

* Grimm, et Diderot, Correspondance Littéraire, etc., vol. III. pp. 11-24, 134-157.
† Wanley, Wonders of the Little World. vol. 1. pp. 260, 341, 356, 402;—Valerius Maximus, Opera, pp. 285, 532;—Whiston's Josephus, vol. iv. pp. 82, 33.

of a deserter, who, during the siege of Jotapata by Vespasian, went over from the Jews to the Romans, and remarks;—" But Vespasian had a suspicion about this deserter, as knowing how faithful the Jews were to one another, and how much they despised any punishments that could be inflicted on them; this last, because one of the people of Jotapata had undergone all sorts of torments, and though they made him pass through a fiery trial of his enemies in his examination, yet would he inform them nothing of the affairs within the city, and, as he was crucified, smiled at them."—That the tortures of impalement and of burning alive are far greater than those of crucifixion, there can be no doubt; yet even these dreadful punishments have often been borne with admirable courage and magnanimity. An example of the former kind occurred a few years since, at the execution of some chiefs taken prisoners from the eastern part of the kingdom of Sennaar by the present Viceroy of Egypt.—" Two of these chiefs the pacha ordered to be impaled in the market-place of Sennaar. They suffered this horrid death with great firmness. One of them said nothing but,—There is no God but God, and Mohammed is his apostle,—which he frequently repeated before impalement; while the other, named Abdallah, insulted, defied, and cursed his executioners, calling them robbers and murderers, till too weak to speak, when he expressed his feelings by spitting at them." *

By these and many other instances recorded in history it is abundantly proved that persons of both sexes, and all ages, have often endured the most severe torments with invincible fortitude; and it cannot, therefore, be supposed that the Saviour of the world, whose human nature was perfect both in body and mind, was deficient in so common an endowment. Some commentators have, nevertheless, injudiciously ascribed the agony of Christ in the garden of Gethsemane to his dread of the ordinary sufferings of crucifixion, which awaited him on the following day; but the opinion is so manifestly erroneous that, without further argument on the subject, the following facts will alone suffice for its refutation. They are derived from the well-known narrative of the last days of Dr. Rowland Taylor, rector of Hadley in Suffolk, and one of the early victims of the Marian persecution. On account of his refusal to conform to the Church of Rome, the domination of which was at that time promoted by the whole force of the government, this venerable and exemplary clergyman was, after a tedious imprisonment of nearly two years, condemned to be burned at a stake in the very town where he had exercised his ministry; and the cruel sentence was carried into effect on the 9th of February, 1555, O. S. It could not in this case

* Narrative of an Expedition to Dongola and Sennaar, etc., pp. 177, 178.

be pretended that natural sensibility was blunted by ferocity of character, defect of education, or a low and brutal course of life; for Dr. Taylor was a pious and learned Christian minister, remarkable for his faithful and benevolent attention to his pastoral duties, and greatly beloved by his parishioners. He was also a married man, advanced in years, and had been the father of nine children. If under such circumstances, and in the immediate prospect of so horrible a death, he had given way to fear and dejection, it would have been very natural and excusable; but, instead of this, he uniformly evinced a degree of cheerfulness and courage which some persons might even be disposed to condemn, as bordering on levity. His conduct on the occasion could not, however, be duly appreciated, without quoting the lively description of Fox, the martyrologist, which will form a suitable conclusion to these remarks. When Dr. Taylor was travelling to the place of his execution, he was conducted from London to Chelmsford by the sheriff of Essex, with his yeomen.— "At Chelmsford"—says the historian,—" the sheriff of Suffolk met them, there to receive them, and to carry him forth into Suffolk. And being at supper, the sheriff of Essex very earnestly persuaded him to return to the popish religion, thinking with fair words to persuade him."—After doing this, the sheriff and all the yeomen of the guard drank to his health.—" When they had all drunk to him, and the cup was come to him, he stayed a little, as one studying what answer he might give. At last, he thus answered and said;—Mr. Sheriff, and my masters all, I heartily thank you for your good will. I have hearkened to your words, and marked well your counsels. And, to be plain with you, I do perceive that I have been deceived myself, and am like to deceive a great many of Hadley of their expectation.—With that word they all rejoiced. . . . At last,—Good Mr. Doctor,—quoth the sheriff,—what meant ye by this, that ye say ye think ye have been deceived yourself, and think ye shall deceive many one in Hadley?—Would ye know my meaning plainly?—quoth he.—Yea,—quoth the sheriff,—good Mr. Doctor, tell it us plainly.—Then said Dr. Taylor,—I will tell you how I have been deceived, and, as I think, I shall deceive a great many. I am, as you see, a man that hath a very great carcass, which I thought should have been buried in Hadley church-yard, if I had died in my bed, as I well hoped I should have done. But herein I see I was deceived. And there are a great number of worms in Hadley church-yard, which should have had jolly feeding upon this carrion which they have looked for many a day. But now I know we be deceived, both I and they; for this carcass must be burnt to ashes, and so shall they lose their bait and feeding that they looked to have had of it.—When the sheriff and his company heard him say so, they were amazed, and looked at one another, marvelling at the man's constant mind, that thus without all fear made but a jest at the cruel torment and death now at hand prepared for him. Thus was their expectation clean disappointed."—Nor was this a solitary instance of his intrepidity, for the same author soon after adds;—" They that were present and familiarly conversant with this Dr. Taylor reported of him, that they never did see in him any fear of death; but especially, and above all the rest which besides him suffered at the same time, always showed himself merry and cheerful. In the time of his imprisonment, as well before his condemnation as after, he kept one countenance, and like behavior. Whereunto he was the rather confirmed by the company and presence of Mr. John Bradford, who was in the same prison and chamber with him. The morning when he was called up by the sheriff to his burning, being suddenly awaked out of his sound sleep, he sat up in his bed, and putting on his shirt, had these words, speaking somewhat thick after his accustomed manner;—Ah, whoreson thieves! ah, whoreson thieves! rob God of his honor? rob God of his honor?—Afterward, being risen, and tying his points, he cast his arms about a great beam which was in the chamber between Mr. Bradford's bed and his, and there hanging by the hands, said to Mr. Bradford,—O Mr. Bradford—quoth he,—what a notable sway should I give, if I were hanged!—meaning for that he was a corpulent and big man. These things I thought good here to note, to set forth and declare to those who shall read this history, what a notable and singular gift of spirit and courage God had given to this blessed martyr." *

NOTE III.—PAGES 95-97.

ON AGONY AND BLOODY SWEAT.

"OF all the maladies which affect cutaneous transpiration, *diapedesis*, or sweating of blood"—says Dr. Millingen,—"is the most singular; so much so, indeed, that its existence has been doubted, although several well-authenticated cases are on record, both in the ancient and modern annals of medicine. It is mentioned by Theophrastus, Aristotle, and Lucan. . . . The base Charles IX. of France sank under this disorder, as stated by Mezeray. The same historian relates the case of a governor of a town taken by storm, who was condemned to die, but was seized with a profuse sweating of blood the moment he beheld the scaffold. Lombard mentions a general who was affected in a similar manner on losing a

---

* Fox, Book of Martyrs, etc., pp. 128, 129.

battle. The same writer tells us of a nun who was so terrified when falling into the hands of a ruthless banditti, that blood oozed from every pore. Henry ab Heer records the case of a man who not only labored under diapedesis, but small worms [also] accompanied the bloody secretion. In the Memoirs of the Society of Arts of Haarlem, we read of the case of a sailor who, falling down during a storm, was raised from the deck streaming with blood. At first it was supposed that he had been wounded, but on close examination the blood was found to flow from the surface of the body. . . . Dr. Fournier relates the case of a magistrate who was attacked with diapedesis after any excitement, whether of a pleasurable or painful nature. . . . The case of Catherine Merlin, of Chamberg, is well authenticated, and worthy of being recorded. She was a woman forty-six years of age, strong and hale. She received a kick from a bullock in the epigastric region [pit of the stomach], that was followed by vomiting of blood. This discharge having been suddenly stopped by her medical attendants, the blood made its way through the pores of various parts of her body, every limb being affected in turn. The sanguineous discharge was invariably preceded by a prickly and itching sensation. Frequently this exudation proceeded from the scalp. The discharge usually occurred twice in the twenty-four hours, and on pressing the skin the flow of blood could be accelerated and increased."—Dr. Millingen's explanation of bloody sweat, although brief, is judicious.—"It is probable"—says he,—"that this strange disorder arises from a violent commotion of the nervous system, turning the streams of blood out of their natural course, and forcing the red particles into the cutaneous excretories. A mere relaxation of the fibres could not produce so powerful a revulsion. It may also arise in cases of extreme debility, in connection with a thinner condition of the blood." *—It is in like manner remarked by Schwencke, that a dissolved state of the blood cannot in all instances be assigned as the cause.—"Nec tamen omnis eruptio sanguinea quæ vulgo creditur a dissolutione sanguinis fieri talis est, ut ex sequenti historia satis singulari patebit. Puella quindecim annorum, a tribus annis jam menstruam purgationem largiter, imo, nimium passa, ex quinque retro annis convulsionibus correpta, tenuis habitus, acris ingenii, et facile animo mota, extra paroxysmum bene valens, quacunque diei atque noctis hora, per quoscunque superficiei corporis locos subinde sanguinem fundebat per cutim erumpentem, idque vel brevi post convulsiones, vel eodem simul cum convulsionibus tempore, nec ulla corporis pars est quæ hanc evacuationem non experta est; namque ex oculis, naribus, auribus, labiis, lingua, mammis, ano, et omnibus extremitatibus, instar sudoris profluebat.

* Dr. Millingen, Curiosities of Medical Experience, vol. II. pp. 338-342.

Prædicebat sæpissime ex quanam parte sanguis proflueret; erantque signa præsagii ordinaria, anxietas, vomitus, gravitas, pruritus, et calor partis, fere nullo cum tumore; tumque dein ex ea parte sanguinis sudoris specie expulsio fiebat, brevi sponte cessans; neque ullum vitium aut vestigium sudoris sanguinei relictum animadvertebatur, quamvis aliquando viginti quatuor horarum spatio ante paroxysmum sanguinis eruptionem prædiceret. Per quinque annos hunc effectum durasse norunt multi, quem tamen ex dissolutione, præsertim putrefaciente, fuisse natum nemo concedet, præcipue si attento percipiat animo atque perpendat, post paroxysmum eam bene valuisse, eamque sudoris sanguinei evacuationem sequuta fuisse nulla alia symptomata, sed et omnis generis eam medicamenta deglutivisse."—A case very similar to the foregoing is quoted in the Medico-Chirurgical Review, from the French "Transactions Médicales" for November, 1830.—"A young woman, aged twenty-one years, irregular in menstruation, and of indolent habits, and obstinate temper, had been much irritated by some reflections made by her parents, on account of her abjuring the Protestant religion. She left her paternal roof, and after wandering about for some time, took up her residence in a hospital. She was then suffering violent attacks of hysteria, attended with general convulsions, and exquisite sensibility in the pubic and hypogastric regions [lower part of the belly]. After paroxysms of hysteria, which sometimes lasted twenty-four or thirty-six hours, this female fell into a kind of ecstasy, in which she lay with her eyes fixed, sensibility and motion suspended. Sometimes she muttered a prayer, but the most remarkable phenomenon was an exudation of blood from the cheeks and the epigastrium [pit of the stomach], in the form of perspiration. The blood exuded in drops, and tinged the linen. The cutaneous surface appeared injected in those parts whence the blood escaped, being red, and showing a net-work of arborescent vessels. This bloody perspiration took place whenever the hysteric paroxysm lasted a considerable time. This state continued for three months, and ultimately gave way, it is said, to local bleeding. . . . together with strong revulsive measures." *—Such cases are valuable, by proving the possibility and actual occurrence of bloody sweat which, although attested by authors of the highest eminence and credibility, some persons have on speculative grounds disputed, or denied. Thus Baron Haller declares that passions of the mind sometimes force blood from the skin, and infers that the sudoriferous tubes are not much smaller than the capillary blood-vessels.—"Sanguis ipse in summo æstu, in motu vehementi, a vita vinolenta, ex terrore et anxietate [in Ser-

---

* Schwencke, Hæmatologia, pp. 130, 13;—Medico-Chirurgical Review, from July to October, 1831, p. 496.

vatoris exemplo], ex dissolutione sanguinis, variisque causis per sudoris vias sequi, etiam minime malo eventu; manifesto argumento vasa sudorifera arteriolis rubris non valde minora esse, summa violentia sanguinem **indigere, ut in** ea succedat."—" Affectus animi, qui nihil mutant nisi nervorum stricturas, miras secretionum mutationes faciunt, sanguinem per **cutis vasa expellunt,** bilemque." *

For the satisfaction of those readers who love to ascertain the authenticity and value of the evidence submitted to them, the original accounts of most of the cases of bloody sweat mentioned in the text are here subjoined, with two or three additional ones. The first are from the German Ephemerides.—"Præter naturam aliquos sanguinem sudasse annotarunt Aristoteles, lib. iij. de part. animal. cap. v.; et. lib. iij. de histor. animal. cap. xvj.; Rondelet, de dignosc. morb. cap. xj.; Fernel. lib. vj. de part. morb. et symptom, cap. iv.; Marcellus Donatus, lib. j. de medic. histor. mirab. cap. ij.; Mercurialis, lib. iv. variar. lect. cap. xij.; Greg. Horstius. lib. j. part. ij.; Obs. 15; Thomas Bartholinus, cent. ij. epist. xij. p. 440. Henricus Ab Heer, Observ. 23, meminit cujasdam nobilis, qui sanguinem, cumque eo pediciilos ruberrimos sudavit."—" Juvenis quidam studiosus, cum propter, insolentias nocturnas et alia tentata carceri injiceretur, talem timorem et anxietatem cordis passus est ac si ad mortem usque deliquisset ut sparsim in pectore manibus et brachiis guttulæ sanguinis erumperent et transudarent. Re ad inclytum magistratum delata, jussus sum eum visitare, **et historiam explorare: quæ omnia cum oculis** meis vidissem, et incarceratum in periculo, vitæ constitutum deprehendissem, **ad instantiam** meam (poena quidem reservata) dimissus, **et tenuior** factus sanguis, sublata omni anxietate, ad pristinum statum reductus est." —" Observatum fuit puellulum, dum duo sui fratres majores **laqueo** suspenderentur, quia delicti erat particeps, et in poena juxta patibulum spectaculo **adstabat, sanguinem toto corpore sudasse."**—" Joachimus Scacerna, Ferrariensis, anno ætatis sexagesimo secundo, alioquin sanus, vexabatur forti animi pathemate ob criminationem alicujus, ut asserebat, testificationis falsæ; qua de re mense Novembris **sub meridiem mihi obviam factus, et** lugens, suum narrabat infortunium, et consilium poscebat, veritus ne in carcerem conjiceretur. Ego interim, misertus ejus calamitatis, observavi ex oculis lachrymas exire rubicundas, ad instar sanguinis. **Eum** consolatus discessi. Postea vero a satellitibus in carcerem ductus, **sanguineas** effundens lachrymas, dolore cordis vexatus, rigore in toto corpore afficitur, et exinde maligna febri, quæ trium dierum spatio illum necavit." †

* Haller, Element. Physiolog. Corp. Human. vol. v. p. 50;—Primæ Linæ Physiologiæ, p. 126.

† Ephemerid. Acad. Natur. Curios. Ann. 2, p. 84;—Dec. ij. Ann. 10, p. 354;—Dec. iij. Ann. 7 and 8; Append. p. 121; Edit. 2da. Norimb. vol. j. p. 84.

— In another volume of the same work is related the case of a boy, twelve years of age, who was relieved from a severe comatose and convulsive disorder by a bloody sweat, which broke out August the 2nd, 1746. After describing this occurrence, the author, J. C. Schilling, observes;— "Quum deinde mensis hujus die 17° sudor hic cessasset, acerbissimi recurrerunt capitis dolores, pectoris oppressiones et anxietates, immo aliquot motuum convulsivorum paroxysmi, quos sanguinis excreatio et, ejecto cum tussi sequuta, itemque sanguinis per alvum secessio; quales excretiones sanguinis, modo per os, modo per alvum, modo per poros cutis hinc inde, ad æquinoctium hujus anni vernale usque et ultra alternatim, sæpius recurrerunt; et, licet puer per aliquot interdum hebdomadas liber fuerit, non prius tamen quam post illud tempus prorsus convaluit. Jam vero, quæ singularis Dei gratia est, optime valet." *

The two cases of bloody sweat from mental emotion mentioned by De Thou are, in his own words, as follows: The first is that of the commander at Monte-Maro in Piedmont, who was treacherously seized and threatened with an ignominious death by the general of the besieging army.—"Capta Dragonera, Magio negotium datum ut Montem-Marinum, munitissimum locum, aggrederetur; qui secum ducto Augusto, Saluciarum principis notho filio, eo tendit; evocatoque quasi ad colloquium præsidiariorum duce ab Augusto, quicum arctissima intercedebat amicitia, Magius ex compacto superveniens eum comprehendi jussit; et ut locum dederet hortatus, cum nihil proficeret, postremo minas addidit, et ipsum vinctum quasi ad supplicium in oppidi conspectum deduci imperavit. Tam miserabili spectaculo victi oppidani, ut ducem suum periculo eximerent, deditionem fecere. Observatum tam indignæ mortis vehementi metu adeo concussum animo eum fuisse, ut sanguineum sudorem toto corpore funderet."—The second case is that of the Florentine youth at Rome, who for a trifling offence was publicly executed by order of Pope Pius the Sixth.—"Insigne severitatis signum dedit in causa juvenis cujusdam Florentini; qui, quod in heri sui ædibus in Transtiberina regione latrunculitoribus de asino quid postulantibus, aut exsequi volentibus, sola denegatione simpliciter restiterat, quanquam postea, non aquarii qui amissum asinum reposcebat, sed heri sui eum fuisse constitisset, nihilominus ad mortem damnatus est, ita Sixto volente ac jubente; nam quo minus recuperatores in juvenem mortis sententiam ferrent urbana lex obstabat, quæ quenquam ob ejusmodi crimina ante vicesimum annum completum morte affici vetat. Cum duceretur ad supplicium juvenis, multorum commiserationem excitavit; ipse præ doloris vehementia lachrymas cruentas fundere, et sanguinem pro sudore toto corpore

* Ephemerid. Acad. Natur. Curios. edit. 2da. vol. j. p. 84: vol. viij. p. 425, etc.

mittere visus est; quod multi pro certo documento acceperunt naturæ festinati crudeliter judicii severitatem impugnantis, et de magistratu ipso, quasi percussore, **ultionem reposcentis."** *

Next come the somewhat similar instances furnished by Maldonato, Zacchias, and Schenck. In illustration of the bloody sweat of Christ the former observes:—"Audio de his qui viderunt aut cognoverunt ante annos duos, Lutetiæ Parisiorum, hominem robustum et bene valentem, audita in se capitali sententia, sudore sanguineo fuisse perfusum."—After distinguishing between real and fictitious cases of this kind, Zacchias remarks:—"Si ergo talia symptomata abessent, per artem procuratum fuisse talem sudorem esset suspicandum; qui tamen non ita extra naturam est, quin aliquando observatum sit illum ex ingenti animi angore in iis qui morte damnati sunt prorupisse; ut in juvene Belba, igni destinato, non multis abhinc annis quicunque voluit adnotavit; et notavit etiam Cardanus, *De subtilitate*, et alibi."—The case of the nun, to which Dr. Millingen seems to have referred, is thus described in the work of Schenck à Grafenberg.—"Soror quædam religiosa, cum incidisset in militum manus, et evaginatos gladios ac machærulas vibratas mortem intentantes videret, adeo territa fuit et commota, ut sanguis ab omnibus corporis partium meatibus manaret; ita ut, in oculis hostium exsanguis effecta, vitam finiret mortalem."—To these may be added the original account given by De Mezeray, concerning the death of Charles IX. of France. After mentioning the various projects which this unprincipled but active monarch contemplated during his last illness, the historian observes:—"Mais c'étoit en vain qu'il faisoit tous ces grands projets; le ciel en avoit autrement disposé. Il se consumoit à petit feu, et pour ainsi dire, il fondoit à vue d'œil. Tous les remèdes de ses médecins pallioient son mal, mais ils ne le guérissoient pas; et après que la vigueur de sa jeunesse et la grandeur de son courage eurent longtemps combattu contre sa maladie, il en fut enfin abattu au lit dans le chateau de Vincennes, vers le huitième jour de Mai [1574]. La nature fit d'étranges efforts pendant les deux dernières semaines de sa vie. Il tressailloit et se roidissoit avec une extrême violence. Il s'agitoit et se remuoit sans cesse, et le sang lui jaillissoit par tous les conduits, même par les pores, de sorte qu'on le trouva une fois qui baignoit dedans." †

The statement that the agony of Christ was **a violent conflict between opposite mental emotions,** and that his sweat was literally mixed with

---

* Thuanus, Hist. sui Temp. vol. j. p. 373; vol. iv. p. 300.

† Joannes Maldonatus, Comment. in quatuor Evangelist. p. 601;—Paulus Zacchias, Quæstiones Medico-legales, lib. ilj. p. 154;—Joannes Schenck à Grafenberg, Observ. Medic. etc., lib. ilj. p. 458;—De Mezeray, Histoire de France, vol. iij. p. 306.

blood in a half-coagulated state, is strongly confirmed by the consideration that Luke, the only sacred writer by whom the awful scene is described, was a physician, and that the terms which he employs, and which occur in no other part of the New Testament, are strictly medical. Their proper import is attested by all the lexicons, as for example by that of Castello.—" Agonia, ἀγωνία, *angorem* significat, et verbum ἀγωνιᾷν, juxta Galen. lib. 2, *de symptom. caus.* cap. 5, *ad finem*, affectum animi compositum ex ira et timore; illa quidem sanguinem et spiritum foras agente et fundente, hoc vero utrumque ad vitæ principium et interiora, cum refrigeratione eorum quæ in summo corpore sunt, reducente et contrahente. Derivatur ab ἀγών, *certamen*, lucta. Unde et ἀγωνία certamen quandoque significat. . . . . Ad summam, *Agonia* significat in genere colluctationem diversorum affectuum animi inter se contrariorum."— " Thrombos. θρόμβος, Vide *Grumus*.—Grumus, θρόμβος, est liquidæ rei in unam massam concretæ et coagulatæ frustum. Ad lac et sanguinem translata vox est medicis; imprimis Hippocrates frequenter de sanguine usus est concreto; 4. aph. 80. Coac. t. 123, lib. 5, *Epid*. 5."—A similar account of these words is given in Poole's Synopsis, at the note on Luke, chap. 22, v. 41.—"'Ἀγών est certamen, periculum, labor. Hinc ἀγωνία, quæ est horror quo homo corripi solet in gravi discrimine. Proprie usurpatur de eo motu animi ad grave periculum, qui tamen fortitudinem non expectoret. Vide Porphyrium ad illud Homeri ; Τρῶας μὲν τρόμος, etc.—Cum esset in æstu.—Significat ἀγωνία summam Christi angustiam, luctantis et cum terroribus mortis, et cum terribili Patris irati judicio. . . . . ὡσεὶ θρόμβοι αἵματος καταβαίνοντες : quasi grumi, vel guttæ, Vulg. Grumi sunt guttæ ampliores sive crassiores sanguinis descendentes, etc., vel decurrentes, fluvii aut forrentis more. . . . Est enim θρόμβος Galeno τὸ αἷμα πεπηγὸς, sanguis concretus, qui-Latinis grumus in Glossario, et in vetere Onomastico. . . . Docet Aristoteles 3 de histor. animal. accedere nonnullis ἱδρῶσαι αἱματώδει περιττώματι· sudare sanguineo excremento, propter malum corporis habitum, et defectum caloris. . . . 'Ἀγωνιῶντες autem maxime sudant, inquit Aristot. Problem. Sect. 2 De sudore. Idemque testantur Artemidorus, Philostratus, et Philo. Sed illud *quasi* non significat hunc non fuisse vere guttas aqueas mistas sanguine ; quod etiam fieri possit per naturam vim intus patientem, ac proinde per poros ejicientem una cum aqua sanguinem, præsertim ubi corpus rarum est ac delicatum, et sanguis subtilis, ut in Christo indubie erat."—Schleusner in like manner remarks that the adverbs ὡς and ὡσεὶ sometimes denote reality, and gives the following references respecting the use of θρόμβοι, in the sense of clots of blood. . . . " In scriptis medicorum Græcorum admodum frequenter vox θρόμβος de gutta spissi et coagulati sanguinis, et de sanguine coagulato in universum usurpatur. V. c. Dioscorid. I, c. 102; Hesych. θρόμβος· αἷμα παχὺ, πεπηγὸς, ὡς βουνοί. Confer. Fœsii Œcon. Hippocr. p. 167."

Note IV.,—Pages 85–131.
ON RUPTURE OF THE HEART FROM MENTAL EMOTION.

Sudden death from violent emotions of mind may be induced in various ways; sometimes by a sort of palsy of the heart, at other times by its over-distention, the latter condition often terminating in rupture. The following references to cases of both kinds are borrowed from Zimmermann.—" Joy,"—says this author,—" is much more dangerous to life than sudden grief. The instances we meet with of the fatal effects of sudden joy are more numerous than those of the latter. Sophocles, being desirous of proving that at an advanced age he was in full possession of his intellectual powers, composed a tragedy, was crowned, and died through joy. The same thing happened to Phillipides, the comic writer. We see Chilo of Lacedæmon embracing his son, who had borne away the prize at the Olympic games, and dying in his arms. Two Roman ladies, seeing their sons return from the battles of Thrasymenus and Cannæ, died in the same manner. M. Juventius Thalna, on being told that a triumph had been decreed to him for having subdued Corsica, fell down dead before the altar at which he was offering up his thanksgiving. Vaterus relates that a brave soldier, who had never been sick, died suddenly in the arms of an only daughter whom he had long wished to see. A worthy family in Holland being reduced to indigence, the elder brother passed over to the East Indies, acquired considerable riches there, and returning home presented his sister with the richest jewels. The young woman at this unexpected change of fortune became motionless, and died. The famous Fouquet died on being told that Louis XIV. had restored him to his liberty. The niece of the celebrated Leibnitz, not suspecting that a philosopher would hoard up treasure, died suddenly on opening a box under her uncle's bed, which contained sixty thousand ducats. Dr. Mead tells us that, in the memorable year of the South Sea bubble, more of those went mad who acquired fortunes, than of those who lost them. . . . Many observations tend to prove that sudden fear has occasioned [syncope] fainting, and even death. The face grows pale, the blood seems to stop in the vena cava, or in the right auricle of the heart, the vessels become distended, and the heart itself in these cases has sometimes burst. Philip II., King of Spain, only said to his first minister, the Cardinal Espinosa, *Cardinal, know that I am matter*, and the minister was so much terrified that he died a few days afterward. The same prince, perceiving that one of his ministers answered him with some hesitation, gave him a severe rebuke: the minister withdrew from the apartment, and died. Philip V. died suddenly on being told that the Spaniards had been defeated; and, on opening him, his heart was found ruptured."*

To collect instances of rupture of the heart from agony of mind is a difficult task; partly, because such instances are, it may reasonably be supposed, of rare occurrence; and partly, because few of those which do occur are either verified or recorded. There cannot, for example, be much ground to doubt that the following case, abridged from the Annual Register, was one of this description; although, owing to the want of actual inspection, it is impossible to speak with absolute certainty on the subject.—Mr. John Palmer, comedian, aged about fifty-six or fifty-seven years, died suddenly on the stage of the Liverpool theatre, August 2d, 1798, while performing the part of *The Stranger*, in the play of that name. He was a man of acute and affectionate feelings, which had been much exercised by the course and events of his life. He had recently lost his wife and a favorite son, labored in consequence under profound grief and depression of mind which he strove to overcome, and had expressed a conviction that these mental sufferings would very shortly bring him to his grave. During some days he seemed, however, to bear up against his misfortunes, and performed in some pieces, including *The Stranger*, with much success. About a week afterward he appeared a second time in that character, when he fell a victim to the poignancy of his feelings. On the morning of the day he was much dejected, but exerted himself with great effect in the first and second acts of the play. In the third act he showed evident marks of depression; and in the fourth, when about to reply to the question of Baron Steinfort relative to his children, appeared unusually agitated. He endeavored to proceed, but his feelings overcame him. The hand of death arrested his progress, and he fell on his back, heaved a convulsive sigh, and instantly expired without a groan. Having been removed to the scene-room, and medical aid immediately procured, his veins were opened, but yielded not a single drop of blood, and every other means of resuscitation was tried without effect. His death was by most persons ascribed to apoplexy; but Dr. Mitchell and Dr. Corry gave it as their opinion that he certainly died of a broken heart, in consequence of the family afflictions which he had recently experienced."—Unfortunately, this highly-probable opinion was

---

* Zimmerman, On Experience in Physic, vol. ii. pp. 268, 269, 274, 275.

merely argued, and not verified, as it ought to have been, by actual inspection. On this point the friends and colleagues of the deceased actor had, it is likely, insurmountable prejudices, and the unopened body was accordingly—"interred on the 6th of August, at the neighboring village of Walton, in a grave seven feet deep, dug in a rock." *—In like manner Mallet's tale of Edwin and Emma, in which the latter is represented as dying of a broken heart owing to the death of her lover, whose union with her had been forbidden by his parents, appears to have been founded on a real occurrence, briefly related in the subjoined extract from a letter, written by the curate of Bowes, in Yorkshire.—"The young lover sickened, and took to his bed about Shrove Tuesday, and died the Sunday seven-night after. On the last day of his illness he desired to see his mistress. She was civilly received by the mother, who bid her welcome when it was too late. But her daughter Hannah lay at his back, to cut them off from all opportunity of exchanging their thoughts. At her return home, on hearing the bell toll out for his departure, she screamed aloud that her heart was burst, and expired some moments after. The then curate of Bowes inserted it in his register that they both died of love, and were buried in the same grave, March 15, 1714."—In this case also, as in many others, the circumstantial evidence is extremely strong, but the positive proof, which might have been furnished by an examination after death, is irrevocably lost.†

Dilatation of some of the chambers of the heart, or of the great vessels connected with them, is a lower degree of the same train of action which, when sudden and intense, occasions rapture; and, like rupture, is often induced by mental anguish and distress, only less violent, and longer continued. The remarkable instance inserted in the text is borrowed from a work by Mr. Bedingfield, who, in a letter to the author, dated April 12, 1839, kindly furnished the following additional particulars.— "Elizabeth Creasey was about twenty-eight years of age, an interesting creature, whose unfortunate situation excited much sympathy. The poor girl had been seduced, and then abandoned; and when admitted into the hospital was in a state of extreme emaciation and debility. Her lips and cheeks were of a bluish color, indicating an imperfect oxygenation of the blood. The action of the heart was labored, the pulse languid, and varying from 90 to 100 in the minute. She never uttered a complaint, seldom spoke, was never known to laugh, nor seen to smile. She did not, although as patient as patience on a monument, even 'smile at grief.' Nothing appeared to excite the slightest emotion, except when

---

* Annual Register for the year 1798,—Chronicle Section, pp. 73–78.
† Johnson's English Poets, vol. 63, pp. 174–176.

any allusion was made to her removal. She would then raise her dark-blue eyes, and throw an imploring look into her countenance, the meaning of which it was impossible to mistake. Neither physician nor visitor ever ordered her discharge from the hospital, where she continued for I think eighteen months, and then sank rapidly. The only morbid appearances met with after death are those detailed in the page to which you have referred;"—namely,—"the right auricle of the heart was of three times its natural dimensions, and contained a large quantity of blood, which had separated into serum, crassamentum, and coagulable lymph, as perfectly as inflamed blood does when drawn from a vein."

Although the term—*broken heart*—is not always used literally, but often in a figurative sense, to denote intense, or perhaps mortal sorrow, it was no doubt originally derived from the actual fact, either accidentally observed, or sagaciously conjectured by poets and moralists, habitually engaged in the study of the human passions, and of their influence on the bodily frame. Rupture of the heart from agony of mind appears to have been familiar to the penetrating genius of Shakespeare, who has frequently depicted it in the most lively manner; and the sacredness of the present subject will not be injured by one or two references, for the sake of illustration, to the works of this master-mind. Thus, the well-known demand which Macbeth, anxious for the relief of his conscience-stricken queen, makes of the physician called to attend her, has a general bearing on the subject.

> " Canst thou not minister to a mind diseased,
> Pluck from the memory a rooted sorrow,
> Raze out the written troubles of the brain,
> And, with some sweet oblivious antidote,
> Cleanse the foul bosom of that perilous stuff
> Which weighs upon the heart ?"—

The admonition of Malcolm to Macduff, when the latter is thrown into consternation on hearing of the murder of his wife and children by order of the usurper is still more explicit.

> " Give sorrow words : the grief that does not speak
> Whispers the o'er-fraught heart and bids it break."

By a poetical license the great dramatist, speaking in the person of Mark Antony, represents the death of Julius Cæsar as occasioned, not by the daggers of the conspirators, but by the anguish of the ambitious chief, on seeing his well-beloved Brutus among their number.

> "This, this was the unkindest cut of all;
> For, when the noble Cæsar saw *him* stab,
> Ingratitude, more strong than traitors' arms,
> Quite vanquished him: then burst his mighty heart,
> And, in his mantle muffling up his face,
> Even at the base of Pompey's statue,
> Which all the while ran blood, great Cæsar fell." *

That Shakespeare was fully aware of the physical fact here intimated, is plainly shown by some other passages of this kind, where it is described with that minute and circumstantial reality which is peculiar to genius of the highest order. See particularly Coriolanus, Act V., Scene 5;—Hamlet, Act I., Scenes 2 and 5;—Julius Cæsar, Act IV., Scene 2;—Lear, Act II., Scene 4; Act V., Scene 3;—Richard III., Act IV., Scene 1;—Titus Andronicus, Act II., Scene 5; Act III., Scene 2.

Several instances have been given in the text, wherein the view here taken of the immediate cause of the Saviour's death has been more or less distinctly anticipated by pious persons, on ordinary grounds, without the advantage of that scientific knowledge of the subject, from which alone demonstrative proof can be obtained. Many more might probably be added, but one or two may suffice. The first specimen is from the psalms and hymns of Dr. Watts.

> "All my reproach is known to thee,
> The scandal and the shame;
> Reproach has broke my bleeding heart,
> And lies defiled my name."
>
> Psalm 69, Part II., C. M. Verse 6.

> "Here, says the kind redeeming Lord,
> And shows his wounded side,
> See here the spring of all your joys,
> That opened when I died."
>
> Hymns, Book III., II. 11, Verse 3.

> "Justice unsheathed its fiery sword,
> And plunged it in my heart:
> Infinite pangs for you I bore,
> And most tormenting smart."
>
> Hymns, Book III. II. 21, Verse 7.

* Shakespeare's Plays, in 21 vols., 1803; vol. x. pp. 248, 270, 271; vol. xvi. pp. 357, 353.

"My Saviour's pierced side
 Poured out a double flood:
By water we are purified,
 And pardoned by the blood."

. . . . . .

"Look up, my soul, to him,
 Whose death was thy desert;
And humbly view the living stream
 Flow from his breaking heart."
    Hymns, Book III., H. 9, Verses 4, 6.

"And here we drink our Saviour's blood;
 We thank thee, Lord, 'tis generous wine
Mingled with love: the fountain flowed
 From that dear bleeding heart of thine."
    Hymns, Book III., H. 18, Verse 2.

A curious example of this kind, although neither the source whence it is derived, nor the form in which it is presented, is entitled to much respect, occurs in the pretended Revelations of St. Bridgit, a Swedish lady, who flourished in the fourteenth century, and founded the religious order which bears her name. In these visions, or prophecies, Christ and his mother are represented as holding conversations in the glorified state concerning his life, sufferings, death, etc., on earth; wherein, among other circumstances, it is repeatedly stated that immediately before he expired on the cross, his heart was ruptured through pain or grief. The following description is ascribed to the mother of Christ.—"Appropinquante autem morte, cum cor præ violentia dolorum rumperetur, tunc omnia membra contremuerunt, et caput ejus, quasi modicum se erigens, inclinabatur. Os ejus apertum videbatur, et lingua tota sanguinolenta. Manus ejus retraxerunt se modicum de loco perforationis, et pondus corporis pedes amplius sustentabant. Digiti et brachia quodammodo extendebant se, et dorsum fortiter stringebatur ad stipitem. Tunc quidam dixerunt ad me, Maria, filius tuus mortuus est. Alii autem dixerunt, Mortuus est, sed resurget. Omnibus itaque dicentibus, unus adveniens, adfixit lanceam in latus ejus tam valide, ut pene per aliud latus ejus transiret. Et cum extraheretur hasta, apparuit cuspis rubea sanguine. Tunc mihi videbatur quasi cor meum perforaretur, cum vidissem cor filii meii charissimi perforatum."—The subsequent reply is attributed to Christ himself.—" Quia, quando, cor meum in cruce præ vehementia doloris rumpebatur, cor tuum ex hoc quasi ferro acutissimo vulnerabatur, et libenter scindi permisisses, si fuisset voluntas mea." *

These passages evidently contain a reference to the prediction, long before addressed to Mary by Simeon in the temple,—" Yea, a sword shall pierce through thine own soul also ;" †—and plainly intimate a conviction that the heart of Christ was ruptured through excess of pain or grief. Nor does it appear wonderful that such a conclusion should have been deduced by persons of piety and intelligence from long and intense meditation on the Scriptures, when it is remembered that the following expressions, some of which have been repeatedly quoted in this treatise, are found in several of the Psalms, more especially in those which relate to the sufferings and death of Christ.

Psalm 38, v. 8. " I am feeble and sore broken. I have roared because of the disquietude of my heart."

v. 10. " My heart panteth : my strength faileth me."

Psalm 40, v. 12. " Innumerable evils have compassed me about: mine iniquities have taken hold upon me, so that I am not able to look up. They are more than the hairs of my head ; therefore my heart faileth me."

Psalm 51, v. 17. " The sacrifices of God are a broken spirit ; a broken and a contrite heart, O God ! thou wilt not despise."

Psalm 69, v. 20. " Reproach hath broken my heart, and I am full of heaviness."

Psalm 109, v. 22. " I am poor and needy, and my heart is wounded within me."

Note V.,—Pages 132-157.

ON THE BLOOD AND WATER WHICH FLOWED FROM THE SIDE OF CHRIST.

The perplexities and errors of commentators respecting this subject have been chiefly owing, either to deficiency of information, or to want of judgment. Many of them have gratuitously imagined that the blood which flowed from the side of Christ was liquid, and the water pure ; and, in order to account for so marvellous an occurrence, have had recourse to miraculous agency, or to other equally untenable suppositions. Their difficulties and mistakes might have been in a great measure avoid-

---

* Memoriale Effigiatum Librorum B. Brigidæ, etc., lib. i. cap. 10, p. 38 ; lib. ii. cap. 20, p. 45.

† Luke, chap. 2, v. 34, 35 ;—John, chap. 19, v. 25-27.

ed, had they perceived that the scriptural expression—" blood and water,"—taken in this connection, simply denotes the crassamentum and serum of blood which has separated into its constituents, and that the same terms are continually used in the same sense both by medical persons, and by others. Of such usage several examples have been given in the text, particularly two cases from the Sepulchretum of Bonet, accompanied by an apposite comment of Morgagni. The original statement is as follows.—" Filia septemdecim annorum, orphana paralytica, sine manifesta causa suffocatur subito. Secto cadavere, cor inveni duplo magis ordinario, auriculas ejus maximas, venas, arteriasque, aqua et sanguine nigro grumosoque admodum distentas. . . . Miles subito post longum mærorem mortuus, visceribus reliquis salvis, habuit in pericardio non aquam modo, sed et copiosum sanguinem concretum."—The comment of Morgagni on the latter of these cases is;—" Ubi, etsi in scholio quoque inculcatum videbis obrutum oppressumque cor fuisse, *tum ob aquæ copia, tum a sanguine*, minime tamen necesse est aliam aquam fuisse credas quam serum, a concreta sanguinis parte reliqua uberiore, et non raro fit, copia separatum."—A remark of Mr. Coleridge on this subject, although in other respects erroneous, furnishes a further illustration of the same usage.—" St. John did not mean "—says he,—" I apprehend, to insinuate that the spear-thrust made the death, merely as such, certain or evident, but that the effusion showed the human nature.—' I saw it '—he would say,—' with my own eyes. It was real blood, composed of lymph and crassamentum, and not a mere celestial ichor, as the Phantasmists allege." *—An example of similar language has already been quoted from Wheeler's Manchester Chronicle; and, as that journal cannot very easily be consulted, the passage is here more fully transcribed.—" A man named James Brown, about twenty-seven years of age, who had been at sea, and lost his left leg, and subsequently lived as a tramper about the country, was drinking with two others in a beer-shop in Blakeley street, when he suddenly complained of illness, lay down on one of the forms and vomited a little; and, ere a surgeon who had been sent for could arrive, expired. Mr. Ollier, on examination of the body, found it wholly free from any mark of violence, the stomach and liver were in a very diseased state, the heart-purse contained about a quart of blood and water, and there was a rupture in the great artery leading from the heart, which was produced by disease, and must have caused death almost instantaneously. An inquest was held on view of the body on Monday, by W. S. Rutter, Esq., Coroner, when the jury found that his death had been

* Bonetus, Sepulchretum, vol. j. pp. 585, 887;—Morgagni, de Caus. et Sed. Morb. vol. iij. p. 465;—Coleridge (S. T.) Specimens of his Table-talk, vol. j. pp. 19, 20.

caused by disease, and not otherwise."—A letter on the subject, addressed to the author by the late J. A. Ransome, Esq., of Manchester, confirms the foregoing narrative, and contains the following note from Mr. Ollier.—" The disease of the aorta was a thickening of its coats, without any ossific deposit. The size of the aperture was very small, and was situated just where it rises from the ventricle, and would not have been observed but for the consequences. The blood was separated, although indistinctly, into serum and crassamentum."—As a proof of the equivalence of the terms, the same surgeon, when delivering his testimony at the Coroner's inquest, judiciously used the more popular language above mentioned,—" The pericardium contained about a quart of blood and water." *

If it is admitted that in the evangelical narrative of the death of Christ the terms blood and water signify crassamentum and serum, a critical examination of the circumstances under which alone such a discharge could have taken place from his dead body, on the side being pierced by a spear, leads inevitably to the conclusion that he died from rupture of the heart. The condition of the blood in dead bodies varies, according to the cause and mode of death. In persons killed by lightning, by blows on the stomach, or by the more simple and direct operation of violent passions, the blood remains liquid. A striking case of the former kind is related in the Philosophical Transactions.—" On the 29th of September, 1772, about two o'clock in the morning, were three remarkably loud claps of thunder, attended with proportionate lightning. Mr. Thomas Heartly, formerly a wine-merchant of Leeds, but lately retired from business to Harrogate, lived there in a hired house, the second northward from the Queen's Head. While he was in bed with his wife she was awaked from sleep by the thunder, and went to the window, but not being afraid she got to bed again, and fell asleep. About five she awaked, and not perceiving her husband to breathe, though warm, endeavored to awake him in vain. She quickly sent for Mr. Hutchinson, a considerable apothecary at Knaresborough, who, upon sight of Mr. Heartly, and some experiments, declared him dead, though still very warm. At her request, however, he opened a vein, and Mr. Heartly bled freely, insomuch that the blood did not cease to ooze out of the orifice till the body was put in the coffin, which was on Thursday evening, October 1st; and it was not then cold." †

Within the heart and vessels of dead bodies the blood is commonly found either wholly liquid or solid, or a portion of liquid blood is inter-

---

* Wheeler's Manchester Chronicle for Saturday, November 22d, 1834.
† Philosophical Transactions, vol. 63, pp. 177, 178.

mixed with pale or dark-colored coagula; but its distinct separation into serum and crassamentum is scarcely ever seen. On this subject few observations occur among the earlier medical writers. In a small treatise on polypous concretions, etc., Dominicus De Marinis remarks,—" Scribit Fernelius, ex rara quadam et abdita morbi causa, se vidisse quempiam post diuturnum languorem de vita exiisse, cui sanguis universus in vasis concreverat, adeo ut demum coralli modo fruticans illinc eximeretur. Physiolog. lib. 6, cap. 7. . . . Non absimilem sanguinis constitutionem, in venis meseraicis in hectica tumefactis, descripsit Platerus. Observ. lib. 2. . . . Audivisse notat Ballonius sanguinem nigrum ita in jugularibus venis concrevisse, ut carbones illic impacti crederentur, Eph. 2." On the other hand, Schwencke, in his Hæmatologia, states somewhat too decidedly,—" Raro vel nunquam sanguis in vasis mortuorum coagulatus reperitur. . . . In cadaveribus, sanguinis in partes secessus stricte non observatur, sed mistus et fluidus in venis reperitur;"—unless, which is not improbable, he herein refers to the complete division of the blood into its constituents.*

The deficiencies of the earlier writers in this respect are, however, amply compensated by two living authors quoted in the text; namely, Dr. John Davy, and James Paget, Esq. The physiological and anatomical researches of the former contain a table, which gives a condensed account of 249 bodies examined at Malta, from the year 1828 to 1835. In 85 of these the state of the blood was not noticed, but in the remaining 164 it was recorded.—" The fatal cases affording the subjects of these observations were,"—says Dr. Davy,—" without exception, soldiers of our regiments serving in Malta, composed of Englishmen, Scotch, and Irish. In the cool season the bodies were commonly inspected in from 12 to 17 hours after death; in the hot season in from 3 to 12."—Among the 164 cases above mentioned, the blood was found coagulated, and containing fibrinous concretions in 105;—coagulated and broken up, as if by the contractions of the heart, feebly continued for some time after apparent death, in 17;—liquid, in 14;—in the state of soft coagulum, or merely grumous and without fibrinous concretions, in 12;—partly liquid and partly coagulated, in 9;—and wholly or nearly deficient in the heart, in 6.—In one instance only there were fibrinous concretions without cruor, that is, without liquid blood or bloody serum. Next follows a tabular account of 35 cases of post-mortem examination, made in the General Hospital at Fort Pitt, Chatham, from January to September, 1838. The various conditions in which the blood was found are still more mi-

---

* Dominic. De Marinis, De Re Monstrosa, etc., p. 74;—Schwencke, Hæmatologia, pp. 81, 91.

nutely described in these cases than in the preceding ones; but in none of either set does clear serum appear to have been discovered, except in one solitary instance, and under very peculiar circumstances; namely, in No. 16, a case of phthisis wherein, says the author,—"a mass of fibrine in the right ventricle contained a collection of transparent serum. The mass was firmest externally. There was some crassamentum, fibrinous concretions, and a good deal of cruor in the right cavities of the heart. Two hours after examination the cruor was found jellied. After twenty-four hours the coagulum had contracted, and serum had separated. When broken up and agitated, some air was given off." *

The testimony of Mr. Paget, equally positive, and in some respects even more precise than that of Dr. Davy, is summed up in the concluding paragraph of his—"Observations on the Coagulation of the Blood after Death,"—published in the London Medical Gazette.—"In all cases it must be remembered that the coagulation which takes place in the body is much slower than that which ensues in blood drawn from it, either during life or after death; so that a quantity of uncolored fibrine is found in the heart and uppermost vessels of the dead body in many cases, in which it is most probable that, had the blood been drawn during life, it would not have presented a buffy coat. In the majority of cases, the blood does not coagulate in the body for the first four hours after its rest has commenced. In many it remains fluid for six, eight, or more hours, and yet coagulates within a few minutes of its being let out of the vessels. But, as this greater slowness of coagulation is common to all, it is not material in a comparison of the blood of the dead with that of the living." †—In a letter on the subject, with which the author has been favored by Mr. Paget, the following additional explanations are supplied. —" I have never found clear serum, such as I could suppose to be separated from the blood in its coagulation, collecting in any part of the body after death; but I have marked passages in my paper which express, though ambiguously, what I believe becomes of that which does separate. I suppose that it gravitates to the dependent parts of the body, and is there imbibed by the adjacent tissues, which are thus rendered moister and more œdematous than those in the upper or anterior parts. That the serum, if at all separated from the blood, would thus pass to the dependent parts, is I suppose certain, and I have never met with any facts to lead me to imagine that it is not separated. All that I have seen leads me to think—that in the very great majority of cases all the blood re-

* Dr. John Davy. Researches Physiological and Anatomical, vol. ii. pp. 190-213.
† James Paget, Esq., On the Coagulation of the Blood after Death;—in the London Medical Gazette for 1840, vol. l. p. 618.

mains fluid till the heart ceases to act;—that then it gradually coagulates, in the same manner as it would out of the body, though much more slowly;—that the coloring particles, descending more and more deeply in direct proportion to the time occupied in the coagulation, leave a certain portion of uncolored fibrine above them; and that, just as happens in blood drawn from the body, the serum is in part separated during the coagulation of the fibrine, and in part squeezed out by the contraction of the clot. The clot, I suppose, is detained in the place in which it forms, either by its adhesion to the adjacent structures, or by being supported by the parts in which it is as it were modelled; and the serum, as it separates, flows down to the most depending portions of the body, and is there either retained in the vessels, or infiltrated into the adjacent porous tissues."

The conclusion that the blood and water which issued from the side of Christ were crassamentum and serum, necessarily implies three conditions; namely, first, that a considerable quantity of his blood separated into its constituents previously to the infliction of the wound;—secondly, that this separation took place within two hours after he expired, the longest period which can be assigned for such an effect, since the entire interval between his death and the commencement of the Jewish sabbath was only three hours;—and thirdly, that the blood and water thus separated were in a situation whence they could easily flow out when the wound was inflicted, according to the statement of the evangelist John,— "One of the soldiers pierced his side with a spear, and immediately there came forth blood and water."—These conditions prove, as has been already shown, that the blood and water flowed from the pericardium, and consequently, that the death of Christ was occasioned by the rupture of his heart, the blood from which had been discharged into its investing capsule, and had there divided into its elements; inasmuch as they perfectly agree with this explanation, and are incompatible with any other. To the supposition that the blood and water proceeded directly from the heart, there are three insuperable objections; namely,—first, that the separation into serum and crassamentum of the blood remaining in the vascular system of dead bodies, is of very rare occurrence;—secondly, that such separation, if it happened at all, could not have happened within the specified period of two hours, since,—"in the majority of cases, the blood [thus situated] does not coagulate for the first four hours after its rest has commenced, [and] in many it remains fluid for six, eight, or more hours;"—and thirdly, that, independently of these difficulties, the escape of such constituents from any of the cavities of the heart would be scanty, slow, and probably indistinct, and therefore at variance with the evangelical narrative. On the other hand, by the explanation here adopted all these objections are avoided; since a much larger quantity of blood would thus be discharged into the pericardium than could possibly be retained in the heart; the blood so effused would long within the time mentioned divide into its constituents; and, on the side being pierced by a spear, these constituents would, by the mere force of gravity, instantly and completely flow out in so conspicuous a manner, as to attract the notice of the most ignorant or indifferent spectator.

A good many examples have been given in the text, tending to show that the separation of blood into serum and crassamentum, or blood and water, which is so rarely observed within the heart and vessels of dead bodies, frequently happens when death has been suddenly induced by internal hæmorrhage, and blood has been extravasated into any of the serous capsules, whether the pleura, the pericardium, or the peritonæum. Some of the original statements, and two or three additional cases, are here annexed; and, as in all of them the general principle is the same, it is a matter of no consequence in reference to the illustration from what quarter the extravasated blood proceeded, nor into which of these capsules it entered. Several instances are, however, adduced in which, as in the great event which it is the object of this treatise to explain, blood was discharged from the ruptured heart into the pericardium, and there divided into its constituents. The two following cases occurred in the Manchester workhouse, and are thus reported by Dr. Francis.—"Samuel J . . . , aged fifty-nine years, a hand-loom weaver, of spare frame, middle height, and temperate habits, at ten A. M., September 22, 1844, was seized with intense pain across the forehead, faintness, and vomiting. . . . He was conveyed to bed, but died in about an hour and a half from the commencement of the seizure, having previously experienced severe pains in the cardiac region. On inspection of the body, the arteries generally were found in a morbid state, especially the coronaries. The aorta was greatly diseased, and about an inch above its valves was ruptured. The external opening did not correspond to the internal, and would just have admitted a crow-quill. The pericardium contained twenty-six ounces of blood, which had escaped through this aperture, and was equally made up of dark clot and serum. . . . Nicholas D . . . , aged thirty-five years, a tall, well-developed, stout young man, of dark complexion, a power-loom weaver, had been in the workhouse during the six weeks preceding his death, complaining of wandering pains in the upper limbs, lumbago, and especially a severe pain commencing at the fourth or fifth dorsal vertebra, and passing along the corresponding intercostal nerves to the sternum. On the 8th of February, 1845, he was more cheerful than usual;

but about nine P. M. was heard to groan, and immediately afterward turned on the left side, and died within a few minutes. On examining the body, an aneurism was found projecting from the interior surface of the aorta, opposite the third dorsal vertebra. In the left pleura, close to the lung at its root, was a slit parallel with the long axis of the artery, four lines in length, through which the aneurism had burst. The left pleural sac contained five imperial pints of blood, separated into a straw-colored serum and a firm clot, which latter had subsided to the depending parts." *

Of the striking contrast which, as remarked by Dr. Carpenter, is sometimes presented in the same subject, between the complete separation of extravasated blood into serum and crassamentum, and the continued fluidity of the blood remaining within the heart and vessels, a good example is furnished by Morgagni, in these terms.—" Mulier consistente ætate, quæ alias in nosocomio Patavino fuerat ob dolorem in sinistra intima thoracis parte, in idem rediit ante medium Januarium, anni 1717, de eodem illo dolore querens, nunc magna cum febre conjuncto. Pulsus erant vibrati, morbusque omnino videbatur gravis, sed non adeo ut mors jam proxima esse crederetur. Fuit tamem; nam postridie quam in nosocomium venerat mulier improviso mortua est. Thorace aperto, hujus quasi hydrops a primo apparuit. Sed, cum infra aquam magna concreti sanguinis copia occurreret, intellectum est hujus serum hydropis specimen repræsentasse. Quærentibus unde sanguis prodiisset magnum se obtulit aortæ aneurysma, idque perruptum. . . . Cæterum nullum in corde vitium, nulla polyposa concretio, si unam excipias longulam quidem sed exilem, quæ ex sinisto ventriculo per aortam ad hujus usque curvaturam pertinebat; quin sanguis in corde et alibi fluidus, non minus quam ater conspectus est."—The same author judiciously explains the cause of death when blood, derived from whatever source, is poured into the pericardial sac, namely, compression of the heart, and consequent arrest of the circulation, whence, as he observes, it arises that—" multo minor intra pericardium, quam plerisque aliis in locis hæmorrhagia, longe citius interitum afferat." †

Perhaps the smallest amount of hæmorrhage into the pericardium, which has ever been known to prove fatal in this manner, is that mentioned in the following case communicated to the Lancet by Mr. Taylor, of Guildford.—" Mrs. Keele, aged fifty-three years, the wife of a farmer's laborer, was taken ill suddenly on the morning of the 20th [of Sept. 1843], and died in the course of half an hour. . . . Her husband stated

---

* Dr. Francis, in the Guy's Hospital Reports, Second Series, No. 5, pp. 89–92.
† Morgagni, De Caus. et Sed. Morborum, vol. iij. pp. 116–118, 442–445; vol. vij. pp. 654–657.

that she had been in **very** good health, and only the day before had walked five miles with a burden."—On inspection of the body,—" the muscular tissue [of the heart] appeared somewhat pale and softened, its fibres being intermixed with fat, the right ventricle rather dilated, and its **walls much** thinned, so that near the point of rupture their thickness did not exceed half a line, and here the accumulation of fat was greatest. . . . The right ventricle was collapsed, and on the middle of its anterior surface, close to the septum, I observed a depression, which proved to be a perforation into its cavity large enough to admit a goose-quill, and showing one of the fleshy columns through it. About an ounce and a half of fluid blood was effused into the pericardium. . . . The **only comment that I have to make on the case is, that a very small quantity of blood was effused from a considerable breach in the ventricle; whence I conclude that death must have been instantaneous, from the heart's action being suspended by pressure of the sudden effusion."** * As a further proof that compression of the heart, irrespectively of the compressing agent, whether blood or not, is in such cases the principal cause of death, another narrative, supplied by R. Allan, Esq., staff-surgeon at Port Louis, **Mauritius, and** probably almost unique in its kind, may be cited from the same work.—" Cumia, aged thirty-five [years], native of Bombay, had been in Mauritius one year, working as a field-laborer, when he came into the Immigration Depot, on the 21st of December, 1844, for the purpose of entering into a new engagement, having walked seven or eight miles on that day. He remained in apparent good health until six o'clock **on the** morning of the 26th, when he began to **complain of pain at the pit of the** stomach, and died at half-past ten A. M. On inspecting the body twenty-one hours after death, about two pints of reddish pus and serum [were found] within the pericardium, the entire of which membrane was slightly inflamed. On laying the pericardium freely open, thick yellowish-green pus was seen oozing from an **aperture large enough to** admit the finger, which led through the **diaphragm into** an abscess in the smaller **lobe of the** liver, capable of containing a pint of fluid. It is probable that the pus of the hepatic abscess had been oozing into the sac of **the** pericardium during some hours before death, causing inflammation, and then annihilating the heart's action by pressure." †

Although **a** small portion of blood effused into the pericardial sac **may** be sufficient to destroy life, it has been shown in the text that the quantity actually collected in that receptacle, owing to rupture of the **heart, is often very considerable, amounting in some** instances to two,

* Mr. H. T. Taylor, in the Lancet for Nov. 11th, 1848, p. 181.
† R. Allan, Esq., in the Lancet for June **7, 1845, p.** 645.

three, or even several pounds by weight. How soon the blood thus extravasated coagulates, has not been precisely ascertained; but, as in such cases death is usually sudden, and the separation of the blood into serum and crassamentum exactly resembles that which occurs out of the body, there is every reason to believe that it takes place with similar rapidity, especially when the quantity is large, and certainly far within the allotted period of two hours. If the separation were slow, and the red particles had time to subside, the serum would probably be turbid and deep-colored, and the crassamentum, as remarked by Mr. Paget, would be covered with a layer of fibrine, commonly termed buffy coat. The absence of these peculiarities may, therefore, be regarded as a sufficient proof that the process is rapid.—" When blood "—says Mr. Wilson,—" passes in a free stream into a basin, and is allowed to remain at rest, it begins to jelly or coagulate in three minutes and a half. . . . In blood taken from a healthy person the coagulation is usually completed in seven minutes, and in twelve minutes (although it will sometimes take a longer period), the mass will be very firm. Soon after this a transparent watery part will be perceived transuding through the pores of the coagulum, the coagulum at the same time contracting itself, leaving the sides of the basin, but still preserving its original shape. The transparent watery part forms the serum; the coagulum retains the red color, and forms the crassamentum. . . . . The experiments made by Mr. Hewson, and those made by Mr. Hay, of Leeds, prove that the coagulation and separation of the blood take place most readily when that fluid is kept in a temperature nearest to its standard heat, viz., 99°. It is, therefore, ascertained that cold does not produce the coagulation."—" The period at which concretion takes place "—observes Mr. Thackrah,—" depends upon circumstances that will be afterward considered, but the common time is from three to eight minutes after the blood has been taken from the body. The subsequent effusion of serum is effected generally in from one to three hours." *— Hence it appears that, in a young and vigorous person, rupture of the heart induced by agony of mind would, within a moderate time, occasion the collection in the pericardium of a large quantity of clotted blood and clear serum, which, on the side being afterward pierced with a spear, would immediately flow out in a full and copious stream. The facility with which in such a case this capsule might be pierced, and the readiness with which its contents would be discharged, are well illustrated in an able work on the situation of the internal organs of the body by Mr.

---

* James Paget, Esq., in the London Medical Gazette for 1840, vol. j. pp. 613–618;— James Wilson, Esq., Lectures on the Blood, etc., pp. 28–31;—C. T. Thackrah, Esq., Inquiry into the Nature and Properties of the Blood, etc., pp. 33, 34, 67.

Sibson, of Nottingham, who, having injected into the pericardium twenty-six ounces of water, found that—"the great volume of the sac surrounding the body of the heart was globular;"—and subjoins the following accurate description of its bulk and position.—" The distention by fluid of the pericardial sac, besides displacing the surrounding organs, pushes forward the sternum and costal walls, elevates the second costal cartilage, and to a less degree the third, fourth, and fifth; widens the spaces between the cartilages and ribs, from the second cartilage to the seventh rib, projects outward the sixth rib, and causes some degree of bulge over the left side, and some protrusion of the slope formed by the lower edges of the costal cartilages." *

After all that has been said, it is perhaps scarcely necessary to insist on the negative proof, that the blood and water which flowed from the side of Christ had no other source than that here assigned. Yet, as authors of considerable note have imagined that the blood might have flowed from the heart, and the water from the pericardium, a few remarks will be added in further refutation of that opinion. Lower states that when animals are suddenly slaughtered amid robust health, a large quantity of gelatinous matter is found in their pericardium. After remarking that the liquor of this capsule is serous, and coagulable by heat, he thus proceeds:—" Super hac reobiter notandum est, aquam in pericardio contentam solummodo huic experimento idoneam esse, quæ in animali bene constituto et violenta morte perempto reperitur, cujus utpote sanguis sero nutricio diluitur; nam in animalibus morbo defunctis, aut longa inappetentia et inedia confectis, quorum nempe sanguis succo chyloso prorsus destituitur, neque eadem ratio est, et impar successus. Cæterum in sanioribus tam manifesta res est ut, aperto jugulati bovis pericardio, magnam plerumque concretæ gelatinæ copiam invenias, quæ extincto tantum calore partis aut sponte sua, aut a frigore, in istam consistentiam condensatur, non aliter quam decoctum cornu cervi, ubi frigido aeri exponitur, in gelatinam subito concrescit." †—On this passage it may be observed, in the first place, that a gelatinous effusion which concretes spontaneously without the aid of heat is neither water, nor serum, but fibrine; and secondly, that, whatever may be the case with respect to oxen slaughtered in the usual manner, there is no evidence that any thing of the kind occurs in the human subject. Haller, however, states that, under the circumstances mentioned by Lower, that is, when persons are suddenly killed while in good health, a small quantity of serum,

* Francis Sibson, Esq., in the Trans. of the Provincial Med. and Surgical Association, vol. xij. pp. 8, 357, 527–531.
† Lower (Richard) de Corde, etc., pp. 6, 7.

namely from two to six drachms, has been found in the pericardium. His words are:—" Neque rari auctores sunt qui aquam in pericardio aut cadaveris, aut denique vivi hominis viderunt, etsi hujus quidem generis experimenta non possunt vulgaria esse. Excitabo vero ea sola quæ a sanis et subita morte enectis hominibus sumpta sunt. In homine fulgurato cochlear plenum visum est; et quindecim omnino cochlearia in alio, quem nimia contentio cursus suffocaverat. In strangulato aqua pericardii adfuit; et in occisa muliere, alioque sano homine subito enecto. Ejusmodi eventus minime raro in hominibus ultimo supplicio adfectis mihi vidisse contigit. . . . Ego quidem vaporem de corde exhalantem sæpissime vidi, neque tamen eo minus etiam aquam veram et in clauso quidem, quod aliorum etiam testimoniis confirmo, pericardio, et maxime in vivis canibus. Copiam non sum metitus, quam a duabus drachmis ad tres unciæ quartas partes alii definiverunt."—The anatomists John and Charles Bell admit, with respect to persons who have labored under long-continued weakness or disease, that a little watery fluid may be found after death in the pericardium, as in all the other cavities of the body;— "but"—they add,—"if you open a living animal, as a dog, or if you open suddenly the body of suicides, or if you have brought to the dissecting-room the body of a criminal who had been just hanged, there is not in the pericardium one single particle of water to be found." *— Bohn, in like manner, affirms that, except under morbid circumstances, serous fluid is rarely observed in the pericardium.—"Videtur enim serum hoc in se quidem succus laudabilis et naturalis, ast situ peccans, et per motus cordis impetuosiores, ac circulationem per pulmones impeditam secretus; pari modo ac in corporis partibus diversis arte talem seri con gestum parare licet, circulo nempe sanguinis per vincula venis injecta intercepto. Adeoque non mirum in cunctis quocunque morbo defunctis illud reperiri, utpote quibus in agone ad minimum respiratio et circulatio per pulmones fatiscit, copiosius tamen in his qui ex hydrope, asthmate, phthisi, similive pathemate strangulatorio peribant, ita ut in phthisico ejus uncias quinque J. D. Horstius, Obs. Anat. 18, testetur. Qui violenta morte pereunt, quia pariter vel aquis submerguntur et strangulantur, vel confossi et decollati, i. e. sine notabili circulationis turbatione expirant, non in his, sed in illis tantum lympham hanc cardiacam animadvertere licet; ut aliquoties in publicis æque ac privatis sectionibus ostendi." †— The distinction here made by Bohn is very judicious, and has been too

---

* Haller, Element. Physiolog. Corp. Human. vol. j. pp. 282, 283;—John and Charles Bell, Anatomy of the Human Body, vol. ij. pp. 53–55.
† Bohn (Johann), De Renunciatione Vulnerum, pp. 226, 227;—Kuinoël, Comment. in Lib. Hist. Nov. Test. John, chap. 19, v. 34.

often neglected by other authors. It is not in every case of violent death, but chiefly in cases where there has been much struggle for breath, as in strangling, drowning, etc., that serum is found in the pericardium, and **even** then the quantity is but small.

So much the more objectionable, therefore, is the statement of the elder Grüner, in his comment on John, chap. 19, v. 34, that after **death preceded by great anxiety the pericardium is full of water.**—"Sine dubio,"—says he,—"lancea militis suffixa hæsit in *latere sinistro*. **Johanne** teste, post illam νύσιν, vel κίντησιν, post ictum, et inflictam **lateri plagam**, illico profluxit sanguis et aqua. Tale profluvium vix fieri **potuit** nisi a *latere sinistro*, sub quo, præter pulmonem, est et *pericardium aquæ plenum, si quis post anxietatem **summam mortuus est**,* et cor cum arcu aortæ copulatum. . . . Pulmo leviter ictus quidem poterat parum sanguinis profundere, aquam minime. **Probabilis ergo præ cæteris, et medicinæ forensi magis consentanea ea conjectura est,** quæ fons sanguinis profusi in **cordis ventriculo, aquæ in** pericardio quæritur."—This author was, like his son, a physician, and the term anxiety, as used by both, is ambiguous, since in medical writings it is equally applied to the body and the mind. That the pericardium is full of water after death preceded by great mental anxiety, is an assertion without proof; but, if the statement refers to bodily anxiety, occasioned by obstructed circulation through the heart and lungs, it corresponds to that already quoted from the Commentary of Hewlett:—" Medical writers afford numerous instances of a large effusion of bloody **lymph into the cavities of the pleura, from** diseases of the lungs, and in cases of violent death with **long struggling.** . . . . A skilful and learned physician informed the editor, that in cases **of violent and painful death there** is usually an effusion of lymph, or of **lymph mixed with blood, into the cavities of the chest** and abdomen." *
—This information was no doubt obtained from the late Dr. Willan, who, in one of the notes annexed to his—" History of the Ministry of Jesus Christ,"—remarks,—" We have instances of watery effusion into the cavities of the pleura to a considerable amount, in cases of violent death **with long struggling.** . . . The phenomenon here mentioned by the evangelist is generally looked on as miraculous."—It is singular that the only testimony cited on the occasion by this accomplished **physician is that of** Wepfer, in reference to a beaver, which having been caught in a net on the banks of the Danube, after making desperate but unavailing efforts **to** escape, fell into the river and was drowned. In a report of the appearances observed **in the body of this animal, nothing** is said of the pericar-

---

* Hewlett's Bible, etc., Notes on John, chap. 19, v. 34, and Acts, chap. 1, v. 18;—Dr. Willan, History of the Ministry of Jesus Christ, etc., p. 195.

dium, but the right pleural sac contained four ounces of bloody serum, and the left about three ounces; which, as no liquid was found in the lungs, the author concludes were effused by the blood-vessels during the animal's violent struggles for life. His words are as follows:—"Incisa aspera arteria, nullam aquam ex pulmonibus exprimere potui: fortius illis manu constrictis, prodiit spuma albicans; adeo ut in flumine suffocata nihil prorsus per laryngem intra asperam arteriam liquoris admisisse videretur. Utrinque quidem in cavo pectoris aqua loturæ carnium similis, scilicet, in dextro latere ad uncias quatuor, in sinistro circiter uncias tres cruoris istius limpidioris inveniebantur; quem potius ex vasis sanguiferis in animali cum violentissima morte luctante expressum existimo quam pulmones transiisse, simulque sanguinis aliquid secum rapuisse, et pectori infusum fuisse; nam in asperæ arteriæ vel trunco, vel ramis, nec aqua pura, nec sanguine tincta, extra vasa apparuit."

With no better explanation than that here suggested, it is not very surprising that both Dr. Willan and Mr. Hewlett were disposed to attribute the death of Christ to miraculous agency; while the Grüners, in direct contradiction of the evangelical narrative, ascribe it to the wound inflicted by the soldier's spear.—" Christus a spiculatore, ictus atque transfossus, e vulnere pectoris profudit sanguinem et aquam simul; ergo tunc temporis, cum jam expirasse credebatur, vixit adhuc lipothymicus (in hoc enim statu datur aliquis sed prædebilis sanguinis motus, in mortuo minime): ergo eo lanceæ ictu vitalis vis demum frangi, spes vitæ revocandæ et redintegrandæ omnino tolli debuit. . . . Ex vulnere profluxit *cum impetu*, ut videtur, sanguis et aqua simul, neque hoc mortui, sed viventis est; ergo Christus, dum cruci affixus a milite fodiebatur, vivebat quidem vitam aliquam sed prædebilem, proximeque casuram; at vero, vulnere pectoris allato, e vita subito ac vere excessisse putandus est. Ex hoc enim vitalem fontem exhauriri, atque vim vitæ perexiguam omnino tolli oportuit." *—In order to refute these and similar erroneous explanations, to which some biblical critics have paid far greater attention than they deserve, little more is necessary than to state them, since it is manifest on the slightest reflection that they are totally inadmissible.—" We have,"—says Dr. Willan,—"instances of watery effusion into the cavities of the pleura to a considerable amount, in cases of violent death with long struggling;"—but in a body nailed and otherwise fastened to a cross there could have been no struggling. Moreover, crucified persons often survived two or three days; and the death of Christ, after a suspension of only six hours, took place in a manner so sudden and extraor-

---

* Wepfer, in Miscellan. Acad. Curios. Naturæ, Annus 2, 1671, pp. 353-355;—Kulnoël, Comment. in Lib. Hist. Nov. Test. John, chap. 19, v. 34, 35.

dinary, that the spectators were astonished, and many, like Dr. Willan himself, have since ascribed it to miraculous agency.—"In persons who die after extreme anxiety,"—say the Grüners,—"the pericardium is full of water;"—but, in the first place, this is a gratuitous assertion, and in the second, the mental condition of Christ immediately before his death was not that of anxiety, but of intense agony. That he was not in a weak and fainting state, owing to an effusion of serum into the pectoral cavities, is evident from the energy and self-possession which he displayed, and from his loud and repeated exclamations. But had it been otherwise, this supposition accounts for the water only, and not for the blood. The latter, according to the Grüners, came from the heart, which they accordingly assume to have been pierced by the spear. Yet, if the pectoral cavities, or even the pericardium alone, was at that time full of water, the heart must have been compressed and empty; or, if it contained any blood at all, that blood could scarcely have been extracted from a dead body. Aware of this difficulty, the authors maintain that at the moment of receiving the wound Christ was still alive; but as their statement is at variance with the scriptural narrative, it ruins the argument which it is intended to support.—" The soldiers"—says the evangelist John,—" came, and broke the legs of the first and of the other who was crucified with Jesus; but on coming to him, *as they perceived that he was already dead*, they did not break his legs: one of the soldiers, however, pierced his side with a spear, and immediately there came forth blood and water." *—But, even if the contrary supposition were admissible, nothing would be gained by it. The heart of a fainting and dying person would not be more able than that of a corpse to expel its blood *with force*, when pierced with a spear. In either case, the blood effused would be scanty and liquid; and, if there were at the time any serum in the pericardium, the two fluids would immediately mix, so that a distinct flow of blood and water could not be observed. It is therefore manifest that all the explanations of this kind which have been proposed are either incapable of accounting for the facts recorded, or inconsistent with them; while, on the other hand, that which is here substituted in their place has been proved to be real, adequate, and in perfect accordance with all the circumstances and requirements of the case.

* John, chap. 19, v. 31-34.

Note VI.,—Pages 124-127, 188.

ON THE DARKNESS OF THE SUN AND MOON, DURING THE SUFFERINGS OF CHRIST.

It has been briefly suggested in the text, that during the hour of Christ's agony in the garden of Gethsemane there was probably a natural eclipse of the moon, and during the last three hours of his crucifixion an extraordinary darkness of the sun, occasioned by a shower of volcanic ashes which at that time overspread the land of Palestine. It has also been remarked that this darkness of the sun and moon on the same day was apparently one of the signs of the times, divinely appointed to indicate the approaching conclusion of the Mosaic, and commencement of the Christian dispensation; and that the prediction of Joel, quoted by the apostle Peter in his address to the Israelitish people assembled at Jerusalem on the memorable day of Pentecost, may thus be satisfactorily explained:—" I will show wonders in the heaven above, and signs on the earth beneath, blood, and fire, and vapor of smoke. The sun shall be turned into darkness, and the moon into blood, before the coming of the great and illustrious day of the Lord; and it shall be that whosoever shall call on the name of the Lord shall be saved." *—In the Hebrew and other Eastern languages, the phrase of the moon being turned into blood signifies a lunar eclipse, and the origin of the expression is well known; namely, that on such occasions the moon is not absolutely black, like the sun, but of a dull red, or blood-color. This appearance is most conspicuous at the equinoctial seasons; and as the Jewish passover always takes place at the vernal equinox, and during the time of full moon, the only time when lunar eclipses occur, the supposition is so far in harmony with the circumstances of the case. That an eclipse of the moon actually happened about the period of the crucifixion, is affirmed by several writers, although concerning the precise day and hour of the event they are not perfectly agreed. Thus, in a physiological treatise on the passion of Christ, published in 1673, by V. H. Vogler, professor of philosophy and medicine in the University of Helmstadt, the author regards the darkness of the sun as miraculous, but ascribes that of the moon to a natural eclipse.—" Venimus ad obscuratum solem, cujus solus Lucas signato, Matthæus autem et Marcus generatim duntaxat tenebrarum factarum, quarum tamen etiam ipse Lucas antea mentionem fecit, meminerunt. Notum vero est alias soli reapse tenebras non offundi, sed lumen ejus duntaxat intercipi, luna inter eum ac terram nostrumque adspectum posita. At solis iste defectus qui tempore passionis Domini evenit, prorsus a na-

---

* Joel, chap. 2, v. 23-32;—Acts, chap. 2, v. 16-21.

turalibus causis fuit alienus; utpote qui plena luna contigerit, quæ et ipsa eopse die, sed naturaliter, eclipsin est passa, id quod aliunde constat." *—A similar statement was made about a century later by a learned English clergyman, the Rev. Mr. Kennedy, in his "System of Astronomical Chronology unfolding the Scriptures," from which the following is an extract.—" In the year of our Saviour's crucifixion, the true astronomical time of the paschal new moon happened some hours before six in the evening, in the meridian of Jerusalem ; while the *mean time*, as computed by the Jews, followed some hours after six in the evening; by which means Neomenia Nisan, the first day of Nisan, began in the second evening after the true conjunction, on which evening the moon was visible, although the Jews did not propose to calculate the visibility, but under the aforementioned circumstances it must necessarily begin in that manner. Now, if to the second evening after the conjunction we add 14 days, it will bring us down to the 15th day of the moon's age, or to the day of the full moon; and that the moon was at the full on the passover day on which our Lord suffered (in the 19th year of Tiberius Cæsar, and the 33d of the vulgar Christian era, as the best chronologers agree to fix it), is not difficult to prove ; for, as there was, by the gospel history, on the noon of that day a supernatural eclipse of the sun, so was there on the evening of that day (as astronomers report), a natural eclipse of the moon, which is a clear proof that it was at the full. So far is it from being true that the moon would be constantly visible at the end of the first day of the month that, on the contrary, the month would sometimes begin on the evening on which the moon was visible. It began so in the year of our Lord's crucifixion, and by the laws of Jewish computation." †—The final determination of this interesting point must be left to astronomers ; but their calculations may perhaps be assisted by the following records, borrowed from Archbishop Usher's Annals, of several lunar eclipses which were observed and reported in the first half century of the Christian era.—(During Herod's last illness, A. M., 4000, A. P. J. 4710, and 4 years before Christ, that is, before A. D., there was an eclipse of the moon); " which eclipse to have been on the 3d day of March, three hours after midnight, the astronomical table doth show." (Herod's death took place A. M. 4001, A. P. J. 4711), "about the 25th of our November. . . . The legions of Pannonia being in a mutiny, are affrighted at a sudden eclipse of the moon, and so submit themselves to Tiberius. This total eclipse was seen on the 27th of September [A. M. 4018, A. P. J. 4728],

* Vogler (V. H.), Physiologia Historiæ Passionis Jesu Christi, p. 23.
† Kennedy (John), A Complete System of Astronomical Chronology, etc., pp. 367, 368.

five hours after midnight, so that the moon set in the very eclipse. . . . Valerius Asiaticus being again consul, the island Therasia rose out of the Ægean sea in a night wherein the moon was eclipsed. This eclipse was seen the very night between the last day of December (which terminated that year in which Valerius Asiaticus was the second time consul), and the kalends of January" [A. M. 4050, A. P. J. 4760].—In the well-known chronological work,—L'Art de Vérifier les Dates,—a total eclipse of the moon is said to have occurred June 14th, A. D. 29, at 8½ P. M.; and another April 14th, A. D. 32, at 9½ A. M.; a partial eclipse December 9th, A. D. 29, at 8½ P. M.; and another, April 25th, A. D. 31, at 9 P. M.*

If in Joel's remarkable prediction the allusion to blood, in connection with the darkening of the moon, signifies a lunar eclipse, the reference to fire and smoke, in connection with the darkening of the sun, may justly be regarded as intimating that this darkness would be occasioned by a volcanic eruption, attended with a discharge of smoke and ashes:— "I will show wonders in the heaven above, and signs on the earth beneath, blood, and fire, and vapor of smoke. The sun shall be turned into darkness, and the moon into blood, before the coming of the great and illustrious day of the Lord."—The terms used by the prophet, as quoted in a Greek translation by the apostle Peter, exactly correspond to those of the three earlier evangelists, when recording the darkness at the crucifixion; as likewise to those of John in the Apocalypse, when describing the appearance in vision of a volcanic eruption. The words from Joel are,—"Καὶ δώσω τέρατα ἐν τῷ οὐρανῷ ἄνω, καὶ σημεῖα ἐπὶ τῆς γῆς κάτω, αἷμα, καὶ πῦρ, καὶ ἀτμίδα καπνοῦ· ὁ ἥλιος μεταστραφήσεται εἰς σκότος, καὶ ἡ σελήνη εἰς αἷμα, πρὶν ἢ ἐλθεῖν τὴν ἡμέραν Κυρίου, τὴν μεγάλην καὶ ἐπιφανῆ," etc.; those of the Apocalypse,—"Καὶ ἤνοιξε τὸ φρέαρ τῆς ἀβύσσου, καὶ ἀνέβη καπνὸς ἐκ τοῦ φρέατος, ὡς καπνὸς καμίνου μεγάλης, καὶ ἐσκοτίσθη ὁ ἥλιος καὶ ὁ ἀὴρ ἐκ τοῦ καπνοῦ τοῦ φρέατος."—"And he opened the bottomless pit, and there arose a smoke out of the pit, like the smoke of a great furnace; and the sun and the air were darkened by the smoke of the pit."

Language precisely similar is employed in the Old Testament to represent the awful convulsions which attended the overthrow of the cities of the plain, and the promulgation of the Mosaic law from Mount Sinai, and which in both cases may reasonably be ascribed to volcanic agency, under the guidance of divine interposition. On the former occasion,—"the Lord rained upon Sodom, and upon Gomorrah, brimstone and fire from the Lord out of heaven: . . . . and Abraham gat up early in the morn-

---

* Usher (Archbishop), Annals of the World, etc., pp. 794, 795, 809, 873;—L'Art de Vérifier les Dates, etc. depuis J. C. vol. 1. p. 271.

ing to the place where he stood before the Lord; and he looked toward Sodom and Gomorrah, and toward all the land of the plain, and behold, and lo! the smoke of the country went up as the smoke of a furnace."— On the latter,—" Moses brought forth the people out of the camp to meet with God, and they stood at the nether part of the mount. And Mount Sinai was altogether on a smoke, because the Lord descended upon it in fire, and the smoke thereof ascended as the smoke of a furnace, and the whole mount quaked greatly." *—That shocks of earthquake actually occurred in the immediate neighborhood of Jerusalem, both at the crucifixion of Christ, and at his resurrection, is distinctly stated by the evangelist Matthew:—" And behold! the veil of the temple split asunder from the top to the bottom, and the earth quaked, and the rocks were rent, and the tombs were opened. . . . When the centurion, and those who were with him guarding Jesus observed the earthquake, and the [other] events, they feared exceedingly," etc.;—and on the morning of the resurrection, it is stated by the same sacred writer,—" Now behold! there had been a great earthquake."—The close resemblance of Luke's description of the darkness at the crucifixion to the passage above quoted from the Apocalypse, naturally suggests the conclusion that the same explanation is applicable to both.—" Ἦν δὲ ὡσεὶ ὥρα ἕκτη, καὶ σκότος ἀγένετο ἐφ' ὅλην τὴν γῆν ἕως ὥρας ἐννάτης· καὶ ἐσκοτίσθη ὁ ἥλιος, καὶ ἐσχίσθη τὸ καταπέτασμα τοῦ ναοῦ μέσον."—" It was about the sixth hour, and a darkness overspread the whole land till the ninth hour, and the sun was obscured, and the veil of the temple split [asunder] in the midst." —This description intimates that the darkness which covered the land gradually increased in density, until the sun became invisible; which is precisely the effect that would be produced by a shower of volcanic ashes, represented in the language of the apostle John as a smoke arising out of the bottomless pit, darkening the sun and the air. The darkness of three days' continuance, which constituted one of the plagues of ancient Egypt at the period of the Exodus,—" even darkness which might be felt,"—was evidently of a similar nature; and by the apocryphal author of the wisdom of Solomon is accordingly said to have proceeded from Hades, that is, from the internal abyss of the earth.—" Οἱ δὲ τὴν ἀδύνατον ὄντως νύκτα, καὶ ἐξ ἀδύτου ᾅδου μυχῶν ἐπελθοῦσαν, τὸν αὐτὸν ὕπνον κοιμώμενοι," etc.;—" But they, sleeping the same sleep that night, which was indeed intolerable, and which came upon them out of the bottoms of inevitable hell, were partly vexed with monstrous apparitions," etc.†

* Daubeny's Description of Active and Extinct Volcanoes, etc., pp. 278-290;—Genesis, chap. 19, v. 23-28;—Exodus, chap. 19, v. 16-18;—Joel, chap. 2, v. 30, 31;—Acts, chap. 2, v. 19, 20;—Revel. chap. 9, v. 1, 2.

† Exodus, chap. 10, v. 21-23;—Wisdom, chap. 17, v. 14, 15;—Matt. chap. 27, v. 51-54; chap. 28, v. 1, 2;—Luke, chap. 23, v. 44, 45.

The view here taken implies that the darkness at the crucifixion was not universal, but limited to the land of Judea, or at furthest of Palestine, in conformity with its presumed import and design; namely, like the star or meteor which preceded the birth of Christ, to mark out that land as the scene of a momentous transaction, wherein the Deity was directly concerned. Such was also the case on the two analogous occasions in Egypt, already noticed; for, when—" Moses stretched forth his hand toward heaven, and there was a thick darkness in all the land of Egypt, three days, [so that] they saw not one another, neither rose any from his place for three days [it is added], but all the children of Israel had light in their dwellings."—So also, when through the prophet Ezekiel God denounced a similar judgment against Pharaoh-Hophrah, the infliction was expressly limited to the country concerned:—" All the bright lights of heaven will I make dark over thee, and set darkness *upon thy land*, saith the Lord God." *—Both in the Scriptures, and in other books, the Greek word γῆ, like the Hebrew ארץ, is, perhaps, more frequently used in a restricted than in an extensive sense, and its actual signification must, therefore, be determined in each particular case by the circumstances and the context. That a preternatural darkness should overspread the entire globe of the earth, one half of which lies always in shadow, is physically impossible; and that even a whole hemisphere should be thus obscured for three hours, without the slightest notice being taken of such an event by the eminent naturalists and historians who flourished in those times, is morally impossible; while, on the other hand, the absence of any record except by the evangelists of a merely local occurrence of this kind, confined to the province of Judea, cannot reasonably excite either doubt or surprise. Neither is it necessary to suppose that the shower of ashes issued from that very land, and accompanied the earthquake mentioned by Matthew; since it might have proceeded from a simultaneous eruption in Asia Minor, or some other neighboring volcanic country, whence it would naturally have been wafted over Palestine by the westerly winds which always prevail at the paschal season. The following instances of similar occurrences in modern times will show how complete and continued a darkness might thus be induced at noonday:

The first took place at Detroit, in North America, in the year 1762; and is thus described in a letter communicated to the Royal Society of London, and inserted in their *Transactions*. [On] " Tuesday last, being the 19th inst., we had almost total darkness for the most of the day. I got up at daybreak. About ten minutes after I observed it get no

* Ezek. chap. 32, v. 7, 8.

lighter than before. The same darkness continued until nine o'clock, when it cleared up a little. We then, for the space of about a quarter of an hour saw the body of the sun, which appeared as red as blood, and more than three times as large as usual. The air all this time, which was very dense, was of a dirty yellowish-green color. I was obliged to light candles to see to dine at one o'clock, notwithstanding the table was placed close by two large windows. About three the darkness became more horrible, which augmented until half-past three, when the wind breezed up from the S. W., and brought on some drops of rain, or rather sulphur and dirt, for it appeared more like the latter than the former, both in smell and quality. I took a leaf of clean paper, and held it out in the rain, which rendered it black whenever the drops fell upon it; but, when held near the fire turned to a yellow color, and when burned, it fizzed on the paper like wet [gun] powder. During this shower the air was almost suffocating, with a strong sulphurous smell: it cleared up a little after the rain. There were various conjectures about the cause of this natural incident, .·. . . but I think it most probable that it might have been occasioned by the eruption of some volcano, or subterraneous fire, whereby the sulphurous matter may have been emitted in the air, and contained therein, until meeting with some watery clouds, it has fallen down together with the rain.—Detroit, October 25, 1762."—The second case occurred at Tripoli, in Africa, and is mentioned in a letter from Miss Tully, the sister of the British resident of that court, to a friend in England, which has been published in the narrative of his proceedings.—" Accounts we have just received from Europe having explained to us a preternatural appearance that happened there some time since, leads me to tell you of the extraordinary manner in which an eruption of Mount Etna affected this country. Nothing could make a more desolate appearance than this town. The sky was extremely thick and dark, and the heavy rain, as it fell, left the white walls of the houses streaked with black, as if from sooty water tinged with red. This phenomenon appears now, without doubt, to have been caused by the eruption of Mount Etna in July last. From the great convulsions of the mountain, showers of hot sand were carried toward Malta; and the amazing column of fire that issued took at last its direction across the sea toward Barbary, when the atmosphere on this coast became heated to an alarming degree, and occasioned great consternation, no one at the instant being able to account for such a phenomenon.— Nov. 22, 1787." *

The remaining examples of this kind are on a larger scale, and of a

---

* Philosophical Transactions for the year 1763, vol. liij. pp. 63, 64;—Tully's Narrative of a Ten Years' Residence at Tripoli in Africa, pp. 153, 154.

still more striking character. The first is derived from a vivid description in Tilloch's Philosophical Magazine, of the dreadful eruption of the Souffrier Mountain, in the island of St. Vincent, on Thursday night, April 30, 1812, which concludes as follows:—"The break of [the next] day, if such it could be called, was truly terrific. Darkness was only visible at eight o'clock, and the birth of May dawned like the day of judgment. A chaotic gloom enveloped the mountain, and an impenetrable haze hung over the sea, with black sluggish clouds of a sulphurous cast. The whole island was covered with favilla, cinders, scoria, and broken masses of volcanic matter. It was not till the afternoon the muttering noise of the mountain sank gradually into a solemn, yet suspicious silence."—From this eruption an enormous shower of ashes drifted with the wind to the island of Barbadoes, distant from St. Vincent about 110 miles, and the darkness thereby produced is thus depicted by a resident planter.—"About half-past seven o'clock [A. M. May 1st] it was so dark that candles were brought in. At eight o'clock it was pitch dark in the open air; or, in other words, so dark that we could not perceive our hands when held up before our faces at two feet distance. No night at home in winter, when neither the moon nor a star is to be seen, was ever more sombre. This darkness continued of the same intenseness until twenty-five minutes past twelve o'clock; that is, for the space of four hours and twenty-five minutes; at which time we perceived very indistinctly the outlines of large and near objects. At half-past twelve o'clock we distinguished them more correctly; from which period the light increased until between three and four o'clock, P. M., but was very obscure. From the time at which I got up in the morning, until we went to bed in the evening, at eight o'clock, there was a constant fall from the clouds of a substance in extremely fine flakes, which, when first gathered from our clothes, had the appearance of the dust of wood-ashes, but which, when suffered to accumulate, assumed the resemblance of powdered rotten-stone, and possessed the same quality of cleaning brass. . . . Assuming the product of an experiment as the medium quantity which fell on a foot square throughout the island, and estimating from our best maps the quantity of land in the island at 106,470 acres, the total quantity of this extraneous substance which is now on its surface, independent of that which is upon the trees, could not be less than 1,739,187,750 gallons wine measure, or 6,811,817,512 pounds avoirdupois."*

The following graphic account of a still more awful eruption of the Tomboro Mountain, in the island of Sumbawa, which occurred in April, 1815, is borrowed from the History of Java, by the late Sir T. S. Raffles.

* Tilloch's Philosophical Magazine, 8vo, London, 1812, vol. xl. pp. 67-76.

—" In order to give the reader some idea of the tremendous violence with which nature sometimes distinguishes the operations of the volcano in these regions, and enable him to form some conjecture from the occurrences of recent experience of the effects they may have produced in past ages, a short account of the extraordinary and wide-spread phenomena that accompanied the eruption of the Tomboro Mountain, in the island of Sumbawa, in April, 1815, may not be uninteresting. Almost every one is acquainted with the intermitting convulsions of Etna and Vesuvius, as they appear in the descriptions of the poet, and the authentic accounts of the naturalist; but the most extraordinary of them can bear no comparison in point of duration and force with that of Tomboro. This eruption extended perceptible evidences of its existence over the whole of the Molucca islands, over Java, a considerable portion of Celebes, Sumatra, and Borneo, to a circumference of a thousand statute miles from its centre, by tremulous motions and the report of explosions; while within the range of its more immediate activity, embracing a space of three hundred miles around it, it produced the most astonishing effects, and excited the most alarming apprehensions. On Java, at the distance of three hundred miles, it seemed to be awfully present. The sky was overcast at noonday with clouds of ashes; the sun was enveloped in an atmosphere whose 'palpable' density he was unable to penetrate; showers of ashes covered the houses, the streets, and the fields, to the depth of several inches; and amid this darkness explosions were heard at intervals, like the report of artillery, or the noise of distant thunder. . . . All conceived that the effects experienced might be caused by eruptions of some of the numerous volcanoes on the island; but no one could have conjectured that the showers of ashes which darkened the air, and covered the ground of the eastern districts of Java, could have proceeded from a mountain in Sumbawa, at the distance of several hundred miles. . . . The first explosions were heard on this island (Java) in the evening of the 5th of April. They were noticed in every quarter, and continued at intervals until the following day. . . . From the 6th the sun became obscured: it had everywhere the appearance of being enveloped in a fog. The weather was sultry, and the atmosphere close, and still the sun seemed shorn of its rays; and the general stillness and pressure of the atmosphere seemed to forebode an earthquake. This lasted several days. The explosions continued occasionally, but less violently and less frequently than at first. Volcanic ashes also began to fall, but in small quantities, and so slightly as to be hardly perceptible in the western districts. This appearance of the atmosphere continued with little variation until the 10th of April, and till then it does not appear that the volcano attracted much observation, or was considered of greater importance than those which have occasionally burst forth in Java. But on the evening of the 10th, the eruptions were heard more loud and more frequent. From Cheribon eastward the air became darkened by the quantity of falling ashes, the sun was nearly darkened; and in some situations, particularly at Solo and Rembang, many said that they felt a tremulous motion of the earth. It was universally remarked in the more eastern districts that the explosions were tremendous, continuing frequently during the 11th, and of such violence as to shake the houses perceptibly. An unusual thick darkness was remarked all the following night, and the greater part of the next day. At Solo candles were lighted at 4 P. M. of the 12th. At Mágelan in Kédu objects could not be seen at three hundred yards' distance. At Grésik, and other districts more eastward, it was dark as night in the greater part of the 12th of April, and this saturated state of the atmosphere lessened as the cloud of ashes passed along, and discharged itself on its way. . . . The distance to which the cloud of ashes was carried so quickly as to produce utter darkness was clearly pointed out to have been the island of Celebes, and the district of Grésik on Java. The former is two hundred and seventeen nautical miles distant from the seat of the volcano; the latter, in a direct line, more than three hundred geographical miles." *

The last occurrence of this nature which will be here cited, and the most dreadful of all, took place in Central America, and is thus described in a communication inserted in the *Edinburgh Philosophical Magazine*.

"Rio Mopan, April 13, 1835.—One of the most stupendous convulsions of the globe ever known in this hemisphere took place last January, on the eruption of the volcano of Cosiguina. This volcano is situated in Nicaragua, one of the states of Central America, and stands near the eastern promontory of the bay of Conchagua, separating the waters of the gulf from the Pacific. I can give no more faithful or vivid description of its appearance and effects in the immediate vicinity than the following translation of a report, dated January 29th, from the Commandant of Union, a seaport situated on the western shore of the bay of Conchagua, and the nearest place of any consequence to the volcano.—'On the 20th instant, day having dawned with usual serenity, at eight o'clock, toward the S. E., a dense cloud was perceived of a pyramidal figure, preceded by a rumbling noise, and it continued rising until it covered the sun, at which elevation, about ten, it separated to the north and south, accompanied by thunder and lightning. The cloud finally covered the

* Sir T. S. Raffles, History of Java, vol. i. pp. 29-33.

NOTES AND ILLUSTRATIONS. 379

whole firmament about eleven, and enveloped every thing in the greatest darkness, so that the nearest objects were imperceptible. The melancholy howling of beasts, the flocks of birds of all species that came to seek as it were an asylum among men, the terror which assailed the latter, the cries of women and children, and the uncertainty of the issue of so rare a phenomenon,—every thing combined to overcome the stoutest soul, and fill it with apprehension; and the more so when at four P. M. the earth began to quake, and continued in a perpetual undulation, which gradually increased. This was followed by a shower of phosphoric sand, which lasted till eight o'clock P. M. on the same day, when there began falling a heavy and fine powder, like flour. The thunder and lightning continued the whole night, and the following day [the 21st], and at eight minutes past three o'clock P. M., there was a long and violent earthquake, [so] that many men who were walking in a penitential procession were thrown down. The darkness lasted forty-three hours, making it indispensable for every one to carry a light, and even these were not sufficient to see clearly with. On the 22d it was somewhat less dark, although the sun was not visible; and toward the morning of the 23d, the tremendously loud thunder-claps were heard in succession like the firing of pieces of artillery of the largest calibre, and this fresh occurrence was accompanied by increased showers of dust. From day-dawn of the 23d until ten o'clock A. M. a dim light only served to show the most melancholy spectacle. The streets, which from the rocky nature of the soil are full of inequalities and stones, appeared quite level, being covered with dust. Men, women, and children, were so disfigured, that it was not easy to recognize any one except by the sound of their voices, or other circumstances. Houses and trees, not to be distinguished through the dust which covered them, had the most horrible appearance. Yet, in spite of these appalling sights, they were preferable to the darkness into which we were again plunged from after the said hour of ten, as during the preceding days. The general distress, which had been assuaged, was renewed; and, although leaving the place was attended by imminent peril from the wild beasts that had sallied from the forests, and sought the towns and high-roads, as happened in the neighboring village of Conchagua and this town into which tigers thrust themselves, yet another terror was superior; and more than half the inhabitants of Union emigrated on foot, abandoning their houses, well persuaded that they should never return to them, since they prognosticated the total destruction of the town, and fled with dismay for refuge to the mountains. At half-past three on the morning of the 24th the moon and a few stars were visible, as if through a curtain, and the day was clear, although the sun could not be seen, since the dust continued falling, having covered the ground all round about, to a thickness of five inches. The 25th and 26th were like the 24th, with frequent though not violent earthquakes. The cause of all this has been the volcano of Cosiguina, which burst out on the 20th. I am also informed that on the island of Tigre, in that direction, the showers of the 21st were of pumice-stones of the size of a pea, and some even as large as a hen's egg. The earth quaked there more than here, but no houses or other edifices have been thrown down. Here there are many people with catarrhs, headaches, sore throats, and pectoral affections, resulting doubtless from the dust. Several persons are seriously unwell, and yesterday a girl of seven years old died, with symptoms of an inflammatory sore throat. Flocks of birds are found dead, lying on the roads, and floating on the sea. The showers of dust lasted till the 27th." *

It is impossible to read with attention the foregoing and similar extracts, without perceiving that the awful scenes described in several parts of Scripture,—the overthrow of Sodom and Gomorrah, the conflagration of Mount Sinai, the extraordinary darkness in Egypt, and that at the crucifixion of Christ, although primarily induced by divine interposition, were in their immediate nature and origin volcanic. The short and simple account given by Moses of the phenomena which occurred at Mount Sinai, during the promulgation of the Israelitish covenant, is decisive in this respect.—"It came to pass in the third day in the morning, that there were thunders, and lightnings, and a thick cloud upon the mount, and the voice of the trumpet exceeding loud, so that all the people that [were] in the camp trembled. And Moses brought forth the people out of the camp to meet with God; and they stood at the nether part of the mount. And Mount Sinai was altogether on a smoke, because the Lord descended upon it in fire, and the smoke thereof ascended as the smoke of a furnace, and the whole mount quaked greatly."—When reminding them a little before his death of the same solemn transaction, he uses similar language:—"Ye came near and stood under the mountain, and the mountain burned with fire unto the midst of heaven, with darkness, clouds, and thick darkness. And the Lord spake unto you out of the midst of the fire: ye heard the voice of the words, but saw no similitude, only [ye heard] a voice. And he declared unto you his covenant, which he commanded you to perform, [even] ten commandments, and he wrote them upon two tables of stone." †—This description, a little mag-

---

* Edinburgh New Philosophical Journal, vol. xx. pp. 165-167. (From Silliman's Journal, July, 1835.)

† Exodus, chap. 19, v. 16-18; chap. 20, v. 18-21; chap. 24, v. 15-17;—Deuteron. chap. 4, v. 10-12; chap. 5, v. 22, 23;—Heb. chap. 12, v. 18-21.

nified, would be perfectly applicable to the eruption of the Souffrier mountain, in the island of St. Vincent. The—"thick darkness"—at Mount Sinai, and the—"darkness which might be felt"—in ancient Egypt, corresponded to—"the palpable density of the atmosphere,"—occasioned by the showers of volcanic ashes which fell in the island of Java, during the eruption of Tomboro. In reference to Egypt, the scriptural statement is remarkably distinct.—"And the Lord said unto Moses, Stretch out thy hand toward heaven, that there may be darkness over the land of Egypt, even darkness [which] may be felt. And Moses stretched forth his hand toward heaven, and there was a thick darkness in all the land of Egypt three days. They saw not one another, neither rose any from his place for three days; but all the children of Israel had light in their dwellings."—The comment on this event in the apocryphal book of the Wisdom of Solomon appears at first sight, like many other oriental narratives, extravagant and hyperbolical:—"Being scared with beasts that passed by, and hissing of serpents, they died for fear. . . . . Whether it were a whistling wind, or a melodious noise of birds among the spreading branches, or a pleasing fall of water running violently, or a terrible sound of stones cast down, or a running that could not be seen of skipping beasts, or a roaring voice of most savage wild beasts, or a rebounding echo from the hollow mountains,—these things made them to swoon for fear."—Nevertheless, with some allowance for the diffuse and florid style of this uninspired but venerable writer, his description bears a close resemblance to that of the eruption of Cosiguina only a few years since; when the appalling sounds which accompanied the heavy showers of dust and pumice, drifting with the wind, were aggravated by the howling of wild beasts, the rushing of domestic animals, and the screaming of birds impelled by terror to seek refuge among the dwellings of men, and thus furnishes an internal evidence of truth.*
The darkness for three hours at the crucifixion finds a parallel in the darkness for more than four hours in Barbadoes, derived from the smoke and ashes of the Souffrier mountain. In the former case its volcanic origin was indicated by the shocks of earthquake which occurred on the spot, yet it might very possibly have been occasioned by a shower of ashes which had travelled from another region; since in Java, at the distance of three hundred miles from the crater, it was, owing to a similar cause, as dark as pitch during a whole day. It is also illustrated by the catastrophe at Union, in Central America; where, in consequence of the eruption of Cosiguina,—"a pyramidal cloud rose gradually until it covered the entire firmament, darkened the sun, and enveloped every thing

* Exodus, chap. 10, v. 21-23;—Wisdom, chap. 17, v. 9, 10, 18, 19.

in the greatest obscurity;"—exactly corresponding to the description of the apocalyptic vision,—"There arose a smoke out of the [bottomless] pit, like the smoke of a great furnace; and the sun and the air were darkened by the smoke of the pit."

The view here taken is strongly confirmed by its remarkable agreement with a conclusion briefly noticed in the text, and which seems to be equally suggested by reason and by Scripture; namely, that in the present condition of the world, all volcanic movements are effects of the malediction which God denounced against the earth at the fall of man, and evidences of his displeasure at human depravity. Not long before that event the globe was, according to the Mosaic narrative, in a state of chaos and ruin, when the Deity interposed; and, having by successive operations reduced it to order, and furnished it with living beings, including mankind as the lords of all, pronounced his blessing on the new creation, and declared it to be very good. Had mankind retained their primitive innocence and friendship with God, this happy state of things would doubtless have continued, and in that case it cannot be supposed that earthquakes or volcanic eruptions would ever have occurred. But the numerous events of this kind which have actually taken place, wherein large tracts of land and myriads of persons have been suddenly destroyed by fire, plainly indicate the reality of the malediction, and the consequent tendency of the earth to relapse into its original chaos. These partial catastrophes are therefore to be regarded as preludes to the final and universal one predicted in Scripture, and which, according to the same authority, is to be followed by the reconstruction of the globe in more than its pristine perfection, as the eternal abode of virtue and happiness. Thus, after referring to the general deluge in the time of Noah, another stupendous intimation of the same kind, the apostle Peter declares;—"The heavens and the earth [which are] now . . . . are kept in store, being reserved to fire, at the day of judgment and perdition of ungodly men. . . . The day of the Lord will come as a thief, wherein the heavens will pass away with a great noise, and the elements will be dissolved by fervent heat, and the earth with [all] its productions will be burnt up: . . . nevertheless we, according to his promise, expect new heavens and a new earth, wherein righteousness will dwell."—The description of the renovated world, given by the apostle John in the figurative language of the Apocalypse, exactly corresponds.—"I saw a new heaven and a new earth, for the first heaven and the first earth had passed away, and there was no more sea. And I saw the holy city, new Jerusalem, descending out of heaven from God, prepared like a bride adorned for her husband, and I heard a loud voice from heaven saying,—

'Behold! the tabernacle of God [is] with men, and he will dwell with them, and they will be his people, and God himself will be with them [as their God], and **will wipe away** all tears from their eyes; and there **will** be no **more death,** neither grief nor crying, nor pain, for the former **things have** passed away.'—And he that sat on the throne said,—' Behold! I make all things new.' . . . And he showed me a river of [the] **water** of life, clear as crystal, flowing from the throne of God and of **the** Lamb; [and] in the midst of the street [of the city] and on each **side** of the river [the] tree of life, producing twelve kinds of fruit, [and] yielding its fruit every month; and the leaves of the tree for the healing of the nations, *and there will be no more curse.*" *

It is still further in favor of this view, if, as there **is much reason to conclude, the majority of epidemic and pestilential diseases are occasioned by volcanic effluvia, emitted either silently or with explosion from the interior of the globe, and wafted by** winds over various regions, until, after **causing great ravages,** they are finally decomposed or dispersed. That **such is the case has been** strongly suspected by physicians and philosophers from the earliest periods down to the present, and no other explanation of the facts equally probable has ever been proposed. The connection observed in all times and countries between pestilential disorders and volcanic agency has been abundantly proved by Short, Webster, Forster, and others, who have also shown that this connection is regular and constant. In several instances the cause of epidemics has been rendered manifest **by their being attended with a fog or cloud, or** with colored rains, fancifully compared to showers of blood; **and during the** prevalence of the Asiatic cholera in England **in the year 1832, the specific** gravity of the atmosphere was found by Dr. Prout to be sensibly increased. This author judiciously observes that the poisonous character of certain **effluvia from volcanoes is well exemplified by two of them,—Selenium and Sulphur.** When dissolved in hydrogen gas, and diffused through **the air, the minutest quantities of these substances, more especially the former, produce the most powerful and deleterious effects on the animal frame.†** Mr. Parkin, who has published a distinct treatise on the subject, remarks that independently of violent eruptions, and of earthquakes, which according to Lyell are merely abortive eruptions, volcanic action accompanied with gaseous exhalations is almost always going on in a silent and invisible manner; and that the occasional presence in the

---

* 2 Peter, chap. 3, v. 7-13;—Revel. chap. 21, v. 1-4; chap. 22, v. 1-3.

† Dr. Prout, Bridgewater Treatise, pp. 347-354;—Orton, On Cholera, pp. 258, 259, 466;—**Parkin, On** Epidemic Diseases, pp. 170-177;—Webster, On Pestilential Diseases, vol. I. pp. 87-90, 100-102, 116-121, 140-146, 165, 166, 191, 192, 226-228, 436, 437, 443-446; vol. II. pp. 13-23.

atmosphere of a virulent poison is proved by the fact, that, during remarkable epidemic periods the lower animals, and even vegetables, suffer as well as man. It may be added, that in some of these cases the waters of lakes, rivers, and of the sea itself, have become contaminated, and that great numbers of fishes have in consequence been infected and destroyed.* That during volcanic eruptions enormous quantities of gas, vapor, or impalpable powder are often discharged from the interior of the earth, and after rising to an immense height are transported to vast distances, is well known; and the extensive diffusion, and sometimes capricious course of epidemic disorders, as well as their variable prevalence and intensity, exactly correspond to the influence of such a cause. A complete demonstration of this theory must, of course, be a work of time and labor; but enough has been done, especially of late years, to render it highly probable, and to encourage further research.

Let the result, however, be what it may, it is an indisputable and appalling fact that, even admitting for the present the formidable effects of malaria, a poison generated on the surface, the interior of the earth is to a great extent a source of disease and death to its inhabitants, and chiefly to the human race. By way of illustration, it is sufficient to mention that two epidemics alone, the Black Death in the fourteenth century, and the Asiatic Cholera in the nineteenth, are each computed to have destroyed within a few years fifty millions of mankind. Concerning the former it is stated by Hecker,—"This great pestilence of the fourteenth century, which desolated Asia, Europe, and Africa, was an Oriental plague. . . . On account of the inflammatory boils and tumors of the glands, and from the black spots indicatory of a putrid decomposition which appeared on the skin, it was called in Germany, and the northern kingdoms of Europe, —The Black Death. From China to the Atlantic the foundations of the earth were shaken. Through Asia and Europe the atmosphere was in commotion. . . . In the inmost depths of the globe that impulse was given in the year 1333, which in uninterrupted succession for twenty-six years shook the surface of the earth, even to the western shores of Europe. . . . It was reported to Pope Clement [VI.] at Avignon, that throughout the East, probably with the exception of China, 23,840,000 had fallen victims to the plague. . . . It may be assumed without exaggeration that Europe lost during the Black Death 25,000,000 of inhabitants."—The mortality occasioned by the Asiatic Cholera, which in the early part of the present century made the entire circuit of the world can scarcely have been less; since in British India alone, during the short

* Parkin, On Epidemic Diseases, pp. 34, 35, 48, 64, 70, 71, 170, 171, 177-184;—Webster, On Pestilential Diseases, vol. i. pp. 131-135, 184-188, 201-206, 219-221, 427-430.

space of fourteen years, it was estimated by Scoutetten and Desruelles at eighteen millions, and the latter author infers that in China it was still more considerable.* **The** connection **of the** Black Death with earthquakes is mentioned above in very striking terms by Hecker; **that of Cholera is thus** noticed by Orton.—" It has been very long and generally **observed that** *earthquakes* either accompany or precede severe epidemical **diseases.** Mr. Webster (who has paid the most minute and laborious **attention** to all the histories of epidemics, and all the remarkable phenomena of Nature of which any records are to be found), is extremely clear and explicit on this head, and his evidence is such as **to place the** truth of at least this part of his interesting speculations **beyond a doubt.** . . . The epidemic Cholera **in India affords the strongest confirmation of this remarkable fact. Earthquakes are in general by no means common in India; but since the appearance of the epidemic they have been extremely so, and in some instances their effects** have been **very** ruinous. . . . **The connection of earthquakes, and** atmospherical disturbances, **and** irregularities of seasons, with epidemics, can scarcely be disputed; **and** if the eruption of volcanoes, particularly of new or extinct ones, forms a part of the concatenation, it lends a degree of probability to the hypothesis of changes in the interior of the earth being the original cause of all." †

This state of things, far from being " very good," is, therefore, **a painful** proof of the reality of the malediction, **and the explanation here** offered merely indicates **the mode in which that malediction usually operates**; for, although such visitations are doubtless always **to be regarded** as divine judgments, they do not, except in special cases, **imply a direct** interposition, nor **do they always imply even in these cases a different** mode of action, but **often merely a new and** supernatural impulse, agreeably **to the rule observed in all genuine miracles; namely, that supernatural agency is employed with the strictest economy, and no further than is absolutely necessary.** This principle is well illustrated by a passage in the book of Isaiah, wherein it is said ;—" Tophet [is] ordained of old, yea, for the king it is prepared : he hath made [it] deep [and] large : the pile thereof [is] fire and much **wood:** the breath **of the Lord, like a stream of brimstone, doth** kindle it."—The immediate **dependence of** pestilential diseases on volcanic agency **is** intimated **in various parts of Scripture. The murrain and** pestilence, for example, in **Egypt,** together

---

* Hecker, On the Black **Death, pp. 4,** 23, 29, 44, 45, 56, 57, 77;—Desruelles, Précis Physiologique du Cholera **Morbus, pp.** 26, 27;—Scoutetten, Histoire du Choléra Morbus, etc., pp. 20-27.

† Orton. On the Epidemic Cholera of India, pp. 258, 259, 466.

with most of the other plagues inflicted on that country in the time of Moses, exhibit this character, and it is distinctly avowed in the sublime hymn of Habakkuk.

"God came from Teman, and the Holy One from Mount Paran:
His glory covered the heavens, and the earth was full of his praise.
[His] brightness was as the light:
He had beams [coming] forth from his hand, and there [was] the hiding of his power.
Before him went the pestilence, and burning diseases went forth at his feet.
He stood, and measured the earth: he beheld, and drove asunder the nations:
The everlasting mountains were scattered; the perpetual hills did bow:
His ways [are] everlasting." *

Similar intimations are found in the New Testament, particularly in Christ's principal prediction of the destruction of Jerusalem, and of the physical and political convulsions which would precede that awful event. —"Nation will rise up against nation, and kingdom against kingdom; and there will be great earthquakes in various places, and famines, and pestilences; there will also be fearful sights, and great signs from heaven, ... in the sun, and in the moon, and in the stars; and on the earth distress of nations with perplexity; the sea and its waves roaring, [and] men fainting through fear, and apprehension of the [events] coming on the earth; for the powers of the heavens will be shaken." †—If, therefore, at the crucifixion of Christ an extraordinary darkness at noonday, expressive of the malediction, was produced by volcanic agency operating under divine direction, it was an occurrence peculiarly suited to the occasion, and in perfect accordance both with general principle, and with ancient prophecy.

NOTE VII.,—PAGES 31–33.

ON PETER'S DENIALS OF CHRIST.

It is seldom desirable that an author should be his own commentator, but there are two subjects of considerable importance mentioned in the

---

* Genesis, chap. 11, v. 10; chap. 19, v. 23–28;—Exodus, chap. 9, v. 1–7, 13–15; chap. 12, v. 29, 30;—Psalm 78, v. 49–51;—Isaiah, chap. 30, v. 33;—Habakkuk, chap. 3, v. 1–6. In the latter passage the marginal readings, which are almost always the best, have been here adopted.

† Matt. chap. 24, v. 3–8;—Mark, chap. 13, v. 3–8;—Luke, chap. 21, v. 7–11, 25, 26.

preceding treatise which require explanation; and, as that explanation could not be conveniently given in the work itself, it is here subjoined. These subjects are the denials of Christ by Peter, and the representation of Christianity as founded, not on a testament, but on a covenant.

Concerning the nature and number of Peter's denials of Christ much misapprehension has prevailed. By the majority of harmonists and commentators they are reckoned as three, and ascribed either to disaffection, timidity, or unbelief; but, if all the circumstances of the case as described by the evangelists are carefully examined, it will plainly appear that they were seven in number, and occasioned by presumption and spiritual pride.

After celebrating his last paschal supper with the apostles, instituting his own supper, and dismissing from the apartment Judas Iscariot, whose intended treachery he had previously intimated, both to the traitor himself and to the beloved disciple, Christ said to the eleven,—" Children, yet a little while I am with you. Ye will seek me, and as I said to the Jews,—Whither I go ye cannot come,—so now I say to you. A new commandment I give you—to love one another; [I mean] to love one another as I have loved you. Hereby all men will know that ye are my disciples, if ye have love to one another.—And the Lord said, 'Simon! Simon! behold Satan hath demanded to have you, that he may sift [you] like wheat, but I have prayed for thee that thy faith may not fail. When [therefore] thou art restored, strengthen thy brethren.'—Simon Peter said to him,—' Lord, whither goest thou?'—Jesus answered him,— 'Whither I go thou canst not follow me now, but thou shalt follow me hereafter.'—Peter said to him,—' Lord! why cannot I follow thee now? I am ready to go with thee both to prison and to death: I will lay down my life for thy sake.'—Jesus answered him,—'Wilt thou lay down thy life for my sake? I assuredly tell thee, the cock will not crow this day before thou wilt thrice deny that thou knowest me."—The important discourses of Christ which followed this conversation terminated in his well-known prayer to the Father, after recording which, the narrative thus proceeds.—" When Jesus had spoken these words he went forth with his disciples, and having sung a hymn, they repaired as usual to the Mount of Olives. He then said to them,—' All of you will this night be offended by me, for it is written,—*I will smite the shepherd, and the sheep of the flock will be scattered:*—but after I am risen [from the dead], I will go before you to Galilee.'—Peter answered him,—' Though all [others] should be offended by thee, I will never be offended.'—Jesus said to him, —' I tell thee truly that to-day, [even] this very night, before the cock crows the second time, thou wilt disown me thrice:'—but he spoke the more positively,—'Though I should die with thee, I will never disown thee:'—so likewise said all the disciples." *

The foregoing passages relate the predictions made by Christ on this subject: the following ones exhibit the accomplishment of these predictions. About an hour after his entrance into the garden of Gethsemane, a formidable band of soldiers and civil officers, dispatched by the military and ecclesiastical authorities at Jerusalem, arrived there to apprehend him. Before surrendering himself to them, he stipulated with characteristic kindness for the safe retreat of his apostles.—" If ye seek me, allow these men to depart;"—thus fulfilling the declaration which he had made,—" Of those whom thou gavest me I have not lost one."— " Then they advanced, laid hands on Jesus, and seized him. On this those who were with him, perceiving what was about to happen, said to him,—' Lord, shall we smite with the sword?'—and Simon Peter, having a sword drew it, and smote the high-priest's slave, and cut off his right ear. The slave's name was Malchus. Then said Jesus to Peter,—' Put the sword into the scabbard, for all who take the sword will perish by the sword. The cup which the Father hath given me, shall I not drink it? Thinkest thou that I cannot even now request my Father, and he would send to my aid more than twelve legions of angels? [but] how then would the Scriptures be fulfilled, [which declare] that thus it must be?'—And he said,—' Suffer [me] thus far,'—and, touching the ear of Malchus, he healed him. Then said Jesus to the chief-priests, commanders of the temple-[guard], and elders, who had come forth against him, —' Are ye come forth as against a robber, with swords and staves, to seize me? I sat daily amongst you, teaching in the temple, and ye did not seize me; but this is your hour, and the power of darkness, in fulfilment of the writings of the prophets.'—Then all the disciples forsook him, and fled." †

In order to represent more distinctly the seven denials of Christ by Peter, which shortly followed these events, they are here separately stated in the words of the evangelists.

FIRST DENIAL.

Annas sent Jesus bound to Caiaphas the high-priest, at whose palace all the chief-priests, scribes, and elders, were assembled.—Now Simon Peter had followed Jesus at a distance; another disciple also [followed

---

* The portions of the four gospels here harmonized are, Matt. chap. 26, v. 30-35;— Mark, chap. 14, v. 26-31;—Luke, chap. 22, v. 31-34, 39;—John, chap. 13, v. 33-38; chap. 18, v. 1.

† The portions of the four gospels here harmonized are, Matt. chap. 26, v. 50-56;— Mark, chap. 14, v. 46-50;—Luke, chap. 22, v. 49-53;—John, chap. 18, v. 7-11.

him] : that disciple was known to the high-priest, and entered with Jesus into the palace, but Peter stood without at the gate; so the other disciple who was known to the high-priest went out, and spoke to the maid-servant who attended the gate, and obtained admission for Peter. Then said the maid-servant to Peter,—" Art thou also [one] of this man's disciples?"—He said,—" I am not."—John, chap. 18, v. 15–17, 24.

SECOND DENIAL.

And he went in, and joined the officers, to see the end. The slaves and officers were standing round a fire of embers which they had kindled in the midst of the hall, for it was cold, and were warming themselves, and Peter stood with them, and warmed himself. Whilst he was there, one of the maid-servants of the high-priest came, and seeing Peter sitting at the fire, after looking steadfastly at him, said,—" This man also was with him,—thou also wast with Jesus of Nazareth;"—but he disowned him before them all, saying,—" Woman, I know him not, neither do I understand what thou meanest."—Matt. chap. 26, v. 58, 69, 70;—Mark, chap. 14, v. 54, 66–68;—Luke, chap. 22, v. 55–57.

THIRD DENIAL.

A little after another person saw him, and said,—" Thou also art [one of] them;"—but Peter said,—" Man, I am not."—Luke, chap. 22, v. 58.

FOURTH DENIAL.

And he went out into the porch, and the cock crew. Whilst he was there, another [maid-servant] saw him, and said to those who were present,—" This man also was with Jesus of Nazareth."—Again he denied [it] with an oath [saying],—" I know not the man."—Matt. chap. 26, v. 71, 72;—Mark, chap. 14, v. 68–70.

The first trial of Christ by the Sanhedrim, occupying about an hour, here intervened.

FIFTH DENIAL.

[Meanwhile] Simon Peter was standing and warming himself. So they said to him,—" Art not thou also [one] of his disciples?"—he denied [it], and said,—" I am not."—John, chap. 18, v. 25.

SIXTH DENIAL.

One of the high-priest's slaves, a relative [of him] whose ear Peter had cut off, said,—" Did not I see thee in the garden with him?"— Again Peter denied [it]—John, chap. 18, v. 26, 27.

SEVENTH DENIAL.

A little after another man confidently affirmed, saying,—"Certainly this man also was with him, for he is a Galilean."—So the by-standers came up, and said again to Peter,—"Certainly thou also art [one] of them, for thy [manner of] speaking is similar, [and] discovereth thee;"—but he began to utter oaths and curses, [saying]—"Man, I know not what thou meanest: I know not this man of whom ye speak:"—and instantly, whilst he was yet speaking, the cock crew the second time. And the Lord turned and looked on Peter: and Peter remembered what the Lord had said to him,—"Before the cock crows the second time thou wilt disown me thrice:"—and he went out, and wept bitterly." *—Matt. chap. 26, v. 73–75; Mark, chap. 14, v. 70–72; Luke, chap. 22, v. 59–62.

The general correctness of this representation of Peter's denials will perhaps be sufficiently obvious on inspection; but there are two points connected with the subject which may seem to require further explanation, namely, the motives of these denials, and their number. The narrative itself suggests as their primary cause, that presumption and self-confidence, which prompted Peter to declare that he would stand by Christ even if all others abandoned him, and to contradict his master when foretelling the reverse; for, on hearing the prediction,—"he spoke the more positively,—'Though I should die with thee, I will never disown thee.'"—But the immediate cause was no doubt the dread of capital punishment, as the natural consequence of his atrocious assault on Malchus in the garden of Gethsemane; for, although this act was providentially arrested, it was evidently one of intentional murder toward the individual, and of open sedition against the lawful governors of the land, both civil and ecclesiastical. It was an act alike opposed to the spirit, and hostile to the success of the gospel; and had not Christ promptly remedied the evil, by rebuking the apostle, and healing the wounded slave, might have seriously injured his character and cause. The apostles were apparently unprepared for his ready submission to the power of his adversaries; and hence, on seeing him calmly resign himself into their hands,—"they all forsook him and fled."—Finding, however, that they were not pursued by the guard, Peter and John speedily returned to the spot, and followed him to his destination; but with a remarkable difference in their demeanor, corresponding to the difference of their previous conduct. John, who had not committed any offence,

---

* The portions of the four gospels here harmonized are, Matt. chap. 26, v. 57, 58, 69–75;—Mark, chap. 14, v. 53, 54, 66–72;—Luke, chap. 22, v. 54–62;—John, chap. 18, v. 15–18, 24–27.

entered boldly with Jesus into the high-priest's palace, where, although well known to be one of his disciples, he was allowed to remain unmolested; while Peter, conscious of the danger which he had incurred by his recent outrage, followed at a distance, and when admitted into the palace, was soon betrayed into a denial of his discipleship.

His danger, both then and long afterward, was indeed great. Owing to the darkness and confusion of the scene in the garden, he fortunately escaped without being recognized as the man who wounded Malchus; for, had he been detected, he might have been legally put to death for a crime precisely similar to that of Barabbas,—" who, on account of a sedition attended with murder which had taken place in the city, was in prison with his accomplices."—The reality and extent of the danger are indicated by the fact that both Christ and the three earlier evangelists carefully abstained from mentioning the name of Peter in connection with this occurrence. When Jesus said,—" Put the sword into the scabbard," etc.,—he did not name him. Matthew, Mark, and Luke, merely intimate that it was one of the disciples who thus acted; and John alone, who wrote at a later period, when the danger was past, expressly names both the apostle and his victim,—" Simon Peter, having a sword drew it, and smote the high-priest's slave, and cut off his right ear. The slave's name was Malchus."—Neither was the danger confined to Peter, but involved also the sacred cause to which he was devoted. His fear on this occasion was therefore natural and rational; and had he been wise, he would, like the apostles generally, have yielded to circumstances, and taken refuge in retirement. But his pride forbade so humiliating a course. He had confidently promised to follow his master both to prison and to death, to lay down his life for his sake, and faithfully to adhere to him though all others forsook him. He was aware that by entering into the high-priest's palace he should run the risk of being detected as the assailant of Malchus, but, on the other hand, could not without a struggle submit to the disgrace of grossly breaking his word, and forfeiting his engagements. He therefore followed the guard afar off; and through the influence of John, who had entered some time before, obtained admission in an evil hour into the dreaded mansion.

In order that the sequel may be better understood, it is proper to notice that this mansion, like that of Eliashib, in the time of Nehemiah, was apparently an official residence within the precincts of the temple, where during the passover and other solemn seasons the attendance of the high-priest was frequently required. Here alone, until the final decline of the Jewish state, the Sanhedrim held their sittings, in a large circular saloon, called by the Jews,—the chamber of free-stone. Here the trial of Stephen was conducted;* and here they were at this time assembled, anxiously awaiting the appearance of Jesus, as a prisoner at their bar. Those who entered this apartment from without passed in succession through a portico or vestibule, and a spacious hall, the roof of which, as well as that of the council-chamber, was probably perforated, and in fair weather partially open to the sky. At the entrance of the vestibule a maid-servant was stationed, as portress, to take cognizance of those who went in or out. In the midst of the hall a fire of embers or charcoal was kindled in a brazier, for the accommodation of the slaves and officers who attended on the high-priest, and the other members of the Sanhedrim. Under the disquietude of mind naturally induced by the perilous position into which he had thrown himself, Peter twice approached the fire in the hall, and twice retired to the vestibule, in which two apartments all his denials were committed. The identity or diversity of these denials, as described with some variety by the four evangelists, is determined by those of the times, places, persons, or other principal circumstances connected with them;—their arrangement is fixed either by the order of narration, when uncontradicted, or by more positive indications of sequence, when these are supplied. The first, fifth, and sixth denials, are peculiar to John's gospel, the third to that of Luke, the second and seventh are related by the three earlier evangelists in common, and the fourth by Matthew and Mark alone.

The first of Peter's denials was addressed to the maid-servant at the gate; and having occurred at the very moment of his entrance into the palace, cannot be confounded with any other. The second, addressed to *another* of the high-priest's maid-servants, is represented by Luke as having happened almost immediately after Peter's first approach to the fire in the hall. It must, of course, have followed the former, and preceded all the rest. The third denial, given in reply to a man, is by Luke expressly dated a little after the last, and about an hour before the seventh. On this ground it is left where it is found in the narrative, annexed to the preceding one; and from the shortness of the interval, and the similar expression applied by the evangelist to the parties, both of whom seem to have observed Peter by the light of the fire, it may reasonably be concluded that both denials occurred in the same situation. From John's statement it is evident that the three concluding denials also took place in the hall, whither Peter, who had previously retired from it, must therefore after a time have returned, the interval of about an hour having been occupied by the first trial of Christ before the Sanhedrim. The two for-

---

* See Calmet's Dictionary, Article Sanhedrim; also Nehemiah, chap. 3, v. 20, 21;—Acts, chap. 6, v. 8–15.

mer of these denials, whereof the second is by John almost confounded with the seventh which so speedily ensued, are consequently the fifth, addressed to the attendants, on their asking Peter whether he were not a follower of Jesus; and the sixth, in reply to a relative of Malchus, on his putting a similar question. The seventh, in reply to the attendants, on their *again* charging him more positively with being a disciple, was manifestly the last denial, having immediately preceded the second crowing of the cock, and the final retirement and penitence of Peter;—" Instantly, while he was yet speaking, the cock crew the second time, ... and he went out, and wept bitterly."

Supposing it to have been now demonstrated that Peter denied Christ seven times, it may reasonably be asked how **this view can be reconciled with the express and seemingly restrictive declarations of all the evangelists, that he denied him thrice, a declaration repeated in not** less than **seven different passages.*** The solution of this difficulty depends on a **right interpretation of the terms** employed, an interpretation which is happily furnished by **some of the** evangelists themselves; among whom **Luke alone intimates** what the Saviour meant by denying him, and **Mark alone** what he meant by the crowing of the cock. Of disowning Christ there were evidently two modes or degrees, the lower degree consisting in a person denying that he was his disciple, the higher in denying that he had any knowledge of him whatever. Among the Jews, as among most other civilized nations, when a man was tried on a capital charge, **it was usual to receive** any respectable testimony **which** might **be adduced** in favor of his general **character.** There were doubtless **many persons in** Jerusalem at that time, who, although they were not **disciples of** Jesus, could bear witness to the purity and beneficence of his life. Even his adversaries, either directly or indirectly, **admitted** the fact. Caiaphas declared that it was expedient to sacrifice him to the **safety of** the nation, implying **that it** was unjust; Judas Iscariot confessed, **when** it was too late, that he had betrayed innocent blood; and Pontius Pilate, after **the** fullest investigation, pronounced him a righteous man. **Yet** Peter, the most eminent and zealous of the apostles, owing to the unhappy predicament into which he had brought himself, rendered less justice to the character of his master than those who were concerned in his death; and thus perhaps contributed unwittingly to the fulfilment of a remarkable passage in Isaiah's prophecy concerning the sufferings of the Messiah, chap. 53, v. 8.

* Matt. chap. 26, v. 34, 75;—Mark, chap. 14, v. 30, 72;—Luke, chap. 22, v. 34, 61;— John, chap. 13, v. 38.

"By an oppressive judgment he was taken off;
And his manner of life who would declare?" *

for he was guilty of denying Christ in both the modes above described, having repeatedly protested, not only that he was no disciple of Christ, but even that he did not know the man. It was the latter more aggravated kind of denial, which, during the paschal supper, the Saviour predicted Peter would commit before cock-crowing the next morning;—"I assuredly tell thee, the cock will not crow this day before thou wilt thrice deny *that thou knowest me.*"—When on the subsequent passage from Jerusalem to Gethsemane this prediction was repeated, the time of its accomplishment was intimated with equal precision;—"I tell thee truly that to-day, [even] this very night, before the cock crows *the second time*, thou wilt disown me thrice."—These two explanatory passages serve to show that, in all the corresponding ones, the more general terms employed for this purpose are to be understood in the special sense here expressed; that by Peter's disowning Christ thrice is meant his thrice denying *that he knew him;* and by the cock-crowing, not the slight and casual crowing which often takes place during the middle watch of the night, but the loud, regular, and repeated cry of that bird which introduces the following watch, *at three o'clock in the morning*, according to the division of the day then in use, as noticed in Mark's gospel; namely, evening, midnight, cock-crowing, and morning.† Jewish writers are said to have objected to the evangelical narrative in this respect, that, on account of the sanctity of Jerusalem, fowls were not allowed to be kept there; but, supposing this to have been the case, the objection is unimportant, since they might have been kept immediately without the walls, from which no part of the city was very remote, and the distance to which the crowing of cocks can be heard in early morning is well known.

The Jewish day commenced at sunset, the period of darkness preceding that of light, according to the mode of expression so often repeated in the Mosaic history of the creation,—"The evening and the morning were the first day," etc.;—and to the divine direction respecting the day of atonement,—"From even to even shall ye celebrate your sabbath."—During the original passion week, as it may be termed, the paschal day began about six o'clock on Wednesday evening, being the fourteenth day of Nisan, which was the first month of the sacred year, and coincided

---

* Bishop Lowth's New Translation of Isaiah, vol. I. p. 171. See also the note in vol. II. pp. 327, 328, which strongly supports the correctness of this interpretation.

† Mark, chap. 6, v. 48; chap. 13, v. 35; chap. 14, v. 29, 30;—Luke, chap. 12, v. 38; chap. 22, v. 34.

with the vernal equinox. The first day of *the feast* of unleavened bread, being an extraordinary sabbath, began at the same hour on Thursday evening; the second day of the feast, which in this instance was the ordinary weekly sabbath, on Friday evening; the third day of the feast, and first of the week, on Saturday evening, and so forth.* Attention to these facts is necessary, in order fully to understand the circumstances described in the gospel narrative of that important period. Thus, notwithstanding the objections of some commentators, it is most clearly and positively stated by the evangelists that Christ and his apostles celebrated the paschal supper on the accustomed day and hour; namely, on the evening of Thursday, the fourteenth of Nisan, the solemnity having naturally been protracted into the ensuing night, that is, into the commencement of Friday, the fifteenth; on which memorable day the whole of our Saviour's sufferings and death were accomplished. The Mosaic law directed that the paschal supper should not commence later than the evening of the fourteenth of Nisan, and that no part of the lamb or kid should remain unconsumed beyond the morning of the fifteenth.†—It is accordingly stated by the three earlier evangelists, that, on the appointed day,—"when the evening was come, [Christ] placed himself at table with the twelve;"—and, long before they quitted the upper chamber where they partook of the paschal supper, John mentions that—"it was night."—Hence appears the perfect accuracy of Christ's second prediction concerning Peter, in reference to *time ;*—" To-day, [even] this very night, before the cock *crows the second time*, thou wilt disown me thrice ;"—corresponding to the accuracy of his first prediction in reference to *mode ;*—" The cock will not crow this day before thou wilt thrice deny that thou knowest me."—These predictions are exceedingly precise, and they were most precisely fulfilled; for on inquiry it will be found that, among the seven denials of Christ by Peter, which preceded the second crowing of the cock, there were just three of the personal kind; and by so critical an accordance with the facts of the case, the truth of the predictions is more strikingly displayed than if there had been no other denials.‡ The proof of this statement is as follows :

Peter's first denial was a general one; for, on being asked by the portress at the gate,—" Art not thou also [one] of this man's disciples ?"—he said,—" I am not."—The second was a personal, and more public dis-

---

* Genesis, chap. 1, v. 5, etc.;—Exodus, chap. 12, v. 14-20;—Levit. chap. 23, v. 4-8, 26-32;—Numbers, chap. 9, v. 1-5;—Deuteron. chap. 16, v. 1-8.

† Exodus, chap. 12, v. 1-28;—Numbers, chap. 28, v. 16-25.

‡ Matt. chap. 26, v. 17-20;—Mark, chap. 14, v. 12-17, 29, 30;—Luke, chap. 22, v. 7-14, 33, 34;—John, chap. 13, v. 25-30.

avowal; for, when another maid-servant, having observed him sitting at the fire in the hall, positively asserted,—"'Thou also wast with Jesus of Nazareth,'—he disowned him before them all, saying,—'Woman, *I know him not*, neither do I understand what thou meanest.'"—The third was general, in reply to another person, who affirmed,—"Thou also art [one] of them:"—but Peter said,—"Man, I am not."—He then went out into the vestibule, or portico; and, as Mark alone relates, the cock crew. Peter had, therefore, in some sort denied Christ three times, even before the first crowing of the cock; but, as has been above shown, this did not fulfil the prediction, neither is it so represented by the evangelists. The fourth denial was personal, when the portress, again observing him in the vestibule, more confidently affirmed to those who were present,—"'This man also was with Jesus of Nazareth:'—again he denied [it] with an oath [saying],—'*I know not the man.*'"—The fifth was general, on Peter's return to the fire in the hall; for, the by-standers having asked him,—"'Art not thou also [one] of his disciples?'—he denied [it] and said.—'I am not.'"—The sixth also was general, when a relative of Malchus having put to him the searching question,—"'Did not I see thee in the garden with him?'—again Peter denied [it]."—The seventh and last denial was, however, in the highest degree personal and decided; for, on the attendants at the fire making the positive charge,—"'Certainly thou also art [one] of them, for thy [manner of] speaking is similar, [and] discovereth thee,'—he began to utter oaths and curses, [saying]—'*I know not this man of whom ye speak.*'"—Peter's conduct on this latter occasion is well illustrated by that of John of Gischala, one of the leaders of the Jews in their final war with the Romans, as thus described by Josephus.—"But now John was afraid for himself, since his treachery had proved unsuccessful; so he took the armed men that were about him, and removed from Tiberias to Gischala, and wrote to me to apologize for himself concerning what had been done, as if it had been done without his approbation, and desired me to have no suspicion of him to his disadvantage. *He also added oaths, and certain horrible curses upon himself*, and supposed he should be thereby believed in the points he wrote about to me."*

The preceding remarks may serve to show that a well-constructed Harmony, or, in other words, a careful analysis and consolidation of the statements of the four evangelists, affords great and peculiar advantages. In many cases, a complete and methodical view of the events which they relate cannot otherwise be obtained; but by this means every occurrence

---

* Whiston's Josephus, vol. iii. pp. 204, 205;—Congregational Magazine for 1836; pp. 85-91, 143-148.

is placed in the clearest and most natural light, and circumstances are often discovered which, without such a process, might easily be overlooked. The character, origin, and design of the several gospels are also hereby thoroughly illustrated; while their veracity is at the same time confirmed by a train of internal evidence which, although minute and subtile, is on that very account the more demonstrative and irresistible.

NOTE VIII.,—PAGES 268–293.

ON THE SCRIPTURAL USE OF THE TERMS COVENANT AND TESTAMENT.

The scriptural term διαθήκη may signify either a covenant or a testament. In the authorized English version, and in some others, both these senses are occasionally adopted; but in the foregoing treatise the former only. It is the object of the following remarks to assign the grounds of this preference, and to show that in an accurate translation of the Bible, the latter term should never be employed, except, perhaps, in the technical appellations,—Old Testament, and New Testament,—which at the present period it might be difficult as well as inconvenient to alter.

The term διαθήκη occurs in thirty-three places of the New Testament, and in three more is evidently implied. In seventeen of these instances the authorized version renders it—*Covenant*,*—in fourteen—*Testament*, and in the remaining five the translators have candidly intimated their doubts, by inserting one of these words in the text, and the other in the margin. In order to obtain a clear view of the question, and to aid the judgment in drawing a correct conclusion, the nineteen passages of the authorized version wherein the word *Testament* occurs will first be collated with the version now proposed; and, as the real import of terms is often overlooked when long use has rendered them familiar, the word *Testament* will on this occasion be exchanged for its equivalent, *Will*, with a view to fix the attention more closely to the subject which it actually represents.

No. 1.—Matt. chap. 26, v. 28.

AUTHORIZED VERSION.

For this is my blood of the new WILL, which is shed for many, for the remission of sins.

PROPOSED VERSION.

For this is my blood, the [blood] of the new COVENANT, which [is] shed for many, for [the] discharge of sins.

* Luke, chap. 1, v. 72;—Acts, chap. 3, v. 25; chap. 7, v. 8;—Rom. chap. 9, v. 4; chap. 11, v. 27;—Galat. chap. 3, v. 17;—Ephes. chap. 2, v. 12;—Heb. chap. 8, v. 7-10; chap. 9, v. 1, 4; chap. 10, v. 16, 29.

No. 2.—Mark, chap. 14, v. 24.

AUTHORIZED VERSION.

This is my blood of the new WILL, which is shed for many.

PROPOSED VERSION.

This is my blood, the [blood] of the new COVENANT, which [is] shed for many.

No. 3.—Luke, chap. 22, v. 20.

This cup [is] the new WILL in my blood, which is shed for you.

This cup [is] the new COVENANT by my blood, which [is] shed for you.

No. 4.—1 Corinth. chap. 11, v. 25.

This cup is the new WILL in my blood.

This cup is the new COVENANT by my blood.

No. 5.—2 Corinth. chap. 3, v. 6.

Who also hath made us able ministers of the new WILL, not of the letter, but of the spirit.

Who also hath qualified us [as] ministers of [the] new COVENANT, not of [the] written [law], but of [the] spirit.

No. 6.—2 Corinth. chap. 3, v. 14.

But their minds were blinded; for until this day remaineth the same vail untaken away, in the reading of the old WILL, which [vail] is done away in Christ.

But their minds were blinded; for even to this day, at the reading of the old COVENANT, the same vail remains unwithdrawn, for by Christ [only] it is abolished.

No. 7.—Galat. chap. 3, v. 15.

Brethren, I speak after the manner of men, though [it be] but a man's WILL, yet [if it be] confirmed, no man disannulleth, or addeth thereto. (*Marginal reading.*)

Brethren, I speak after [the manner of] man, [that when] a human COVENANT [is] confirmed, no one [either] setteth [it] aside, or addeth [to it].

No. 8.—Galat. chap. 4, v. 24.

Which things are an allegory, for these are the two WILLS. (*Marginal reading.*)

Which things are allegorical, for these [women] represent two COVENANTS.

No. 9.—Heb. chap. 7, v. 22.

By so much was Jesus made a surety of a better WILL.

Of a COVENANT so much the better is Jesus [the] surety.

NOTES AND ILLUSTRATIONS. 399

No. 10.—Heb. chap. 8, v. 6.

AUTHORIZED VERSION.

But now hath he obtained a more excellent ministry, by how much also he is the mediator of a better WILL, which was established upon better promises. (*Marginal reading.*)

PROPOSED VERSION.

But [Christ] hath obtained a more exalted ministry [than that of Aaron], inasmuch as he is [the] mediator of a better COVENANT, which was established on better promises.

No. 11.—Heb. chap. 9, v. 15.

And for this cause he is the mediator of the new WILL;

And for this end he is [the] mediator of [the] new covenant;

No. 12.—Heb. chap. 9, v. 15.

that by the means of death, for the redemption of the trangressions [that were] under the first WILL, they which are called might receive the promise of eternal inheritance.

that [in consequence of] a death having taken place, as a ransom for the transgressions [committed] under the first COVENANT, those who are called might attain the promised [gift] of the eternal inheritance.

No. 13.—Heb. chap. 9, v. 16.

For where a WILL [is], there must also of necessity be the death of the TESTATOR:

For where [there is] a COVENANT, [the] death of the COVENANT-VICTIM [must] necessarily take place:

No. 14.—Heb. chap. 9, v. 17.

for a WILL [is] of force after men are dead, otherwise it is of no strength at all while the TESTATOR liveth.

for a COVENANT [is] ratified over dead [victims], not having any force while the VICTIM remains alive.

No. 15.—Heb. chap. 9, v. 18.

Whereupon, neither the first [WILL] was dedicated without blood.

On which account, neither was the first COVENANT solemnized without blood.

No. 16.—Heb. chap. 9, v. 20.

This [is] the blood of the WILL which God hath enjoined unto you.

This [is] the blood of the COVENANT which God hath appointed for you.

No. 17.—Heb. chap. 12, v. 24.

And to Jesus, the mediator of the new WILL, and to the blood of

And to Jesus [the] mediator of [the] new COVENANT, and to [the]

AUTHORIZED VERSION.	PROPOSED VERSION.
sprinkling, that speaketh better things than [that of] Abel. (*Marginal reading.*)	blood of sprinkling, [which] speaketh better things than [that of] Abel.

No. 18.—Heb. chap. 13, v. 20, 21.

Now the God of peace, that brought again from the dead our Lord Jesus, that great shepherd of the sheep, through the blood of the everlasting WILL, make you perfect, etc. (*Marginal reading.*)	May the God of peace, who brought again from the dead our Lord Jesus, the great shepherd of the sheep by [the] blood of the everlasting COVENANT, make you perfect, etc.

No. 19.—Revel. chap. 11, v. 19.

And the temple of God was opened in heaven, and there was seen in his temple the ark of his WILL.	And God's temple in heaven was opened, and the ark of the Lord's COVENANT appeared in his temple.

To the rendering of διαθήκη by Covenant rather than Testament, in the seventeen passages wherein the former term has been adopted by the authorized version, no objection will, it is presumed, be made; and, in the greater part of the nineteen passages above quoted, the superiority of the same rendering will probably be admitted by most readers on a simple comparison, with the exception, perhaps, of Nos. 7, 13, and 14, wherein the other rendering may seem to be admissible at least, if not preferable; and which will, therefore, be reserved for a separate consideration. In the mean while, some general arguments will be adduced, to show that in Scripture the word διαθήκη always signifies a covenant, and never a testament or will.

This conclusion is, in the first place, deducible from the nature of the subject. A covenant is a mutual engagement between parties respecting their subsequent relation and conduct toward each other. A testament is the declaration of a person's will respecting the disposal of his property after his death. According to these commonly-received definitions, a divine covenant is a perfectly conceivable transaction; but a divine testament is an absurdity. All the circumstances of a will are characteristic of the weakness, selfishness, and mortality of inferior beings, but are utterly incompatible with the attributes of him—"from whom, and through whom, and for whom are all things, ... the blessed and only potentate, the King of kings, and Lord of lords, who alone possesseth immortality, dwelling in light inaccessible, whom no man hath seen nor can see, to whom be honor and eternal dominion. Amen." *—A will, notwithstanding its appellation, is an act which is seldom performed willingly. A man gives directions respecting the disposal **of his** property after his death, merely because death compels him **to part** with it; but, **as long as** he lives he has the right, and usually also the inclination **to retain it** in possession; on which account his **will cannot be lawfully** executed before his decease, nor altered after it. The Deity, on **the contrary**, can neither die, nor part with property, nor remove from one world to another. As the absolute lord and proprietor of all things, he is never impoverished by his gifts, which belong to him as much **after** they are granted as before, and which he is always at liberty to bestow or withdraw at his pleasure.

Should it be alleged that Christ is the testator here intended, it must be replied that such a view is at variance with the Scripture, which always represents him as the mediator, not as the principal; and his followers as—" heirs of God, and joint-heirs with Christ."—The general notion is moreover equally unsuitable in this case as in the former one; for, in the immediate prospect of crucifixion, Christ assured his disciples that he would not leave them in the forlorn condition of orphans,† but would speedily return to them as their eternal protector and benefactor; a promise which he performed by rising from the dead the third day, conversing with them during forty days on earth, and granting them, after his ascension to heaven, the extraordinary gifts of the Holy Spirit. From that period, instead of losing or transferring any property by his death, —"**God hath constituted his Son heir** of all things; .... and hath seated him at his own right hand in the heavenly [places], far above all rule, and authority, and power, and dominion, and every name [that is] named, not only in this world, but in that also [which is] to come; hath put all things in subjection under his feet, and hath appointed him to be [the] supreme head of the Church, which is his body, the completion of him who completeth all in all." ‡—If there is any passage in the New Testament which bears the semblance of a bequest made by Christ to his disciples, it is Luke, chap. 22, v. 29;—" Κἀγὼ διατίθεμαι ὑμῖν, καθὼς διέθετό μοι ὁ πατήρ μου, βασιλείαν.—I appoint unto you a kingdom, as my Father hath appointed unto me."—Regarding the term abstractedly, without reference to the context, this passage might certainly be ren-

---

* Rom. chap. 11, v. 36;—1 Tim. chap. 1, v. 17; chap. 6, v. 15, 16;—Heb. chap. 2, v. 10.

† Οὐκ ἀφήσω ὑμᾶς ὀρφανούς· ἔρχομαι πρὸς ὑμᾶς.—John, chap. 14, v. 18;—See also v. 1-4; and chap. 16, v. 19-22.

‡ Rom. chap. 8, v. 14-17;—Galat. chap. 4, v. 1-7;—Ephes. chap. 1, v. 19-23;—Philipp. chap. 2, v. 5-11;—Heb. chap. 1, v. 1-4: chap. 7, v. 23-28, etc.

dered,—"*I bequeath* unto you a kingdom, as my Father *hath bequeathed* unto me."—But the authors of the English Vulgate doubtless perceived that such a translation is inadmissible, both as regards the Father, to whom such an act is utterly inapplicable, and as regards the Son, to whom the very next verse,—"that ye may eat and drink at my table in my kingdom, and sit on thrones, judging the twelve tribes of Israel,"—as well as the corresponding passages in Matt. chap. 19, v. 27–30; Rev. chap. 3, v. 20, 21; and chap. 21, v. 6, 7, etc., plainly shows that it was never intended to be applied; since a bequest is enjoyed, not in conjunction with the testator, but in succession to him.

Secondly, this conclusion is deducible from the fact, that the word διαθήκη is chiefly used by the sacred writers when addressing their Hebrew fellow-countrymen, who, although familiar with covenants, knew nothing of testaments; because among their nation the transmission of property after death was determined by law, and not by the will of the previous possessor. On this ground alone it might reasonably be inferred that, under such circumstances, the word διαθήκη would uniformly be employed in the sense of covenant, and never in that of testament. The frequent occurrence in Scripture of the words heir, and inheritance, in connection with the death of Christ, may not unnaturally have suggested the notion that his followers obtain a heavenly inheritance, as a legacy bequeathed to them by his will; but this error, like some others which disfigure biblical interpretation, has chiefly arisen from inattention to Hebrew customs and idioms, and from neglecting to distinguish things which, although they may have a superficial resemblance, are essentially different. With the exception of some of the Asamonean and Herodian princes, and a few other opulent persons who adopted Gentile manners, Israelites when in their own land, and under the Mosaic dispensation, did not dispose of their property by will. During their lifetime they gave to their younger children such portions as they thought fit, but at their death the bulk of their estate descended, as a matter of course, to their legal heir. Thus, at the very commencement of their history, it is stated that,—"Abraham gave all that he had to Isaac; but unto the sons of his concubines which Abraham had, Abraham gave gifts while he yet lived, and sent them away from Isaac his son eastward, unto the east country."—So, in the parable of the prodigal, the younger son demanded from his father a portion of the family property, and, having received it, withdrew to a distant land; but to the elder son the father said, when endeavoring to appease his resentment,—"Son, thou art ever with me, and all that I have is thine."—Hence, among the people of Israel, the term corresponding to inheritance was applicable to property lawfully

NOTES AND ILLUSTRATIONS. 403

acquired by whatever tenure, but was perhaps most frequently applied to that which children derived, either by gift or by succession, from their father. That **by the** death of Christ those who believe on his name become the **adopted children of God**, and obtain a title and **qualification to a heavenly inheritance, is undoubtedly true, but it is not the whole truth**; and it is owing to this partial and imperfect view of the **doctrine, aided** by a misinterpretation of some of the terms employed, **that the notion** of a will has been introduced. A little reflection, however, is sufficient to prove its incorrectness; since it is evident that these unspeakable blessings are procured by the death of Christ, not as **a testator**, who in the ordinary course of mortality **is compelled to resign a** property, to which other **parties may succeed by a natural claim as soon as the former possessor is deceased, but by his death as an atoning victim, through the infinite value and efficacy of which, penitent sinners, who cordially embrace the offers of divine mercy proclaimed** in the gospel, **are redeemed from the bondage of sin**, and the malediction of the law, **and admitted into a covenant** of reconciliation and friendship with God, **ratified not merely by the death, but also by the life's blood of the Redeemer.**" *

Thirdly, the same conclusion is suggested by the context and connection of all the passages in which the term διαθήκη is found; for they all agree with the notion of **a** covenant, and are opposed **to that of a testament**. The inference here drawn is much facilitated, in consequence of the Scripture describing under this name two dispensations, the Mosaic and the Christian, which are evidently of the same general nature, and concerning one of which no doubt can be entertained. In the Septuagint version of the Old Testament the word διαθήκη frequently occurs; and, like the corresponding Hebrew term ברית, uniformly signifies a covenant, and never a testament, an object to which there is not in the whole of this portion of the sacred volume the slightest allusion. In those passages of the New Testament, more especially Heb. chap. **8 and 9, where the two dispensations are minutely compared, and called by the same name** διαθήκη, **it is** manifest that, if **the meaning of this term is covenant in the former case, it must be equally so in the latter**. Thus, in Galat. chap. 4, v. 24, the apostle Paul, speaking of Abraham's wives Hagar and Sarah, remarks,—" Which things are allegorical, for these [women] represent [δύο διαθῆκαι,] TWO COVENANTS."—In Rom. chap. 9, v. 4, he observes of the Jews,—" Who are Israelites, to whom belong the

---

* Genes. chap. 25, v. 5, 6;—Numb. chap. 27, v. 1-11;—Luke, chap. 15, v. 11-13, 31; —John, chap. 1, v. 10-13;—Rom. chap. 5, v. 8-11;—Galat. chap. 4, v. 1-7;—Titus, chap. 3, v. 3-7.

adoption, and the glory, and [αἱ διαθῆκαι,] THE COVENANTS, and the giving of the law, and the [appointed] worship, and the promises," etc.;—and in Ephes. chap. 2, v. 11, 12, he says to Christian Gentiles,—"Remember that ye who were once Gentiles in flesh, and called uncircumcision by those who derive their name from the circumcision made by hands in the flesh, were at that time without Christ, aliens from the commonwealth of Israel, and [ξένοι τῶν διαθηκῶν τῆς ἐπαγγελίας,] strangers to the COVENANTS of promise, without hope and without God in the world."—The appendages also which are associated by the sacred writers with each of these dispensations, such as temple,—ark,—mediator,—surety,—victim,—atoning blood,—discharge of sins,—reconciliation,—and redemption,—are all appropriate to the notion of a covenant, but inapplicable to that of a testament or will. The same may be said of the various relative or comparative terms so often applied to them in Scripture; for, as it is notorious that there never was any first,—former,—old,—inferior,—or temporary divine WILL, there cannot have been any second,—latter,—new,—better, or everlasting one; whereas, if the word COVENANT is substituted, all these appellations are suitable and true. Hence, whenever the word διαθήκη is accompanied with any such terms or allusions, it must undoubtedly signify a covenant, not a testament; and by this simple rule the import of almost all the passages above quoted may easily be determined.

To avoid prolixity, the majority of these passages will therefore be left without further comment to the reader's investigation; and the following remarks will comprehend three of them only, to which the rule does not so strictly apply, and which are also the only ones wherein the notion of a will, abstractedly considered, seems capable of being seriously entertained. These passages, which in the preceding tabular statement are numbered 7, 13, and 14, will for the sake of perspicuity be here reproduced, both in the authorized and in a modified version.

No. 7.—Gal. chap. 3, v. 15.

AUTHORIZED VERSION.

Brethren, I speak after the manner of men, though [it be] but a man's WILL, yet [if it be] confirmed, no man disannulleth, or addeth thereto. (*Marginal reading.*)

PROPOSED VERSION.

Brethren, I speak after [the manner of] man, [that when] a human COVENANT [is] confirmed, no one [either] setteth [it] aside, or addeth [to it].

In this instance it cannot be difficult to decide which of the two senses is the true one, since one of them only agrees with the context, and with the general subject. Throughout the whole of this and the following chapter the apostle is speaking of the two covenants,—δύο διαθῆ-και,—which God successively made with Abraham. On that and similar grounds he maintains that, notwithstanding the aversion of the Israelitish people to Christianity, there is no opposition between the law and the Gospel; and that, supposing even it were otherwise, the Christian covenant, which God originally established with Abraham and his spiritual seed, that is with Christ, could not be superseded by the Mosaic covenant, which was not introduced until four hundred and thirty years afterward. The apostle enforces his argument by remarking that there are two parties to a covenant ;—that, when it is once confirmed, neither party can alter it without the consent of the other ;—and that, if such a rule is binding in a human covenant, it must, if possible, be still more so in one that is divine. This reasoning is apposite and conclusive ; but, except in reference to the single point of inheritance, common to both subjects, and which has been already explained, any allusion to a testament or will in this connection would have been incongruous and unsuitable ; for, to say that a will cannot be altered after the death of the testator, would afford no proof that God cannot alter a covenant into which he has entered. In all transactions of this kind those who embrace the offer made to them are, it is true, entitled to an inheritance, either in heaven, or in earth ; but it is secured to them by a covenant, not by a testament ; a mode of proceeding which, as previously observed, cannot be ascribed to the Deity without absurdity.

No. 13.—Heb. chap. 9, v. 16.

AUTHORIZED VERSION.

For where a WILL [is], there must also of necessity be the death of the TESTATOR.

PROPOSED VERSION.

For where [there] is a COVENANT, [the] death of the COVENANT VICTIM [must] necessarily take place :

No. 14.—Heb. chap. 9, v. 17

AUTHORIZED VERSION.

for a WILL [is] of force after men are dead, otherwise it is of no strength at all while the TESTATOR liveth.

PROPOSED VERSION.

for a COVENANT [is] ratified over dead [victims] not having any force while the VICTIM remains alive.

These verses present the case which, separately considered, is of all others the most favorable to the notion of a Will, were that notion in any case admissible; but that it is utterly untenable, will appear from its total discrepancy with the phraseology, the argument, and the entire object of these passages; while that of a Covenant is in perfect accordance with each.

Before proceeding with this inquiry, it may be useful to recollect that among the more important ancient covenants were treaties of peace and alliance, adopted by parties previously hostile; who, having at length agreed on terms of reconciliation, pledged themselves by oaths and sacrifices to their faithful observance. On these occasions the victims were divided longitudinally into corresponding halves, between which the contracting parties solemnly passed in succession, thereby literally entering into a covenant, and imprecating on themselves, in the event of breaking their engagements, a similar fate. Hence the Hebrew name for a covenant, and perhaps also the Greek word $\delta\iota\alpha\theta\eta\kappa\eta$, are derived from roots signifying to sever or divide; and hence probably the ancient punishment of cutting or sawing asunder, to which there seems to be some allusion in a few passages of the New Testament, was originally contrived to mark the peculiar atrocity of treachery, or the violation of covenants.*
A memorable example of a covenant of this kind occurs in Jerem. chap. 34, v. 6-22, and may be thus described.—At the commencement of the siege of Jerusalem by Nebuchadnezzar, during the reign of Zedekiah, many of the higher and more opulent classes among the Jews who, in opposition to the law of Moses, had reduced their countrymen and countrywomen to domestic slavery, set them at liberty, and confirmed this act of justice by a solemn covenant, celebrated in the manner above mentioned. This procedure was, however, the result, not of principle, but of fear; and hence, on the subsequent retirement of the Babylonish army from the city, they basely broke their covenant, and reduced to their former slavery the persons whom they had recently emancipated. Such conduct was of course highly offensive to God, who threatened them in consequence through the prophet Jeremiah with the severest judgments, and in the course of these denunciations used the following remarkable

---

* Matt. chap. 24, v. 45-51;—Luke, chap. 12, v. 41-46;—Acts, chap. 1, v. 16-20;—Rom. chap. 1. v. 31;—2 Tim. chap. 3, v. 3.

expressions,—chap. 34, v. 18,—" I will give the men that have transgressed my covenant, who have not performed the words of the covenant which they had made before me, when they cut the calf in twain, and passed between the parts thereof, 19. the princes of Judah and the princes of Jerusalem, the eunuchs and the priests, and all the people of the land, who passed between the parts of the calf, 20. I will even give them into the hand of their enemies, and into the hand of them that seek their life; and their dead bodies shall be for meat unto the fowls of the heaven, and to the beasts of the earth," etc.

Such having been the established practice in ancient times and Eastern countries, it pleased God in making his primitive covenant with Abraham to adopt similar observances. The condescension of God, both in providing a method of reconciliation between himself and sinful men, and in pressing it on their acceptance, is indeed almost too great to be believed; and hence a second act of condescension became necessary, especially before the birth of Christ, in order to prove the reality and certainty of the first. The fact is thus noticed by the apostle Paul.—" When God made a promise to Abraham, since there was none greater by whom he could swear, he swore by himself, saying—' I will assuredly bless thee and multiply thee;'—and accordingly, after patiently waiting, [Abraham] obtained the promised [blessing]. For men swear by a superior, and an oath furnishes them with a confirmation beyond all dispute. On which account God, being desirous to prove more fully to the heirs of the promise the unchangeableness of his purpose, had recourse to an oath, that by means of two unchangeable acts, wherein [it was] impossible that God should deal falsely, we, who have fled [for refuge] to lay hold of the hope set before [us], might have a strong consolation."—Nor was this all; for the patriarch having by God's direction slain and divided victims in the usual manner, the Shechinah, or emblem of the divine presence, actually went, like a human party, between the several halves.—" It came to pass that when the sun went down, and it was dark, behold! a smoking furnace and a burning lamp that passed between those pieces. In the same day the Lord made a covenant with Abram."—Thus by every conceivable token, both in word and in deed, the gracious engagement of God with repenting sinners is throughout Scripture represented as a covenant of reconciliation; and the short description which he himself gives of them is,—" Those who have made a covenant with me by sacrifice." *

Returning to the two passages in the Epistle to the Hebrews which are now under consideration, it will be recollected that in this portion of

---

* Gen. chap. 15, v. 7-21;—Psalm 50, v. 5;—Rom. chap. 5, v. 1-11;—2 Cor. chap. 5, v. 14-21;—Ephes. chap. 2, v. 11-18;—Heb. chap. 6, v. 13-20.

Scripture the apostle Paul is addressing Israelitish Christians, more especially perhaps those of Palestine, with a view to confirm them in the faith and practice of the gospel, and probably also to produce through them a favorable impression on the minds of their unbelieving countrymen. For this purpose, he draws a full and minute comparison between the two covenants, the Mosaic and the Christian; shows that the Mosaic covenant, and the whole ceremonial law annexed to it, were merely typical and temporary institutions, preparatory to the great and spiritual realities of Christianity; and intimates that, as the substance was now come, the shadow would speedily vanish away. This discussion is chiefly pursued in the long section which extends from the eighth chapter to the middle of the tenth, and includes the two verses in question, together with the following context:—"Christ having arrived [as] high-priest of the blessings to come, by the greater and more perfect tabernacle not made with hands, that is, not of this institution, neither by the blood of goats and calves, but by his own blood, entered once for all into the most holy place, having achieved an everlasting redemption. For, if the blood of bulls and goats, and the ashes of a heifer, sprinkled on those who are unclean, sanctify to the purification of the flesh, how much more will the blood of Christ, who through the eternal Spirit offered himself [as] a spotless [sacrifice] to God, purify your consciences from dead works, to worship the living God? And for this end he is [the] mediator of [the] new covenant; that, [in consequence of] a death having taken place as a ransom for the transgressions [committed] under the first covenant, those who are called might attain the promised [gift] of the eternal inheritance. For, where [there is] a covenant, [the] death of the covenant-victim [must] necessarily take place; for a covenant [is] ratified over dead [victims], not having any force while the victim remains alive. On which account, neither was the first [covenant] solemnized without blood; for, when every commandment of the law had been recited to all the people by Moses, he took the blood of calves and goats, with water, and scarlet wool, and hyssop, and sprinkled both the book, and all the people, saying—'This [is] the blood of the covenant which God hath appointed for you.'—And in like manner he sprinkled with the blood both the tabernacle, and all the implements of the sacred service; and [indeed], according to the law, almost all things are purified by blood, and without effusion of blood there is no discharge [of sins]." *—The whole tenor of this important passage proves that the term $\delta\iota\alpha\theta\acute{\eta}\kappa\eta$ is therein used in the same sense as in all the passages previously cited. Christ is here described, not as the testator of a will, but as the mediator, the

* Heb. chap. 9, v. 11-22.

surety, the high-priest, and the victim of a covenant. That the transaction was a covenant, not a testament, is determined by its collation with the Mosaic covenant, concerning which there cannot be any dispute. For the ratification of such a covenant, the apostle observes that the violent death of a suitable victim, attended with the effusion of its life's blood, was indispensable; that until these conditions were fulfilled the covenant was not valid; and that the *first* covenant was ratified by the blood of animals, but the *new* covenant by that of Christ. These circumstances have no relation or analogy to those of a will, nor are they explained by stating that a will is not in force until after the death of the testator. If any one doubts this, let him consider which of the following answers to the questions implied in the **foregoing passage is the most rational and satisfactory:**

QUERIES.—Why did Christ become the mediator of the new covenant, and make atonement for the sins of mankind by the effusion of his blood? —and why was the Mosaic covenant solemnized by shedding the blood of calves and goats?

ANSWER I.—Because a will is not in force until after the death of the testator.

ANSWER II.—Because a covenant of reconciliation is not ratified without the sacrifice of the appointed victim, or, in other words, without a suitable atonement.

The natural conclusion is, that the inspired writer could not have intended to construct a solid argument by the combination of such heterogeneous materials, and that the term διαθήκη, which in every other part of Scripture signifies a covenant, cannot on this single occasion, without warning, and against reason, have been employed in a sense so different and incongruous as that of a will.

Such being the case, it is not a little surprising that some eminent theologians of the present day either hesitate to admit this conclusion, or even adopt the opposite one. The latter course is taken by Dr. Moses Stuart, in his *Commentary on the Epistle to the Hebrews*, but with a feebleness which forms a striking contrast to the general merit of his excellent work, and with concessions which greatly detract from the weight of his authority on this point. For, in the first place, although he zealously advocates the notion of a testament, and although with a view to consistency the authorized version has actually inserted the word in several places, he has never introduced it in his own translation, except in these two solitary verses; and admits that—" this mode of illustration or comparison depends entirely on the sense of the *Greek* word διαθήκη, and is not at all supported by any meaning of the Hebrew, ברית,"—the corresponding term in the Old Testament.* But the very language which he employs in support of this opinion affords a convincing proof of its unsoundness; for the divine transaction denoted by either of these terms, whether Hebrew or Greek, is in Scripture uniformly represented as a sacred reality; and, as in this case the notion of a will or testament could at best be nothing more than—"a mode of illustration or comparison,"—and that a very inapposite one, it cannot be the object intended. In commenting on the text,—" Ὅπου γὰρ διαθήκη, θάνατον ἀνάγκη φέρεσθαι τοῦ διαθεμένου,"—Heb. chap. 9, v. 16, Dr. Stuart in like manner makes the following concession.—" Φέρεσθαι, in the sense of *intervening, happening, taking place* (which must necessarily be attached to it here), has no exact parallel, that I can find, either in classic or sacred usage. It is as to such a meaning a true ἅπαξ λεγόμενον,"—a singular expression. Were this statement strictly correct, it would strengthen the argument for interpreting the word διαθέμενος in the peculiar sense, wherein the context shows that it must here have been employed. But, although the terms —"intervening, happening, or taking place,"—may tolerably well represent the general meaning of the verb φέρομαι, they do not express its full meaning, the character of which is not passive, but forcible, and in this particular case might very properly be rendered—"to be brought about or induced,"—in other words,—"to be inflicted;"—a meaning which perfectly agrees with the death of a victim, but not at all with that of a testator. Again, in the following verse 17,—" Διαθήκη γὰρ ἐπὶ νεκροῖς βεβαία," etc.,—the expression, ἐπὶ νεκροῖς, which has been translated—"over dead victims,"—and literally means—"over dead bodies,"—is inapplicable to a deceased testator, whose will is certainly not confirmed over his corpse, but fully accords with the victims, often numerous, over whose dead and dissevered bodies a covenant of reconciliation was anciently ratified. The version of this passage, proposed after much deliberation by Dr. Stuart, and which is probably the best that could be contrived in favor of the opinion which he endeavors to support,—"because a testament is valid in respect to those only who are dead,"—affords a further proof that the opinion is untenable; since, if such were the fact, a will could never be executed.†

Dr. Pye Smith, in his admirable work on the Priesthood of Christ, evidently inclines to the opposite opinion; but, with his usual modesty and candor, mentions two difficulties with which he and others conceive it to be pressed, namely,—"the necessity of making ὁ διαθέμενος and

---

* Dr. Moses Stuart, Commentary on the Epistle to the Hebrews, vol. ii. pp. 225-228.

† Ibid., pp. 7, 226.

νεκροί to signify the animal sacrifices by which the most solemn covenants in early times were ratified; whereas the phrase διαθέσθαι διαθήκην is common in the Septuagint, and always refers to the act of the person who constitutes the covenant, and νεκροί, or νεκρά, is never applied to the dead **bodies of** any but mankind."—He adds,—"Perhaps we must humbly say that this passage is among 'the things hard to be **understood**' of the apostle Paul's writings, and that the satisfactory elucidation of it is not yet attained." *—With much deference to so respected an authority, it may be replied that neither of these remarks is strictly accurate; for, in the Septuagint version, the phrase διαθέσθαι διαθήκην or its equivalents is often applied to either or both of the parties engaging in a covenant, as well as to the mediator or agent by whom it is administered. Of its application to the principal party, and more especially to the Deity, the instances are too numerous and familiar to require quotation. **In the following cases the term is** applied to both parties. **Abraham and Abimelech entered into a covenant** at Beersheba;—" and both of them made a covenant; καὶ διέθεντο ἀμφότεροι διαθήκην."—Jacob and Laban, at the proposal of the latter, entered into a covenant on Mount Gilead;—"Now therefore come thou, let us make a covenant I and thou; Νῦν [οὖν δεῦρο, διαθώμεθα διαθήκην ἐγὼ καὶ σύ."—David and Jonathan, in the wilderness of Ziph;—" And they two made a covenant before the Lord; Καὶ διέθεντο ἀμφότεροι διαθήκην ἐνώπιον Κυρίου."—and Solomon and Hiram, through the medium of ambassadors;—" And they two made a league together; Καὶ διέθεντο διαθήκην ἀνὰ μέσον ἑαυτῶν." †— In some instances the expression is employed in reference to parties making a covenant with God. Thus Hezekiah, in an address to the priests and Levites at the commencement of his reign, intimated,—" Now [it is] in my heart to make a covenant with the Lord God of Israel; Ἐπὶ τούτοις, νῦν ἔστιν ἐπὶ καρδίας διαθέσθαι διαθήκην μου, διαθήκην Κυρίου, Θεοῦ Ἰσραὴλ."—Josiah, on mounting the throne, followed the example of his pious ancestor;—" And the king stood by a pillar, and **made a covenant before the Lord**; Καὶ ἔστη ὁ βασιλεὺς πρὸς τὸν στῦλον, καὶ διέθετο διαθήκην ἐνώπιον Κυρίου."—And, after the return of the Jews from the Babylonish captivity, Shechaniah, in an address to Ezra, recommended a similar proceeding to those among them who had married foreign wives; —" Now, therefore, let us make a covenant with our God, etc.; Καὶ νῦν διαθώμεθα διαθήκην τῷ Θεῷ ἡμῶν." ‡

* Dr. J. P. Smith, On the Sacrifice and Priesthood of Jesus Christ, pp. 110–120.
† Gen. chap. 21, v. 27, 32; chap. 31, v. 43, 44;—1 Sam. chap. 23, v. 16-18;—1 Kings, chap. 5, v. 12.
‡ 2 Kings, chap. 23, v. 1-3;—2 Chron. chap. 29, v. 10; chap. 34, v. 29-32;—Ezra, chap. 10, v. 1-3.

There are other cases again, and more to the present purpose, where the term is applied to those who act as mediators, or ministers, in bringing other parties into a covenant. Thus, in the national covenant established between God and the people of Israel at Mount Sinai, and afterward renewed on the plains of Moab, Moses was the appointed mediator. This circumstance, to which allusion is made in Galat. chap. 3, v. 19, 20, is described on the first occasion in the book of Exodus, and on the second, in the following manner, in that of Deuteronomy;—" These [are] the words of the covenant which the Lord commanded Moses to make with the children of Israel in the land of Moab, besides the covenant which he made with them in Horeb. . . . Keep therefore the words of this covenant, and do them, that ye may prosper in all that ye do. . . . Neither with you only do I make this covenant, and this oath; Καὶ οὐχ ὑμῖν μόνοις ἐγὼ διατίθεμαι τὴν διαθήκην ταύτην, καὶ τὴν ἀρὰν ταύτην."— Joshua, a little before his death, imitated the conduct of his illustrious predecessor, and persuaded the people of Israel to renew their covenant with God.—" So Joshua made a covenant with the people that day; Καὶ διέθετο Ἰησοῦς διαθήκην πρὸς τὸν λαὸν ἐν τῇ ἡμέρᾳ ἐκείνῃ."—Jehoiada the high-priest performed a similar act after the deposition of the idolatrous Athaliah, and the restoration of true religion under Joash the rightful sovereign.—" And Jehoiada made a covenant between the Lord, and the king, and the people, that they should be the Lord's people; Καὶ διέθετο Ἰωαδαὲ διαθήκην ἀνὰ μέσον Κυρίου, καὶ ἀνὰ μέσον τοῦ βασιλέως, καὶ ἀνὰ μέσον τοῦ λαοῦ, τοῦ εἶναι εἰς λαὸν τῷ Κυρίῳ."—And lastly, during the siege of Jerusalem by the Babylonians, Zedekiah the king brought the people, as above related, into a solemn covenant with God, to emancipate their Hebrew slaves.* It hence appears that the scriptural use of the phrase διαθέσθαι διαθήκην is more extensive than was supposed by Dr. Smith; a fact which may be still further illustrated by the text already cited; namely, Psalm 50, v. 5. " Gather my saints together unto me, those that have made a covenant with me by sacrifice; τοὺς διατιθεμένους τὴν διαθήκην αὐτοῦ ἐπὶ θυσίαις"—literally—" over slaughtered victims;" —an expression exactly corresponding to that in Heb. chap. 9, v. 17. " A covenant [is] ratified over dead [victims]; διαθήκη ἐπὶ νεκροῖς βεβαία." —Dr. Smith's objection to such an application of the term νεκροῖς, on the ground that it is always restricted to the dead bodies of mankind, is in like manner obviated by three opposite examples; to which several others might doubtless be added. Two of these are derived from Æsop's Fables;—" Ὁ αἴλουρος . . . . προσεποιεῖτο αὐτὸν ΝΕΚΡΟΝ εἶναι. The cat

---

* Deuteron. chap. 29, v. 1-15;—Joshua, chap. 24, v. 25;—2 Kings, chap. 11, v. 4, 17, 18;—2 Chron. chap. 23, v. 1-3, 16;—Jerem. chap. 34, v. 8, 9;—Hosea, chap. 2, v. 18.

.... pretended to be dead;"—"ἐπειδὴ εἶδε τὴν χελιδόνα ΝΕΚΡΑΝ ἐρημουμένην· when he saw the swallow left dead;"—and the third from the Septuagint translation of the book of Ecclesiastes;—" Ὁ κύων ὁ ζῶν, αὐτὸς ἀγαθὸς ὑπὲρ τὸν λέοντα τὸν ΝΕΚΡΟΝ. A living dog is better than a dead lion." *

Supposing the other difficulties connected with the interpretation of this passage to have been now removed, there remains only that of explaining the exact signification of the term ὁ διαθέμενος, and of accounting for its being so applied. But, if διαθήκη here means a covenant of reconciliation, ὁ διαθέμενος cannot mean the testator; for, as has been well observed by the Rev. Archibald M'Lean, in his judicious commentary on this epistle, the expressions *mediator of a testament*, and *testator of a covenant*, are alike unintelligible.† It must, therefore, mean *the covenant victim;* since, of all the parties concerned in such a transaction, the victim is the only one whose death is necessary for the purpose of ratification, and by the effusion of whose blood atonement is made for the offences which occasioned the previous hostility. This usage of the term is perhaps somewhat uncommon; but it should be remembered that the sacred writers of the New Testament do not confine themselves to classical Greek, that the subject is one of great complexity, and of supreme importance, that it was difficult to find Greek idioms perfectly adapted to the case, and that in addressing Hebrew Christians familiar with the topics under discussion, and accustomed to the Hellenistic dialect, the apostle might very naturally have been induced to employ an expression which, although a little irregular, would probably convey to their minds more precisely than any other, the object which he had in view. This object was to show that, whereas under the Mosaic covenant the blood of inferior victims offered on the altar accomplished a figurative and ceremonial atonement, the blood of Christ, who was at once the mediator, surety, high-priest, and victim of the new covenant, accomplished a real one, whereby all who cordially embrace it are reconciled to God, and entitled as his adopted children to an eternal inheritance. Nor was this proceeding arbitrary, or unreasonable, but founded on the intrinsic nature of the case, and analogous to human usages on similar occasions. Except through a suitable mediator, God could not, consistently with the perfection and dignity of his character, have made overtures of friendship to depraved and sinful men;—unless security had been given for the full satisfaction of divine justice, the negotiation could

---

* Æsopicæ Fabulæ, Fab. 67, and 123;—Ecclesiast. chap. 9, v. 4.
† Rev. Archibald M'Lean, Paraphrase and Commentary on the Epistle to the Hebrews, vol. i. pp. 259, 260; vol. ii. pp. 38–41.

not have proceeded;—unless the pledge so given had been thoroughly redeemed by the death of Christ as an atoning victim, it could not have been completed;—and it is obvious that he who thus consecrates and presents acceptable worshippers to God, is a high-priest. As all these offices are virtually united in that of a reconciler of hostile parties through the medium of a sacrificial covenant, the term διαθεμένος, which in this sense is generally applicable to every covenant-victim, is peculiarly applicable to Christ. The texts recently quoted from the Septuagint show that the corresponding verb is occasionally there used in reference to the office of a mediator; and both the verb and its participles are often employed by the ancient Greek authors in the sense of composing animosities, and reconciling parties who have been at variance. Among the meanings assigned to the middle verb διατίθεμαι in Stephens's Thesaurus, are—*componere, ad concordiam reducere, concorditer constituere, placare;*—among those mentioned in Donnegan's Lexicon,—*to conciliate, to reconcile, to accommodate a difference;*—and, by the evidence thus supplied, the use of this term by the apostle Paul in the sense here assigned may, therefore, be regarded as sufficiently explained. At all events, it is far better to admit that in such a use of the term the apostle committed a slight irregularity, if it really is one, than to consign the whole of a most important passage to obscurity, or absurdity.

Nor is this view of the passage now proposed for the first time, having long since been adopted by several eminent authors, and among others by Mr. Taylor, in his well-known edition and continuation of Calmet's Dictionary of the Bible, as appears from the following extract, which will form a suitable conclusion to the present remarks:—" ' Now, where there is a . . . . COVENANT, the death of . . . . the CONFIRMER OF THE COVENANT is necessary; for a . . . . *covenant* is of no authority while the confirmer of the . . . . *covenant* is living:'—i. e. while that beast was not slain, between whose divided parts the persons *covenanting* were to pass, the *covenant* wanted the most solemn token of its ratification." *—But, as in a modern translation of Scripture such expressions as covenant-confirmer, or covenant-ratificator, would be harsh, and scarcely intelligible, the term COVENANT-VICTIM, which is nearly equivalent, and actually implied, is here substituted.

* Calmet's Dictionary of the Bible, edited by Taylor; Article Covenant;—also Fragments, vol. i. pp. 205–210, 539–542;—Evangelical Register for 1830; vol. iv. pp. 69–73, 103–109

LIST OF AUTHORS AND WORKS,

TO WHICH

REFERENCE IS MADE IN DR. STROUD'S TREATISE.

A.

ABERCROMBIE (Dr. John), Cases of Rupture of the Heart;—in the Trans. of the Medico-Chirurg. Society of Edinburgh, vol. i.
Academia Naturæ Curiosorum,—Ephemerides; sive Acta Physico-Medica; in many volumes.
Acta Sanctorum (curâ Bollandi), 50 vol. fol. Antuerp. 1643, etc.
Adams (Mr.), Case of Rupture of the Heart;—in the Journal of Morbid Anatomy, Ophthalmic Medicine, etc. Art. 5.
Æsopicæ Fabulæ (curâ Francisci De Furia); 8vo. Lips. 1810.
Allan (Mr.), Case of Hepatic Abscess bursting into the Pericardium;—in the Lancet for 1845.
Annual Register for the year 1798; 2d Edit. 8vo. Lond. 1806.
Arnott (Mr.), Case of Hæmorrhage into the Pericardium;—in the Lond. Med. and Phys. Journal for 1826.
Art de Vérifier les dates, in many volumes; 8vo. Paris, 1818, etc.

B.

Bardus (Hieronymus), Epistola ad Thomam Bartholinum, 12mo. Ludg. Bat. 1646.
Baricelli (Julius Cæsar), De Hydronosa Natura, etc. 4to. Neapol. 1814.
Bartholinus (Thomas), De Latere Christi Aperto, etc. 12mo. Ludg. Bat. 1646.
—— Epistola ad Hieron. Bardium; ibid.
Bedingfield (James), Compendium of Medical Practice; 8vo. Lond. 1816
Bell (Sir Charles), On the Nervous System of the Human Body; 4to Lond. 1830.
—— Anatomy and Philosophy of Expression, etc.; large 8vo. Lond. 1844.
—— (John and Charles), Anatomy of the Human Body; 4 vols. 8vo. Edinb. 1797.

Biblia Sacra, juxta Vulgatam Editionem; fol. Paris, 1549.
Biblia Sacra, Vet. Test. juxta Septuaginta Interpretes (curâ Grabe), fol. Oxon. 1707.
Biscoe (Rev. Richard), Twenty-four Sermons on the Acts of the Apostles; 2 vols. 8vo. Lond. 1742.
Blanchinus (Josephus), Evangeliarium Quadruplex Latinæ Versionis Antiquæ, etc.; 4 vols. fol. Romæ, 1749.
Bohn (Johannes), De Renunciatione Vulnerum, etc.; 12mo. Amstelod. 1710.
Bonetus (Theophilus), Sepulchretum (curâ Manget), 3 vols. fol. Genevæ, 1700.
Bosius (Jacobus), Crux Triumphans et Glorioso; fol. Antuerp. 1617.
Brigida (Beata), Memoriale Effigiatum Librorum Prophetiarum, etc.; fol. Romæ, 1556.
Burns (Allan), On Diseases of the Heart, 8vo. Edinb. 1809.
Butler (Rev. Alban), Lives of the Fathers, etc.; 12 vols. 8vo. Lond. 1812-1815.

C.

Calmet (August.), Dictionary of the Holy Bible, edited and enlarged by C. Taylor; 5 vols. 4to. Lond. 1823.
Calvinus (Joannes), Comment. in Quatuor Evangelistas; fol. Amstelod. 1667.
Carpenter (Dr. W. B.), Principles of Human Physiology, etc.; 8vo. Lond. 1842.
Castellus (Barthol.), Lexicon Medicum; 4to. Genev. 1746.
Chrysostomus (Joannes), Opera (curâ Montfaucon); 13 vols. fol. Paris, 1727.
Clarke (Dr. Adam), The New Testament, with a Commentary, etc.; 3 vols. 4to. Lond. 1817.
Cogan (Dr. Thomas), Philosophical Treatise on the Passions; 8vo. Bath, 1802.
Coleridge (S. T.), Specimens of his Table Talk; 2 vols. 12mo. Lond. 1835.
Comment. [Lipsienses], de Rebus in Scientia Naturali et Medicina gestis, etc.; 40 vols. 8vo. Lips. 1752-1792.
Congregational Magazine; 28 vols. 8vo. Lond. 1818-1845.
Copland (Dr. James), Dictionary of Practical Medicine; in several vols. 8vo. Lond. 1832-1847.
Corvisart (J. N.), Sur les Maladies du Cœur, et des Gros Vaisseaux; 12mo. Paris, 1811.
Crevier (J. B. L.), History of the Roman Emperors, etc. (trans. by Mill), 10 vols. 8vo. Lond. 1814.
Crichton (Dr. Alexander), On Mental Derangement; 2 vols. 8vo. Lond. 1798.
Curling (Mr.), Case of Hæmorrhage into the Pericardium;—in the London Medical Gazette for 1838.
Cyprianus, Opera, fol. Paris, 1726.

D.

Davy (Dr. John), Researches Physiological and Anatomical; 2 vols. 8vo. Lond. 1839.

Daubeny (Dr. Charles), Description of Active and Extinct Volcanoes, etc.;
    8vo. Lond. 1826.
De Marinis (Dominicus), De Re Monstrosa, etc.; 32mo. Romæ, 1678.
De Mezeray, Histoire de France; 3 vols. fol. Paris, 1685.
Denham and Clapperton, Travels and Discoveries in Northern and Central
    Africa; 4to. Lond. 1826.
Desruelles (Dr.), Précis Physiologique du Choléra Morbus; 8vo. Paris,
    1831.
Dickson (Sir D. J. H.), Case of Aneurism of the Aorta bursting into the
    right Pleural Sac;—in the Edinb. Med. and Surg. Journal for 1843.
Dionis, Anatomy of Human Bodies, etc. (trans. from the French); 8vo.
    Lond. 1703.
Doddridge (Dr. Philip), Family Expositor of the New Testament, etc.; 6
    vols. 4to. Lond. 1761.
Dongola and Sennaar, Narrative of an Expedition to, in 1820; 8vo. Lond.
    1822.
Dublin Medical Transactions (New Series); 8vo. Dublin, 1830, etc.
Durrius (G. T.), Case of Bloody Sweat;—in the Ephemerid. Acad. Natur.
    Curios.

E.

Edinburgh Medical and Surgical Journal.
Edinburgh New Philosophical Journal (by Brewster).
Edwards (Jonathan), Works; 8 vols. 8vo. Lond. 1817.
Elliotson (Dr. John), Lumleyan Lectures on Diseases of the Heart; fol.
    Lond. 1830.
Ellis (Rev. W.), History of Madagascar; 2 vols. 8vo. Lond. and Paris,
    1838.
English Poets, Works of, edited by Dr. S. Johnson; 75 vols. 12mo.
    Lond. 1790.
Erskine (Thomas, Esq.), On the Internal Evidence for the Truth of Re-
    vealed Religion; 18mo. Edinb. 1829.
—— Essay on Faith; 18mo. Edinb. 1829.
—— On the Unconditional Freeness of the Gospel; 12mo. Edinb. 1829.
Evangelical Register, or Magazine for the Connection of the Countess of
    Huntington; 4 vols. 8vo. Lond. 1824–1831.

F.

Ferguson (J. C.), Two Cases of Pulmonary Apoplexy;—in the Dublin
    Medical Transactions for 1830.
Fischer (Dr. Daniel), Case of Hæmorrhage into the Pericardium;—in the
    Ephemerid. Acad. Natur. Curios.
Fischer (Dr.), Case of Rupture of the Heart;—in the London Medical
    Repository, vols. xi. and xii.
Fitzpatrick (Mr.), Case of Hæmorrhage into the Pericardium;—in the
    London Medical Repository, vol. xvii.
Forster (T.), Illustrations of the Atmospherical Origin of Epidemic Dis-
    orders, etc.; 8vo. Chelmsford, 1829.
Foxe (Rev. John), The Book of Martyrs in the Reign of Queen Mary the
    First (edited by Madan), small folio. Lond. 1760.
Francis (Dr.), Cases of Hæmorrhage into the Pericardium, etc.;—in the
    Guy's Hospital Reports for 1845.

G.

Galeati (D. G.), Case of Rupture of the Heart;—in the Comment. Lipsiens. for 1758.
Gesenius (Rev. Dr.), Hebrew and English Lexicon; 8vo. Lond. 1827
Gibbon (Edward), History of the Decline and Fall of the Roman Empire; 12 vols. 8vo. Lond. 1807.
Gill (Dr. John), Exposition of the New Testament; 3 vols. fol. Lond. 1746.
Grimm, and Diderot, Correspondance Littéraire, etc., depuis 1770, jusqu'en 1790; 6 vols. 8vo. Paris, 1813.
Grotius (Hugo), Opera Theologica, etc.; 4 vols. fol. Lond. 1679.
Grüner (Father and Son), On the Death of Christ, etc.;—in Kuinoël's Lib. Historic. Nov. Test.
Guy's Hospital Reports.

H.

Haller (Baron), Element. Physiolog. Corp. Human; 8 vols. 4to. Lausann. 1757.
——— On the Motion of the Blood, etc.; 8vo. Lond. 1757.
Harvæus (Gulielmus), Opera; 4to. Lond. 1766.
——— De Motu Cordis et Sanguinis in Animalibus; 32mo. Roterodam. 1648.
Harwood (Edward), On the Probable Causes of our Saviour's Agony; 8vo. Lond. 1772.
Hecker (Dr. J. F. C.), The Black Death in the 14th Century (translated by Dr. Babington); 12mo. Lond. 1833.
Henderson (Rev. Dr.), Translation of Isaiah, etc.; 8vo. Lond. 1840.
Henry (Rev. Matthew), Exposition on the New Testament; 2 vols fol. Lond. 1763.
Herodotus, History (translated by Beloe); 4 vols. 8vo. Lond. 1806.
Hewlett (Rev. Mr.), Bible, with Notes; 3 vols. 4to. Lond. 1812.
Hewson (William), Inquiry into the Properties of the Blood, etc.; 8vo. Lond. 1772.
Hey (William), Observations on the Blood; 8vo. Lond. 1779.
——— Short Defence of the Doctrine of Atonement, etc.; 8vo. Leeds, 1774.
Hieronymus, Opera (curâ Erasmi); 9 vols. fol. Paris, 1546.
Hope (Dr.), On the Diseases of the Heart and Great Vessels; 3d edit. 8vo. Lond. 1839.
Horne (Bishop), Commentary on the Book of Psalms; 2 vols. 8vo. Lond. 1802.
Hunter (John), Works (edited by Palmer); 4 vols. 8vo. Lond. 1835.

I.

Irenæus, Opera (curâ Grabe); fol. Oxon. 1702.

J.

Josephus, Works (translated by Whiston); 4 vols. 8vo. Lond. 1806.
Journal of Morbid Anatomy, Ophthalmic Medicine, etc.; 8vo. Lond. 1828.
Journal Universel des Sciences Médicales; 32 vols. 8vo. Paris, 1816, etc.
Justinus, Historiæ Philippicæ; 8vo. Lugd. Bat. 1760.
Justinus (Martyr), Cum Tryphone Judæo Dialogus (curâ Sam. Jebb.); 8vo. Lond. 1719.

K.

Kannegiesser (G. H.), On Bloody Sweat ;—in the Ephemerid. Acad. Natur. Curios.
Kennedy (John), Complete System of Astronomical Chronology, etc. Lond. 1762.
Kipping (M. H.), De Cruce et Cruciariis ; 12mo. Bremæ, 1671.
Klefeker (J. P.), De Halitu Pericardii ; 4to. Lugd. Bat. 1758.
Kuinoë (C. T.), Comment. in Lib. Historic. Nov. Test. ; 4 vols. 8vo. Lips. 1816.

L.

Lancisi (J. M.), Opera ; 2 vols. 4to. Genevæ, 1718.
Lanzoni (Joseph), Case of Bloody Sweat ;—in the Ephemerid. Acad. Natur. Curios.
Lardner (Dr. Nathaniel), Works ; 11 vols. 8vo. Lond. 1788.
Lentilius (Rosinus), Cases of Bloody Sweat ;—in the Ephemerid. Acad. Natur. Curios.
Leti (Gregorio), Life of Pope Sixtus V. (translated by Farneworth) ; fol. Lond. 1754.
Lightfoot (Dr. John), Works ; 2 vols. fol. Lond. 1684.
Lipsius (Justus), De Cruce ; 12mo. Amstelod. 1670.
London Medical and Physical Journal ; 67 vols. 8vo. Lond. 1799-1832.
London Medical Repository ; 29 vols. 8vo. Lond. 1814-'28.
Lower (Richard), De Corde, etc. ; 12mo. Lugd. Bat. 1728.
Lowth (Bishop), New Translation of Isaiah ; 2 vols. 8vo. Lond. 1795.
Ludwig (C. D.), Adversaria Medico-Practica ; 3 vols. 8vo. Lips. 1769-'74.

M.

M'Lean (Rev. Archibald) Paraphrase and Commentary on the Epistle to the Hebrews ; 2 vols. 8vo. Lond. 1820.
Maldonatus (Joannes). Comment. in Quatuor Evangelistas ; fol. Paris, 1639.
Maundrell (Rev. H.), Journey from Aleppo to Jerusalem, etc. ; 8vo. Lond. 1810.
Mayo (Herbert), Outlines of Human Physiology ; 8vo. Lond. 1827.
Medical Observations and Inquiries ; 4th edit. 6 vols. 8vo. 1776-'84.
Medico-Chirurgical Review.
Medico-Chirurgical Society of Edinburgh,—Transactions ; 8vo. Edinb. 1824.
Michaelis (Sir J. D.), Translation of Isaiah, quoted in Dr. J. P. Smith's Treatise on the Priesthood of Christ.
Millingen (Dr. J. G.), Curiosities of Medical Experience ; 2 vols. 8vo. Lond. 1837.
Moore (Thomas), On the Nature and Causes of our Saviour's Agony in the Garden ; 8vo. Lond. 1757.
Morgagni (J. B.), De Causis et Sedibus Morborum ; 8 vols. 8vo. Paris, 1821.
Morgan (J.), Complete History of Algiers ; 4to. Lond. 1731.

N.

Novum Testamentum, Græce, juxta recensionem J. J. Griesbach ; 2 vols. 8vo. Lond. 1809.

O.

Ollier (Mr.), Case of Hæmorrhage into the Pericardium ;—in the Manchester Chronicle for Nov. 22, 1834.
Origenes, Opera, Gr. Lat. ; 2 vols. fol.   Basil. 1545.
Orton (Reginald), On the Epidemic Cholera of India ; 2d edit. 8vo. Lond. 1831.
Outram (Gulielmus), De Sacrificiis ; 12mo.   Amstelod. 1688.

P.

Paget (James), On the Coagulation of the Blood after Death ;—in the London Med. Gazette for 1840.
Paley (Rev. Dr.), View of the Evidences of Christianity, etc. ; 2 vols. 8vo. Lond. 1805.
Parkin (John), On the Remote Cause of Epidemic Diseases ; 8vo. Lond. 1841.
Patissier (Dr.), Case of Rupture of the Heart ;—in the London Med. and Phys. Journal, vol. 47.
Pearson (Bishop), Exposition of the Creed ; fol.   Lond. 1741.
Penn (Granville), Book of the New Covenant, etc. ; 8vo.   Lond. 1836.
—— Annotations to ditto ; 8vo.   Lond. 1837.
Philosophical Magazine ; 68 vols. 8vo.   Lond. 1798–1826.
Philosophical Transactions of the Royal Society of London.
Pictorial Bible, by Knight and Co. ; 3 vols. large 8vo.   Lond. 1838.
Poole (Matthew), Synopsis Criticorum ; 5 vols. fol.   Lond. 1649.
Portal (Dr. A.), Sur la Nature et le Traitement de plusieurs Maladies ; 5 vols. 12mo.   Paris, 1800–'25.
Priestley (Dr. Joseph), Discourse on the Evidence of the Resurrection of Jesus ; 8vo.   Birmingham, 1791.
Provincial Med. and Surg. Association ;—Transactions.
Prout (Dr. W.), Bridgewater Treatise : On Chemistry, Meteorology, etc. ; 8vo.   Lond. 1834.

R.

Raffles (Sir T. S.), History of Java ; 2 vols. 8vo.   Lond. 1830.
Ramazzini (Bernard), Opera ; 4to.   Genevæ, 1716.
Rambach (J.), Considerations on the Sufferings of Christ (translated from the German) ; 3 vols. 8vo.   Lond. 1759.
Richter (G. G.), Opuscula Medica ; 3 vols. 4to.   Lips. 1780, 1781 ; vol. iii. pp. 313–366.
Robinson (Nich.), System of the Spleen, etc. ; 12mo.   Lond. 1729.
Rostan, Mémoires sur les Ruptures du Cœur ; 12mo.   Paris, 1820.
Ruggieri (Dr. C.), Narrative of the Crucifixion of Matthew Lovat, etc. (translated from the Italian) ;—in the Pamphleteer ; vol. iii. 8vo. Lond. 1814.
Russell (Dr. Alexander), Natural History of Aleppo ; 2d edit. 2 vols. 4to. Lond. 1794.
Russell (Dr. David), Letters, chiefly Practical and Consolatory ; 3 vols. 12mo.   Edinb. 1825.

S.

Salmasius (Claudius), De Cruce, etc. ; 12mo.   Lugd. Bat. 1646.
Schenck (Joann. à Grafenberg) Observ. Medicæ Rariores, etc. ; fol.   Francofurt, 1609.

Schilling (J. C.), Case of Bloody Sweat;—in the Ephemerid. Acad. Natur. Curios.
Schleusner (J. F.), Lexicon of the Greek Testament; 2 vols. 8vo. Glasgow, 1817.
Schwencke (Thomas), Hæmatologia; 12mo. Hag. Com. 1743.
Scoutetten (Dr.), Histoire Médicale et Topographique du Choléra Morbus, etc.; 8vo. Metz, 1831.
Seiler (Dr. G. F.), Translation of Isaiah;—quoted in Dr. J. P. Smith's Treatise on the Priesthood of Christ.
Senac (Pierre), Traité de Cœur, etc.; 2 vols. 4to. Paris, 1783.
Shakespeare (William), Plays, in 21 vols. 8vo. Lond. 1803.
Short (Thomas), General Chronological History of the Air, Weather, etc.; 2 vols. 8vo. Lond. 1749.
Sibson (Francis), On the Changes induced in the Situation and Structure of the Internal Organs, etc.; 8vo. Worcester, 1844;—in the Trans. of the Provinc. Med. and Surg. Association; vol. xii.
Slade (Adolphus), Records of Travels in Turkey, Greece, etc.; 2 vols. 8vo. Lond. 1833.
Smith (Dr. J. P.), Four Discourses on the Sacrifice and Priesthood of Jesus Christ, etc.; 12mo. Lond. 1842.
Stuart (Dr. Moses), Commentary on the Epistle to the Hebrews; 2 vols. 8vo. Lond. 1828.

T.

Taxil St. Vincent, Cases of Rupture of the Heart;—in the Journal Universel des Sciences Médicales; vol. xix.
Taylor (Bishop Jeremy), Works (edited by Bishop Heber); 15 vols. 8vo. Lond. 1824.
Taylor (Mr.), Case of Rupture of the Heart;—in the Lancet for 1843.
Tertullianus, Opera; fol. Paris, 1675.
Thackrah (C. T.), Inquiry into the Nature and Properties of the Blood, etc.; 8vo. Lond. 1834.
Theophylact, Opera; fol. Paris, 1635.
Thuanus (J. A.), Historia sui Temporis (curâ Buckley); 7 vols. fol. Lond. 1733.
Thurnam (Dr. John), On Rupture of the Heart, and Hæmorrhage into the Pericardium;—in the London Medical Gazette for 1838.
Tissot (S. A. D.) Traité des Nerfs, etc.; 12mo. Avignon, 1800.
Townsend (P. S.), On the Influence of the Passions in the Production and Modification of Disease; 8vo. New York, 1816.
Tully (Miss), Narrative of a Ten Years' Residence at Tripoli, in Africa; 4to. Lond. 1816.

U.

Usher (Archbishop), Annals of the World, etc.; fol. Lond. 1658.

V.

Valerius Maximus, Opera; 12mo. Lugd. Bat. 1660.
Van Geuns (Matt.), De Morte Corporea, etc.; 4to. Lugd. Bat. 1761.

Vater (Christian), Case of Hæmorrhage into the Pericardium and Rupture of the Heart;—in the Ephemerid. Acad. Natur. Curios.
Voetius (Gisbert), On the Flow of Blood and Water from the Side of Christ;—quoted in Kipping, De Cruce et Cruciariis.
Vogler (V. H.), Physiologia Historiæ Passionis Jesu Christi; small 4to. Helmestad. 1673.
Voltaire (F. M.), Œuvres complètes; 71 vols. 8vo. Basle, 1785.

W.

Wanley (Rev. Nathaniel), Wonders of the Little World, etc. (edited by Johnston); 2 vols. 8vo. Lond. 1806.
Watson (Bishop), Apologies for Christianity and the Bible; 8vo. Lond. 1816.
Watson (Mr.), Case of Hæmorrhage into the Pericardium;—in the London Medical Repository for 1814.
Watts (Dr. Isaac), Psalms and Hymns.
Webster (Noah), Brief History of Epidemic and Pestilential Diseases, etc.; 2 vols. 8vo. Lond. 1800.
Wepfer (J. J.), Anatomia aliquot Castorum;—in the Ephemerid. Acad. Natur. Curios.
Willan (Dr. Robert), History of the Ministry of Jesus Christ, etc.; 12mo. Lond. 1786.
Wilson (James), Lectures on the Blood, etc.; 8vo. Lond. 1819.
Wiseman (Bishop), Twelve Lectures on the Connection between Science and Revealed Religion; 2 vols. 8vo. Lond. 1836.
Wright (J.), Case of Rupture of the Heart;—in the Med. Obs. and Inquiries, vol. vi.

Z.

Zacchias (Paulus), Quæstiones Medico-Legales; fol. Avenion. 1657.
Zecchinelli (G. M.), Sulla Angina del Petto, etc.; 8vo. Padova, 1813 and 1814.
Zimmermann (J. G.), On Experience in Physic (translated from the German); 2 vols. 8vo. Lond. 1782.

THE END.

A Complete Biblical Library.

THE
TREASURY OF BIBLE KNOWLEDGE:
BEING
A DICTIONARY
OF

The Books, Persons, Places, Events, and other matters, of which mention is made in Holy Scripture. Intended to establish its authority and illustrate its contents.

By REV. JOHN AYRE, M. A.,
OF GONVILLE AND CAIUS COLLEGE, CAMBRIDGE.

Illustrated with many hundred woodcuts and fifteen full-page steel plates, drawn by Justyne, from original photographs by Graham, and five colored maps. 1 thick volume, 12mo, 944 pages. Price, Cloth, $4.00; Half Calf, $5.

Sent free by mail on receipt of the price.

"The general object of this work is to promote the intelligent use of the Sacred Volume by furnishing a mass of information respecting Palestine, and the manners, customs, religion, literature, arts, and attainments of the inhabitants; an account of the countries and races with which the Hebrews had relations, together with some notice of all the persons and places mentioned in the Bible and Apocrypha. The history and authority of the books themselves are discussed conjointly and severally. I have been anxious to study the best authorities for what is asserted, and to bring up the information to the most modern standard. I have not written hastily, therefore, but have spent some years in the compilation of this volume."—*Extract from the Preface.*

"Among the books which should find a place in the collection of every Christian man, who seeks to have in his possession any thing beyond a Bible and hymn-book, we know of none more valuable than 'The Treasury of Bible Knowledge.' It is in all respects the best, as it is the most convenient manual for the Biblical student yet published. We hope to see this work in the hands of every Sunday-school and Bible-class teacher."—*American Baptist.*

"* * * One of the most valuable publications ever issued by that house."—*New Yorker.*

D. APPLETON & COMPANY,
Publishers and Booksellers,
549 & 551 *Broadway, New York*

BIBLE TEACHINGS IN NATURE.

By the Rev. HUGH MacMILLAN.

1 Vol., 12mo. Cloth. Price, $1.50.

From the N. Y. Observer.

"These are truly original and delightful discourses, in which investigations of natural science are skilfully and often eloquently employed to establish divine revelation, and to illustrate its truths."

From the Hartford Morning Post.

"This is a work of rare merit in its way, and may be read with great profit and interest by lovers of Nature—by those who have the gift of *insight*, and who can look up 'through Nature to Nature's God' and see the 'invisible power and Godhead in the things which He has made.'"

From the Eastern Argus.

"The healthy mind delights in the beauties and mysteries of Nature, and this volume will be found both instructive and interesting."

From the Daily Enquirer.

"This is a beautifully written work, intended to make the studies of the Bible and of Nature doubly attractive, by pointing out the harmony which exists between them as revealed to the earnest students of both."

From the Norfolk County Journal.

"The author sees God everywhere revealed in the development of Nature,—finds Him in the works of pure and unobtrusive beauty; in the grand and impressive in scenery, and in the wonderful manifestations with which the world abounds."

Cowles's Notes on the Old Testament

I. THE MINOR PROPHETS.
1 vol., 12mo. $2.00.

II. EZEKIEL AND DANIEL.
1 vol., 12mo. $2.25.

III. ISAIAH.
1 vol., 12mo. $2.25.

IV. PROVERBS, ECCLESIASTES, AND THE SONG OF SOLOMON.
1 vol., 12mo. $2.00.

By Rev. HENRY COWLES, D. D.

From The Christian Intelligencer, N. Y.

"These works are designed for both pastor and people. They embody the results of much research, and elucidate the text of sacred Scripture with admirable force and simplicity. The learned professor, having devoted many years to the close and devout study of the Bible, seems to have become thoroughly furnished with all needful materials to produce a useful and trustworthy commentary."

From Dr. Leonard Bacon, of Yale College.

"There is, within my knowledge, no other work on the same portions of the Bible, combining so much of the results of accurate scholarship with so much common-sense and so much of a practical and devotional spirit."

From Rev. Dr. S. Wolcott, of Cleveland, Ohio.

"The author, who ranks as a scholar with the most eminent graduates of Yale College, has devoted years to the study of the Sacred Scriptures in the original tongues, and the fruits of careful and independent research appear in this work. With sound scholarship the writer combines the unction of deep religious experience, an earnest love of the truth, with a remarkable freedom from all fanciful speculation, a candid judgment, and the faculty of expressing his thoughts clearly and forcibly."

From President E. B. Fairfield, of Hillsdale College.

"I am very much pleased with your Commentary. It meets a want which has long been felt. For various reasons, the writings of the prophets have constituted a sealed book to a large part of the ministry as well as most of the common people. They are not sufficiently understood to make them appreciated. Your brief notes relieve them of all their want of interest to common readers. I think you have said just enough."

D. APPLETON & CO.'S PUBLICATIONS.

CHRISTIAN BALLADS,

BY THE

RIGHT REV. ARTHUR CLEVELAND COXE, D. D.,

BISHOP OF WESTERN NEW YORK.

Beautifully Illustrated with fourteen full-page Engravings, and nearly sixty head and tail pieces, by JOHN A. HOWS.

Mor. Super Extra, $7; Crushed Levant, $8; Cloth Extra, $3.50

"These Ballads have gained for the author an enviable distinction, and have opened his way to multitudes of hearts and homes in the Old World, as well as in the New, where in cottage, castle, and hall he has found the same warm and hearty welcome. * * * * This work stands almost without a rival. In bringing out this illustrated edition, the publishers have called to their aid the best talent. All lovers of fine books will experience a genuine pleasure in turning over the leaves of this elegant work."—*Christian Times.*

"We have seen nothing so beautiful as this for some time. * * It is produced in a beautiful and attractive style. Hardly a family will consent to be without it among the choice volumes for the family parlor or sitting-room. We know of nothing more beautiful for a Christmas or New Year's present. The title-page, in mediæval text, illuminated, is a marvel of beauty, while the numerous illustrations through the volume heighten the effect of true poetry and high art."—*Gospel Messenger.*

"We welcome with peculiar satisfaction the new and exquisitely illustrated edition of CHRISTIAN BALLADS, published as a Gift-Book, in their best style, by D. APPLETON & Co., New York. The volume is the best religious souvenir of the season."—*Boston Transcript.*

"That the Ballads have lived so long, and are worthy of reproduction in elegant style, is proof of their merit; and on looking over the contents we find that they are well worthy of this honor. Not alone do they breathe a beautiful religious and Christian-like spirit, there is much real and true poetry in them. * * * * It only remains to be said that the book is profusely illustrated by that talented young artist, Mr. JOHN A. HOWS."—*Home Journal.*

"It is a magnificent revised edition of an old favorite of the reading world. We think they are destined to remain among the permanent writings of our age, a position which is theirs through their undoubted merits."—*Boston Journal.*

RELIGIOUS WORKS

PUBLISHED BY

D. APPLETON & COMPANY,

549 & 551 Broadway, New York.

The Good Report; Morning and Evening Lessons for Lent. By ALICE B. HAVEN. 1 vol., 12mo, 318 pages. Cloth, $1.25.

Thoughts on Personal Religion: Being a Treatise on the Christian life in its two chief elements—Devotion and Practice. With two new chapters not in previous editions. By EDWARD MEYRICK GOULBURN, D. D. Fourth American Edition, enlarged. With a Prefatory Note by GEORGE H. HOUGHTON, D. D., Rector of the Church of the Transfiguration in the City of New York. 1 vol., 12mo. Cloth, $1.00.

Office of the Holy Communion in the Book of Common Prayer. A Series of Lectures delivered in the Church of St. John the Evangelist. By EDWARD MEYRICK GOULBURN, D. D. Adapted by the author for the Episcopal Service in the United States. 1 vol., 12mo. Cloth, $1.00.

Sermons Preached on Various Occasions during the Last Twenty Years. By EDWARD MEYRICK GOULBURN, D. D. 1 vol., 12mo. Cloth, $1.00.

The Idle Word: Short, Religious Essays on the Gift of Speech and its Employment in Conversation. By EDWARD MEYRICK GOULBURN, D. D. 1 vol., 12mo. Cloth, 75 cents.

An Introduction to the Devotional Study of the Holy Scriptures. By EDWARD MEYRICK GOULBURN, D. D. First American from the Seventh London Edition. 1 vol., 12mo. Cloth, $1.00.

Either of the above sent free by Mail on receipt of the price.

"A BOOK WHICH IS AS READABLE AS A NOVEL."

HISTORY OF EUROPEAN MORALS,

From Augustus to Charlemagne.

By W. E. H. LECKY, M. A.

2 vols., 8vo. 500 pages each. Price, $6.00.

CONTENTS:

The Utilitarian School—Objections to the School—Consequence of acting on Utilitarian Principles—Utilitarian Sanctions—Intuitive School—Alleged Diversities of Moral Judgment—Each of the Two Schools of Morals related to the General Condition of Society—The Order in which Moral Feelings are developed.

THE PAGAN EMPIRE.

Stoicism—Growth of a Gentler and more Cosmopolitan Spirit in Rome—Rise of Eclectic Moralists—The People still very corrupt—Causes of the Corruption—Effects of Stoicism on the Corruption of Society—Passion for Oriental Religions—Neoplatonism.

THE CONVERSION OF ROME.

Examination of the Theory which ascribes part of the Teaching of the Hated Pagan Moralists to Christian Influence—Theory which attributes the Conversion of the Empire to the Evidence of Miracles—The Persecution the Church underwent not of a Nature to crush it—History of the Persecutions.

FROM CONSTANTINE TO CHARLEMAGNE.

First Consequence of Christianity, a New Sense of the Sanctity of Human Life—The Second Consequence of Christianity, to teach Universal Brotherhood—Two Qualifications of our Admiration of the Charity of the Church—The Growth of Asceticism—The Saints of the Desert—Decline of the Civic Virtues—General Moral Condition of the Byzantine Empire—Distinctive Excellences of the Ascetic Period—Monachism—Relation of Monachism to the Intellectual Virtues—The Monasteries the Receptacles of Learning—Moral Condition of Western Europe—Growth of a Military and Aristocratic Spirit—Consecration of Secular Rank.

THE POSITION OF WOMEN.

The Courtesans—Roman Public Opinion much purer—Christian Influence—Relation of Christianity to the Female Virtues.

D. APPLETON & CO., Publishers,
549 & 551 Broadway, New York.

Sent free by mail to any address in the United States on receipt of the price

LITERATURE IN LETTERS:

OR,

MANNERS, ART, CRITICISM, BIOGRAPHY, HISTORY, AND MORALS,

ILLUSTRATED IN THE

CORRESPONDENCE OF EMINENT PERSONS.

EDITED BY

JAMES P. HOLCOMBE, LL.D.

1 vol., large 12mo. 520 pages, handsomely printed on tinted paper. Cloth extra, gilt top. Price $2.

"Such Letters," says Lord Bacon, "as are written from wise men, are, of all the words of man, in my judgment the best; for they are more natural than orations and public speeches, and more advised than conferences or private ones." The sources of pleasure and instruction to be found in the private correspondence of eminent persons have never been fully explained; much less have they been rendered accessible to the bulk of the reading public. Our language abounds in letters which contain the most vivid pictures of manners, and the most faithful and striking deliniations of character, which are full of wit, wisdom, fancy, useful knowledge, noble and pious sentiment."—*Extract from Preface.*

"The idea of this work is a happy one, and it has been well carried out by the accomplished editor. To concentrate into one compact volume the cream and marrow of a hundred different letter-writers, whose epistles fill many hundred tomes, involved the necessity of a course of reading so extensive that most people would shrink from undertaking it; Dr. Holcombe, however, has accomplished the task, and here presents us with the golden grain winnowed from the masses of chaff which he has dared to encounter in his progress."—*New York Times.*

"This volume—which, by the way, is very handsomely issued in all respects—is constructed on a novel plan, with entire success. The work is divided into six books: the first comprising 'letters of gossip, society, and manners;' the second 'pleasantry, sentiment, and fancy;' the third 'nature, art, and travel;' the fourth 'those of public history;' the fifth 'literary biography, anecdote, and criticism;' the sixth 'moral and devotional reflection.' Thus it will be seen that we have here the most interesting topics of life, treated of not in the cold form of essay, but in special letters written warm from one mind to another. All the great letter-writers in our language are represented whose names are 'household words.'"—*Boston Journal.*

"This is one of the most charming books in the language. Dr. Holcombe has taken the most sprightly, racy, readable letters, abounding in wit, fancy, anecdote, allusions to men, women, and events—just the reading that intelligent, cultivated people most admire. It is issued in beautiful dress, and will easily find its way to the hands of thousands of delighted readers."—*New York Observer.*

"This is an extremely interesting work, and gives an insight into the private thoughts and feelings of some of the greatest authors and prominent men and women of the last century. The sources of pleasure and instruction to be found in the private correspondence of eminent persons, have never been fully explored, much less have they been rendered accessible to the bulk of the reading public. His task has been a laborious one, and eminently successful. We commend the volume as a valuable addition to the list of American publications, and worthy a place in the library of every household."—*St. Louis Press.*

A STANDARD BOOK OF REFERENCE.

THE
HOUSEHOLD BOOK OF POETRY.

Collected and Edited by CHARLES A. DANA.

Tenth Edition. Royal 8vo. 798 pp. Beautifully printed.

Half mor., gilt top, $6; half calf, extra, $8; mor. ant., $10.

"The purpose of this book is to comprise within the bounds of a single volume whatever is truly beautiful and admirable among the minor poems of the English language. * * * Especial care has also been taken to give every poem entire and unmutilated, as well as in the most authentic form which could be procured."—*Extract from Preface.*

"This work is an immense improvement on all its predecessors. The editor, who is one of the most erudite of scholars, and a man of excellent taste, has arranged his selections under ten heads, namely: Poems of Nature, of Childhood, of Friendship, of Love, of Ambition, of Comedy, of Tragedy and Sorrow, of the Imagination, of Sentiment and Reflection, and of Religion. The entire number of poems given is about two thousand, taken from the writings of English and American poets, and including some of the finest versions of poems from ancient and modern languages. The selections appear to be admirably made, nor do we think that it would be possible for any one to improve upon this collection."—*Boston Traveller.*

"Within a similar compass, there is no collection of poetry in the language that equals this in variety, in richness of thought and expression, and of poetic imagery."—*Worcester Palladium.*

"This is a choice collection of the finest poems in the English language, and supplies in some measure the place of an extensive library. Mr. Dana has done a capital service in bringing within the reach of all the richest thoughts that grace our standard poetical literature."—*Chicago Press.*

"A work that has long been required, and, we are convinced from the selections made, and the admirable manner in which they are arranged, will commend itself at once to the public."—*Detroit Advertiser.*

"Never was a book more appropriately named. By the exercise of a sound and skilful judgment, and a thorough familiarity with the poetical productions of all nations, the compiler of this work has succeeded in combining, within the space of a single volume, nearly every poem of established worth and compatible length in the English language."—*Philadelphia Journal.*

"It gives us in an elegant and compact form such a body of verse as can be found in no other volume or series of volumes. It is by far the most complete collection that has ever been made of English lyrical poetry."—*Boston Transcript.*

"Among the similar works which have appeared we do not hesitate to give this the highest place."—*Providence Journal.*

"We are acquainted with no selections which, in point of completeness and good taste, excel the 'Household Book of Poetry.'"—*Northwestern Home Journal.*

"It is almost needless to say that it is a mine of poetic wealth."—*Boston Post.*

www.ingramcontent.com/pod-product-compliance
Lightning Source LLC
Chambersburg PA
CBHW051739300426
44115CB00007B/622